DATA AND APPLICATIONS SECURITY

DEVELOPMENTS AND DIRECTIONS

IFIP TC11 / WG11.3 Fourteenth Annual Working Conference on Database Security Schoorl, The Netherlands, August 21–23, 2000

Edited by:

Bhavani Thuraisingham
The MITRE Corporation, USA

Reind van de Riet
Vrije Universiteit, The Netherlands

Klaus R. Dittrich
Universität Zürich, Switzerland

Zahir Tari
RMIT University, Australia

SPRINGER SCIENCE+BUSINESS MEDIA, LLC

DOI 10.1007/978-0-306-47008-0

Library of Congress Cataloging-in-Publication Data

A C.I.P. Catalogue record for this book is available from the Library of Congress.

Originally published by Kluwer Academic Publishers in 2001
MyCopy version of the original edition 2001

Printed on acid-free paper.
www.springer.com/mycopy

CONTENTS

PREFACE

This book consists of the enhanced versions of the papers presented at the 14th IFIP Conference on Data and Applications Security. The preliminary versions of these papers were published in the Informal Proceedings and distributed at the conference. We have also included papers describing the two panel discussions as well as a summary of the conference. The conference was held in Schoorl, Netherlands from August 21 to 23, 2000.

We thank all those who submitted papers, presented papers as well as participated at the conference. We thank the three keynote speakers, the sponsors of this conference, and all those who provided administrative support to this conference both at The MITRE Corporation as well as at Vrije University. With special thanks to Laura-Cristina Nyiredi of The MITRE Corporation for her work compiling the camera-ready manuscript. Finally, we thank IFIP for its support as well as Kluwer Academic Publishers for this book.

Bhavani Thuraisingham (Program Chair)
Reind van de Riet (General Chair)
Klaus Dittrich (Program Chair, Europe/Africa)
Zahir Tari (Program Chair, Australasia)

CONTRIBUTORS

Chapter Number/Name(s)/Affiliation

1. **Gio Wiederhold**; Dept. of Computer Science, Stanford University, Stanford CA, USA

2. **E. Bertino, M. Braun, S. Castano, E. Ferrari**; Dept. of Information Science, University of Milan, ITALY
   M Mesiti; Dept. of Information Science; University of Genova, Genova ITALY

3. **Indrajit Ray, Indrakshi Ray**; Dept. of Computer and Information Information Science, University of Michigan-Dearborn USA
   Natarajan Narasimhamurthi; Dept. of Electrical and Computer Engineering, University of Michigan-Dearborn, USA

4. **Ernesto Damiani**; Computer Science Dept., George Mason University, Fairfax VA, USA and Dept. of Information Science, University of Milano, Milano ITALY
   Sabrina De Capitani di Vimercati; University of Brescia, Dept. of Electronic Automation, Brescia, ITALY
   Stefano Paraboschi; Milano Polytechnic, Dept. of Electronic Informaiton, Milano, ITALY
   Pierangela Samarati; Dept. of Information Science, University of Milano, Milano ITALY

5. **Alexandre Hardy, Martin S Olivier**; Dept. of Computer Science, Rand Afrikaans University, Johannesburg SOUTH AFRICA

6. **Susan Chapin, Don Faatz, Sushil Jajodia**; The MITRE Corporation, McLean, VA, USA

7. **Christian Altenschmidt, Joachim Biskup, Yucel Karabulut**; University of Dortmund, Dortmund, GERMANY

8. **M Papa, O Bremer, S Magill, J Hale, S Shenoi**; Center for Information Security; Dept. of Computer Science, University of Tulsa, Tulsa, OK, USA

9. **Premkumar Devanbu, Michael Gertz, Charles (Chip) Martel**, Dept. of Computer Science, University of California, Davis, CA, USA
Stuart Stubblebine; Cert Co, New York, NY, USA

10. **Daniel Barbara, Rajni Goel, Sushil Jajodia**; Center for Secure Information Systems; George Mason University, Fairfax, VA, USA

11. **Bhavani Thuraisingham**, The MITRE Corporation, Bedford, MA USA

12. **Ken Moody**; Computer Laboratory, University of Cambridge, Cambridge, ENGLAND

13. **Marta Oliva**; Dept. of Information and Industrial Engineering, University of Lleida, Lleida (Catalonia) SPAIN
Felix Saltor; Dept. of Information System Engineering; Catalunya Polytechnic University, Barcelona (Catalonia) SPAIN

14. **Martin S Olivier**; Dept. of Computer Science, Rand Afrikaans University, Johannesburg SOUTH AFRICA
Ehud Gudes; Mathmatics and Computer Science, Ben-Gurion University, Beer-Sheva, ISRAEL

15. **LiWu Chang, Ira S Moskowitz**; Center for High Assurance Computer Systems, Naval Research Laboratory, Washington, DC, USA

16. **Christina Yip Chung, Michael Gertz, Karl Levitt**; Dept. of Computer Science; University of California, Davis, CA, USA

17. **Steve Barker**; Cavendish School of Computer Science, University of Westminster, London, ENGLAND

18. **Adrian Spalka, Armin B Cremers**; Dept. of Computer Science, University of Bonn, Bonn, GERMANY

19. **Arnon Rosenthal**; The MITRE Corporation, Bedford, MA, USA
Edward Sciore; Boston College, Boston, MA, USA and The MITRE Corporation, Bedford, MA, USA

20. **John Hale, Rodrigo Chandia, Clinton Campbell, Mauricio Papa, Sujeet Shenoi**; Center for Information Security, Dept. of Computer Science, University of Tulsa, Tulsa, OK, USA

21. **Soon Ae Chun, Vijayalakshmi Atluri**; MSIS Department, Rutgers University and Center for Information Managemnt, Inegration and Connectivity, Newark, NJ, USA

22. **Sylvia Osborn**; Dept. of Computer Science, The University of Western Ontario, London, Ontario, CANADA

23. **Profs. S.A. Demurjian, T.C. Ting, J. Balthazar, H. Ren, C. Phillips**; Computer Science & Engineering Dept. The University of Connecticut, Storrs, CT, USA
P. Barr; The MITRE Corporation, Eatontown, NJ, USA

24. **Wouter Teepe**; Dept. of Technical Cognition Science, University of Groningen, Groningen, THE NETHERLANDS
Reind van de Riet; Dept. of Mathmatics and Computer Science, Vrije University, Amsterdam, THE NETHERLANDS
Martin Olivier; Dept. of Mathmatics and Computer Science, Rand University, Johannesburg, SOUTH AFRICA

25. **Jurgen Steger, Holger Gunzel, Andreas Bauer**; Dept. of Database Systems, University of Erlangen-Nuremberg, Erlangen, GERMANY

26. **Marc Donner, David Nochin, Wendy Walasek**; Morgan Stanley Dean Witter, NY, NY USA
Dennis Shasha; New York University, NY, NY, USA

27. **John R Campbell**; Department of Defense, Fort Mead, MD, USA

28. **Hasan M Jamil**; Dept. of Computer Science; Mississippi State University, MS, USA

29. **James B Michael, Leonard T Gaines**; Naval Postgraduate School, Computer Science Dept., Monterey, CA, USA

30. **Daniel Cvrcek**; PhD Student at Dept. of Computer Science and Engineering, Brno University of Technology, Brno, CZECH REPUBLIC

31. **Ari Moesriami Barmawi, Shingo Takada, Norihisa Doi**; Dept. of Computer Science, Graduate School of Science and Technology, Keio University, JAPAN

32. **Sejong Oh, Seog Park**; Sogang University, Seoul, KOREA

33. **Keiji Izaki, Katsuya Tanaka, Makoto Takizawa**; Dept. of Computers and Systems Engineering, Denki University, Tokyo, JAPAN

34. **Reind van de Riet**; Dept. of Mathmatics and Computer Science, Vrije University, Amsterdam, THE NETHERLANDS
Radu Serban; Dept. of Mathmatics and Computer Science, Vrije University, Amsterdam, THE NETHERLANDS
Sylvia Osborn; Dept. of Computer Science, The University of Western Ontario, London, Ontario, CANADA
Arnon Rosenthal; The MITRE Corporation, Bedford, MA, USA
Vijayalakshmi Atluri; MSIS Department, Rutgers University and Center for Information Managemnt, Inegration and Connectivity, Newark, NJ, USA
Joachim Biskup; University of Dortmund, Dortmund, GERMANY

35 **Bhavani Thuraisingham**, The MITRE Corporation, Bedford, MA, USA

CHAPTER 1

Protecting Information when Access is Granted for Collaboration

Keynote 1

Gio Wiederhold

Dept. of Computer Science, Stanford University, Stanford CA 94305; gio@cs.stanford.edu

Abstract: There are settings where we have to collaborate with individuals and organizations who, while not being enemies, should not be fully trusted. Collaborators must be authorized to access information systems that contain information that they should be able to receive. However, these systems typically also contain information that should be withheld. Collaborations can be rapidly created, requiring dynamic alterations to security policies. Classifying data to cover all current and possible access privileges is both awkward and costly, and always unreliable.

An alternative approach to protection, complementing basic access control, is to provide filtering of results. Filtering of contents is also costly, but provides a number of benefits not obtainable with access control alone. The most important one is that the complexity of setting up and maintaining specific, isolated information cells for every combination of access rights held by collaborators is avoided. New classes of external collaborators can be added without requiring a reorganization of the entire information structure. There is no overhead for internal use, i.e., for participants that are wholly trusted. Finally, since documents contents rather than their labels are being checked, cases of misfiled information will not cause inappropriate release.

The approach used in the TIHI/SAW projects at Stanford uses simple rules to drive filtering primitives. The filters run on a modest, but dedicated computer managed by the organization's security officer. The rules implement the institution's security policy and must balance manual effort and complexity. By not relying on the database systems and network facilities, and their administrators a better functional allocation of responsibilities ensues.

1. Introduction

There are data sources that are primarily intended for external access, such as public web pages, reports, bibliographies, etc. These are organized according to external access criteria. If some of the information is not intended to be public, then security provisions are put into place. In more complex settings several mandatory layers will exist, and protection may require discretionary access control as well. When we deal with collaborators more discretionary partitions will be needed, and those are likely to overlap, creating combinatorial cells. Examples in the medical domain include external research groups, various public health agencies, pharmaceutical companies performing drug surveillance, as well as third-party payors.

These collaborators are increasingly important in our complex enterprises, and cannot be viewed as enemies. They may be part of a supply chain, they may provide essential, complementary information, or may supply specialized services, beyond our own capabilities. However, their roles are often specific, so that they do not fit neatly into existing security categories. The problem of managing security becomes impossibly complex.

Today, security provisions for computing focus on controlling access. At least five technological requirements interact in the process, and all of these are will recognized in the literature:

1. Secure Communication, c.f. [He:97].
2. Perimeter Control, c.f. [CheswickB:94].
3. Reliable Authentication, c.f. [CastanoFMS:95]
4. Authorization to information cells, c.f. [GriffithW:76]
5. Partitioning of the information into cells, c.f. [LuniewskiEa:93]

The fifth requirement, often under-emphasized, is that there must be a highly reliable categorization of all information to those cells [Oracle:99]. It is in the management of that categorization where many failures occur, and where collaborative requirements raise the greatest problem.

Relying on access control makes the assumption that all these five conditions are fulfilled. Unfortunately, there are many situations where the last one, namely perfect partitioning of the information into cells for disjoint access is not realistic. A corporation may have large, existing databases which were established before external access needed to be considered. In modern environments access will be needed for off-site staff, corporate salespersons, vendors which have contract relationships, government inspectors, and an ever-increasing number of collaborators. The trend to outsourcing of tasks that used to be internal exacerbates the problem. Reorganizing corporate databases to deal with developing needs for external access is costly and disruptive, since it will affect existing users and their application. It is not surprising that security concerns were the cited as the prime reason for lack of progress in establishing *virtual enterprises* [HardwickS:96].

We encountered the problem initially in the manufacturing area, where security concerns caused the interchange of manufacturing data to a subcontractor to take many weeks, although they had installed compatible CAD systems and high-speed datalinks. All drawings had to be printed, inspected by a security specialist, verified, and edited if the design contained information inappropriate for the subcontractor. The edited drawings could then be copied and shipped to the contractor, who had to scan the paper copies into their systems. The source of the problem is, of course, that the design engineer makes drawings of the equipment to be built, with justifications, finishing information, and explicit and implicit performance criteria. The drawings are not initially produced to satisfy the capabilities of an unknown subcontractor.

Our actual initial application domain was actually in healthcare. Medical records are needed for many purposes: diagnosis, care delivery, drug supplies, infection control, room assignments, billing, insurance claims, validation of proper care, research, and public health records. Patient care demands that the record be accessible in a comprehensive form and up-to-date [Rindfleisch:97]. Historical information is important for disease management, but not for many billing tasks. It is obviously impossible to split the record into access categories that match every dimension of access. Even if that would be possible, the cost and risks to the internal operations in a hospital or clinic would be prohibitive. Expecting a physician to carry out this task is unrealistic, and, if required, would greatly increase the cost of healthcare.

Partitioning of the information into cells

The process of assigning categories to information involves every person who creates, enters, or maintains information. When there are few cells, these originators can understand what is at stake, and will perform the categorization function adequately, although error in filing will still occur. When there are many cells, the categorization task becomes onerous and error prone. When new coalitions are created, and new collaborators must share existing information system, the categorization task becomes impossible.

A solution to excessive partitioning might be to assign accessors combinations of access rights. This approach appears to invert the multi-level security approach. Numerous research results deal with multi-level security within a computer system [LuntEa:90]. Several simple implementations are commercially available, but have not found broad acceptance, likely because of a high perceived cost/benefit ratio [Elseviers:94]. These systems do not accommodate very many distinct cells, and mainly support mandatory security levels [KeefeTT:89]. Leaks due to inference are still possible, and research into methods to cope with this issue is progressing [Hinke:88]. However few cases of exploiting these weaknesses have been documented [Neuman:00].

However, break-ins still occur. Most of them are initiated via legitimate access paths, since the information in our systems must be shared with customers and collaborators. In that case the first three technologies provide no protection, and the burden falls on the mappings and the categorization if the information. Once users are permitted into the system, protection becomes more difficult.

A complementary technology

The solution we provide to this dilemma is ***result checking*** [WiederholdBSQ:96]. In addition to the conventional tasks of access control the results of any information requests are filtered before releasing them to the requestor. We also check a large number of parameters about the release. This task mimics the manual function of a security officer when checking the briefcases of collaborating participants leaving a secure meeting, on exiting the secure facility. Note that checking of result contents is not performed in standard security processing. Multi-level secure systems may check for unwanted inferences when results are composed from data at distinct levels, but rely on level designations and record keys. Note that result checking need not depend on the sources of the result, so that it remains robust with respect to information categorization, software errors, and misfiling of data.

2. Filtering System Architecture

We incorporate result checking in a *security mediator* workstation, to be managed by a security officer. The *security mediator* system interposes security checking between external accessors and the data resources to be protected, as shown in Fig.1. It carries out functions of authentication and access control, to the extent that such services are not, or not reliably, provided by network and database services. Physically a security mediator is designed to operate on a distinct workstation, owned and operated by the enterprise security officer (S.O.). It is positioned as a pass gate within the enterprise firewall, if there is such a firewall. In our initial commercial installation the security mediator also provided traditional firewall functions, by limiting the IP addresses of requestors [WiederholdBD:98].

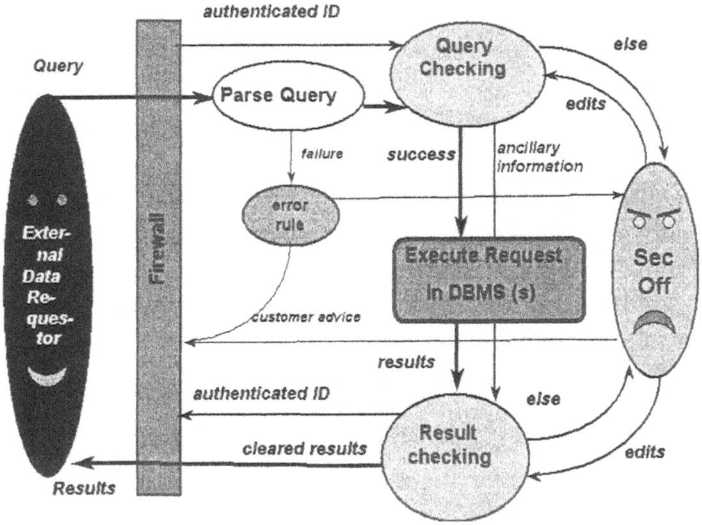

Figure 1. Functions provided by a TIHI/SAW Security Mediator

The mediator system and the source databases are expected to reside on different machines. Thus, since all queries that arrive from the external world, and their results, are processed by the security mediator, the databases behind a firewall need not be secure unless there are further internal requirements. When combined with an integrating mediator, a security mediator can also serve multiple data resources behind a firewall [Ullman:96]. Combining the results of a query requiring multiple sources prior to result checking improves the scope of result validation.

The supporting database systems can still implement their view-based protection facilities [GriffithsW:76]. These need not be fully trusted, but their mechanisms add efficiency.

Operation

Within the workstation is a rule-base system which investigates queries coming in and results to be transmitted to the external world. Any request and any result, which cannot be vetted by the rule system, is displayed to the security officer, for manual handling. The security officer decides to approve, edit, or reject the information. An associated logging subsystem provides an audit trail for all information that enters or leaves the domain.

The log provides input to the security officer to aid in evolving the rule set, and increasing the effectiveness of the system.

The software of our security mediator is composed of modules that perform the following tasks

1. Optionally (if there is no firewall): Authentication of the requestor
2. Determination of authorization type (clique) for the requestor
3. Processing of a request for information (pre-processing) using the policy rules
4. If the request is dubious: interaction with the security officer
5. Communication to internal databases (submission of certified request)
6. Communication from internal databases (retrieval of unfiltered results)
7. Processing of results (post-processing) using the policy rules
8. If the result is dubious: interaction with the security officer
9. Writing query, origin, actions, and results into a log file
10. Transmission of vetted information to the requestor

Item 7, the post-processing of the results obtained from the databases, possibly integrated, is the critical additional function. Such processing is potentially quite costly, since it has to deal thoroughly with a wide variety of data. Applying such filters selectively, specifically for he problems raised in collaborations, as well as the capabilities of modern computers and text-processing algorithms, makes use of the technology feasible. A rule-based system is used in TIHI to control the filtering, allowing the security policies to be set so that a reasonable balance of cost to benefit is achieved. It will be described in the next section.

Having rules, however is optional. Without rules the mediator system will operate in fully paranoid mode. Each query and each result will be submitted to the security officer. The security officer will view the contents on-line, and approved, edit, or reject the material. Adding rules enables automation. The extent of automation depends the coverage of the rule-set. A reasonable goal is the automatic processing of say, 90% of queries and 95% responses.

Unusual requests, perhaps issued because of a new coalition, assigned to a new clique, will initially not have applicable rules, but can be immediately processed by the security officer. In time, simple rules can be entered to reduce the load on the officer.

Traditional systems, based on access control to precisely defined cells, require a long time to before the data are set up, and when the effort is great, may never be automated. In many situations we are aware of, security mechanisms are ignored when requests for information are deemed to be important, but cannot be served by existing methods. Keeping the security officer in control allows any needed bypassing to be handled formally. This capability recognizes that in a dynamic, interactive world there will always be cases that are not foreseen or situations the rules are too stringent.

Keeping the management of exceptions within the system greatly reduces confusion, errors, and liabilities.

Even when operating automatically, the security mediator remains under the control of the enterprise since the rules are modifiable by the security officer at all times. In addition, logs are accessible to the officer, who can keep track of the transactions. If some rules are found to be to liberal, policy can be tightened. If rules are too stringent, as evidenced by an excessive load on the security officer, they can be relaxed or elaborated.

3. The Rule System

The rules system is composed of the rules themselves, an interpreter for the rules, and primitives, which are invoked by the rules. The rules embody the security policy of the enterprise. They are hence not preset into the software of the security mediator.

In order to automate the process of controlling access and ensuring the security of information, the security officer enters rules into the system. These rules are trigger analyses of requests, their results, and a number of associated parameters. The interpreting software uses these rules to determine the validity of every request and make the decisions pertaining to the disposition of the results. Auxiliary functions help the security officer enter appropriate rules and update them as the security needs of the organization change.

The rules are simple, short and comprehensive. They are stored in a database local to the security mediator system with all edit rights restricted to the security officer. Some rules may overlap; in which case the most restrictive rule automatically applies. The rules may pertain to requestors, cliques of requestors having certain roles, sessions, databases tables or any combinations of these.

Rules are selected based on the authorization clique determined for the requestor. All the applicable rules will be checked for every request issued by the requestor in every session. All rules will be enforced for every requestor and the request will be forwarded to the source databases only if it passes all tests. Any request not fully vetted is posted immediately to the log and sent the security officer. The failure message is directed to the security officer and not to the requestor, so that the requestors in such cases will not see the failure and its cause. This prevents that the requestor could interpret failure patterns and make meaningful inferences, or rephrase the request to try to bypass the filter [KeefeTT:89].

The novel aspect of our approach is that security mediator checks outgoing results as well. This is crucial since, from the security-point-of-view, requests are inclusive, not exclusive selectors of content and may retrieve unexpected information. In helpful, user-friendly information systems getting more than asked for is considered beneficial, but from a security point-of-view being generous is risky. Thus, even when the request has been validated, the results are also subject to screening by a set of rules. As before, all rules are enforced for every requestor and the results are accessible only if they pass all tests. Again, if the results violate a rule, a failure message is logged and sent to the security officer but not to the requestor.

Primitives

The rules invoke executable primitive functions which operate on requests, data, the log, and other information sources. As new security functions and technologies appear, or if specialized needs arise, new primitives can be inserted in the security mediator for subsequent rule invocation. In fact, we do not expect to be the source of all primitives. We do hope that all primitives will be sufficiently simple that their correct function can be verified.

Primitives that have been used include:

- Assignment of a requestor to a clique
- Limit access for clique to certain database table segments or columns
- Limit request to statistical (average, median, ..) information
- Provide number of data instances (database rows) used in a statistical result
- Provide number of tables used (joins) for result for further checking
- Limit number of requests per session
- Limit number of sessions per period
- Limit requests by requestor per period
- Block requests from all but listed sites
- Block delivery of results to all but listed sites
- Block receipt of requests by local time at request site
- Block delivery of results by local time at delivery site
- Constrain request to data which is keyed to requestor name
- Constrain request to data which is keyed to request site name
- Filter all result terms through a clique-specific good-word dictionary
- Disallow results containing terms in a clique-specific bad-word dictionary
- Convert text by replacing identifies with non-identifying surrogates [Sweeney:96]
- Convert text by replacing objectionable terms with surrogates
- Randomize responses for legal protection [Leiss:82]
- Extract text out of x-ray images (for further filtering) [WangWL:98]

- Notify the security officer immediately of failure reports
- Place failure reports only in the log

Not all primitives will have a role in all applications.

Primitives can vary greatly in cost of application, although modern technology helps. Checking for terms in results is costly in principle, but modern spell-checkers show that it can be done fairly fast. For this task we create clique-specific dictionaries, by initially processing a substantial amount of approved results. In initial use the security officer will still get false failure reports, due to innocent terms that are not yet in the dictionary. Those will be incrementally added, so that in time the incidence of such failures will be minimal.

For example, we have in use a dictionary for ophtamology, to allow authenticated researchers in that field to have access to patient data. That dictionary does not include terms that would signal, say HIV infection or pregnancies, information which the patients would not like to see released to unknown research groups. Also, all proper names, places of employment, etc. are effectively filtered.

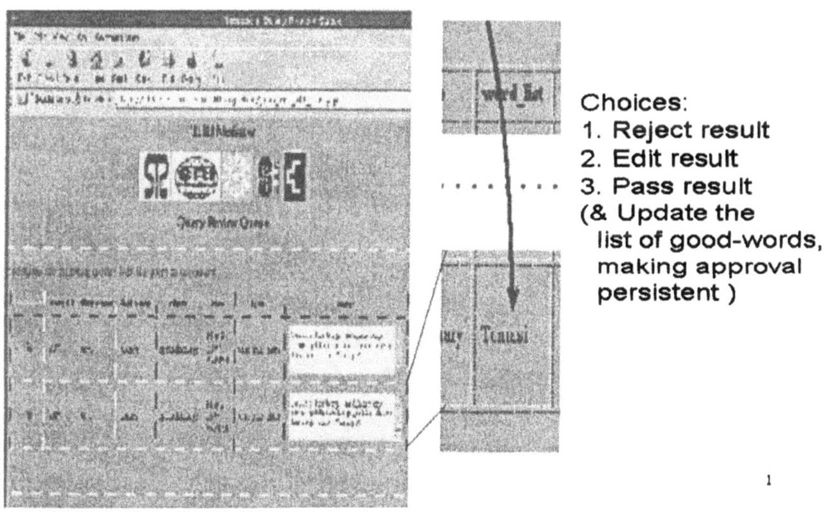

Figure 2. Extract from a report to the Security Officer

Several of these primitives are designed to help control inference problems in statistical database queries [AdamW:89]. While neither we, nor any feasible system can prevent leaks due to inference, we believe that careful management can make reduce the probability [Hinke:88]. Furthermore, providing the tools for analysis, as logging all accesses will reduce the practical threat [Hinke:88], [Sweeney:97]. The primitive to enforce dynamic limits on access frequencies will often have to refer to the log, so that efficient access to the log, for instance by maintaining a large write-through cache for the log, will be important. Here again the function of traditional database support and security mediation diverges, since database transaction are best isolated, where as inference control requires history maintenance.

4. Logging

Throughout, the failures, as well as the request text and source, and actions taken by the security officer, are logged by the system for audit purposes. Having a security log that is distinct from the database log is important since:

- A database system logs all transactions, not just external requests, and is hence confusingly voluminous
- Most database systems do not log attempted and failed requests fully, because they appear not to have affected the databases
- Reasons for failure of requests in database logs are implicit, and do not give the rules that caused them.

We provide user-friendly utilities to scan the security log by time, by requestor, by clique, and by data source. Offending terms in results are marked.

No system, except one that provides complete isolation, can be 100% foolproof. The provision of security is, unfortunately, a cat-and-mouse game, where new threats and new technologies keep arising. Logging provides the feedback, which converts a static approach to a dynamic and stable system, which can maintain an adequate level of protection. Logs will have to be inspected regularly to achieve stability.

Bypassing of the entire system and hence the log remains a threat. Removal of information on portable media is easy. Only a few enterprises can afford to place controls on all personnel leaving daily for home, lunch, or competitive employment. However, having an effective and adaptable security filter removes the excuse that information had to be downloaded and shipped out because the system was too stringent for legitimate purposes. Some enterprises are considering limiting internal workstations to be diskless. It is unclear how effective this approach will be outside of small, highly secure domains in an enterprise. Such a domain will then have to be protected with its own firewall and a security mediator as well, because collaboration between the general and highly secure internal domains must be enabled.

5. Current State and Further Work

Our initial demonstrations have been in the healthcare domain, and a commercial version of TIHI is now in use to protect records of genomic analyses in a pharmaceutical company. As the expectations for protection of the privacy of patient data are being solidified into governmental regulations we expect that our approach will gain popularity [Braithwaite:96]. Today the healthcare establishment still hopes that commercial encryption tools will be adequate for the protection of medical records, since the complexity of managing access requirements has not yet been faced [RindKSSCB:97]. Expenditures for security in medical enterprises are minimal [NRC:97]. Funding of adequate provisions in an industry under heavy economic pressures, populated with many individuals who do not attach much value to the privacy of others, will remain a source of stress.

Non-textual contents

Identifying information is routinely deleted from medical records that are disseminated for research and education. However, here a gap existed as well: X-ray, MRI, and similar images accompany many records, and these also include information identifying the patient. We have developed software that recognizes such text using wavelet-based decomposition and analysis, extracts it, and can submit to the filtering system developed in TIHI. Information, which is determined to be benign, can be retained, and other text is effectively removed by omitting high-frequency components in the affected areas [WangWL:98].

We have also investigated our original motivating application area, namely manufacturing information. Here the simple web-based interfaces that are effective for the customer and the security officer interfaces in health care are not adequate. We have demonstrated interfaces for the general viewing and editing of design drawings and any attached textual information. In drawings significant text may be incorporated in the drawings themselves. When delivering an edited drawing electronically, we also have to assure that there is no hidden information. Many design formats allow *undo* operations, which would allow apparently deleted information to reappear.

Before moving to substantial automation for collaboration in manufacturing, we will have to understand the parameters for reliable filtering of such information better. However, as pointed out initially, even a fully manual security mediator will provide a substantial benefit to enterprises that are trying to institute shared efforts rapidly.

6. Conclusions

Security mediation provides an architectural function as well as a specific service. Architecturally, expanding the role of a gateway in the firewall from a passive filter to an active pass gate service allows concentration of the responsibility for security to a single node, owned by the security officer. Assigning responsibilities for security to database or network personnel, who have primary responsibilities of making data and communication available, will conflict with security concerns and is unwise. These people are promoted to their positions because they have a helpful attitude and know how to overcome problems of system failures and inadequacies. This attitude is inherently in conflict with corporate and legal concerns for the protection of data.

Existing services, as constraining views over databases, encryption for transmission in networks, password management in operating systems can be managed via the security mediator node.

The specific, novel service presented here, result checking, complements traditional access control. We have received a patent to cover the concept. Checking results is especially relevant in systems with many types of users, including external collaborators, and complex information structures. In such settings the requirement that systems that are limited to access-control impose, namely that all data are correctly partitioned and filed is not achievable in practice. Result checking does not address all issues of security of course, as protection from erroneous or malicious updates, although it is likely that such attacks will be preceded by processes that extract information. A side-effect of result checking that it provides a level of intrusion detection.

The rule-based approach allows balancing of the need for preserving data security and privacy and for making data available. Data, which is too tightly controlled, reduces the benefits of sharable information in collaborative settings. Rules, which are too liberal, can violate security and expectation of privacy. Having a balanced policy will require directions from management. Having a single focus for execution of the policy in electronic transmission will improve the consistency of the application of the policy.

Result filtering does not solve all problems, in security, of course. They rely still on a minimum level of reliability in the supporting systems. They cannot compensate when information is missing or not found because of misidentification. In general, a security mediator cannot protect from inadvertent or intentional denial of information by a mismanaged database system.

Acknowledgements

Research leading to security mediators was supported by an NSF HPCC challenge grant and by DARPA ITO via Arpa order E017, as a subcontract via SRI International. Steve Dawson was the PI at SRI. The commercial transition was performed by Maggie Johnson, Chris Donahue, and Jerry Cain under contracts with SST (www.2ST.com). Work on editing and filtering graphics is due to Jahnavi Akalla and James Z. Wang, This paper is a version of a broader paper being submitted to an IEEE Transaction.

References

[CastanoFMS:95] S.Castano, M.G. Fugini, G.Martella, and P. Samarati: *Database Security;* Addison Wesley Publishing Company - ACM Press, 1995 pp. 456

[CheswickB:94].William R.Cheswick and Steven M. Bellovin: *Stalking the Wily Hacker*; Addison-Wesley, 1994.

[Didriksen:97] Tor Didriksen: "Rule-based Database Access control – A practical Approach""; *Proc. 2nd ACM workshop on Rule-based Access Control*, 1997, pp.143-151.

[Elseviers:94] Elseviers Advanced Technology Publications: Trusted Oracle 7; *Computer Fraud and Technology Bulle*tin, March 1994.

[GriffithsW:76] Patricia P. Griffiths and Bradford W. Wade: "An Authorization Mechanism for a Relational Database System"; *ACM Trans. on Database Systems*, Vol.1 No.3, Sept.1976, pp.242-255.

[HardwickS:96] M. Hardwick, D.L. Spooner, T. Rando, and KC Morris: "Sharing Manufacturing Information In Virtual Enterprises"; *Comm. ACM*, Vol.39 no.2, pp.46-54, February 1996.

[He:97] J. He: "Performance and Manageability Design in an Enterprise Network Security System"; *IEEE Enterprise Networking Miniconference 1997* (ENM-97), IEEE, 1997.

[Hinke:88] T. Hinke: "Inference Aggregation Detection in Database management Systems"; *Proc. IEEE Symposium on Security and Privacy*, Oakland CA, April 1988.

[JohnsonSV:95?] Johnson DR, Sayjdari FF, Van Tassel JP.: Missi security policy: A formal approach. Technical Report R2SPO-TR001, National Security Agency Central Service, July 1995.

[KeefeTT:89] T. Keefe, B.Thuraisingham, and W.Tsai: "Secure Query Processing Strategies"; *IEEE Computer*, Vol.22 No.3, March 1989, pp.63-70.

[LandwehrHM:84] Carl E. Landwehr, C.L. Heitmyer, and J.McLean: "A Security Model for Military Message Systems"; *ACM Trans. on Computer Systems*, Vol.2 No.3, Aug. 1984, pp. 198-222.

[LuniewskiEa:93] Luniewski, A. et al. "Information organization using Rufus" SIGMOD '93, *ACM SIGMOD Record*, June 1993, vol.22, no.2 p. 560-1

[LuntEa:90] Therea Lunt et al.: "The SeaView Security Model"; *IEEE Trans. on Software Eng.*, Vol.16 No.6, 1990, pp.593-607.

[Neuman:00] Peter Neumann: Illustrative Risks to the Public in the Use of Computer Systems and Related Technology"; SRI International, May 2000, http://www.csl.ri.com/neumann/illustrative.html.

[Oracle:99] *Oracle 8I Fine-grained Access Control*, Oracle corporation, February 1999.

[QianW:97] Qian, XioaLei and Gio Wiederhold: "Protecting Collaboration"; abstract for *IEEE Information Survivability Workshop, ISW'97*, Feb.1997, San Diego.

[RindKSSCB:97] David M. Rind, Isaac S. Kohane, Peter Szolovits, Charles Safran, Henry C. Chueh, and G. Octo Barnett: "Maintaining the Confidentiality of Medical Records Shared over the Internet and the World Wide Web"; *Annals of Internal Medicine* 15 July 1997. 127:138-141.

[Rindfleisch:97] Thomas C. Rindfleisch: Privacy, Information Technology, and Health Care; *Comm. ACM;* Vol.40 No. 8 , Aug.1997, pp.92-100.

[SchaeferS:95] M. Schaefer, G. Smith: "Assured discretionary access control for trusted RDBMS"; in *Proceedings of the Ninth IFIP WG 11.3 Working Conference on Database Security*, 1995:275-289.

[Seligman:99] Len Seligman, Paul Lehner, Ken Smith, Chris Elsaesser, and David Mattox: "Decision-Centric Information Monitoring"; *Jour. of Intelligent Information Systems (JIIS)*, Vol.14, No.1.; also at http://www.mitre.org/pubs/edge/june_99/dcim.doc

[Sweeney:96] Latanya Sweeney: "Replacing personally-identifying information in medical records, the *SCRUB* system"; Cimino, JJ, ed. *Proceedings, Journal of the American Medical Informatics Association*, Washington, DC: Hanley & Belfus, 1996, Pp.333-337.

[Sweeney:97] Latanya Sweeney: "Guaranteeing anonymity when sharing medical data, the *DATAFLY* system"; *Proceedings, Journal of the American Medical Informatics Association*, Washington DC, Hanley & Belfus, 1997.

[Ullman:97?] Jeffrey Ullman: Information Integration Using Logical Views; *International Conference on Database Theory (ICDT '97)* Delphi, Greece, ACM and IEEE Computer Society, 1997.

[WangWL:98] James Z. Wang, Gio Wiederhold and Jia Li: Wavelet-based Progressive Transmission and Security Filtering for Medical Image Distribution"; in Stephen Wong (ed.): *Medical Image Databases*; Kluwer publishers, 1998, pp.303- 324.

[WiederholdBC:98] Gio Wiederhold, Michel Bilello, and Chris Donahue: "Web Implementation of a Security Mediator for Medical Databases"; in T.Y. Lin and Shelly Qian:Database Security XI, Status and Prospects, IFIP / Chapman & Hall, 1998, pp.60-72.

[WiederholdBSQ:96] Gio Wiederhold, Michel Bilello, Vatsala Sarathy, and XiaoLei Qian: A Security Mediator for Health Care Information"; Journal of the AMIAecurity Mediator for Health Care Information"; Journal of the AMIA issue containing the Proceedings of the 1996 AMIA Conference, Oct. 1996, pp.120-124.

[WiederholdEa:96] Gio Wiederhold, Michel Bilello, Vatsala Sarathy, and XiaoLei Qian: Protecting Collaboration; postscript); presented and published at the National Information Systems Security Conference, 21 Oct.1996; as Proceedings of the NISSC'96, Baltimore MD, Oct. 1996, pp.561-569.

CHAPTER 2

Author-$\mathcal{X}$: A JAVA-BASED SYSTEM FOR XML DATA PROTECTION*

E. Bertino, M. Braun, S. Castano, E. Ferrari, M. Mesiti

Abstract Author-$\mathcal{X}$ is a Java-based system for access control to XML documents. Author-$\mathcal{X}$ implements a discretionary access control model specifically tailored to the characteristics of XML documents. In particular, our system allows (i) a set-oriented and single-oriented document protection, by supporting authorizations both at document type and document level; (ii) a differentiated protection of document/document type contents by supporting multi-granularity protection objects and positive/ negative authorizations; (iii) a controlled propagation of authorizations among protection objects, by enforcing multiple propagation options.

Keywords: XML, access control, authorization base, eXcelon, Java.

1. Introduction

Since the Web is becoming the main information dissemination means for most organizations, an increasing number of applications at Internet and Intranet level need access control mechanisms enforcing a selective access to information retrieved/exchanged over the Web. XML [9] has recently emerged as the most relevant standardization effort in the area of markup languages, and it is increasingly used as the language for information exchange over the Web. In this context, developing an access control mechanism in terms of XML is an important step for Web information security.

In this paper, we present Author-$\mathcal{X}$, a Java-based system for discretionary access control to XML documents. Author-$\mathcal{X}$ takes into account XML document characteristics, the presence of document types (called *Document Type Definitions* (DTDs)), and the types of actions that can be executed on XML documents (i.e., navigation and browsing), for implementing an access control mechanism tailored to XML. In particular,

*This work has been partially supported by a grant from Microsoft Research.

Author-$\mathcal{X}$ has the following distinguishing features: both a *set-oriented* and *instance-oriented* document protection, by supporting DTD-level as well as document-level authorizations; *differentiated protection* of XML document and DTD contents by supporting positive and negative authorizations and fine grained protection objects, identified on the basis of the graph structure of XML documents and DTDs; *controlled propagation* of authorizations among protection objects at different granularity levels, by enforcing multiple propagation options stating how an authorization defined on a document/DTD applies by default to protection objects at a finer granularity level within the document/DTD.

Author-$\mathcal{X}$ exploits authorizations stored in an XML authorization base and their propagation options to evaluate access requests issued by users and determines if they can be completely satisfied, partially satisfied, or not satisfied at all. In case of a partially satisfied request, only a view of the requested document(s) is returned by Author-$\mathcal{X}$. Author-$\mathcal{X}$ is implemented in Java on top of the eXcelon data server [4], which is used to store both the sources to be protected and the XML authorization base of the system. Architectural and implementation issues of Author-$\mathcal{X}$ are described, with particular attention to the authorization base and the access control mechanism. An application of Author-$\mathcal{X}$ to the protection of a real XML source, derived from the *Sigmod Record Articles XML Database* [7], is presented.

As far as we know, Author-$\mathcal{X}$ is the first tool, we are aware of, supporting XML document protection. In fact, research work in this field has concentrated more on the development of access control models for Web documents [6]. XML documents have a richer structure than HTML documents and can be coupled with DTDs describing their structures. Such aspects require the definition and enforcement of more sophisticated access control mechanisms for XML, than the ones devised for HTML. An access control model for XML documents has been recently proposed in [3]. Such model borrows some ideas from previous models for object-oriented databases and does not actually take into account some peculiarities of XML. For example, the case of documents not conforming/partially conforming to a DTD is not considered, and no support is provided to the Security Officer for protecting such documents.

The paper is organized as follows. Section 2 summarizes characteristics of the Author-$\mathcal{X}$ discretionary access control model and describes the overall system architecture. Section 3 describes the structure of an XML source and of the authorization base. Section 4 presents the access control module of Author-$\mathcal{X}$. Section 5 illustrates expected interactions of the Security Officer with Author-$\mathcal{X}$ for authorization management.

Finally, Section 6 concludes the paper and outlines future research directions.

2. Overview of Author-$\mathcal{X}$

In the following we first briefly review the access control model of Author-$\mathcal{X}$ [1]. Then, we present its overall architecture.

2.1. Author-$\mathcal{X}$ access control model

Authorizations in the Author-$\mathcal{X}$ model have the following format:

$$< \texttt{users}, \texttt{protection-objs}, \texttt{priv}, \texttt{prop-opt}, \texttt{sign} >$$

Component `users` denotes a (set of) user(s) to which the authorization applies. Component `protection-objs` denotes the (portions of) documents/DTDs (called *protection objects*) to which the authorization applies. The `priv` component denotes the access modes that can be exercised on the protection objects specified in the authorization. We support two different kinds of privileges: *browsing* and *authoring* privileges. Browsing privileges allow users to read the information in an element (`read` privilege) or to navigate through its links (`navigate` privilege). Authoring privileges allow users to modify (or delete) the content of an element (`write` privilege) or to append new information in an element (`append` privilege). The `prop-opt` component allows one to specify how authorizations specified at a given level propagate to lower level elements. The following options are provided: *i)* CASCADE: the authorization propagates to all the direct and indirect subelements of the element(s) specified in the authorization; *2)* FIRST_LEV: the authorization propagates only to all the direct subelements of the element(s) specified in the authorization; *3)* NO_PROP: no authorization propagation occurs. Finally, the component `sign` $\in$ {`+`, `-`} specifies whether the authorization is a permission (`sign` = `+`) or a prohibition (`sign` =`-`).

In addition to such "explicit" propagation, Author-$\mathcal{X}$ supports a form of "implicit" propagation according to which an authorization specified on a certain protection object o "applies by default" to a set of protection objects that have a relationship with o. In Author-$\mathcal{X}$, the relationships considered for propagation are the *element-to-subelements*, *element-to-attributes*, *element-to-links* relationships, deriving from the graph structure of documents and DTDs, and the *DTD-to-instances* relationship, holding between a DTD and the set of its valid instances. Note that, the possibility of specifying both positive and negative authorizations allows the Security Officer to always override these "by default" propagation principles.

The possibility of specifying both positive and negative authorizations introduces potential conflicts among authorizations, in that a user may have two authorizations for the same privilege on the same protection object but with different signs. These conflicting authorizations can be either explicit or derived through propagation. We do not consider the simultaneous presence of conflicting authorizations as an inconsistency; rather we define a conflict resolution policy which is based on the notion of *most specific authorization.* The conflict resolution policy of Author-$\mathcal{X}$ is based on the following principles: authorizations specified at the document level prevail over authorizations specified at the DTD level; authorizations specified at a given level in the DTD/document hierarchy prevail over authorizations specified at higher levels; when conflicts are not solved by the previous rules, we consider as prevailing negative authorizations.

2.2. Architecture of Author-$\mathcal{X}$

Author-$\mathcal{X}$ is built on top of eXcelon [4], an XML data server for building Web applications. EXcelon manages an XMLstore where the XML data can be indexed and manipulated using the Document Object Model (DOM) [8], and queried using the XQL language [5]. Programmers can extend eXcelon functionalities by writing Java server extensions. The purpose of server extensions is to extend the eXcelon server with custom modules to cover specific application requirements.

Figure 1 shows the general architecture of an eXcelon document server enhanced with Author-$\mathcal{X}$. Author-$\mathcal{X}$ components of the architecture are:

- *XMLStore*, which is organized in two components: *XML source*, which stores XML documents and DTDs to be protected, and $\mathcal{X}$*-base*, the authorization base storing authorizations.

- $\mathcal{X}$*-core*, which is the main component of the architecture. It is composed of two Java server extensions, $\mathcal{X}$*-access* and $\mathcal{X}$*-admin*. $\mathcal{X}$*-access* is the server extension implementing access control over the *XML source* based on authorizations contained in $\mathcal{X}$*-base*. $\mathcal{X}$*-admin* is the server extension providing support functionalities to the Security Officer for authorization management.

$\mathcal{X}$*-core* is part of the eXcelon data server and interacts with the external environment by means of an eXcelon client API. Users and the Security Officer interact with $\mathcal{X}$*-core* by means of specific user applications, or through the Web, using an eXcelon explorer or a Web server extension. Users submit access requests which are processed by the $\mathcal{X}$*-access* component of $\mathcal{X}$*-core*, and receive back the (portion of) re-

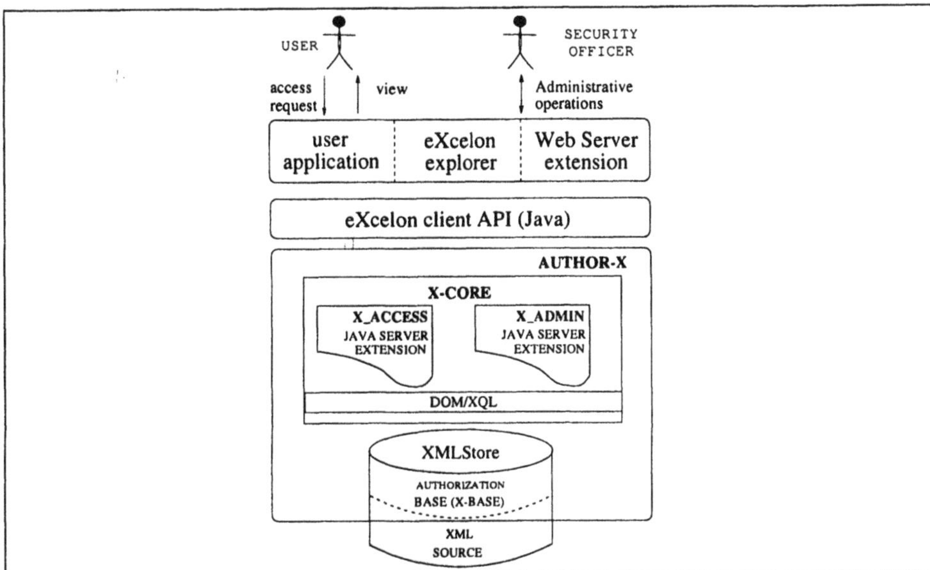

Figure 1: Architecture of an eXcelon document server enhanced with Author-$\mathcal{X}$

quested data in the *XML source* they are authorized for. The Security Officer interacts with the $\mathcal{X}$*-admin* component of $\mathcal{X}$*-core*, for performing administrative operations on authorizations in the $\mathcal{X}$*-base*.

3. Structure of Author-$\mathcal{X}$ XMLStore

In this section, we describe in more detail the structure of the XML-Store, i.e., the *XML source* and the $\mathcal{X}$*-base*.

3.1. XML source

The *XML source* component of the XMLStore contains XML documents to be protected with their DTDs, if defined. In particular, the source can contain well-formed or valid documents. A *well-formed* document is a document that follows the grammar rules of XML [9], while, *valid documents* have an associated DTD defining their structure.

To illustrate functionalities of Author-$\mathcal{X}$, we have defined an *XML source* derived from the *Sigmod Record Articles XML Database* [7], containing sigmod record documents and associated DTDs. Figure 2(a) shows a portion of an XML document in the *XML source*. For each sigmod record issue, the document provides information about the number and volume, and about articles therein contained. Each article is characterized by information about title, authors, abstract, initial page and final page in the issue. Moreover, information about related articles

```
<SigmodRecord>
 <issue>
  <volume>11</volume>
  <number>1</number>
  <articles>
   <article id="WB99" related="KG98">
    <title>Annotated...</title>
    <initPage>45</initPage>
    <endPage>77</endPage>
    <abstract>...</abstract>
    <authors>
     <author position="00">
      Anthony I. Wasserman
     </author>
     <author position="01">
      Karen Botnich
     </author>
    </authors>
   </article>
   ....
   <article id="KG98"> ...  </article>
   ...
  </articles>
 </issue>
 ....
</SigmodRecord>
```

(a)

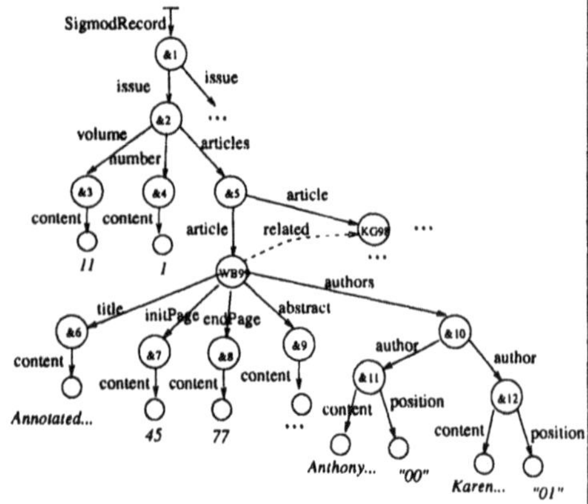

(b)

Figure 2: (a) An example of SigmodRecord XML document and (b) its corresponding graph representation

is provided in the document. Figure 2(b) shows a graph representation of the XML document in Figure 2(a). This representation is compliant with the Document Object Model (DOM) specification [8] adopted by eXcelon to internally represent XML documents.

3.2. $\mathcal{X}$-base

The $\mathcal{X}$-*base* part of the XMLStore is an XML file (`auth.xml`) storing authorizations on the XML source contents. Authorizations in the $\mathcal{X}$-*base* conform to the DTD presented in Figure 3.

According to the DTD of Figure 3, authorizations are organized into an `authorizations` XML document with a subelement `users`, denoting users, and a subelement `auths`, denoting access authorizations. The `users` subelement contains a `user` subelement for each user to be authorized to access the *XML source.* Each `user` element is identified by the login of the corresponding user (attribute `id`) and contains the password of the user (attribute `passwd`). The `auths` element contains an `authspec` subelement for each authorization given to a certain user on the *XML source.* Each `authspec` element is characterized by the following attributes:

- `userid`: it contains a reference to the user to which the authorization refers;

```
<!DOCTYPE authorizations[
<!ELEMENT authorizations (users,auths)>
<!ELEMENT users (user)+>
<!ELEMENT user EMPTY>
<!ELEMENT auths (authspec)*>
<!ELEMENT authspec EMPTY>
<!ATTLIST user id ID #REQUIRED passwd CDATA #REQUIRED>
<!ATTLIST authspec userid IDREF #REQUIRED target CDATA #REQUIRED path CDATA #REQUIRED
          priv (READ | NAVIGATE | APPEND | WRITE) #REQUIRED
          type (GRANT | DENY) #REQUIRED
          prop (NO_PROP | ONE_LEVEL | CASCADE) #REQUIRED> ]>
```

Figure 3: $\mathcal{X}$-*base* DTD

- `target`: it stores the file name of the XML document/DTD to which the authorization refers;
- `path`: it stores a path within the `target` document corresponding to the specific protection object(s) to which the authorization applies. `path` is based on the following notation, compliant with Xpath [10] and XQL language [5]:

  /[{`elem`['[`expr`]']/}]`TRGelem`['[`expr`]'][/@`TRGattr`['[`expr`]']}

  where: first symbol '/' denotes the root element; `TRGelem` denotes the name of a target element; `TRGattr` denotes the name of a target attribute;[1] {`elem/`} denote optional intermediate element(s) (separated by '/') in the path from the root element to the target element/attribute in the considered file, and `[expr]` is an optional condition on an element/attribute content to select specific document portions in the considered XML source files.
- `perm`: it stores the authorization privilege (i.e., READ, NAVIGATE, APPEND, or WRITE);
- `type`: it stores the authorization type (i.e., GRANT, or DENY);
- `prop`: it stores the propagation option of the authorization (i.e., NO_PROP, ONE_LEVEL, or CASCADE).

Example 1 *An example of $\mathcal{X}$-base is shown in Figure 4. According to this authorization base, users* `Mary` *and* `Rose` *are authorized to read all information about issues contained in the Sigmod Record document of the* XML source, *except articles'* `abstract`. *Additionally,* `Mary` *is authorized to read all the information about the article identified by* `WB99`. ○

[1]Symbol @ denotes attribute names as in Xpath and XQL.

```
<authorizations>
 <users>
  <user id="Mary" passwd="%$#$%"/ >
  <user id="Rose" passwd="&#$%"/ >
 </users>
 <auths>
  <auth-spec userid="Mary" target="SigmodRecord.dtd" path="/issue"
    priv="READ" type="GRANT" prop="CASCADE"/ >
  <auth-spec userid="Rose" target="SigmodRecord.dtd" path="/issue"
    priv="READ" type="GRANT" prop="CASCADE"/ >
  <auth-spec userid="Mary" target="SigmodRecord.dtd" path="/issue/articles/article/abstract"
    priv="READ" type="DENY" prop="NO_PROP"/ >
  <auth-spec userid="Rose" target="SigmodRecord.dtd" path="/issue/articles/article/abstract"
    priv="READ" type="DENY" prop="NO_PROP"/ >
  <auth-spec userid="Mary" target="SigmodRecord.xml"
    path="/issue/articles/article[@id='WB99']" priv="READ" type="GRANT" prop="CASCADE"/ >
 </auths>
</authorizations>
```

Figure 4: An example of $\mathcal{X}$*-base*

4. The $\mathcal{X}$-access component of Author-$\mathcal{X}$

The $\mathcal{X}$-access component of Author-$\mathcal{X}$ enforces access control on the *XML source.*

Users request access to documents under two different modalities: *browsing* and *authoring.* A user requests a browsing access when he/she wants to access a document (and navigating its links), without modifying it, whereas, requests an authoring access when a modification of the document is required. Access can also be requested wrt a specific portion(s) of a document. Thus, an access request `r` is represented as a tuple `r=` ⟨`user,target,path,acc_modality`⟩, where `user` is the user requesting the access, `target` is the XML document to which the access is requested, `path` is a path within the requested document (specified through an XQL query [5]) which eventually selects specific portions of the requested document, and `acc_modality` ∈ {`browsing,authoring`} specifies whether a browsing or authoring access is requested.

Upon issuing an access request `r`, $\mathcal{X}$-access checks which authorizations (both positive and negative) `user` has on the `target` document. Such authorizations can be either explicitly stored in the $\mathcal{X}$*-base* or implicitly given by the propagation policies enforced by Author-$\mathcal{X}$ model. Based on such authorizations, `user` can receive a *view* of the requested document that contains only those portions for which he/she has a corresponding positive authorization which is not overridden by a negative conflicting authorization. In the case of totally authorized requests, the view coincides with the whole document (or with all the requested portions in the case the user does not require the access to the whole document). When, no positive authorizations are found for the requested document, or all of them are overwritten by negative authorizations, the access is denied.

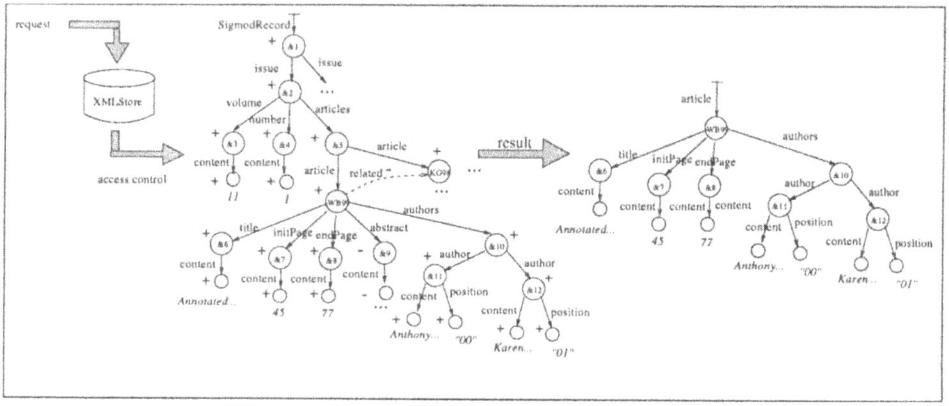

Figure 5: The access control process

To enforce access control, Author-$\mathcal{X}$ adopts the following strategy: all the elements and/or attributes for which `user` does not have an appropriate authorization are removed from the `target` document, before evaluating the `path` contained in the access request. The `path` is then evaluated against such pruned version and the result is returned to `user`. This strategy allows us to define an access control mechanism independent from any query language. This possibility is very important, because XQL is not yet a standard query language.

For lack of space we do not report here the access control algorithm implementing the above strategies. A detailed description of the algorithm can be found in [1].

Example 2 *Suppose that* `Rose` *submits the access request*

⟨`Rose`, `SigmodRecord.xml`, `/issue/articles/article[@id =' WB99']`, `browsing`⟩

Figure 5 shows the access control process. Author-$\mathcal{X}$ extracts the browsing authorizations for `Rose` *(from the $\mathcal{X}$-base reported in Figure 4) and evaluates them against the file* `SigmodRecord.xml`*. The result of the evaluation is a graph, where each node is labeled with symbol "−", if a negative authorization applies to the corresponding attribute/element, or with symbol "+", if a positive authorization applies to the corresponding attribute/element. The view to be returned to* `Rose` *is obtained by pruning from the graph nodes with a label different from "+", and by extracting from the resulting graph the elements/attributes identified by the path:* `/issue/articles/ article[@id='WB99']`*. As a result, a view of article* `WB99` *is returned to* `Rose` *(shown on the right hand side of Figure 5) that does not contain the* `abstract` *element.* ○

Figure 6 shows the graphical interface provided by Author-$\mathcal{X}$ for access request submission (the access request is the one of Example 2).

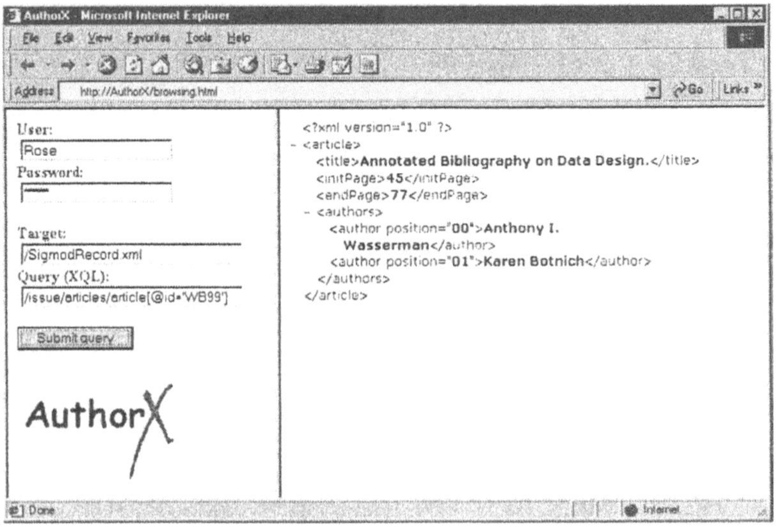

Figure 6: Access request submission in Author-$\mathcal{X}$

The left hand side of the figure shows how the user can submit his/her request, whereas the right hand side shows the corresponding result.

5. The $\mathcal{X}$-admin component of Author-$\mathcal{X}$

The $\mathcal{X}$-admin component of Author-$\mathcal{X}$ is designed to support administrative operations on authorizations under responsibility of the Security Officer. In particular, $\mathcal{X}$-admin supports the Security Officer in defining new authorizations to protect XML documents in the *XML source*.

Author-$\mathcal{X}$ supports two kinds of policies for authorization specification: a *DTD-based policy*, in which authorizations are specified at the DTD level, and propagated within the DTD due to the element-to-subelements and the element-to-attributes/links relationships as well as to all XML documents that are valid instances of the DTD, due to the DTD-to-instances relationship, and a *document-based policy*, in which authorizations are specified at the document level, and apply only to the considered document. In this case, authorization propagation occurs only due to the element-to-subelements and the element-to-attributes/links relationships within the considered document.

Based on these policies, authorization management for valid and well-formed documents can be enforced by the Security Officer in Author-$\mathcal{X}$ as follows:

- **Valid document protection**: the DTD-based policy is adopted, in that valid documents are instances of some DTD in the source.

As a consequence, the Security Officer specifies authorizations at the DTD level which apply by default to all its valid document instances. Exceptions to the policy defined at the DTD level are modeled by specific authorizations defined in the *$\mathcal{X}$-base* on the involved document instances. For instance, if all information in a set of valid documents have the same protection requirements, then the Security Officer invokes the definition of authorizations at the DTD level, with the CASCADE option. By contrast, when different subelement(s) (respectively, attributes/links) of a DTD need different authorization policies, it is convenient to guarantee a minimal common protection on the whole DTD by defining an authorization with the NO_PROP or FIRST_LEV propagation option. A number of additional authorizations are then defined on the subelement(s) (respectively, attribute(s)/link(s)) of the DTD with the most appropriate privileges and sign to enforce the policy holding on the specific subelement(s) (respectively, attribute(s)/link(s)).

- **Well-formed documents**: different approaches are supported by Author-$\mathcal{X}$. According to a *classification-based approach*, the Security Officer decides to adopt the DTD-based policy also for well-formed documents. To this end, well-formed documents to be protected are first classified against available DTDs in the source, with the goal of finding the "best matching" DTD. If such a DTD is found by the tool, protection of a well-formed document is enforced by propagating authorizations defined for the selected DTD to the document. This propagation can be total or partial, depending on the level of conformance between the well-formed document and the selected DTD (conformance vs. partial conformance). In case of partial conformance, the Security Officer can manually define additional authorizations on non-matching portions of the well-formed document, if necessary. According to an *instance-based approach*, the Security Officer defines from scratch authorizations needed to implement the access control policy for the considered well-formed document (document-based policy). The document-based policy is also adopted when no conforming DTD is found after the classification process, and also when exceptions for the policy defined in the selected DTD have to be specified, when the classification-based approach is taken.
  The classification-based approach exploits the propagation principle to limit the manual activity of the Security Officer in the definition of the authorization policy for a well-formed document. The classification-based approach relies on suitable mechanisms to

automatically derive all required authorizations for all the involved users. The Security Officer can interactively validate derived authorizations to check their suitability to the well-formed document to be protected.

6. Concluding Remarks

In this paper, we have presented Author-$\mathcal{X}$, a Java-based system for access control to XML sources. Author-$\mathcal{X}$ supports positive and negative authorizations for browsing and authoring privileges with a controlled propagation. Core functionalities of access control and authorization base management have been implemented as Java server extensions on top of the eXcelon data server. Currently, we are setting up a comprehensive administration environment, by developing interactive tool support for the Security Officer to guide the choice of the best policy to be adopted for document protection, based on the results of document classification process.

References

[1] E. Bertino, M. Brawn, S. Castano, E. Ferrari, and M. Mesiti. Author-$\mathcal{X}$: a Java-Based System for XML Data Protection. In pre-Proc. of 14th IFIP WG11.3 Working Conference on Database and Application Security. Schoorl, The Netherlands, August, 2000.

[2] E. Bertino, S. Castano, E. Ferrari, and M. Mesiti. Specifying and Enforcing Access Control Policies for XML Document Sources. *World Wide Web Journal*, 3(3), 2000.

[3] E. Damiani, S. De Capitani di Vimercati, S. Paraboschi, and P. Samarati. Securing XML Documents. In *Proc. of EDBT*, 2000.

[4] Object Design Inc. An XML Data Server for Building Enterprise Web Applications, 1998. `http://www.odi.com/excelon`.

[5] J. Robie. XQL Tutorial, 2000. `http://www.ibiblio.org/xql/xql-tutorial.htm`

[6] P. Samarati, E. Bertino, and S. Jajodia. An Authorization Model for a Distributed Hypertext System. *IEEE TKDE*, 8(4):555–562, 1996.

[7] Sigmod Record XML Database. `http://www.dia.uniroma3.it/Areneus/Sigmod`

[8] W3C. Document Object Model 1, 1998. `http://www.w3.org/DOM/`.

[9] W3C. Extensible Markup Language 1.0, 1998. `http://www.w3.org/TR/REC-xml`.

[10] W3C. XML Path Language, 1.0, 1999. `http://www.w3.org/TR/xpath`.

Chapter 3

A FAIR-EXCHANGE E-COMMERCE PROTOCOL WITH AUTOMATED DISPUTE RESOLUTION

Indrajit Ray
Department of Computer and Information Science
University of Michigan-Dearborn
indrajit@umich.edu

Indrakshi Ray
Department of Computer and Information Science
University of Michigan-Dearborn
iray@umich.edu

Natarajan Narasimhamurthi
Department of Electrical and Computer Engineering
University of Michigan-Dearborn
nnarasim@engin.umd.umich.edu

Abstract

In this paper, we present a fair-exchange electronic commerce (e-commerce) protocol, based on using an online trusted third party, that ensures fairness and prevents any party from gaining advantage by quitting prematurely from the transaction or otherwise misbehaving. An important contribution of this protocol is that the dispute resolution is taken care of within the protocol itself and does not require manual intervention. Thus even if one of the parties disappear after the transaction completion, the other party does not suffer in any manner. Another noteworthy contribution is that the protocol allows the customer to verify that the product he is about to receive is the one he actually ordered, before the customer pays for the product. At the same time it ensures that the customer receives the product if and only if the merchant gets paid for the product. All these features are achieved without significantly increasing the communication overhead or interactions with the third party as compared with similar protocols.

1. INTRODUCTION

In an electronic commerce environment the merchants and the customers are reluctant to trust each other and the following scenario is not uncommon. A customer is not willing to pay for a product without being sure it is the correct product sent by the merchant. A merchant is not willing to give the product unless he is sure that he will receive payment. If the merchant delivers the product without receiving the payment, the fraudulent customer may receive the product and then disappear without trace, causing loss for the merchant. If the customer pays before receiving the product, the merchant may not deliver or may deliver some wrong product. To address this problem we propose a fair exchange protocol that ensures the two parties get their respective items without allowing either party to gain an advantage by quitting or otherwise misbehaving.

Fair exchange protocols have been proposed in the context of electronic mails [2, 8] and electronic transactions [1, 3]. Most of these works [1, 2, 8] focus on storing evidence that is to be used in case one party misbehaves. If a dispute occurs, a judge looks at the evidence and delivers his judgment. This dispute resolution is done after the protocol execution, that is, after the customer has obtained his product or the merchant his money. However, such "after-the-fact" protection [3, 4] may be inadequate in an e-commerce environment where the customer and the merchant may not have identifiable places of existence and may be unreachable after the transaction. This motivates us to propose a protocol in which dispute resolution is within the scope of the protocol.

The e-commerce protocol that we develop is based on a theory of cross validation. A merchant has several products. He places a description of his products and the encrypted products in a catalog server. If the customer is interested in a product, he downloads the encrypted version of the product. When the customer agress to purchase the product, the merchant sends it encrypted with a second key such that this key bears a mathematical relation with the key the merchant used when putting up the encrypted product on the catalog server. The mathematical relation between the keys is such that the encrypted messages compare if and only if the unencrypted messages compare. Thus, by comparing the encrypted product received with the encrypted product that the customer downloaded from the catalog, the customer can be sure that the product he is about to pay for is indeed the product he wanted. Once the customer is satisfied with his comparison, he sends his payment token to a trusted third party. At the same time, the merchant sends the decrypting key to the third party. The third party verifies the customer's financial information and forwards the payment token to the merchant and the decrypting key to the customer. Thus we ensure that fairness is established in the protocol.

Tygar [7] has identified three desirable properties of a secure e-commerce protocol. These are the *money atomicity, goods atomicity* and *certified delivery* properties. To prevent any misbehavior during the execution of the protocol, we propose a new property which we call the *validated receipt* property. This property allows the customer to verify the contents of the product the merchant is about to deliver *before* making the payment. We reason that our protocol satisfies all of these properties.

The rest of the paper is organized as follows: Section 2 presents the theory for cross validation and then introduces the validated receipt property. This section also describes briefly the product validation process based on this validated receipt property. Section 3 describes the complete protocol. Section 4 shows informally that the protocol has all the desirable properties of secure e-commerce protocols. This section also discusses how transaction disputes are resolved automatically without human arbitration. Finally, Section 5 concludes the paper.

2. THEORY FOR CROSS VALIDATION

Before presenting our protocol we establish the theory of cross-validation on which the protocol is based. For lack of space we omit the proofs for the theorems presented here. The interested reader is referred to [6].

We assume that the item that needs to be validated by the customer, is transferred from the merchant to the customer in the form of a message. Examples of such products are digital library items such as, electronic papers, magazines, books, images, internet movies, music etc.

Definition 1 The set of *messages* $\mathcal{M}$ is the set of non negative integers m that are less than an upper bound N, i.e.

$$\mathcal{M} = \{m | 0 \leq m < N\} \tag{1}$$

Definition 2 For positive integers a, b and N, we say a is *equivalent* to b, modulo N, denoted by $a \equiv b \bmod n$, if $a \bmod n = b \bmod n$.

Definition 3 For positive integers a, x, n and $n > 1$, if $\gcd(a, n) = 1$ and $a.x \equiv 1 \bmod n$, then x is referred to as the *multiplicative inverse of a modulo n*. Two integers a, b are said to be *relatively prime* if their only common divisor is 1, that is, $\gcd(a, b) = 1$. The integers n_1,n_2,. . .,n_k are said to be *pairwise relatively prime*, if $\gcd(n_i, n_j) = 1$ for $i \neq j$.

Definition 4 The Euler's totient function $\phi(N)$ is defined as the number of integers that are less than N and relatively prime to N.

Theorem 1 Euler's theorem states that for every a and N that are relatively prime,

$$a^{\phi(n)} \equiv 1 \bmod N$$

Corollary 1 If $0 < m < N$ and $N = N_1 N_2 \ldots N_k$ and $N_1, N_2, \ldots, N_k$ are primes, then $m^{x\phi(N)+1} \equiv m \bmod N$.

Definition 5 A *key* K is defined to be the ordered pair $< e, N >$, where N is a product of distinct primes, $N \geq M$, where M is the largest message in the set of messages $\mathcal{M}$, and e is relatively prime to $\phi(N)$; e is the *exponent* and N is the *base* of the key K.

Definition 6 The *encryption* of a message m with the key $K = < e, N >$, denoted as $[m,K]$, is defined as

$$[m, < e, N >] = m^e \bmod N \tag{2}$$

Definition 7 The *inverse* of a key $K =< e, N >$, denoted by K^{-1}, is an ordered pair $< d, N >$, satisfying $ed \equiv 1 \bmod \phi(N)$.

Theorem 2 For any message m.

$$\left[[m, K], K^{-1}\right] = \left[\left[m, K^{-1}\right], K\right] = m \tag{3}$$

where $K =< e, N >$ and $K^{-1} =< d, N >$.

Corollary 2 An encryption, $[m, K]$, is *one-to-one* if it satisfies the relation

$$\left[[m, K], K^{-1}\right] = \left[\left[m, K^{-1}\right], K\right] = m$$

Definition 8 Two keys $K_1 =< e_1, N_1 >$ and $K_2 =< e_2, N_2 >$ are said to be *compatible* if $e_1 = e_2$ and N_1 and N_2 are relatively prime.

Definition 9 If two keys $K_1 =< e, N_1 >$ and $K_2 =< e, N_2 >$ are *compatible*, then the *product* key, $K_1 \times K_2$, is defined as $< e, N_1 N_2 >$.

Lemma 1 For positive integers a, N_1 and N_2,

$$(a \bmod N_1 N_2) \equiv a \bmod N_1$$

Theorem 3 For any two messages m and $\hat{m}$, such that $m, \hat{m} < N_1, N_2$,

$$[m, K_1 \times K_2] \equiv [\hat{m}, K_1] \bmod N_1 \text{ if and only if } m = \hat{m} \tag{4}$$

$$[m, K_1 \times K_2] \equiv [\hat{m}, K_2] \bmod N_2 \text{ if and only if } m = \hat{m} \tag{5}$$

where K_1 is the key $< e, N_1 >$, K_2 is the key $< e, N_2 >$ and $K_1 \times K_2$ is the product key $< e, N_1 N_2 >$.

2.1. VALIDATED RECEIPT PROPERTY

The validated receipt property is stated as follows:

Validated Receipt A customer is able to ensure that the product he is about to receive from the merchant is the same as the product he ordered, before the customer pays for the product.

Our protocol achieves the validated receipt property using the results of theorem 3. Let m be the product to be delivered. The values N_1 and N_2 are public. The merchant generates the set of keys (K_1, K_1^{-1}), and sends m, K_1 and K_1^{-1} to a trusted third party. The trusted third party computes $T = [m, K_1]$ (that is encrypts m with the key K_1) and places T at a public place, henceforth called the catalog, as an advertisement for m. When the customer decides to purchase m from the merchant, the customer acquires T from the catalog and keeps it for future validation of the product received.

To sell m to the customer, the merchant selects a second set of keys (K_2, K_2^{-1}) such that K_2 is compatible with K_1 according to definition 8. The merchant escrows the key K_2^{-1} with the trusted third party and provides the customer with $C = [m, K_1 \times K_2]$.

The customer verifies that T and C are encryption of the same message m by verifying: $T \equiv C \bmod N_1$, as per equation (4)

When satisfied, the customer requests the key K_2^{-1} from the trusted third party and decrypts C to obtain m using

$$m = \left[C, K_2^{-1}\right]$$

The proof of correctness follows from theorem 3:

$$[m, K_1 \times K_2] \equiv [\hat{m}, K_2] \bmod N_2 \text{ if and only if } m = \hat{m}$$

3. THE COMPLETE PROTOCOL

3.1. ASSUMPTIONS

We make the following assumptions in the protocol:

1 We assume the existence of an on-line trusted third party.

2 Before the protocol is initiated, mutual authentication takes place between the trusted third party, the customer and the merchant and secure channels are set up between them. All communications are assumed to occur over these secure channels so that confidentiality of messages in transit is ensured. Note, we do not assume that integrity of messages will be ensured; nor do we assume that the secure channels are immune to replay attacks.

3 We assume that a message transmitted over a channel is guaranteed to be delivered.

4 We assume that all encryptions are strong enough that the receiver of an encrypted message is unable to decrypt the message without the appropriate key.

5 All parties use the same algorithm for encryption as well as for generating cryptographic checksums.

6 Financial institutions are assumed to be trusted. The customer and its financial institution shares a secret key that was established when the customer opened an account with the financial institution.

7 Payment for product is in the form of a token, $\mathcal{P}$, that is accepted by the merchant.

8 The merchant advertises the product with the trusted third party by keeping an encrypted copy of the product, $[m, K_1]$, with the trusted third party, together with a description of the product. Note that the merchant actually creates the key pair K_1 and K_1^{-1} and sends m, K_1 and K_1^{-1} to the trusted party. The trusted third party performs the encryption before advertising the product on the catalog. We prefer this approach over the merchant providing the encrypted copy of the product, because, in this manner, the trusted third party is able to certify that the product meets its claims.

Table 3.1 lists the notations used in the description of the protocol.

3.2. PHASE 1: INTENT TO PURCHASE PRODUCT

1 TP $\Longrightarrow$ C: PID, $[m, K_1]$

2 C $\Longrightarrow$ M: PO = {purchase-order,[CC(purchase-order),C_{prv}]}, where purchase-order = {PID,C,M,Agreed_Price,ψ_C}

Message 1 The customer browses the product catalog located at the trusted third party, and chooses the product m he wants to buy. Then he gets the encrypted form of the product, namely, $[m, K_1]$, together with the product identifier, PID.
Message 2 The customer decides on a price (Agreed_Price) to pay for the product and prepares a purchase order. The purchase order contains the following information:

(i) the product identifier, PID

(ii) the customer's identity, C

Table 3.1. Symbols used in protocol description

C, M and TP	Ids for customer, merchant and trusted third party
A_{prv}, A_{pub}	A's private and public keys
$A \Longrightarrow B$: X	A sends X to B
m	Product the customer purchases
PID	The id for product m
C_{Act}	Customer's account information with customer's financial institution
CF	A secret key shared between the customer and its financial institution
F_C	An Id for customer's financial institution
$\mathcal{P}$	Payment token used for paying for goods
[X,K]	encryption of X with key K
CC(X)	A cryptographic checksum of X, using an algorithm such as the Secure Hash [5]
K^{-1}	decryption key corresponding to encryption key K
ψ_A	a nonce for entity A. Each entity's nonces are unique and different from other entities' nonces.

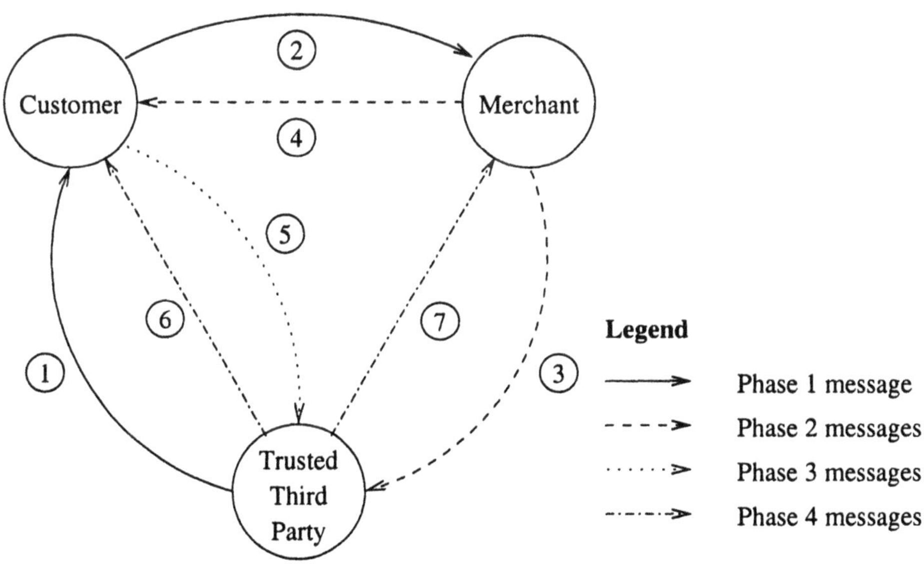

Figure 3.1. Messages exchanged in the e-commerce protocol

(iii) the identity of the merchant, M

(iv) the price of the product, Agreed_Price, and

(v) a nonce, ψ_C, from the customer.

The customer generates a cryptographic checksum of the purchase-order and then digitally signs the digest. The cryptographic checksum of the purchase-order forestalls debate over the details of the order, or whether the order was received completely and correctly. The customer's signature forestalls debate over whether the customer expressed intention to purchase the product. The nonce, ψ_C, in the purchase order forestalls a replay of the purchase order with the merchant.

The purchase order and its signed checksum, together henceforth called PO, is then forwarded to the merchant.

3.3. PHASE 2: KEY ESCROW AND PRODUCT DELIVERY

3 M $\Longrightarrow$ TP: [[CC(purchase-order),C_{prv}],M_{prv}], K_2^{-1}, [CC([m,$K_1 \times K_2$]),M_{prv}]

4 M $\Longrightarrow$ C: [m,$K_1 \times K_2$], [CC([m,$K_1 \times K_2$]),M_{prv}]

Message 3 The merchant endorses the purchase order received from the customer, provided the merchant agrees to all its contents (that is, the Agreed_Price is indeed the price agreed upon for the product m); the merchant then digitally signs the cryptographic checksum of the purchase-order bearing the customer's signature, that is [CC(purchase-order),C_{prv}] and forwards it to the trusted third party. This prevents the merchant claiming later on that he hadn't agreed to the terms and conditions of the transaction.

The merchant, at this time, generates a second set of keys K_2 and K_2^{-1} such that K_1 and K_2 are compatible. He encrypts m with the product key, $K_1 \times K_2$ and prepares a cryptographic checksum, CC([m,$K_1 \times K_2$]), from it. The merchant digitally signs this digest and forwards it, together with the key K_2^{-1}, to the trusted third party. The signed digest for [m,$K_1 \times K_2$] provides certified delivery.

Message 4 To the customer the merchant sends the encrypted product [m,$K_1 \times K_2$] together with its signed cryptographic checksum [CC([m,$K_1 \times K_2$]),M_{prv}]. The signed cryptographic checksum establishes origin of the product and also forestalls debate over the product being corrupted in transit.

3.4. PHASE 3: PRODUCT VALIDATION AND PAYMENT FOR PRODUCT

5 C $\Longrightarrow$ TP: PO, [CC([m, $K_1 \times K_2$]),C_{prv}], [$\mathcal{P}$,C_{prv}], [CC($\mathcal{P}$),C_{prv}], where $\mathcal{P}$ = {F_C,C,[C_{Act},CF],Agreed_Price,ψ_C}

Message 5 The customer validates the product by comparing $[m, K_1]$ with $[m, K_1 \times K_2]$ (as outlined in Section 2.1). If the two compare, the customer requests the decrypting key, K_2^{-1}, from the trusted third party. To do this, the customer forwards to the trusted third party, PO (as generated in Phase 1 above), signed payment token, $\mathcal{P}$ together with its cryptographic checksum, and a signed cryptographic checksum of the encrypted product received, $[m, K_1 \times K_2]$.

The payment token contains the following information:

(i) the identity of the customer's financial institution, F_C

(ii) the customer's identity, C

(iii) the customer's account information with the financial institution, C_{Act}

(iv) the amount to be debited from the customer's account, Agreed_Price and

(v) a nonce of the customer, ψ_C.

The customer's account information is encrypted with the secret key, CF, shared between the customer and his financial institution. This ensures that nobody other than the customer and his financial institution can access this information. The nonce, ψ_C, in the payment token ensures that it is not susceptible to replay attacks. The customer prepares a digest of the payment token, CC($\mathcal{P}$) and then digitally signs the token and the digest. The digest forestalls debate over the contents of the payment token and the customer's signature forestalls debate by customer regarding amount debited from his account.

The signed cryptographic checksum of the product received, $[m, K_1 \times K_2]$ ensures certified delivery.

3.5. PHASE 4: PRODUCT AND PAYMENT RECEIPT

6 TP $\Longrightarrow$ C: $[K_2^{-1}, TP_{prv}]$

7 TP $\Longrightarrow$ M: $[\mathcal{P}, TP_{prv}]$

Messages 6 and 7 The trusted third party first compares the digest included in PO from the customer (received in Message 5), with the digest of the same from the merchant (as received in Message 3). If the two do not compare the trusted third party aborts the transaction. If they do, the trusted third party next validates the payment token with the customer's financial institution by presenting the token as well as the agreed upon sale price, Agreed_Price (from the purchase-order). The financial institution validates the token only if the two prices (the one from the payment token and the one supplied by the trusted third party) match and the customer has sufficient funds in his account for the payment. If the token is not validated, the trusted third party aborts the protocol by informing the merchant about this. If token is validated, the trusted third party sends the decrypting key K_2^{-1} to the customer and the payment token $\mathcal{P}$ to the merchant, both digitally signed with the trusted third party's private key.

4. PROTOCOL ANALYSIS

The e-commerce protocol presented here satisfies all the desirable properties of secure e-commerce protocols. Secure channels guarantee the confidentiality of all messages. Transmission freshness of request and/or response is guaranteed by including nonces within the relevant messages. Non-repudiation of the origin for the request and/or response is provided because, wherever required, such requests and/or responses are digitally signed by the sender's private keys.

The protocol ensures money atomicity as follows: The payment token generated by the customer contains the amount to be debited from the customer's account and credited to the merchants account. Consequently no money is created or destroyed in the system (comprising of the merchant's account and the customer's account) by this protocol. Moreover, the nonces in the payment token ensure that the merchant cannot debit the customer's account multiple times for the same purchase.

Goods atomicity is ensured because the trusted third party hands over the payment token only when the customer acknowledges the receipt of the product; the protocol also ensures that the product is actually available to the customer for use, only when the customer gives the go-ahead for payment (by acknowledging the receipt of the good).

Certified delivery is achieved as follows. The trusted third party receives a cryptographic checksum of the product from the merchant. Also the customer independently generates a checksum of the product received and sends it to the trusted third party. Using these two copies of the cryptographic checksums available at the trusted third party both the merchant and the consumer are able to give non-repudiable proof of the contents of the delivered goods.

Finally validated receipt is ensured in the protocol. This has been illustrated earlier in section 2.1.

4.1. DISPUTE HANDLING

Our e-commerce protocol, is able to handle almost all possible dispute scenarios without human arbitration.

Customer complains that product is not as advertised Such a complaint is prevented in the protocol because the trusted third party is involved in advertising the product on the catalog. Recall that the trusted third party receives m, K_1 and K_1^{-1} from the merchant together with a description of m. The trusted third party compares m with its description before encrypting m with key K_1 and placing it on the catalog.

Customer complains about incorrect or damaged product The validated receipt property ensures that the customer requests the decryption key, K_2^{-1} only after the customer is satisfied that the product received is correct. Consequently, if such a complaint is ever made, it is not entertained.

Customer complains about incorrect decryption key K_2^{-1} The trusted third party takes the following steps:

1. From the copy, $[m, K_1]$ that the trusted third party has on the catalog, it gets the product m and sends it to the customer.
2. The trusted third party may optionally take appropriate action with the merchant to prevent such problem/fraud in future.

Customer complains that he was charged more than what he agreed to The trusted third party has a copy of the purchase order, PO, signed by the customer and hence a proof of what the customer agreed to pay. Consequently, such a claim is not entertained.

Customer complains that he has been wrongly charged The trusted third party can settle this dispute by producing the signed purchase order.

Merchant complains of inadequate payment Such a claim is not entertained because the trusted third party validates the payment token with the customer's financial institution.

Merchant complains that payment token was not received The trusted third party re-delivers the payment token. Note that even if the merchant receives the payment token multiple times, it can be used only once because of the presence of the customer's nonce in the payment token.

5. CONCLUSION AND FUTURE WORK

In this work we have proposed a new e-commerce protocol for performing business over the Internet. The protocol relies on an online trusted third party. An important feature of this protocol is that it tries to avoid disputes between the transacting parties. If disputes still arise, the protocol can handle these automatically, without manual intervention and within the protocol itself. The protocol allows the customer to be confident that he is paying for the correct product before actually paying for it. The protocol also ensures that the customer does not get the product unless he pays for it and that the merchant does not get paid unless he delivers the product.

A major bottleneck in the protocol is the trusted third party. Not only is the performance of the trusted third party an issue, but also its vulnerability to denial of service attacks. However, this is not a problem which is limited to our protocol. This bottleneck is present in all e-commerce protocols that require a trusted third party for their operation. We are currently investigating two approaches to reduce this problem. In the first approach we are looking at ways to modify the protocol to reduce the interactions with the trusted third party. In the second approach we are looking at the multiple roles played by the trusted third party and ways to distribute these roles over a number of (possibly) semi-trusted third parties. This second approach will also help in making our protocol fault-tolerant.

Acknowledgment

The works of Indrajit Ray and Indrakshi Ray were partially supported by the NSF under grant EIA 9977548 and by a Faculty Research Grant from the University of Michigan-Dearborn.

References

[1] B. Cox, J. D. Tygar, and M. Sirbu. NetBill Security and Transaction Protocol. In *Proceedings of the First USENIX Workshop in Electronic Commerce*, pages 77–88, July 1995.

[2] R. H. Deng, L. Gong, A. A. Lazar, and W. Wang. Practical Protocols for Certified Electronic Mail. *Journal of Network and System Management*, 4(3), 1996.

[3] S. Ketchpel. Transaction Protection for Information Buyers and Sellers. In *Proceedings of the Dartmouth Institute for Advanced Graduate Studies '95: Electronic Publishing and the Information Superhighway, 1995*, 1995.

[4] S. Ketchpel and H. Garcia-Molina. Making Trust Explicit in Distributed Commerce Transactions. In *Proceedings of the Sixteenth International Conference on Distributed Computing Systems*, pages 270–281, 1996.

[5] National Institute of Standards. FIPS 180: Secure Hash Standard, April 1993. Federal Information Processing Standard.

[6] I. Ray, I. Ray, and N. Narasimhamurthi. A Fair-exchange E-commerce Protocol with Automated Dispute Resolution. Technical Report CIS-TR-010-00, Computer and Information Science Department, University of Michigan-Dearborn, 2000.

[7] J. D. Tygar. Atomicity in Electronic Commerce. In *Proceedings of the 15th Annual ACM Symposium on Principles of Distributed Computing*, pages 8–26, May 1996.

[8] J. Zhou and D. Gollmann. A Fair Non-repudiation Protocol. In *Proceedings of the 1996 IEEE Symposium on Security and Privacy*, pages 55–61, Oakland, California, May 1996.

CHAPTER 4

XML ACCESS CONTROL SYSTEMS: A COMPONENT-BASED APPROACH

E. Damiani[1] S. De Capitani di Vimercati[2] S. Paraboschi[3] P. Samarati[1]
(1) Università di Milano, Polo di Crema, 26013 Crema - Italy
(2) Università di Brescia, 25123 Brescia - Italy
(3) Politecnico di Milano, 20133 Milano - Italy

Abstract We recently proposed an access control model for XML information that permits the definition of authorizations at a fine granularity. We here describe the design and implementation of an *Access Control Processor* based on the above-mentioned model. We also present the major issues arising when integrating it into the framework of a component-based Web server system.

1. INTRODUCTION

XML [2] promises to have a great impact on the way information is exchanged between applications, going well beyond the original goal of being a replacement for HTML. Given the ubiquitous nature of XML, the protection of XML information will become a critical aspect of many security infrastructures. Thus, the investigation of techniques that can offer protection in a way adequate to the peculiarities of the XML data model is an important research goal.

Current solutions do not address the peculiarities of the security of XML information. Web servers may easily export XML documents, but their protection can typically be defined only at the file system level. Our proposal, presented in [3, 4], introduces an access control model for XML data that exploits the characteristics of XML documents, allowing the definition of access control policies that operate with a fine granularity, permitting the definition of authorizations at the level of the single element/attribute of an XML document.

The focus of this paper is the design and implementation of a system offering the services of our access control model. We first give in Section 2 a brief description of the approach. Then, in Section 3 we describe the high-level software architecture. Section 4 presents the IDL interfaces of the classes which implement the services of the access control system. Finally, Section 5 is dedicated to the integration of the access control system with Web based systems.

The analysis contained in this paper derives from the experience we gained in the implementation of the current prototype of the system; our results should be helpful to those considering the implementation of security mechanisms in the WWW/XML context.

2. XML ACCESS CONTROL MODEL

The access control model we present is based on the definition of authorizations at the level of the elements and attributes of an XML document.

A natural interpretation for XML documents is to consider them as trees, where elements and attributes correspond to nodes, and the containment relation between nodes is represented by the tree arcs. Authorizations can be *local*, if the access privilege they represent applies only to a specific element node and its attributes, or can be *recursive*, if the access is granted/denied to the node and all the nodes descending from it (i.e., the nodes that in the textual representation of an XML document are enclosed between the start and end tags).

We identified two levels at which authorizations on XML documents can be defined, instance and DTD (Document Type Definition, a syntax defining the structure of the document). DTD level authorizations specify the privileges of all the documents following a given DTD, whereas instance level authorizations denote privileges that apply only to a specific document. The distinction between the two authorization types may correspond to the distribution of responsibilities in an organization, as DTD authorizations may be considered derived from the requirements of the global enterprise, whereas authorizations on the instance may be the responsibility of the creator of the document. We also hypothesize that normal DTD authorizations are dominated by instance level ones (following the general principle that more specific authorizations win [6, 9] and that an instance level authorization is more specific than a DTD level one), but we also consider the need for an organization to have assurance that some of the DTD authorizations are not overruled. Thus, we permit the definition of *hard* DTD authorizations, which dominate instance level ones. For cases where instance level authorizations must be explicitly defined as valid only if not in conflict with DTD level ones, we designed *soft* instance level authorizations.

Each authorization has five components: *subject*, *object*, *type*, *action* and *sign*. The subject is composed by a triple that describes the user or the group of users to which the authorization applies, combined with the numeric (IP) and symbolic (DNS) addresses of the machine originating the request. This triple can thus permit to define controls that consider both the user and the location. Wild card character `*` permits the definition of patterns for addresses (e.g., `131.*` for all IP addresses having `131` as first component, or `*.it` for all addresses in the Italian domain). The authorization applies on the request only if the triple of parameters of the requester is equal or more specific in all three components of the authorization subject. For example, an authorization with subject `<Student,131.175.*,*.polimi.it>` will be applied to a request from `<Ennio,131.175.16.43,pcenn.elet.polimi.it>`, if `Ennio` is a member of group `Student`. The object is identified by means of an XPath [13] expression. XPath expressions may be used to identify document components in a declarative way, but they can also use navigation functions, like `child`, offering a standard and powerful way to identify the elements and attributes of an XML document. The type can be one of eight values, arising from the combination of three binary properties: DTD level or instance level; local or recursive; normal or soft/hard. The eight types, in order of priority, are: local DTD level hard (LDH), recursive DTD level hard

(RDH), local instance level (L), recursive instance level (R), local DTD level (LD), recursive DTD level (RD), local instance level soft (LS), recursive instance level soft (RS). Since currently, most XML applications offer read-only access, the action currently supported by our prototype is only *read*.
A positive authorization sign specifies that the authorization permits access, a negative sign instead forbids it.

Authorizations are then evaluated according to the following principles:

- If two authorizations are of a different type, the one with the higher priority wins (e.g., between LD and LS, LD wins).
- If two authorizations have the same type, but the object of one is more specific, the more specific wins (e.g., a recursive authorization for an element is dominated by authorizations on its subelements).
- If two authorizations have the same type and are on the same object, but the subject of one is more specific, the more specific wins (e.g., an authorization for the `Public` group is dominated by an authorization for the specific user `Ennio`).
- When none of the above criteria is met, a site-specific general resolution policy is used (e.g., assuming a closed access control policy, the negative authorization wins).

We refer to the presentations in [3, 4] for a complete overview of the characteristics of our solution. In this paper we intend to focus on the design and implementation of a system for access control.

3. SOFTWARE ARCHITECTURE: AN OUTLINE

For the access control technique outlined in Section 2 to be of any interest from the software designer point of view, it must be suitable for clean integration in the framework of XML-based WWW applications. To clarify this point, we shall briefly introduce the use of an *XML Access Control Processor* (ACP) as a part of a *component-based Web service* [5], where a set of reusable components are responsible of processing user *requests*.

The sample *UML Sequence Diagram* shown in Figure 1 gives a general idea of the internal operation of our processor and of its integration in a Web server system. For the sake of simplicity, in this Section we shall not deal with the transformation of the XML document, which is hidden inside a container ACP object. Also, Figure 1 does not show provisions for persistence management and caching. The ACP object wraps up entirely the computation of access permissions to individual elements and the final transformation to be performed on the XML document. The standard operation of a Web server receiving a HTTP request (**1**) from a user is represented in Figure 1 by the creation of a transient *Connection Handler* object (**2**). Then, a *Processor* is activated by the Connection Handler, and an *ACP object* is instantiated (**3**). In turn, ACP creates a *Subjects* object which fully encapsulates the subjects' hierarchy (**4**). After getting the available data about the user/group of the requestor, together with the IP address and symbolic name (**5**), ACP signals to a static *Loader/Parser* object to upload the requested XML document (**6**). The Loader/Parser translates the document into a low level object data structure based on the *Document Object model (DOM)* (not shown in Figure 1) more suitable for modification. Then, the ACP

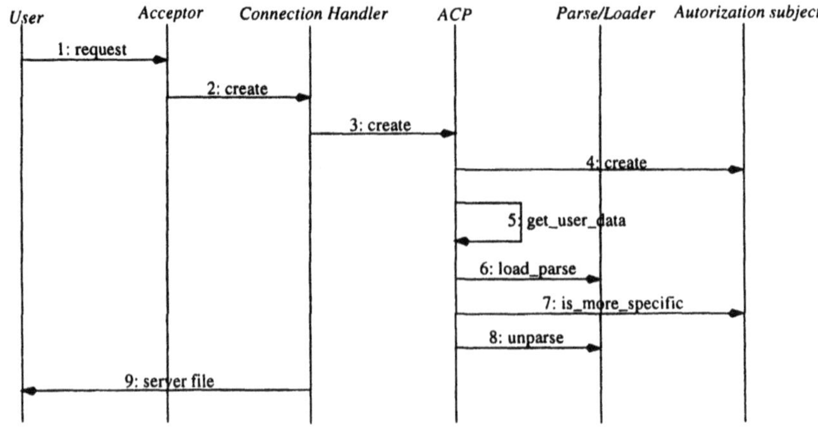

Figure 1 Sequence diagram

modifies the data structure according to the permissions, using the services of the transient *Subjects* object which fully encapsulates the subjects' hierarchy. Messages sent to the *Subjects* object (**7**) allow the ACP object to position the requestor in the subjects' hierarchy. After computing the transformation, the ACP object signals to the Parser (**8**) that the data structure can be returned to its text format, ready to be served to the user by the Connection Handler (**9**).

From the architectural point of view, it should be noted that our design is fully *server side*: all the message exchanges of Figure 1 except the connection itself (**1**) take place on the server. *Client-side* processing strategies (including client-side caching, and caching proxy servers) have been traditionally used for HTML. However, client-side solutions have been found to be less apt at XML-based Web services [5], where the contents to be transferred usually require extra processing. There may well be cases where *negotiation* could be envisioned between the client and the server as to the kinds of XML content transformations that are possible by the server and acceptable to the client; but it is clear that client-side techniques must be excluded from any sound implementation of access control. As we will see in Section 4.3, the fictitious ACP object is indeed a complex object inheriting from Java *Servlet* class.

4. THE XML-AC PACKAGE

The interface offered by the XML-AC system can be represented by a set of classes modeling the entities and concepts introduced by the access control model. Two major class families are used: one constitutes an extension of the DOM Interface defined by the W3C, the other describes all the concepts on which the ACP system is based.

4.1. ARCHITECTURAL OBJECTS: THE SECUREDOM HIERARCHY

Our system, like most XML applications, internally represents XML documents and DTDs as object trees, according to the Document Object Model (DOM) specification [12]. DOM provides an object-oriented *Application Program Interface* (API) for HTML and XML documents. Namely, DOM defines a set of object definitions (e.g.,

Element, **Attr**, and **Text**) to build an object-oriented representation which closely models the document structure. While DOM trees are topologically equivalent to XML trees, they represent element containment by means of the object-oriented *part-of* relationship. For example, a document element is represented in DOM by an **Element** object, an element contained within another element is represented as a child **Element** object, and text contained in an element is represented as a child **Text** object. The root class of the DOM hierarchy is **Node**, which represents the generic component of an XML document and provides basic methods for insertion, deletion and editing; via inheritance, such methods are also defined for more specialized classes in the hierarchy, like **Element**, **Attr** and **Text**. **Node** also provides a powerful set of navigation methods, such as **parentNode**, **firstChild** and **nextSibling**. Navigation methods allow application programs to visit the DOM representation of XML documents via a sequence of calls to the interface. Specifically, the **NodeList** method, which returns an array containing all the children of the current node, is often used to explore the structure of an XML document from the root to the leaves.

We extended the DOM hierarchy associating to the members of the class hierarchy a **Secure** variant. Each **Secure** variant extends the base class with references to all the authorizations which can be applied to the node. Internally, each class separates the references to authorizations into 8 containers, depending on the authorization type. Each container internally keeps a list of positive and negative authorizations of the type. The IDL interface common to all *Secure* classes, written in IDL, the OMG-CORBA standard *Interface Definition Language*, is:

```
interface Secure{
    void addAuthorization (in Authorization AuthToAdd);
    AuthorizationLabel defineFinalLabel
                       (in AuthorizationLabel FatherAuthRecHard,
                        in AuthorizationLabel FatherAuthRec,
                        in AuthorizationLabel FatherAuthRecDTD,
                        in AuthorizationLabel FatherAuthRecSoft);
    void prune();}
```

From this interface is possible to define the interfaces of each **Secure** variant of the DOM classes, using multiple inheritance in IDL definitions. For example, the definition of the **SecureNode** class is **interface SecureNode: Node, Secure** {}.

The extension imposes a limited increase in the cost of the document representation. Indeed, the containers can be implemented with dynamic structures, occupying space only when authorizations are actually associated with the node. The node contains references to the full description of the authorizations, kept in a separate area of memory. In this way, there are no redundancies and, since in the evaluation of access control authorizations must not be modified, the use of references is fully adequate.

4.2. APPLICATION OBJECTS: THE ACCESS CONTROL CLASSES

We describe here the main classes of the Access Control Processor: **UserGroup**, **User**, **AuthorizationLabel**, **AuthorizationType**, **AuthorizationSubject** and finally **Authorization**.

Class **UserGroup** describes the features common to a user and a group: both have a name and appear in the user/group hierarchy. The services offered by the class are the storage of the hierarchy on users/groups, method **addDescendent** that permits to add a new user/group in the hierarchy, and method **isEqualOrMoreSpecific** that permits to determine if a user/group belongs, directly or indirectly, to another user/group.

```
interface UserGroup{
    attribute string Name;
    void addChild (in UserGroup ChildToAdd);
    boolean isEqualOrMoreSpecific (in UserGroup UserGroupToCompare);}
```

Class `User` is a specialization of class `UserGroup` and extends it with all the information specific to users, like the real person name. Method `checkPassword` implements the cryptographic function that determines if the password returned by the user corresponds to the stored value.

```
interface User:  UserGroup{
    attribute string FirstName;
    attribute string LastName;
    boolean checkPassword(in string PasswordToCheck);
    void setPassword(in string NewPassword);}
```

Class `AuthorizationLabel` contains an enumerative type that describes the three values (positive, negative, and undefined) of the security label that can be assigned to a node, after the evaluation of the existing authorizations. Its methods permit to set and retrieve the value.

```
interface AuthorizationLabel{
    enum Label_t (positive, negative, undefined);
    attribute Label_t label;
    void setPositive();
    void setNegative();
    void setUndefined();
    boolean isPositive();
    boolean isNegative();
    boolean isUndefined();}
```

Class `AuthorizationType` describes the possible types of authorization. Its methods permit to set and to retrieve the authorization type (local or recursive, on the document or on the DTD, and hard or soft).

```
interface AuthorizationType{
    enum AuthType_t (LDH, RDH, L, R, LD, RD, LS, RS);
    void setLocal();
    void setRecursive();
    void setOnInstance();
    void setOnInstanceSoft();
    void setOnDTD(); }
    void setOnDTDHard(); }
    boolean isLocal();
    boolean isRecursive();
    boolean isOnInstance();
    boolean isOnInstanceSoft();
    boolean isOnDTD();
    boolean isOnDTDHard(); }
```

Class `AuthorizationSubject` describes the triple ⟨user-group, IP address, symbolic address⟩ that identifies the subjects to which the authorizations must be applied. The class offers methods to get and assign the components of the addresses and a method `isEqualOrMoreSpecific` to determine if one subject is equal or more specific than another subject.

```
interface AuthorizationSubject{
    void setUserGroup(in UserGroup userGroupToSet);
    UserGroup getAuthUser();
    void setIpAddress(in string IPAddrToSet);
```

```
        string getIpAddress();
        void setSnAddress(in string SymbAddrToSet);
        string getSnAddress();
        boolean isEqualOrMoreSpecific(in AuthorizationSubject AuthSubjToCmp);}
```

Class `Authorization` represents the authorizations that are defined on the system. Each authorization is characterized by a subject (class `AuthorizationSubject`), an object (represented by an XPath expression, managed by classes defined in an external XSL implementation), the sign (represented by an `AuthorizationLabel` component for which value *undefined* is not admitted), the action (currently a simple string), and finally the type (represented by a component of class `AuthorizationType`).

```
interface Authorization{
    attribute AuthorizationSubject subject;
    attribute XPathExpr object;
    attribute AuthorizationLabel sign;
    attribute AuthorizationType type;
    attribute string action; }
```

4.3. DEPLOYING THE PACKAGE

We implemented the above classes in Java and used them to realize a prototype of the Access Control Processor with a Java servlet solution. Java servlets, designed by Sun and part of the Java environment, appear as a set of predefined classes that offer services that are needed for the exchange of information between a Web server and a Java application. Examples of these classes are `HttpSession` and `HttpRequest`. Java servlets constitute a simple and efficient mechanism for the extension of the services of a generic Web server; the Web server must be configured to launch the execution of a Java Virtual Machine when a request for a URL served by a servlet arrives, passing the parameters of the request with a specified internal protocol.

The Java classes we implemented can also be used in a different framework, using a solution like JSP (Java Server Pages). Actually, JSP is internally based on servlets, but it offers an easier interface to the programmer, requiring the definition of HTML/XML templates which embed the invocation of servlet services. We have already demonstrated the use of the prototype inside a JSP server.

There are several other architectures that could be used and whose applicability we plan to investigate in the future. Since we gave an IDL description of the classes that constitute the implementation of our system, it is natural to envision a solution based on the distributed object paradigm, using protocols like RMI/IIOP (for the Java implementation) or the services of a generic CORBA broker (where the services are implemented by objects written in a generic programming language).

5. INTEGRATION WITH WEB-BASED SYSTEMS

We are now ready to describe how our access control system can be integrated in a Web-based framework for distribution and management of XML information. This architecture needs to include a number of components and a careful study of their interaction with access control is of paramount importance to achieve an efficient implementation.

5.1. LINKING XAS TO XML DOCUMENTS AND DTDS

As XASs contain access control information for XML documents and DTDs, links must be provided allowing the system, upon receipt of a HTTP request for an XML document, to locate the XAS associated with both the document itself and its DTD. In current XML practice, association between XML documents and their DTDs is made by either *direct inclusion* (the DTD is embedded in the XML document) or by *hypertext link* (the XML document contains the URL of its DTD). Neither technique seems appropriate for linking documents and DTDs to XASs as they would interfere with the normal processing of XML documents, and pose the problem of managing access control for legacy documents not linked to any XAS specification. Luckily enough, we can rely on the abstract nature of XML *XLink* specification to define *out-of-line* links that reside *outside* the documents they connect, making links themselves a viable and manageable resource. The repertoire of out-of-line links defining access control mappings is itself an XML document, easily managed and updated by the system manager; nonetheless it is easily secured by standard file-system level access control. We propose to set up a suitable *namespace*, called AC, which is for the time being aimed at reserving the standard tag name <XAS> to denote off-line links between documents, DTDs and XASs. The DTD of the documents containing the mappings from XML documents to DTDs and to XASs can be written as follows:

```
<!ENTITY % xlink " type    CDATA  # FIXED 'arc'
                   role    CDATA  'access control'
                   title   CDATA  'access control'
                   actuate CDATA  # FIXED 'auto'
                   from    CDATA  # REQUIRED
                   to      CDATA  # REQUIRED">

<!ELEMENT XAS EMPTY>
<!ATTLIST XAS  % xlink
          xmlns:xlink CDATA  'http://www.w3.org/TR/xlink' >
```

Note that, in the private documents specifying link sets for each site and at the DTD level, the name of the XAS element will be preceded by the mention of the AC namespace in order to avoid ambiguity. In the above DTD definition, we rely on a reusable XML *entity* to group the attributes needed to set up an out-of-line link between a document and its access control information. Namely, out-of-line links are identified by the type attribute being set to "arc", and by the presence of required from and to attributes instead of the usual href used for embedded links. The actuate attribute is set to "auto", meaning that the traversal of the link will be automatically made by the system and not revealed to the user. Finally, the role and title attributes are used primarily for descriptive purposes and are therefore not mandatory.

5.2. XML-AC SUPPORT FOR SESSIONS

In the current prototype, sessions are managed by class HttpSession, a component of the Java servlet environment. Class HttpSession keeps track of the series of requests originating from the same user. Using the services of HttpSession it is possible to ask only once to the user to declare his identity and password. The implementation of class HttpSession permits to manage sessions in two modes, with or without cookies. When the client has cookies enabled, HttpSession may store a session identifier in the client cookies and use it to identify the request; if cookies are not enabled, sessions are identified by storing the session identifier as a parameter of the requests that are embedded into the page which is returned to the user. Since users often do not enable cookies, it is important to be able to manage sessions independently.

We observe that the solution we implemented, based on the services of class `HttpSession`, is adequate for our context, where the goal was a demonstration of the capabilities of the access control model. An environment with strong security requirements should probably plan a different implementation of the session management services, using adequate cryptographic techniques to protect the connection.

5.3. A MULTITHREADED SERVER FRAMEWORK

To guarantee efficient and effective integration of access-control in the framework of Web-based systems, two basic problems must be solved:

Quality of Service The emergence of the World Wide Web as a mainstream technology has highlighted the problem of providing a high quality of service (*QoS*) to application users. This factor alone cautioned us about the risk of increasing substantially the processing load of Web server.

Seamless Integration A second point to be mentioned regards how to provide XML access control as seamlessly as possible, without interfering with the operation of other presentation or data-processing services. Moreover, the access control service should be introduced on existing servers with minimal or no interruption of their operation.

To deal with these problems, we chose an integrated (yet modular) approach, that supports reuse allowing for different deployment solutions according to implementation platforms' performance profiles. In fact, besides being deployed as a single-thread servlet invoked by the Connection Handler, as in our current prototype, our processor can be easily interfaced to a *Dispatcher* registered with an *Event Handler*. Dispatcher-based multi-threading can be managed *synchronously*, according to the well known *Reactor/Proactor* design pattern [7] or *asynchronously*, as in the *Active Object* pattern. In this section we shall focus on the former choice, as it facilitates integration of our XML access control code in the framework of existing general-purpose server-side transformers based on the same design pattern like *Cocoon* [1]. Figure 2 depicts the Reactor-based multi-threading technique.

In order to avoid being a potential bottleneck for the server operation, our Access Control system needs to manage effectively a high number of *concurrent requests*. Multi-threaded designs are currently the preferred choice to implement Web-based, high-concurrency systems. This is also our design choice for our components. However, it must be noted that no Java-based design of multi-threading components has full control on thread management: when running on an operating system that supports threads, the *Java Virtual Machine* automatically maps Java threads to native threads [8], while when no native thread support is available, the JVM has to emulate threads. In the latter case, the emulation technique chosen by the JVM implementors can make significant difference in performance. In the sequel, we shall briefly describe the Java thread management technique used for the implementation of our processor, providing full synchronization between threads when accessing the same DOM and `AuthorizationSubject` objects. To clarify the synchronization problem associated with multi-threading, consider two access control tasks that need to be executed in

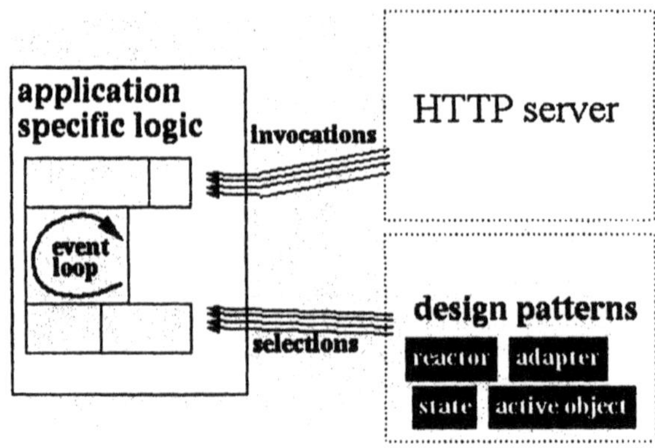

Figure 2 Cocoon-style multi-threading technique

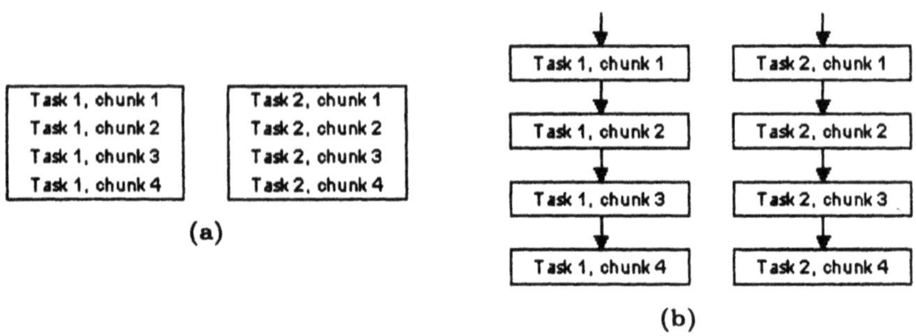

Figure 3 Two AC tasks to be executed in parallel (a) and their subdivision into four atomic sub-tasks (b)

parallel (see Figure 3(a)). For the sake of simplicity both tasks are naturally subdivided into four *atomic* non-interruptible sub-tasks, loosely corresponding to actions from **(4)** to **(7)** of Section 3. In a "naive" multi-threaded implementation of our processor, each task would be executed on its own thread. However, the only way to preserve atomicity using this technique would be to explicitly synchronize threads by means of *semaphores*. Fortunately, the additional complexity and overhead involved in explicit synchronization can be easily avoided in our case.

Synchronous dispatching A synchronous dispatcher can be used to solve the synchronization problem by simulating multi-threading within a single Java thread. To illustrate the evolution of our design from a single task divided into portions to a synchronous dispatcher, consider first the subdivision of each task of Figure 3(a) into four independent sub-tasks, depicted in Figure 3(b). From the Java implementation point of view, each sub-task can now be straightforwardly defined as the `run()` method of a `Runnable` object [10]. Then, the objects can be stored into an array, and a *scheduler* module can be added executing the objects one at a time. `Sleep()` or `yield()` calls mark the transition between sub-tasks.

As anticipated, this code is a simple implementation of Schmidt's Reactor design pattern [7]. The effect is essentially the same as several threads waiting on a single *ordered binary semaphore* that is set to `true` by an event. Here, the programmer

```
Runnable[] task = new Runnable[]
{
 new Runnable(){ public void run(){ /* execute sub-task 1 */ } },
 new Runnable(){ public void run(){ /* execute sub-task 2 */ } },
 new Runnable(){ public void run(){ /* execute sub-task 3 */ } },
 new Runnable(){ public void run(){ /* execute sub-task 4 */ } },
};
for( int i = 0; i < task.length; i++ )
{task[i].run();
 Thread.getCurrentThread().yield();
}
```

Figure 4 Sample Java code for the synchronous dispatcher

```
Runnable[] two_tasks = new Runnable[]
{
 new Runnable(){ public void run(){ /* execute task 1, sub-task 1 */ } },
 new Runnable(){ public void run(){ /* execute task 2, sub-task 1 */ } },
 new Runnable(){ public void run(){ /* execute task 1, sub-task 2 */ } },
 new Runnable(){ public void run(){ /* execute task 2, sub-task 2 */ } },
 new Runnable(){ public void run(){ /* execute task 1, sub-task 3 */ } },
 new Runnable(){ public void run(){ /* execute task 2, sub-task 3 */ } },
 new Runnable(){ public void run(){ /* execute task 1, sub-task 4 */ } },
 new Runnable(){ public void run(){ /* execute task 2, sub-task 4 */ } },
};
for( int i = 0; i < two_task.length; i++ )
 { two_tasks[i].run();
 Thread.getCurrentThread().yield();
}
```

Figure 5 The interleaving dispatcher

retains full control over the sequence of subtask execution after the event. In our AC processor, however, a slightly more complex technique should be used, as we need to execute complex transformation tasks concurrently, each of them being subdivided into atomic sub-tasks. To deal with this problem, the synchronous dispatcher of Figure 4 can be easily modified [10] to provide *interleaving* (Figure 5).

The behavior of the code in Figure 5 allows for a multi-threading *cooperative* system (in which threads explicitly yield control to other threads). Of course, this synchronous dispatching technique is aimed at native multi-threaded operating systems, where all the subtasks are executing on a single operating system-level thread. In this case, there is no synchronization overhead at all, and no expensive context switch into the host operating system's kernel. It should be noted that several dispatchers could be used, each running on its own thread (as in Sun's *green thread* model [11]), so that cooperative and preemptive threads may share the same process.

6. CONCLUSION

In this paper we presented the major results of the study we did before the implementation of the processor for the proposed access control model for XML data. Most of the considerations we present are not specific to our system, but can be of interest in any context where services for the security of XML must be implemented.

There are several directions where our work can be extended and that offer interesting opportunities. For instance, we focused on multi-threading techniques to obtain efficient concurrent execution of access control tasks. However, synchronization overhead is obviously not the only performance problem. Other techniques rather than round-robin interleaving could be adopted: e.g., the XML access-control service could adaptively optimize itself to provide higher priorities for smaller requests. These techniques combined could potentially produce a system highly responsive and with an adequate throughput. The next release of the ACP plans to implement the prioritized strategy.

Acknowledgments

The authors wish to thank Daniel Menasce' for interesting discussions about XML processing performance issues.

References

[1] Apache Software Foundation. Cocoon, a Java publishing framework. http://xml.apache.org/cocoon, 2000.

[2] T. Bray et.al. (ed.). *Extensible Markup Language (XML) 1.0.* World Wide Web Consortium (W3C), February 1998. http://www.w3.org/TR/REC-xml.

[3] E. Damiani, S. De Capitani di Vimercati, S. Paraboschi, and P. Samarati. Design and implementation of an access control processor for XML documents. In *Proc. of the Ninth Int. Conference on the World Wide Web*, Amsterdam, May 2000.

[4] E. Damiani, S. De Capitani Di Vimercati, S. Paraboschi, and P. Samarati. Securing XML documents. In *Proc. of EDBT 2000*, Konstanz, Germany, March 2000.

[5] J. Hu, I. Pyarale, and D. Schmidt. Applying the proactor pattern to high performance web services. In *Proc. of the 10th International Conference on Parallel and Distributed Computing*, Las Vegas, Nevada, October 1998.

[6] S. Jajodia, P. Samarati, and V. S. Subrahmanian. A Logical Language for Expressing Authorizations. In *Proc. of the IEEE Symposium on Security and Privacy*, pages 31–42, Oakland, CA, May 1997.

[7] R. G. Lavender and D. Schmidt. Reactor: A object behavioral pattern for concurrent programming. In J. Vlissides, D. Coplien, and M. Kerth, editors, *Pattern Languages of Program Design 2.* Addison Wesley, 1995.

[8] D. Lea. *Concurrent Programming in Java.* Addison Wesley, 1996.

[9] T.F. Lunt. Access Control Policies for Database Systems. In C.E. Landwehr, editor, *Database Security, II: Status and Prospects*, pages 41–52. North-Holland, Amsterdam, 1989.

[10] B. Marchant. Multithreading in java. http://www.javacats.com/US/articles/multithreading.html, 1996.

[11] M. L. Powell, S. Kleiman, S. Barton, D. Shah, D. Stein, and M. Weeks. *SunOS Multi-thread Architecture.* Sun Microsystems, 1998.

[12] World Wide Web Consortium (W3C). *Document Object Model (DOM) Level 1 Specification Version 1.0*, October 1998. http://www.w3.org/TR/REC-DOM-Level-1.

[13] World Wide Web Consortium (W3C). *XML Path Language (XPath)*, November 1999. http://www.w3.org/TR/xpath.

CHAPTER 5

A Configurable Security Architecture Prototype

Alexandre Hardy
ah@adam.rau.ac.za

Martin S Olivier
molivier@rkw.rau.ac.za
Department of Computer Science
Rand Afrikaans University
PO Box 524, Auckland Park, Johannesburg, South Africa

Abstract Traditional security systems are integrated closely with the applications that they protect or they are a separate component that provides system protection. As a separate component, the security system may be configurable and support various security models. The component does not directly support the application. Instead, operating system objects (such as files) are protected. Security systems that are integrated with the applications that they protect avoid this shortcoming, but are usually not configurable. They also cannot provide the same level of protection that a system provided security component can enforce, as the application does not have access to the hardware that supports these features. The Configurable Security Architecture (ConSA [1]) defines an architecture that provides the flexibility of a system security component while still supporting application security. Such an architecture provides obvious benefits. Security policies can be constructed from off-the-shelf components, supporting a diverse array of security needs. Before this or a similar architecture can be accepted by the industry, the concept must be proven to work theoretically and practically. Olivier [1] has developed the theoretical model and illustrates its usefulness. This paper describes an implementation of ConSA and in so doing, proves that ConSA can be implemented in practice.

Keywords: Access Control, Security, Security Model, Prototype

1. INTRODUCTION

An architecture that supports arbitrary security policies through the use of off the shelf components will greatly simplify the implementation of security systems. Such an architecture will allow developers of security models to concentrate on the access control algorithms of such a model, without concern for the method in which access control will be enforced. The ConSA (Configurable Security Architecture) architecture [1] is one such system. Olivier [1] describes the model and provides a formal description of the various components. The model will not be described again in this paper, due to lack of space. Section 2 will however briefly illustrate how ConSA functions. This paper will instead describe a proof of concept prototype that illustrates that ConSA can be implemented on existing systems. The prototype is implemented in the Linux operating system, and can be moved to another of the many UNIX [9, 11] like operating systems available. Furthermore, the prototype illustrates the use of ConSA for application level security and system level security.

In section 2 a brief background to security is presented, section 3 discusses the prototype and the three significant changes to the ConSA model: the ConSA kernel, Protect Table and Message Dispatcher. Section 4 presents the conclusions drawn from the prototype.

2. BACKGROUND

A security policy determines who may access (and who may not) objects or entities in a system. A security system on a computer must enforce such a policy, ensuring integrity and availability of data. The process of enforcing the security policy is known as *Access Control.* Several security models have been proposed that may be used to implement certain security policies. These models have generally been classified as *Discretionary Access Control* (DAC) and *Mandatory Access Control* (MAC - also known as multilevel access control).

Discretionary Access Control associates an owner with each object in the system. The owner may then grant (or revoke) access to (from) other subjects in the system so that they may access (may not access) that object. The object may have an *Access Control List* associated with it that contains a list of all subjects that may access that object.

Mandatory Access Control associates a clearance level with each subject and a classification with each object. A subject may obtain read access to an object if the clearance of the subject dominates the classification of the object (known as the *simple security property*). Write access may be obtained if the clearance of the subject is lower than the classification of the object (known as the *star property*). The simple security property prevents unauthorized subjects from viewing sensitive information, while the star property prevents subjects of high classification from making sensitive information available to subjects of lower classification.

Flow control ensures that if data is written to an object, then all the subjects who could not access the data in its previous location will still be unable to do so. Further information on security models and other aspects of security can be found in [3, 4, 5, 6].

The concept of *labels* can be applied to most security models. A label encodes security information and may be associated with subjects or objects and perhaps others. Labels are well suited to implementing more advanced and dynamic security models [7, 8].

Traditional security systems have only implemented one security model, ConSA provides a security architecture that may be used to support and enforce a variety of security models. We refer to [1, 2] for details on the ConSA model, and only provide a short description here.

The ConSA system has two types of labels, *Entity Labels* protect objects and determine who may access those objects. *Subject Labels* are tokens presented by subjects that may grant them access to certain objects. The *Subject Management Module* determines which Subject Labels a subject will use. The *Authorization Control Module* determines the initial protection attributes of an object that has just been created. The Protect Table associates Entity Labels with the objects that they protect and controls access to these objects. The *Message Dispatcher* is responsible for relaying messages between objects and enforcing the security model on those messages. And finally, the *Information Flow Manager* enforces flow control on messages.

Typical system interaction may occur as follows: A subject logs onto the system and is presented with a subject label by the Subject Management Module. When the subject sends a message to an object, the Message Dispatcher determines which label protects the object by consulting the Protect Table, and then determines if the message will be relayed by consulting the Entity Label and Information Flow Manager.

3. THE PROTOTYPE

The most important modifications to the ConSA model for the prototype are the introduction of a kernel component that controls the ConSA system, modifications to the role of the Protect Table, and a specification for the Message Dispatcher. The kernel component allows for the specification of how the various ConSA components interact. This interaction is controlled by the ConSA kernel and can be specified by

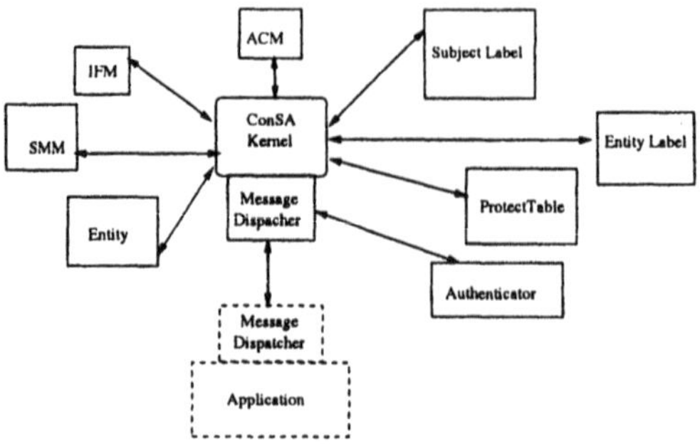

Figure 1. Prototype ConSA architecture

```
Class Entity
Public
    Create(resource)
    Destroy(resource)
    Open(resource,mode)
    Read(data,len)
    Write(data,len)
    Control(cmd,arg)
    Close()
```

Figure 2. Entity interface

sequential algorithms. The Protect Table and ConSA kernel describe how the task of the original Protect Table may be achieved. Lastly the Message Dispatcher is specified so that interaction between applications and the security system may be achieved. Space restrictions preclude a discussion of the other components of the ConSA architecture.

3.1. THE ConSA KERNEL

The ConSA model allows various modules to work together to determine and enforce a security policy. It is clear that a Message Dispatcher component is needed to transfer messages between the ConSA system and user programs. It will be useful to define a new component that integrates the existing components, and defines how these components interact. This component shall be referred to as the ConSA kernel. Now the only concern of the Message Dispatcher is to facilitate the passing of messages between components. The ConSA kernel will handle requests and delegate to the necessary components. In this way, only the Message Dispatcher need be rewritten to support new message transferring methods. These may include network transports, API calls or system calls.

The system can be implemented at different levels to increase the inherent security or efficiency of the system. For example a Message Dispatcher in the form of a linkable library (including the rest of the ConSA system) would increase efficiency. A library would be supplied that clients may use to access the ConSA system. This also allows the system to be easily subverted. Another option would be to integrate the ConSA system into the Linux kernel so that existing system routines may be protected by ConSA (and perhaps more). This approach is slightly less efficient, but inherently much more secure, since the kernel memory is inaccessible to user space programs. Now some component must decide whether messages are to be permitted or denied. The Entity Label module and Information Flow Manager both have an effect on the outcome of this decision. Modularity of the ConSA system would be improved if these two modules did not have to communicate in order to reach a decision. This can be achieved if we allow the ConSA kernel to make the decision, with 'advice' from these two modules. This process will be illustrated a little later.

Furthermore it is difficult to allow the Protect Table to intercept messages to enforce security concerns. The result is that the ConSA modules in the prototype are trusted. The modules themselves are responsible for correctly implementing the security model when inter-module communication occurs. The ConSA kernel will however facilitate this to some extent. Figure 1 illustrates the architecture selected for the prototype.

The Message Dispatcher is responsible for communication between the user and the ConSA system, and the Protect Table simply remembers which labels protect which entities. The ConSA kernel accepts messages from the Message Dispatcher and coordinates with the other modules to achieve the desired result.

3.1.1 Entities. Arbitrary messages are usually difficult to intercept or not very efficient. These problems may be simplified by defining a communication interface for objects, that can be easily monitored and still support arbitrary messages. To support the Message Dispatcher and facilitate message passing to Entities, an Entity interface is defined, as illustrated in figure 2. The Entity Label and Subject Label do not have to conform to this specification. This Entity interface is required for resources in the system to be accessed uniformly by the ConSA kernel. Arbitrary messages can be implemented at a higher level by using this interface as a transport.

The methods listed in figure 2 are self explanatory. Resources are accessed using a resource locator format of *class:resource.* For example *file:example.txt* refers to an entity of class *file*, and the resource to be accessed is *example.txt.* Now that entities have been defined the services that the ConSA kernel provide can be examined.

3.1.2 ConSA Kernel Services. There are a large number of services defined to support module interaction and internal administrative tasks. A discussion of all these services is beyond the scope of this paper, and cannot be presented due to space constraints. The services that implement the ConSA interface are of much greater interest, and so only these services will be discussed. Once again, only selected services

```
function KOpen(token,resource,mode)
      SubjectLabel subject;
      EntityLabel label;
      InformationFlowManager IFM;
      if (InValidToken(token)) then return FAILURE;
      subject=SubjectLabelOf(token);
      IFM=IFMAssociatedWith(subject);
      label=GetLabel(resource);
      if (label is not valid) then
            if (policy=DENY) then return FAILURE;
      if ((label is valid) and
                  (not label->CheckAccess(subject,mode))) then
            return FAILURE;
      IFMresult=IFM->ActivateFlow(FLOW_OPEN,GetLabel(resource),
                  subject,FALSE);
      if (IFMresult is FAILURE) then return FAILURE;
      return OpenEntity(resource);
end function
```

Figure 3. KOpen algorithm

will be presented as a result of space restrictions. Please refer to [2] for details on all these algorithms. The `KOpen` and `KGrantAccess` algorithms will be presented as they are fairly representative of the structure of these algorithms.

`KOpen(subject,resource,mode)`
The `KOpen` service opens a resource for access specified by `mode`. This service must ensure that the specified subject has been granted the required access to the resource. The Protect Table is enlisted to determine which labels protect the requested resource. The algorithm is listed in figure 3.

The first action taken is to validate the subject token provided, by attempting to locate the associated subject label and Information Flow Manager. Next the label protecting the entity, and specifically the `open` method (if any) is located via the `GetLabel` call. If no suitable label is found, then the default policy of the ConSA system determines if access is granted or not. If the label permits access, then the Information Flow Manager is consulted. In this service the Information Flow Man-

```
function KGrantAccess(token,resource,user_for_ACL,mode)
      SubjectLabel subject;
      SubjectLabel usertoadd;
      EntityLabel label;
      EntityLabel protlabel;
      InformationFlowManager IFM;
      if (InValidToken(token)) then return FAILURE;
      subject=SubjectLabelOf(token);
      IFM=IFMAssociatedWith(subject);
          label=GetLabel(resource);
      //If there is no label: default policy would
      //determine if access is granted or not
      if (label is not valid) then
            if (policy=DENY) then return FAILURE;
            else return SUCCESS;
          protlabel=GetLabel(label);
      //IFM is consulted first, for proper
      // logical and construction
      if (not IFM->ActivateFlow(FLOW_GRANT,protlabel,
                  subject,TRUE)) then return FAILURE;
      if (protlabel is not valid) then
            //Policy determines if grant will take place
            if (policy=ALLOW) then begin
                  usertoadd=SMM->Translate(user_for_ACL);
                  return label->GrantAccess(usertoadd,mode);
            end else
                  return FAILURE;
      if (not protlabel->CheckAccess(subject,MODE_GRANT)) then
            return FAILURE;
      else begin
            usertoadd=SMM->Translate(user_for_ACL);
            return label->GrantAccess(usertoadd,mode);
      end
end function
```

Figure 4. KGrantAccess Algorithm

ager cannot deny the request, and still indicate that the operation was successful.

`KGrantAccess(subject,resource,user_for_ACL,mode)` **(figure 4)**
It must be possible for the System Security Officer, and perhaps for other subjects (as in Discretionary Access Control) to change the access control list associated with a resource. The entity label provides these services, but the application cannot communicate directly with the label. The ConSA kernel provides access to the entity label, and also determines whether the subject may in fact access the entity label (which is also a resource). For access to the ACL, the Information Flow Manager is consulted first. It does not matter in which order the Information Flow Manager and entity label are consulted. The operation is always the logical **and** of the results. It is important to see that the label protecting the resource is the entity which is being checked. Once the label has been found, the label protecting this label is in turn found. This label is then the label that determines if access to modify, or read the label is granted or not. This label is the variable `protlabel` in the algorithm. The Subject Manager provides the subject label for the subject that is to be queried, added or removed from the ACL. The user only knows some token that identifies the subject. The entity label may be modified to accept extra parameters specifying which type of access is to be granted (to pass to the `protlabel` variable in this case). Another simpler alternative may also be followed, specific modes of access combining say granting and reading, may be combined to form a new mode: grant read access. If numerical values are used for modes, a bitwise or operation may perhaps be used to obtain the new mode. A further question to ask is, how may we implement Discretionary Access Control with this algorithm? To allow subjects to grant access, the `protlabel` needs to be modified. The algorithm does not modify this label at any stage. Two options are however possible:

- Construct a new resource for accessing and modifying labels. This new resource will allow subjects to query and modify labels at all levels.

- The label protecting the object can determine which label protects it. If the label is to grant access for grant mode then the label simply grants access to the label protecting it. Some method must be developed to differentiate between a label requesting the grant access and another portion of the program from requesting grant access, otherwise the label will recursively grant access to the parent.

3.2. PROTECT TABLE

Entity Labels protect objects in the system. The Entity Labels cannot practically be stored with the objects they protect due to the diversity of the security models that may be implemented. Some other method must be devised to associate objects with their Entity Labels. One solution is a Protect Table that associates labels with objects. The entire table is stored on secondary storage in some representation that may be implemented independently of the file system. This also allows queries to quickly locate labels associated with an object, without first locating the object. The next section lists the services required from a Protect Table.

3.2.1 Protect Table Services.

One method has been identified in [1] for the Protect Table, namely `Protect`. `Protect` associates an Entity Label with an object. The association means that the specified Entity Label controls access to the object it is associated with. It is assumed that at most one Entity Label will protect an object. If two labels L_1, L_2 could protect an object then we could construct a single new label L_3 such that $subj(L_3) := subj(L_1) \bigcap subj(L_2)$[1]. If the label module cannot support this, then a new label module may be constructed that can implement the new label. This specification is relatively simple, but in a practical implementation there are several difficulties. It is difficult to capture attempts to access an object. A universal communication scheme may be implemented to help trap messages, but this cannot be enforced. One object may be instantiated several times in the system, and may have a different identifier at each instantiation. The identifier is provided by the operating system. The information the Protect Table stores must not be lost if the system is halted.

The prototype attempts to address these problems by enforcing protection with the ConSA kernel and Message Dispatcher. A new object identification scheme was implemented to provide objects with identifiers that remained the same even after system reboot. The Protect Table has also been extended to explicitly support protection of objects, classes and methods. The services implemented are listed in table 1.

3.3. MESSAGE DISPATCHER

The Message Dispatcher is responsible for forwarding messages to the correct objects, and enforcing the selected security model on these messages. It is very difficult to intercept messages in an already existing system. A better approach is to implement a new message transmission technique that is difficult to circumvent, and to make services available

Table 1. Protect Table extended methods

Service	Parameters
`ProtectClass`	`(Class,Label)`
`ProtectObject`	`(Object,Label)`
`ProtectClassMethod`	`(Class,Method,Label)`
`ProtectObjectMethod`	`(Object,Method,Label)`
`GetLabel`	`(Object,Class,Method)`

through this system. The efficiency of such a system is also important. The Message Dispatcher has no specific methods that can be identified, rather it is an inherent part of the ConSA system, and facilitates all communication between ConSA and the application. As such, the implementation is very dependent on the system selected for implementation. For the prototype, three message transports were implemented offering various degrees of security and efficiency:

- Dynamic Link Library - As a library, the ConSA system is linked into the application at compile time. The application uses the ConSA system to enforce a security policy. The application may choose not to use the ConSA security system, and this cannot be prevented. Pluggable Authentication Module in Linux [10] is implemented in a similar fashion.

- Device Driver - The device driver developed for Linux supports communication with the Message Dispatcher. The security of the communication mechanism is a lot higher. The device driver is a compiled object module that can be inserted into the Linux kernel at run time. A character device can then be created in the file system, through which communication occurs. Two applications are now required, a server application that responds to requests on one device, and a client application that communicates with the server program. The client application may still access other system resources, but the Linux security system may be used to limit access so that the character devices are the only valid means for communication.

- Kernel Integration - The ultimate level of security is integrating the ConSA system with the operating system. The messages may then be implemented in the same way as existing operating system calls are implemented, and existing system calls may be intercepted to implement the security model on all aspects of the operating system. Now the ConSA system can also protect files that define the behavior of the system. In the prototype, the Linux syscall table was replaced to intercept system commands.

The prototype system implements each of these transports, which demonstrates the flexibility of the architecture. To provide a uniform communication system, whatever the transport, the following services have been identified for implementation:

- Message Dispatcher maintenance routines
  `MessageDispatcherInit()`
  `MessageDispatcherClose()`
  `DispatchMessage()`
  The `DispatchMessage` method is provided so that Message Dispatchers that are not automatically aware of messages, and cannot automatically dispatch the messages, may poll for messages and dispatch them if any are found.

- ConSA Kernel access routines

The ConSA kernel services are used extensively in the Message Dispatcher. By identifying these services, communication can be strictly controlled, and may be more efficient than supporting arbitrary method invocations directly. The communication with an Entity could also have been implemented by writing a device driver for each entity, but this would complicate development of entities. Instead the goal was to keep development of all modules in the ConSA system relatively transparent and independent of the level of implementation selected. This has been achieved in the prototype to a large extent. There are very few items that need replacing if the transport is changed; the various Message Dispatchers can be changed with ease to support the desired transport.

4. CONCLUSION

A prototype implementation of the ConSA system proves that the ConSA is a viable security architecture. Solutions to many of the problems with an implementation have been found. Such a system will be able to implement many security models, including newer techniques such as those presented in [8].

Notes

1. $subj(L)$ Denotes all the subjects that the label L grants access to.

References

[1] M. S. Olivier, *Towards a Configurable Security Architecture*, Data & Knowledge Engineering, To appear

[2] A. Hardy, *An Implementation and Analysis of the Configurable Security Architecture, Masters dissertation*, Rand Afrikaans University, 1999

[3] S. H. von Solms and J. H. P. Eloff, *Information Security*, Rand Afrikaans University, 1998

[4] D. E. Bell and L. J. LaPadula, "Secure computer system: unified exposition and Multics interpretation", *Rep. ESD-TR-75-306*, March 1976, MITRE Corporation

[5] D. E. Bell and L. J. LaPadula, "Secure Computer Systems: Mathematical Foundations", *Secure Computer Systems: Mathematical Foundations(Mitre technical Report 2547, Volume I)*, March 1973, MITRE Corporation

[6] D. E. Bell and L. J. LaPadula, "Secure Computer Systems: A Mathematical Model", *Secure Computer Systems: Mathematical Foundations(Mitre technical Report 2547, Volume II)*, May 1973, MITRE Corporation

[7] L. Gong and X.Qian, "Enriching the Expressive power of Security Labels", *IEEE Transactions on Knowledge and Data Engineering, 7(5)* , October 1995

[8] S. N. Foley, L. Gong and X.Qian, "A Security Model of Dynamic Labeling Providing a Tiered Approach to Verification", Technical Report SRI-CSL-95-15, SRI International, 1995

[9] *The Single UNIXR Specification, Version 2*, The Open Group, 1997, *www.opengroup.org*

[10] Andrew G. Morgan, *The Linux-PAM System Administrators' Guide*, (Distributed with the PAM software package), 1998

[11] Chris Hare, Emmett Dunlaney, George Eckel, Steven Lee, Lee Ray, *Inside Unix*, New Riders Publishing, 1994

CHAPTER 6

Distributed Policies for Data Management – Making Policies Mobile[1]

Susan Chapin, Don Faatz, and Sushil Jajodia

Abstract: This paper presents the challenges facing developers of multi-tier information systems in providing effective consistent data policy enforcement, such as access control in these architectures. It introduces "Mobile Policy" (MoP) as a potential solution and presents a framework for using mobile policy in the business logic tier of multi-tier information systems.

Key words: Security, access control, mobile policy, n-tier architecture

1. INTRODUCTION

In typical multi-tier architectures, the client is reduced to no more than a Web browser and the database management system (DBMS) is returned to its primary function of storing data. Business logic is moved from the client and the database to a middle tier, hosted on a different platform from the DBMS as shown in Figure 1.

Multi-tier architectures require changes in the way security and other policies are managed. Mechanisms are needed that can achieve consistent policy across elements of a distributed environment and support flexible policies other than access control. The need for consistent policy management across distributed components is analogous to the need for consistent transaction management across distributed components. The need for flexible policies arises from the complex functionality of many multi-tier applications. While control over access to data remains a very important policy, support for other types of policies, such as requiring certain files to

[1] This work was funded by the MITRE technology program under project number 51MSR871.

have a copyright notice or be sanitized in some way before being returned to certain clients, is also needed.

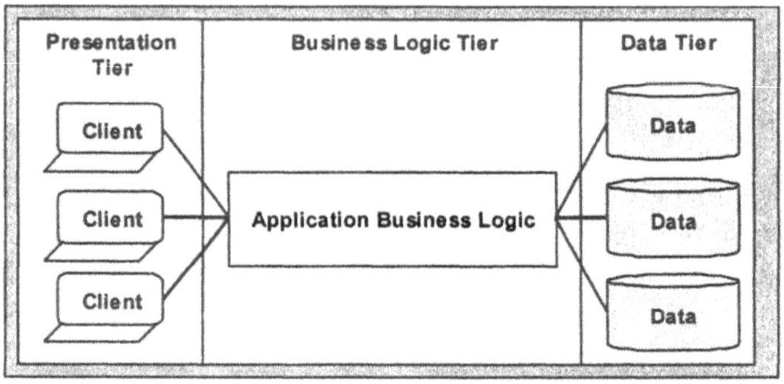

Figure 1. Multi-tier Architectures for Multiple Clients and Databases

Specific requirements for making policies consistent across different components include making policies mobile, so that they may travel with the data from one component to another rather than being applied before the data are released from the DBMS, and making security contexts mobile, so that references to users and roles have the same meaning to all components. Making policies flexible requires enabling those who manage data to define the kinds of policies supported, rather than relying on DBMS vendors.

Traditional data tier policy management does not well support these needs. Supported policies, defined by DBMS vendors, are limited to access control policies; access control is applied by the DBMS at the time access to the data is requested, requiring that the source of the request be known to the DBMS; and traditional data tier users, roles, and policies are all locally defined within the DBMS based on local security context.

We propose an application framework that extends the capabilities for policy management in multi-tier applications without interfering with existing access control policy mechanisms. Policy management is decomposed into three functions, defining policies, associating policies with data, and applying policies. Security context management is enhanced by including third-party mechanisms, such as digital certificates provided by a public key infrastructure (PKI), that can be referred to by all components; the description of the context management can be found in [2]. Almost any policy can be supported, limited only by the ability of developers to implement the policy in software. The framework allows policies to be applied in any tier of the application, determined by the application developers in conjunction with the database administrators. As of this writing, we have developed our proposed framework design in sufficient detail to support a proof-of-concept prototype.

The rest of this paper is organized as follows. Section 2 describes the needs for policy management in multi-tier architectures. Section 3 describes the limitations of existing mechanisms for dealing with policy management in multi-tier architectures. Section 4 presents an overview of our proposed framework and describes how security contexts, as well as policies, can be shared among application components. Section 5 summarizes what we have achieved and what we want to achieve in the future.

2. MULTI-TIER ARCHITECTURES

The downside of multi-tier application architectures is that they can be quite complex. The presentation tier can consist of any one of a number of browser products on any one of a number of platforms. The data tier can consist of multiple databases in different DBMSs on different platforms. The business logic tier can consist of multiple components on multiple different platforms.

The problem is that all these different components need to be composed together into a single application. Where security is involved, the composition must be seamless and reliable. Composing policies in multi-tier applications can be an issue, because the developers of the different components of the business tier and the different databases have different responsibilities and knowledge about the policies that should apply. We address policy composition in multi-tier architectures by providing a framework that allows the developers of each component to concentrate on policy matters that are properly their responsibilities.

2.1 Aligning the Authority for Policy with the Responsibility

Reserving policy application to the DBMS requires extensive communication among various subgroups within the enterprise. Managing a policy has three components, and each component is, ultimately, the responsibility of different enterprise subgroups. *Policy specification* is properly the responsibility of enterprise management. *Policy association* is the process of associating enterprise policy with data. It is properly the responsibility of the data owners, usually represented by the database administrator (DBA). *Policy application* is the process of applying the policy to data at the appropriate time. It is properly the responsibility of the business logic developer or whoever is in charge of the point(s) at which the data are used. Applying the policy at time of use is an ongoing activity; the data may be considered to be "used" when they are accessed within the DBMS, but they are also "used" within the application, whether the application code is located within the DBMS or in a separate middle tier component, and whether the application uses the data immediately or holds on to it for several days before use.

Policy enforcement is only complete when all three elements, definition, association, and application, work harmoniously together. The problem is that building coordinated support for policies can require close cooperation among those responsible for each component. It is not that any of the policy management problems are inherently impossible to solve. The problem is that they require cooperative design decisions affecting application code in both the middle tier and the DBMS, and these two portions of the application may be developed by different groups of people on different time schedules. The result is a greater risk of miscommunication and decreased assurance in the resulting product.

A mechanism is needed that decouples the development of software that implements the policy, the process of associating the policy with data, and the development of software that applies the policy at time of use.

2.2 Making Policies General

"Policy" is often taken to mean "security policy," and "security" is often taken to mean "access control," and all access control is assumed to be handled by the same mechanisms. Although security policies are important policies, and access control policies are important to an enterprise's overall security, these are not the only policies that an enterprise may want to enforce. Furthermore, not all policies, access control or other types, are equally important.

A substantial part of most middle-tier application development involves implementing various kinds of policies. Some policies are enterprise policies that are specified by enterprise management as rules that must be followed. Examples of enterprise policies include requirements for ensuring files have the proper copyright notice before they are released outside the enterprise, degrading the resolution of certain images before they are released to specified classes of clients, and scanning files for viruses before they are used.

Other rules are local to the application but span both the business logic tier and the data tier. It is a bit of a stretch to call these application rules "policies," but it is convenient for our discussion because they share many of the characteristics of enterprise policies. In particular, they may be as critically important and as much in need of assurance that they are working correctly as enterprise policies, and can equally well be handled by our proposed framework.

An example of one of these other "policies" is a rule that defines the confidence that the middle tier application can have in the accuracy of a data item retrieved from a DBMS. Imagine an application that controls airplane takeoffs for various destinations. One of the data items it needs is the amount of fuel in the plane's tank. The rule might be that the confidence level of this type of data is a function of metadata, such as the time since the data were last updated, rather than something that can be derived from the data themselves. The application as a whole, including both the middle tier and the DBMS, needs a mechanism to calculate the confidence factor and get that information to the middle tier before the middle tier releases the plane for takeoff, or some considerable unpleasantness might ensue.

Support is needed for any policies that may be applicable to data, using the same techniques for any policy, without requiring that policy types be predefined by DBMS vendors.

A characteristic of this expanded definition of policies is that not all policies are equally critical. Some types of policies may be less critical than others in an enterprise; for example, the need to check files for copyright notice may be less critical than protecting write access to the salary file. Even within access control, some data may need to be protected more carefully than others. For example, the author of a document may wish it to be restricted to only a small group of people while it is under development, but the accidental release of the partially written document to other employees would not have as severe consequences as the accidental release of the company product's source code to the general public.

Therefore, a mechanism that is not deemed sufficiently secure for one policy may still be acceptable, and very valuable, for other policies. The requirement is that the mechanisms must not interfere with each other.

3. RELATED WORK

Several research efforts are currently under way to centralize the administration of policy. The Open Group's Adage project [7, 9] is a typical example of this research. The notion of mobile policy is not particularly new [1,4,5-7,10]. Several approaches to sharing policy information have been developed. However, none is as general as the approach proposed here.

One problem common to all attempts to centralized policy definition and storage is the need for a semantically rich policy specification language capable of representing all policies that may apply within the multi-tier system. Such a language is very difficult to define and has so far eluded researchers. Mobile policy tries to avoid this problem by encapsulating policy in an executable module. These modules can be coded using any programming or policy definition language that the policy administrator chooses. Instead of defining an all-powerful magic policy language, the problem is transformed into defining a shared vocabulary of inputs to and outputs from policy modules. These vocabularies should be more tractable than a general-purpose policy language.

The next section describes our framework for use of mobile policy in multi-tier information systems.

4. THE PROPOSED FRAMEWORK

We call our proposed framework *MoP,* for mobile policies. With MoP, when data move from one component or tier to another, any associated policies travel along with the data until the policies are applied. The movement of policies is shown in Figure 2.

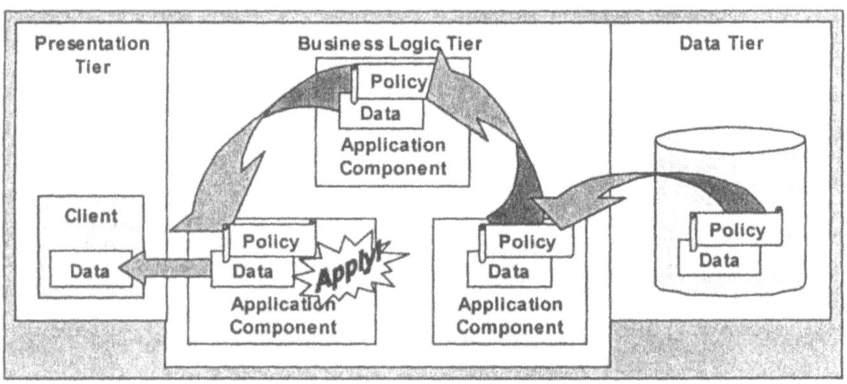

Figure 2. Mobile Policy

MoP is designed to minimize effort on the part of application developers, support assurance that the system works as intended, work harmoniously alongside existing policy mechanisms, support multiple application and DBMS platforms, and minimize the impact on performance. The framework consists of code component types and vocabulary standards that represent the minimal knowledge that must be shared among the developers of systems that use MoP. The component types are shown in Figure 3. The vocabulary standard is the glue that makes the system work. The next sections describe each of these elements.

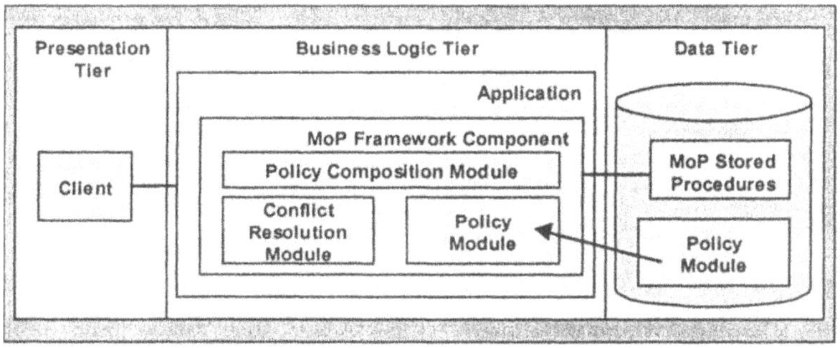

Figure 3. MoP Component Types

4.1 Policy Module

Policy modules implement policy rules. Each policy module is an executable code module, written for the platform of choice of the application, that implements one specific policy rule. For example, a policy module may determine whether a requested access is granted based on user identity, or whether access is granted based on the type of connection between the client and the application, or it may add the correct copyright notice to a file. Thus, each policy module is a self-contained package with a limited, specific function, which has the nice benefit that it simplifies validation of correct behavior.

Policy modules are classified into types by the end function they perform, not by the rule that governs how they perform it. The three examples above include only two policy types: determine whether access is granted and add a copyright notice. The two access granting rules, one of which looks at user identity and the other of which looks at the client connection, would be implemented in two separate policy modules, both of which are of type "access grant."

All policy modules of the same function type return the same output parameters with the same syntax and semantics. An application programmer needs to know what the module does in order to determine whether the module is applicable to the planned use of the data, and what output parameters the module returns and what they mean in order to code an appropriate response, but the application programmer does not need to know the policy rule the module implements.

In contrast, not all policy modules of the same type require the same input parameters. All policy modules implement a method that returns a list of input parameters. The application must be able to accept a list of parameters and return a value for each.

To summarize, a policy module is an executable code module that implements a single rule, has a well-known type and set of output parameters, and produces a list of required input parameters.

4.2 Policy Composition Module

Policy composition modules deal with issues such as the order in which policies are to be applied. We have not yet designed or prototyped this capability, and do not discuss it further.

4.3 Conflict Resolution Module

Conflict resolution modules resolve conflicts among policy modules. Multiple policy modules may be associated with the same data set. If it should happen that more than one policy module of the same type is associated with the same dataset, then any conflicts must be resolved before the correct single output parameter set is defined. This conflict resolution is performed by a *conflict resolution module*.

We assume that different policy module types are independent of each other. Any interactions between, say, a copyright notice rule and an access grant rule we consider to be idiosyncratic, complex, and outside the scope of the MoP framework. MoP, of course, does not prevent the application developer from writing code to resolve any such conflicts.

Conflict resolution module development is closely linked to policy module development. Conflict resolution modules implement the resolution of conflicts among policy rules, and therefore conflict resolution rules are policy rules.

4.4 DBMS Stored Procedures

When data are accessed, the MoP application component needs to retrieve the policy modules associated with the data. Two DBMS stored procedures provide this capability. One receives a SQL request and returns identifiers associated with relevant policy modules, the other receives a policy module identifier and returns the specified policy module.

MoP therefore requires three or more database queries instead of one for each request: access the data, request relevant policy module identifiers, and request each needed policy module. The MoP application component makes all three (or more) requests within the same transaction, thereby eliminating potential synchronization difficulties.

The separation of function not only supports flexibility but also decreases performance overhead by allowing the application to make only those requests it actually needs and to make them in any order. For example, for READ requests the policy may be run before the data are retrieved, because the result of the policy may make retrieving the data unnecessary, or the application may first retrieve data and review it to determine which of the associated policies are relevant to its intended use of the data before requesting the policy modules.

Separating the request for policy module identifiers from the request for specific policy modules allows the application to cache policy modules and to request only those policy modules it actually needs, a potentially significant performance enhancement.

4.5 Application Framework Component (MoP)

The MoP application framework component encapsulates MoP implementation details that are not application dependent. The MoP component exposes methods that support accessing data, identifying relevant policy modules, retrieving relevant policy modules, and running selected policy types.

As of this writing, the application is responsible for setting up pointers to permanent objects (in the current version, the permanent objects are caches and connections to databases), providing an object that actualizes parameters, and calling the MoP retrieve time and MoP apply time methods.

4.6 MoP Shared Vocabularies

MoP shared vocabularies are the heart of our solution for sharing policy among developers responsible for different application tiers while minimizing the knowledge they must share with each other. Encapsulating policy rules into components allows us to reduce the semantics that must be shared from understanding policy logic, which requires a "magic language" and is very difficult, to understanding a small vocabulary of shared terms, which is a relatively easy and familiar technology. We define three vocabularies: a policy module types vocabulary, an output parameters vocabulary, and an input parameters vocabulary.

In the *policy module types* vocabulary, each term specifies what the policy module does, such as add a copyright notice or determine whether access is granted and implies a set of output parameters.

In the *output parameters* vocabulary, each term specifies both syntax and meaning of a parameter returned from a policy module. Output parameters are the same for all policy modules of the same type. The application uses the output parameters to apply the policy. The output parameter vocabulary is important because for many policy types, such as access control, the application must be prepared to take action based on returned output parameters.

In the *input parameters* vocabulary, each term specifies an input parameter needed by the policy module. The application provides a method to be called by the MoP component that accepts a list of input parameters and returns a list of matching values. The input parameter vocabulary is important because two modules with the same function may have different input parameters.

4.7 Allocation of Responsibilities

Supporting separation of duty by allocating specific policy management responsibilities to different development groups is MoP's prime benefit. With MoP, each group of developers needs to understand only the subset of policy management that falls properly within the group's purview.

MoP allocates responsibilities to policy-makers, database administrators, DBMS developers, and application developers. MoP does not impose any requirements on the client tier.

Policy-makers specify the policy rules that are implemented by MoP policy modules. They also have the ultimate responsibility for locating or creating policy modules that implement the rules and conflict resolution modules that implement the resolution of conflicts among policy rules.

DBMS developers create stored procedures that implement the two DBMS functions required by MoP, returning identifiers for the policy modules associated with a data access request and returning a policy module on request.

Database administrators create and install the MoP stored procedures into the DBMS, insert policy modules identified by the policy-makers, and associate policy modules with data. Mechanisms for these functions will vary from DBMS to DBMS. This process is out of the scope of MoP.

Application developers call the MoP application component, pass it required parameters, and use policy module outputs to apply policy.

4.8 The Implementation

We are using a prototype implementation of the MoP components to validate our framework design as we develop it. We do not consider any portion of our design complete until it has been included in the prototype.

The current prototype is an all-COM solution built using Microsoft Visual Basic Enterprise 6.0 and Microsoft Access 8.0. Early work has focused on building the MoP application component, using stubs for database support and policy modules, and a demonstration application that exercises each feature of the MoP application component.

Our target databases are Oracle and SQL Server. Access does not provide stored procedures or sophisticated policy management mechanisms, but its functionality is adequate to support work on the MoP application component.

5. CONCLUSIONS AND FUTURE WORK

This paper proposes the use of mobile policy in multi-tier information systems. Specifically, it separates policy administration from policy enforcement. Policy is specified and administered at the element of a distributed system where the data being controlled by policy is defined. That policy is then shared with consumers of the data so that they can enforce the appropriate policy when using the data.

Performing authentication and access control in the database is suitable where the data are extremely sensitive or the number of potential clients is limited. However, it can be restrictively expensive where the application resides in a middle tier instead of the database or the number of potential clients is large. Therefore, where company policy permits, a solution such as MoP can enhance overall security by expanding practical policy enforcement beyond access control within the DBMS.

Although we have not completed work on the basic MoP framework, we have identified a number of enhancements that we would like to add once the basic framework is complete: dynamically-generated policy modules, dynamic determination of conflict resolution metadata, a policy composition module that manages relationships among different policy modules, and support for associating policy modules with subsets of retrieved data.

Dynamically generated policy modules are interesting because they would eliminate parallel implementations of the same policy. DBMS systems already have a mechanism that associates access control policies with data. We would like to develop a mechanism that extracts the access control information relevant to an SQL query and packages it as a MoP policy module. In addition to convenience value, automatic generation of MoP policy modules potentially could enhance assurance because the information would not have to be associated with the data twice, once as a policy module and once as DBMS access control lists.

Dynamic determination of conflict resolution metadata is interesting because it would simplify the task of policy module developers. As it stands today, MoP requires linked code development in policy modules on one type and their associated conflict resolution modules. We think it would be desirable to provide a cleaner interface so that policy module and conflict resolution module development can be more independent.

Support for associating policy modules with subsets of retrieved data is interesting because it would support applications, such as data warehouses, where a large block of data is retrieved all at once and stored internally in database table format. Later, when the data are to be used, the application extracts subsets of the data for each specific use. MoP as currently designed does not support this kind of application.

Before our framework can be shown to be useful in production environments, a number of issues need to be addressed: performance, multi-platform application support, and assurance.

Performance is an issue, because a prime reason for using multi-tier architectures is to gain enhanced scalability and efficiency. If making policies mobile slows processing down any appreciable amount, any benefits will not be worth the cost.

Multi-platform support is an issue because another prime reason for using multi-tier architectures is to gain application development flexibility. If the MoP application component can be called only by COM applications, and not by EJB or CORBA applications, its usefulness will be limited.

Assurance is an issue because many MoP policies are security policies. A mechanism for implementing security policies that cannot itself be shown to meet enterprise requirements for security will not be very useful.

REFERENCES

1. Black, D. L., D. B. Golub, D. P. Julin, R. F. Rashid, R., P. Draves, R. W. Dean, A. Forin, J. Barrera, H. Tokuda, G. Malan, and D. Bohman, "Microkernel Operating System Architecture and Mach," Journal of Information Processing, Volume 14, Number 4, 1995.
2. Doshi, Vinti, Amgad Fayad, and Sushil Jajodia, "Using Attribute Certificates with Mobile Policies in Electronic Commerce Applications," Proc. 16th Annual Computer Security Applications Conf., New Orleans, LA, December 2000.
3. Minear, Spencer E., "Providing Policy Control Over Object Operations in a Mach Based System," Secure Computing Corporation, Roseville, MN, April 1995.
4. Minear, Spencer E., "Controlling Mach Operations for use in Secure and Safety-Critical Systems," Secure Computing Corporation, Roseville, MN, June 1994.

5. Object Management Group (OMG), Resource Access Decision (RAD), OMG document corbamed/99-03-02, March 1999.

6. Object Management Group (OMG), Transaction Service Specification.

7. Simon, Richard and Mary Ellen Zurko, "Separation of duty in role-based environments," Proceedings of the 10th Computer Security Foundations Workshop, June 1997.

8. U.S. Department of Commerce/National Institute for Standards and Technology, Standard Security Label for Information Transfer, FIPS PUB 188, September 1994.

9. Zurko, Mary Ellen, Rich Simon, Tom Sanfilippo, "A user-centered, modular authorization service built on an RBAC foundation," Proc. IEEE Symp. on Security and Privacy, May 1999.

CHAPTER 7

SECURITY ARCHITECTURE OF THE MULTIMEDIA MEDIATOR

Christian Altenschmidt
Joachim Biskup
Yücel Karabulut
Fachbereich Informatik
Universität Dortmund
D-44221 Dortmund
Germany
altensch, biskup, karabulu@ls6.cs.uni-dortmund.de

Abstract Mediation is a powerful paradigm for advanced interoperable information systems. This paper presents the security module of the multimedia mediator which enforces a previously reported approach to secure mediation. In this approach, a user submits cryptographically signed credentials containing both personal authorization attributes and his public encryption key, and data sources decide on the query access on the basis of shown personal authorization attributes and return encrypted answers. The security module uniformly represents the query access authorizations of the sources, controls the intermediate usage of credentials, assists users in submitting appropriate credentials, selects and forwards credentials for subqueries, and exploits credentials for query optimization.

Keywords: Security, Mediator, Credential, Authorization, Access Control

1. INTRODUCTION

Mediation is a powerful paradigm for advanced interoperable information systems [Wie92]. A *mediator* manages queries on behalf of a user by identifying and addressing appropriate subqueries to heterogeneous and autonomous data sources and by subsequently collecting and integrating the returned answers. A previously reported approach to *secure mediation* [BFK99, BFK98] is based on a public-key infrastructure and cryptographically signed *credentials* that encode the eligibility of users. These technologies potentially provide for an inherently scalable and secure mechanism for widely distributing assured authentication and authorization attributes. Secure mediation is roughly outlined as follows [BFK99, BFK98]. A user submits evidence of being eligible for seeing the answer to a query by submitting certified *personal authorization attributes* which are encoded in credentials. A mediator examines, selects and forwards submitted credentials together with appropriate subqueries to the data sources. A data source autonomously bases *access decisons* for requested data on shown credentials, and it returns subquery answers in *encrypted form* to the mediator. For encryption it applies the user's *public key* for an asymmetric encryption scheme which is also contained in the credentials. Then the mediator processes the returned encrypted data in order to produce the final, still encrypted query answer.

In our Multimedia Mediator, MMM, project [BFKS97] a specific kind of a mediator has been designed and implemented as a prototype. A *security module* for the MMM is being constructed under the following requirements: (1) implement the design [BFK99] as outlined above, (2) smoothly integrate the security features into the functionalities of the MMM prototype, (3) meet emerging standards [IET00, RL98, PKI00] for credentials.

In this paper, we present and discuss the architecture of this security module emphasizing the following original contributions:

- an *authorization model* that allows to consider *credentials* as grantees, to be used for representing the query access authorizations of the sources;
- specifications of query access authorizations as *annotated ODL declarations*, which can be communicated from the sources to the MMM, in particular;
- a *schema authorization policy for mediation*, which allows to dynamically generate external schemas for spontaneous users;
- an *instance authorization policy for mediation*, which conjunctively combines the access restrictions of the mediator and the sources;
- an *isolated co-existence* of the functional layers and the security layers treating authorization data in close correspondance to functional data;
- an enrichment of (so far only functional) *embeddings* [ABFS98] from an application object into the proxy objects for source items, as maintained by the MMM, for evaluating expected access decisions of the sources;
- user support for *credential management* by determining implications among sets of personal authorization attributes;
- and exploitation of credentials for *query optimization*.

2. ENVIRONMENT OF SECURE MEDIATION

The Multimedia Mediator prototype. The Multimedia Mediator, MMM, is implemented as an autonomously operating *agent*. It is based on the object-oriented database management system O2. Figure 2 shows its environment and its functional and security architecture. Seen from the user, the MMM appears as an object-oriented database which consists of an *application schema* with a mostly virtual *instance*. Basically, in addition to persistent data owned by the MMM, this instance is only transiently and partially materialized by *proxy objects* representing items of the data sources. A user addresses the MMM by means of his personal *user agent*. And data sources are connected to the MMM with the help of *wrapper agents*. Interoperability is supported by employing CORBA [OMG98] for data exchanges, KQML [FLM97] for agent communications, and ODL/OQL [CB00] for schema declarations and query expressions.

Authorization model. Credentials [IET00, RL98, Cha85, PKI00, BFL96] are powerful means to receive and to present assured digital certificates about a wide range of personal properties. Such properties may include the ownership of a public key (and the corresponding secret key) for an asymmetric cryptographic scheme, a unique identification for authentication, personal properties like date of birth, gender, educational degrees, profession and so on, and received or payed permissions to get access to digital services. Moreover credentials can be used to approve that several of such properties belong together.

For mediated information systems we employ credentials that contain a *public key* and additional properties of any kind as follows: they approve that the owner of the public key enjoys the additional attributes. When shown to a data source, as well as to a mediator, the additional attributes are interpreted as *personal authorization attributes* proving that the owner of the private key is eligible for querying certain data. Thus for our purpose we abstract *credentials* as pairs of the form [*public (encryption) key, set of personal authorization attributes*] which are digitally signed by the issuer.

Any agent autonomously decides on the specific interpretation, i.e., which data it is willing to return. This means in terms of the usual authorization models that an *authorization subject* can be modelled as a set of personal authorization attributes, like identified users or roles in more traditional approaches. Accordingly, any agent needs two features to decide on an actual permission of a requested query:

- An *authorization database* of granted query access authorizations that have sets of personal authorization attributes as grantees, and
- *authorization policies* to evaluate the request with respect to the authorization database.

Figure 1 shows a coarse model for the *authorization database*. As usual, an *authorization* specifies a grantor, a privilege and a grantee. A *privilege* is composed of an *authorization object* and a set of applicable access *methods*. The *grantor* is supposed to be an identified *user* that in most cases is the *owner* of the privilege (here usually the administrators of the MMM and of the

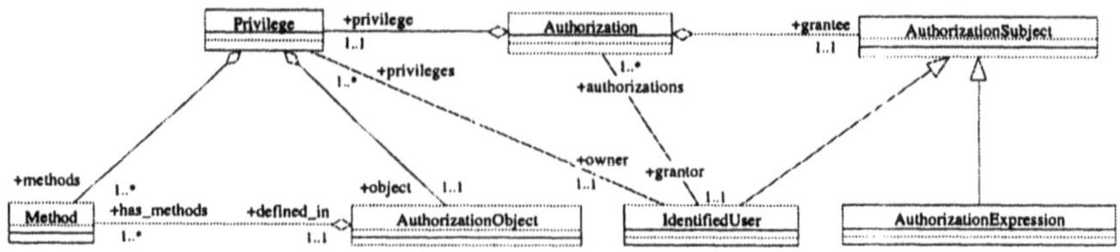

Figure 1. Coarse model for the authorization database

sources, respectively). The *grantee* might be an identified user, as usual, but additionally, as a particularity of our credential based access control, a *Boolean expression over personal authorization attributes* (*authorization expression* for short). For the sake of simple exposition, we only consider authorization expressions over atomic personal authorization attributes which are in *disjunctive normal form without negations*. Such an authorization expression can be identified with a set (representing the disjunction) which contains sets (representing the conjunctions) of personal authorization attributes as elements.

A particular instance (p, g, a) with privilege p, grantor g, and authorization expression a as grantee means that g *has granted* privilege p to any request which is accompanied with an authorization expression r such that "r *qualifies for* a". In the full model, the exact definition of the relationship "*qualifies*" formalizes the rough intuition of "*logical implies* under additional assumptions".

Then any *authorization policy* evaluates a request *on the basis* of the valid *qualifications* between the accompanying authorization expression and the required authorization expression, for all needed privileges. There is a special authorization policy, called *pure*, that *only* checks the envolved qualifications, i.e., the request is permitted iff all these qualifications are valid (and there are no further conditions).

Now we make a subtle distinction for the MMM:

- For each connected source, the MMM maintains a *representation* of the source's authorization database, and the MMM *expects* that the source applies the *pure* authorization policy.
- The mediator itself applies two more elaborated *authorization policies for mediation*, one for querying *schemas* and another one for querying *instances*, which combine the *envolved qualifications* with *additional considerations*, to be presented in subsequent sections.

Annotated ODL declarations. We mostly follow the ODMG proposal to achieve interoperability among our agents with respect to schema declarations. Thus all schema declarations are supposed to be convertable into a canonical form expressed in ODL. For the current prototype we use the following basic ODL features: *class*; *class attribute*; *attribute type* built from classes and atomic types (`boolean`, `string`, `integer`,...) using constructors like `set_of`, `list`, `struct` (`tuple_of`); *relationship* (specifying inverse attributes); *key*; *extent* for denoting an access path to a full class extension; *persistent root* for denoting an access path to an arbitrary subset of a class extension. (Strictly speaking, "persistent root" is an O2 feature which is not explicitly mentioned in [CB00].) Further advanced features (*method, inheritance, interface, exception,...*) could be added to future versions of the prototype.

For specifying access authorizations in the context of the MMM, we have to identify the possibly relevant instances (p, g, a), with privilege $p = (o, m)$ for accessing an authorization object o by method m, grantor g, and authorization expression a. For the current prototype, as well as for the sake of short presentation, we make the following simplifying assumptions: (1) We restrict to *schema based* authorizations (refraining from content based authorizations which depend on actual data values). Thus as *authorization objects* we allow concrete incarnations of all ODL features, except for types where only components of struct-declarations are considered. (2) We assume some generic *access* method for all authorization objects (refraining from specializing the generic method into *read, navigate*, and so on). (3) As a default, we postulate an administrator who acts as *owner* of any object and as *grantor* of any authorization. Thus we can ignore these components further on. (4) In summary, we can specify authorizations as (o, a) where o is a considered ODL feature (more precisely a concrete incarnation of it) and a is an authorization expression. Giving these assumptions, we can succinctly express access authorization by adding two kinds of annotations to ODL schema declarations, each of which consists of an authorization expression:

- a *schema access annotation* grants a privilege to access some part of the schema itself, and
- an *instance access annotation* grants a privilege to access some part of the (mostly virtual) instance.

More precisely we offer the following possibilities: A *schema access annotation* on any ODL feature grants the privilege to access (read and use) the declaration of this very instance. An *instance access annotation* on a class c grants the privilege to access (activate) any instance object of the class extension. An *instance access annotation* on a class attribute $attr$ grants the privilege to access (execute) the attribute for any of the class's instance objects that already has been accessed before. Depending on the type of the attribute, either the stored (complex) value is returned or the stored object identifier is dereferenced resulting in an access to the identified object. An *instance access annotation* on a relationship rel is treated as if rel was an attribute. An *instance access annotation* on a component *com* of a struct-declaration of an attribute type grants the privilege to access that component of an instance object provided the struct part has been accessed before. An *instance access annotation* on an extent or persistent root *ext* grants the privilege to access that data structure, i.e., to execute all available set operations including scanning, searching and so on.

At this point we emphasize that so far we have only described how an annotation updates the *authorization database*. In section 3 we define the *authorization policies* which finally regulate the actual access decisions.

3. SECURE MEDIATION

For secure mediation we distinguish the initialization phase and, afterwards, preparatory phases for sources and users, respectively, and query request phases and corresponding answer delivery phases.

Initialization phase. In the *initialization* phase, a mediation administrator *instantiates* the MMM by declaring an *application schema* expressed in ODL which captures the information needs of the anticipated users. For many parts of the application schema, there will be no persistent instance in general but the corresponding data is dynamically retrieved from sources at query time.

But for some parts of the schema, the administrator may want to maintain data owned by the MMM itself. Technically, for such parts the administrator additionally declares a *twin schema* as a subschema of the application schema, and he inserts an instance for this twin schema. Later on, query processing treats the twin schema and its instance, also referred to as *twin source*, nearly like the other sources.

While specifying the application schema and the twin schema the administrator also grants the *(query access) authorizations* using annotated ODL declarations as introduced in section 2 for both schemas. If there is no annotation for a concept, then there will be no query access restrictions. Conceptually, the authorizations for both the application schema and the twin schema are stated independently, though, in practice, they usually will be closely related.

Preparatory phase for a source. In a *preparatory phase for a source*, a data source can be connected with the MMM for further cooperation provided the source can comply with the functional requirements of the instantiated MMM. Furthermore, the source must provide a credential based authorization policy. The basic functional requirements are that appropriate parts of the application schema can be *embedded* in matching parts of the (virtual or existing) source schema. If the requirements are met, an appropriate *wrapper* agent is created which is devoted to convert source items into a form that is canonical for the mediator, and vice versa.

Thus, in this phase, firstly the wrapper provides a canonical form of the matching source schema parts, again expressed in ODL, which subsequently are internally represented within the MMM and there connected to the matching application schema parts by so-called embeddings [ABFS98]. Secondly, as far as possible, the wrapper also converts the source's authorization database into a canonical form. For this purpose, the wrapper adds pertinent annotations to the ODL representation of the source schema, which are subsequently internally represented within the MMM.

Preparatory phase for a user. In a *preparatory phase for a user*, a spontaneously emerging user asks for inspecting the application schema of the MMM because he wants to know how it captures his information needs. In order to do so, he presents some of his credentials. Let us assume that these credentials contain the set of personal authorization attributes which is denoted by the authorization expression a. Then the MMM returns the largest *subschema* of the application schema permitted to that user according to the following *schema authorization policy for mediation*:

- A subschema is *permitted* (for an authorization expression a) iff it is allowed according to the pure authorization policy applied to the authorization database generated from the annotations declared for the application schema (so far the privileges for all subschema items are granted individually) and, additionally, 1.) the subschema is syntactically correct (closed with respect to the ODL rules) and 2.) privileges are consistently granted (closed with respect to inferences in the sense of [OvS94, CG98]).

Thus the user gets a dynamically generated *external view* about the *functionality* of the mediator. This view is *closed* in the following sense: 1.) If an item is shown, then all other items needed to access that item are also shown. 2.) It is impossible to infer the existence of further items that are not shown. The *dynamic* generation of subschemas is in the spirit of the open computing environments for mediation. Hence we favour this novel dynamic approach rather than declaring a limited set of external views in advance.

On demand, the user also gets the *authorization requirements* for the corresponding (virtual) instances, i.e., the user can ask to be informed about which personal authorization attributes are *likely to be sufficient* to access which parts of the corresponding (virtual) instance. Then the user can assemble credentials with his personal authorization attributes *potentially* providing evidence of his eligibility to see answers to submitted queries.

Query request phase. In a *query request phase*, a prepared user sends a global *request* to the MMM. A global request includes a global query with respect to the application schema and a set of credentials. The MMM analyzes the request with respect to functional and authorization requirements, thereby identifying subrequests to be forwarded to connected sources. Hereby, the twin source maintained by the MMM itself is treated like any external source, except that no wrapper is involved.

Accordingly, a *subrequest* to a source includes a local query with respect to the internal representation of the source schema and appropriately selected credentials, which are subsequently converted by the responsible wrapper.

Concerning the authorization requirements, the MMM relates the global authorizations of the MMM to the local authorizations of the connected sources using the following *instance authorization policy for mediation*:

- A request is (globally) *permitted* (for an authorization expression a) iff it is allowed according to the *pure* authorization policy applied to the authorization database generated from the annotations declared for the application schema and, additionally, all subrequests are (locally) permitted.
- A subrequest to the twin source is (locally) permitted iff it is allowed according to the *pure* authorization policy applied to the authorization database generated from the annotations declared for the twin schema.
- A subrequest to an external data source is (locally) permitted iff the MMM *expects* that the source will permit the access as requested by the included local query based on the included credentials. The *expectation* is based on the *pure* authorization policy applied to the authorization database generated from the annotations specified for the representation of the source schema.
- If a request is (globally) permitted, then all subrequests are forwarded and then autonomously evaluated by the sources. Otherwise the request is (globally) *denied*, and the user will be informed that no answer can be returned due to the lack of personal authorization attributes.
- An external data source, as well as the twin source, autonomously decides on permitting subrequests.
- Subanswers from the twin source and external sources are processed in the mediator and forwarded to the user without any further restrictions.

Thus, seen from the user, the authorization requirements of the mediator and the sources are *conjunctively* combined: access to source data via the mediator is permitted iff it is allowed by *both* the mediator *and* the source. Accordingly, the security module of the mediator acts as a kind of *filter* put in front of the sources. There are obvious tradeoffs between the strength of the filters as defined by the global authorizations, the overall run-time complexity of mediated query evalution and the response quality. These tradeoffs can be exploited for query optimization as discussed in the preproceedings.

Answer delivery phase. A query request phase is followed by the corresponding *answer delivery phase* (allowing the interleaving of several requests). In this phase, a source produces a *protected subanswer*:

- All *content data* for attribute values is piecewise *probabilistically encrypted* with the public encryption key of the user which is connected with those personal authorization attributes on the basis of which query access permissions have been decided.
- All *structural parts* are left *open as plain text.*

The MMM uses the protected subanswers to generate new proxy objects, and if necessary new application pseudo objects which are associated with the corresponding proxy objects. Pertinent embeddings are determined by the types of the application pseudo objects and the types of their corresponding proxy objects in order to define (usually encrypted) attribute values for old and new application pseudo objects. As soon as all subanswers are available (or after some timeout) a suitably modified version of the original (global) query is evaluated on the basis of the current instance, the embeddings into the proxy objects and the retrieved method values for the proxy objects.

Surely, the functionality of this phase is essentially restricted by the attribute values being encrypted with public keys of the user. Basically, the full functionality is preserved as far as the modified version of the original query does not have to perform comparisons for selections and joins on encrypted values. For the strategies to avoid the restrictions we refer to the preproceedings.

4. THE SECURITY MODULE

In this section we provide some more details on how *secure mediation* as explained in section 3 is actually implemented as part of the MMM. Figure 2 gives a first rough overview about the data flow between functional and security components. We only describe the main security components. Further details are given in the preproceedings.

The security module of the MMM has three main components, the security knowledge base, SECKNOB, the credential manager, CREMA, and the mediator authorization decision engine, MAIDEN.

The security knowledge base, SECKNOB, maintains the following parts: (1) The *authorization databases* that are generated from the annotated declarations of the application schema, the twin schema and the representations of the external source schemas. (2) The *credentials* submitted by a user. (3) The *authorization attributes* extracted from the credentials together with links associating them with the credentials they are extracted from. (4) A (Horn clause) *rule base* that specifies implications among authorization expressions which are invoked when an instance of the relationship "*qualifies for*" between

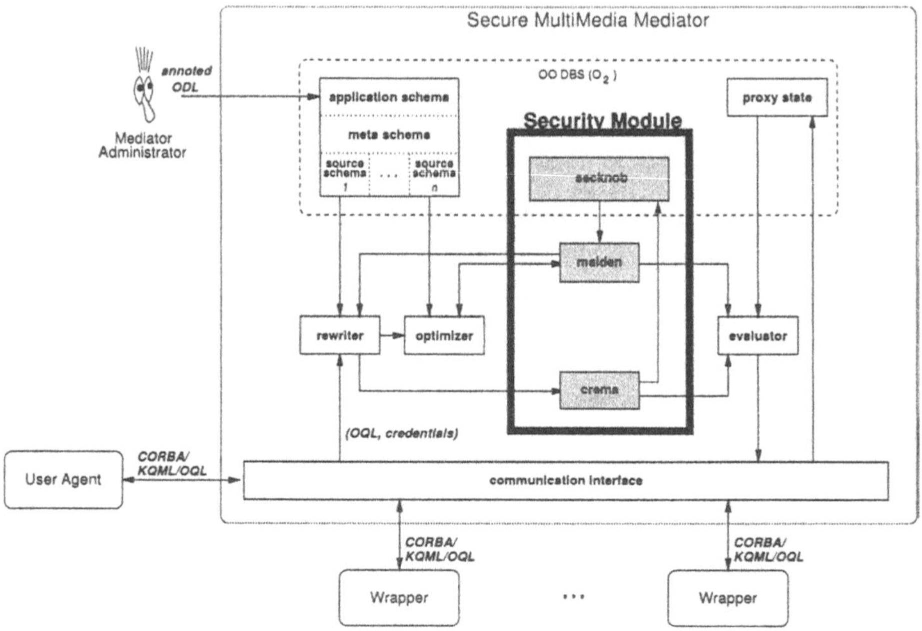

Figure 2. Security architecture of the Multimedia Mediator

authorization expressions must be decided. The rule base is intended to take advantage of "real world" properties of authorization attributes, and to encode known access control features like structured objects, groups or roles, for each of which we can define hierarchies and corresponding inheritance rules. (5) A collection of *protocol converters* which unify the various formats proposed in existing and emerging standards for credentials [IET00, RL98, PKI00].

The credential manager, CREMA, verifies the authenticity and validity of submitted credentials by checking the approving digital signatures and expiration dates. Moreover, it extracts authorization attributes from credentials, inserts credentials, their authorization attributes and the pertinent links into SECKNOB, and determines credentials to be included to subqueries.

The mediator authorization decision engine, MAIDEN, implements the *authorization policies for mediation*, both for *schemas* and for *instances*, and the underlying *pure* authorization policy together with its basic relationship "*qualifies for*" among authorization expressions.

Additionally, we need an appropriate access control shell for the underlying object-oriented database management system. Unfortunately, this shell is not provided by O2 which we use for our prototype.

5. RELATED WORK AND CONCLUSION

Security in interoperable information systems has mostly been investigated within federated database contexts, where the emphasis laid on resolving heterogeneity [Jon98, TF97]. For contributions to security in mediated systems see [CJS96, WBD98, DSS00]. The security mechanisms presented in the works above are identity based rather than credential based.

With our credential based approach we can model both *identity based authorization* as well as *attribute based authorization*. In contrast to the efforts above, our approach makes a specific contribution towards interoperation by combining the credential based authentic authorization with some kind of anonymity and of asymmetric encryption for confidentiality. The concept of credentials has also been adopted previously for various purposes in interoperable systems [SWW97].

The ongoing implementation is based on several original contributions, in particular the identification of suitable schema and instance *authorization policies for mediation*, ODL declarations with schema access and instance *access annotations*, and an analysis of the impact of authorization for *query optimization*. There are a lot of issues for further research and development. Among them are the exploitation of the full scope of ODL, rapid construction of "authorization wrappers", refined optimization, more sophisticated treatment of encrypted subanswers, and user support for presenting appropriate credentials.

References

[ABFS98] C. Altenschmidt, J. Biskup, J. Freitag, and B. Sprick. Weakly constraining multimedia types based on a type embedding ordering. In *Proceedings of the 4th International Workshop on Multimedia Information Systems*, pages 121–129, Istanbul, Turkey, September 1998.

[BFK98] J. Biskup, U. Flegel, and Y. Karabulut. Towards secure mediation. In *1st Workshop on Sicherheit und Electronic Commerce*, pages 93–106, Essen, Germany, October 1998. Vieweg-Verlag.

[BFK99] J. Biskup, U. Flegel, and Y. Karabulut. Secure Mediation: Requirements and Design. In *Proceedings of the 12th Annual IFIP WG 11.3 Working Conference on Database Security*, pages 127–140, Chalkidiki, Greece, 1999. Kluwer Academic Press.

[BFKS97] J. Biskup, J. Freitag, Y. Karabulut, and B. Sprick. Query evaluation in an object-oriented multimedia mediator. In *Proceedings of the 4th International Conference on Object-Oriented Information Systems*, pages 31–43, Brisbane, Australia, November 1997. Springer Verlag.

[BFL96] M. Blaze, J. Feigenbaum, and J. Lacy. Decentralized trust management. In *17th IEEE Symposium on Security and Privacy*, pages 164–173, Los Alamitos, 1996.

[CB00] R. G. G. Cattell and Douglas Barry, editors. *The Object Data Standard: ODMG 3.0.* Morgan Kaufmann, San Francisco, 2000.

[CG98] F. Cuppens and A. Gabillon. Rules for designing multilevel object-oriented databases. In Jean-Jacques Quisquater, Yves Deswarte, Catherine Meadows, and Dieter Gollmann, editors, *Proceedings of the 5th European Symposium on Research in Computer Security (ESORICS'98)*, number 1485 in LNCS, pages 159–174, Louvain-la-Neuve, Belgium, September 1998. Springer-Verlag.

[Cha85] David Chaum. Security without identification: Transaction systems to make big brother obsolete. *Communications of the ACM*, 28(10):1030–1044, October 1985.

[CJS96] K. S. Candan, Sushil Jajodia, and V. S. Subrahmanian. Secure mediated databases. In Stanley Y. W. Su, editor, *12th International Conference on Data Eng.*, pages 28–37, New Orleans, Louisiana, USA, Feb. - Mar. 1996. IEEE, IEEE Computer Society Press.

[DSS00] S. Dawson, Qian S., and P. Samarati. Providing security and interoperation of heterogeneous systems. *Distributed and Parallel Databases*, 8(1):119–145, January 2000.

[FLM97] Tim Finin, Yannis Labrou, and James Mayfield. KQML as an agent communication language. In J. M. Bradshaw, editor, *Software Agents*. MIT Press, Cambridge, 1997. `http://www.cs.umbc.edu/kqml/papers/`.

[IET00] IETF SPKI Working Group. SPKI certificate documentation. `http://world.std.com/~cme/html/spki.html`, July 2000.

[Jon98] D. Jonscher. *Access Control in Object-Oriented Federated Database Systems*. PhD thesis, University of Zurich, Department of Computer Science, Zurich, May 1998. DISDBIS 49, Infix-Verlag.

[OMG98] Object Management Group. The common object request broker, architecture and specification. CORBA 2.3.1/IIOP specification. `http://www.omg.org/library/c2indx.html`, December 1998.

[OvS94] M.S. Olivier and S.H. von Solms. A taxonomy for secure object-oriented databases. *ACM Transactions on Database Systems*, 19(1):3–46, 1994.

[PKI00] PKIX Working Group. An internet attribute certificate profile for authorization. Internet draft, work in progress. `http://www.ietf.org/internet-drafts/draft-ietf-pkix-ac509prof-03.txt`, May 2000.

[RL98] R. L. Rivest and B. Lampson. A simple distributed security infrastructure (SDSI). `http://theory.lcs.mit.edu/~cis/sdsi.html`, 1998.

[SWW97] K. E. Seamons, W. Winsborough, and M. Winslett. Internet credential acceptance policies. In *Proceedings of the Workshop on Logic Programming for Internet Applications*, Leuven, Belgium, July 1997.

[TF97] Z. Tari and G. Fernandez. Security enforcement in the DOK federated database system. In P. Samarati and R. S. Sandhu, editors, *Database Security, X: Status and Prospects, Proceedings of the 10th IFIP WG 11.3 Working Conference on Database Security*, pages 23–42, Como, Italy, 1997. Chapman & Hall.

[WBD98] Gio Wiederhold, Michel Bilello, and Chris Donahue. Web implementation of a security mediator for medical databases. In T. Y. Lin and Shelly Qian, editors, *Database Security, XI: Status and Prospects, Proceedings of the 11th Annual IFIP WG 11.3 Working Conference on Database Security*, pages 60–72, Lake Tahoe, California, 1998. IFIP, Chapman & Hall.

[Wie92] G. Wiederhold. Mediators in the architecture of future information systems. *IEEE Computer*, 25(3):38–49, 1992.

CHAPTER 8
SIMULATION AND ANALYSIS OF CRYPTOGRAPHIC PROTOCOLS

M. Papa, O. Bremer, S. Magill, J. Hale and S. Shenoi

Abstract This paper integrates logic and process calculus components to permit the comprehensive simulation and analysis of cryptographic protocols. The approach permits proofs about the information transmitted in protocols as well as the behavior of participating principals.

Keywords: Cryptographic protocols, simulation, verification, logics, process calculi

1. INTRODUCTION

Cryptographic protocols are unambiguous, mutually subscribed series of steps, involving the exchange of messages between communicating agents (principals). They are indispensable to distributed computing applications ranging from electronic commerce to national defense [14,15].

Most protocols fail due to design flaws, not because of weaknesses in encryption [3,8,9,14]. A subtle flaw in the Needham-Schroeder protocol [8] went undiscovered for nine years, potentially allowing malicious entities to steal keys, corrupt sensitive data, even sabotage military systems.

Higher order logics [3,5,15] are used to reason about protocols. BAN logic [3] is a many-sorted modal logic for analyzing authentication protocols. It assumes that authentication is a function of integrity and freshness of messages. Inference rules are specified for tracing these attributes through all the steps of a protocol. BAN also defines inference rules for reasoning about the information held by principals ("beliefs"). BAN has detected flaws and exposed redundancies in several protocols, including Needham-Schroeder, Yahalom and Kerberos protocols [3,14].

Despite their success, BAN logic and its derivatives (e.g., GNY [5] and SVO logics [15]) have two major limitations. First, protocols must be idealized prior to analysis. The translation of a real protocol to its idealized counterpart is a difficult process, susceptible to misinterpretation and errors [5,14]. Moreover, a single protocol may have multiple idealized representations, each with slightly different properties. The second limitation arises from the logics' inability to express the actions and evolution of principals. Message passing is modeled as an atomic event; the exchange of a message only affects the information held by the principals. When the actions and evolution of principals are ignored, it is not possible to make formal guarantees about their behavior.

Another promising approach to protocol verification involves modeling principals as agents using a process calculus [1,2,10-12]. An axiomatization of the process calculus is then used to obtain proofs about agent behavior. The π-calculus [11,12] exemplifies this approach. It models distributed systems as primitive concurrent agents with complex message passing. Computation is simulated by agent communication: agents exchange messages and evolve to simpler forms, until all communication ceases. A deep embedding of π-calculus using Higher Order Logic (HOL) [6] permits proofs about agents, distributed systems, and the π-calculus itself [10]. The ROC process calculus [7] extends the π-calculus for distributed objects with complex message passing. The *Spi*-calculus [2] augments the π-calculus with cryptographic primitives, permitting encrypted messages.

Process calculi give the ability to comprehensively model and reason about the behavior of principals (agents) without protocol idealization. However, process calculi lack constructs for reasoning about messages. While the *Spi*-calculus can model principals exchanging encrypted messages, it can neither model nor reason about the information held by principals. Thus, only limited properties can be proven about protocols.

This paper integrates logic and process calculus components, combining their strengths to permit the comprehensive simulation and analysis of cryptographic protocols. Protocols need not be idealized prior to modeling and verification. Moreover, it is possible to prove properties about individual messages, principals, and the protocol itself.

2. MESSAGE MODELING

Following the style of process calculi [7,11,12], we model message passing using synchronous communication. Asynchronous communication protocols can be constructed with synchronously communicating agents.

Communication occurs when a message output by one agent matches a pattern exposed by another. This section describes the syntax of messages and patterns, and the pattern-matching conventions.

Definition 2.1: A *key* ($k \in key$) is a public/private key (K_n/K_n^{-1}), a shared or secret key (K_n^s), the concatenation of two keys ($k_1 : k_2$), a placeholder for a key that is not yet known ($k?$), or *nokey*, corresponding to a cleartext message:

$$k \ ::= \ K_n \mid K_n^{-1} \mid K_n^s \mid k_1 : k_2 \mid k? \mid nokey$$

We assume the existence of an infinite set of *names* ($n \in name$) as a basic type. It is used to create unique keys, and data items for messages and patterns.

Definition 2.2: A *message* ($m \in message$) is a tuple $\{v_1, v_2, ..., v_j\}_k$ encrypted under key k. A *value* ($v \in value$) is a key (k), a message (m), a name (n) or a fresh name ($\#n$):

$$\begin{aligned} m \ &::= \ \{v_1, v_2, ..., v_j\}_k \\ v \ &::= \ k \mid m \mid n \mid \#n \end{aligned}$$

To permit complex structures, messages are defined as nested tuples of "values" ($v \in value$). Note that fresh names (nonces and time stamps) are also incorporated in the BAN and GNY logics [3,5]. A newly generated value is considered to be fresh throughout a protocol run. A list of fresh names associated with each run must be maintained to permit reasoning about freshness.

Patterns permit the capture of messages and their contents. A pattern exposed by a receiver expresses the information it has about message format and content.

Definition 2.3: A *pattern* ($p \in pattern$) is a tuple $\{p_1, p_2, ..., p_j\}_k$ encrypted under key k, a key (k), a wildcard ($n?$) for capturing values, or a datum (n):

$$p \ ::= \ \{p_1, p_2, ..., p_j\}_k \mid k \mid n? \mid n$$

Figure 1 illustrates the modeling of messages and patterns. In the example, the Law Enforcement Agency Field (LEAF) for a Clipper transmission [14,15] is output by *Phone* as $\{\{K_s^s\}_{K_{c_1}^s : K_{c_2}^s}, ID, AUTH\}_{K_f^s}$, where $\{K_s^s\}_{K_{c_1}^s : K_{c_2}^s}$ is the session key K_s^s encrypted under the Clipper chip's unit key $K_{c_1}^s : K_{c_2}^s$, ID is the Clipper serial number, and AUTH is the escrow authenticator. All these items are encrypted under the Clipper family key K_f^s.

Since the law enforcement agency knows the LEAF format and the family key K_f^s, it can expose the pattern $\{ekey?, id?, auth?\}_{K_f^s}$ to receive

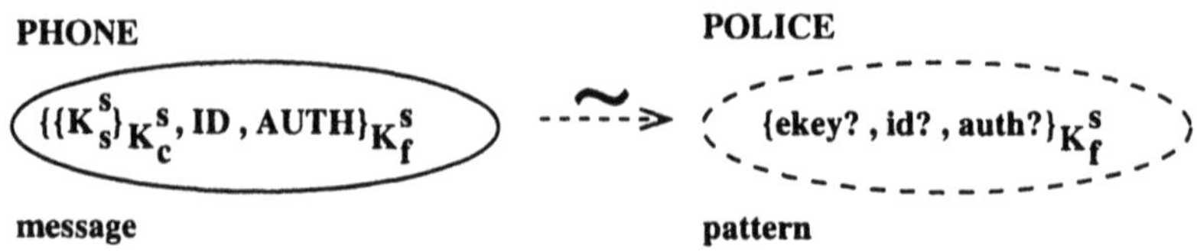

Figure 1. Modeling message passing.

the message as input. The wildcards *ekey?*, *id?* and *auth?* are placeholders for receiving the individual LEAF items. Communication occurs when the *message* output by *Phone* in Figure 1 matches the *pattern* exposed by *Police*.

The following rules define the matching of messages and patterns. First, we define the matching of keys. Intuitively, the key matching operator establishes that an agent can decrypt an encrypted message if it possesses the right key.

Definition 2.4: Key matching ($\overset{K}{\sim}$) is defined by the following rules:

$$K_a \overset{K}{\sim} K_b^{-1} \text{ iff } a = b$$
$$K_a^s \overset{K}{\sim} K_b^s \text{ iff } a = b$$
$$nokey \overset{K}{\sim} nokey$$

Definition 2.5: The matching of messages and patterns ($\sim$) is defined by the following rules ($v \in value$, $p \in pattern$, $k \in key$, $m \in message$ and $n \in name$):

$$\{v_1, v_2, ..., v_j\}_{k_1} \sim \{p_1, p_2, ..., p_j\}_{k_2} \text{ iff } k_1 \overset{K}{\sim} k_2 \wedge v_i \sim p_i \ \forall\, i = 1..j$$
$$m \sim n?$$
$$v \sim n?$$
$$v \sim n \text{ iff } v = n$$
$$k \sim k?$$
$$k_1 \sim k_2 \text{ iff } k_1 = k_2$$

Communication occurs only when a message is matched by an exposed pattern. Free occurrences of a wildcard $n?$ in the pattern p are replaced with the corresponding matching value v throughout the pattern. For example, in Figure 1, the message $\{\{K_s^s\}_{K_c^s}, ID, AUTH\}_{K_f^s}$ is matched by the pattern $\{ekey?, id?, auth?\}_{K_f^s}$ exposed by *Police*, causing $\{K_s^s\}_{K_c^s}$, ID and $AUTH$ to be bound to *ekey*, *id* and *auth*, respectively.

3. PROTOCOL MODELING

Protocols are modeled as sequences of messages exchanged by agents. We model the messages exchanged and the behavior of the agents.

The starting point is a sequence of messages or patterns that are output ($\hat{}$) or input ($\rightarrow$) by an agent. Note that the term $a \equiv m\hat{}\ seq$ denotes that agent a outputs the message m. Likewise, $a \equiv m\hat{}\ p \rightarrow seq$ denotes that a first outputs the message m and then exposes the pattern p for input.

Definition 3.1: Let $m \in message$, $p \in pattern$ and $lstn$: List of $n \in name$. Then, *sequences* (seq), *annotated sequences* ($aseq$) and *concurrent sequences* ($cseq$) of messages and/or patterns are defined by:

$$\begin{aligned} seq &::= m\hat{}seq \mid p \rightarrow seq \mid nil \\ aseq &::= [seq].[lstn] \mid [seq]_\infty \\ cseq &::= aseq \diamond cseq \mid nil \end{aligned}$$

where nil is the empty list, $[seq]_\infty$ is an infinite sequence, and $\diamond$ is the commutative concurrency operator for sequences.

A sequence (seq) is defined as a sequence with an output message ($m\hat{}seq$) or an input pattern ($p \rightarrow seq$) or empty (nil). An annotated sequence ($aseq$) is a sequence of messages and/or patterns followed by a list of names ($[seq].[lstn]$); the list $[lstn]$ stores fresh names for the corresponding sequence ($[seq]$). The term $[seq]_\infty$ for an annotated sequence denotes a sequence that has to be executed repeatedly, e.g., to model a server. A concurrent sequence ($cseq$), the concurrent composition ($\diamond$) of an annotated sequence and a concurrent sequence, models threads of execution for a single agent. It can express multiple runs of one protocol or parallel runs of different protocols.

Definition 3.2: The following property holds for an infinite sequence $[seq]_\infty$:

$$[seq]_\infty \equiv [seq].[nil] \diamond [seq]_\infty$$

Definition 3.3: An agent a is defined by:

$$a ::= c(id, lstv)$$

where $c \in cseq$, $id \in name$ and $lstv$: List of $v \in value$.

The term id identifies the agent a, $lstv$ is a list of values representing the information possessed by the agent. As in the BAN and GNY logics

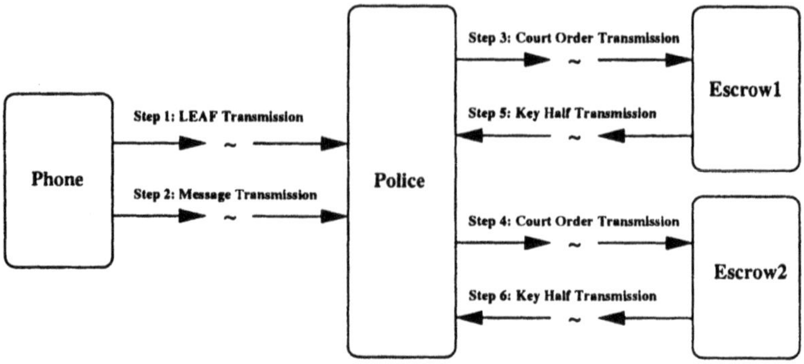

Figure 2. Simplified Clipper protocol.

[3,5], maintaining the list $lstv$ permits reasoning about agents, especially about what they know, say and have been told.

The modeling of cryptographic protocols with this syntax is highlighted using the simplified Clipper protocol in Figure 2.

Four agents participate in the protocol: a Clipper telephone (*Phone*), a law enforcement agent (*Police*) and two key escrow agents ($Escrow1$ and $Escrow2$). The protocol has six steps. *Police* exposes patterns to capture the LEAF (Step 1) and the encrypted message (Step 2) from *Phone*. Next, *Police* transmits *Phone*'s identification and a court order to $Escrow1$ and $Escrow2$ (Steps 3 and 4), each of which hold one-half of *Phone*'s unit key. In Steps 5 and 6, $Escrow1$ and $Escrow2$ transmit one-half of *Phone*'s unit key to *Police*.

Figure 3 shows the formal model of the protocol. *Phone* is defined as: *cseq*(*PhoneId*, *lstv*). *cseq* is composed of two output messages, the LEAF ($\{\{K_s^s\}_{K_{c_1}^s:K_{c_2}^s}, ID, AUTH\}_{K_f^s}$) and a message M encrypted under session key K_s^s ($\{M\}_{K_s^s}$). No fresh names are used in this particular protocol, thus $lstn = [nil]$. List $lstv = [K_s^s, K_{c_1}^s : K_{c_2}^s, K_f^s]$ contains all the the keys required for *Phone* to implement Clipper transmissions. Note that the concatenation of the key halves $K_{c_1}^s : K_{c_2}^s$ yields K_c^s, *Phone*'s unit key.

Police is defined by *cseq*(*PoliceId*, *lstv*). Its $lstv$ only contains the Clipper family key (K_f^s) and two keys: $K_{e_1}^s$ and $K_{e_2}^s$ for communicating with $Escrow1$ and $Escrow2$, respectively. *Police*'s *cseq* contains two patterns: $\{ekey?, id?, auth?\}_{K_f^s}$ to capture the LEAF and $emsg?$ to capture *Phone*'s encrypted message ($\{M\}_{K_s^s}$). The *cseq* also contains two more concurrent sequences, each with a message output followed by a pattern exposure. The first $\{id, auth, CO\}_{K_{e_1}^s} \hat{} \{id, kc_1?\}_{K_{e_1}^s} \rightarrow$ is directed at $Escrow1$ to send *Phone*'s ID and $AUTH$ (which were previously bound to the wildcards $id?$ and $auth?$) and the court order (CO)

$$
\begin{aligned}
Phone &\equiv [\{\{K_s^s\}_{K_{c_1}^s : K_{c_2}^s}, ID, AUTH\}_{K_f^s} \hat{}\, \{M\}_{K_s^s} \hat{}\,].[nil](PhoneId, [K_s^s, K_{c_1}^s : K_{c_2}^s, K_f^s]) \\
Police &\equiv [\{ekey?, id?, auth?\}_{K_f^s} \rightarrow emsg? \rightarrow].[nil] \diamond \\
&\quad [\{id, auth, CO\}_{K_{e_1}^s} \hat{}\, \{id, kc_1?\}_{K_{e_1}^s} \rightarrow].[nil] \diamond \\
&\quad [\{id, auth, CO\}_{K_{e_2}^s} \hat{}\, \{id, kc_2?\}_{K_{e_2}^s} \rightarrow].[nil](PoliceId, [K_f^s, K_{e_1}^s, K_{e_2}^s]) \\
Escrow1 &\equiv [\{id?, auth?, CO\}_{K_{e_1}^s} \rightarrow \{id, K_{c_1}^s\}_{K_{e_1}^s} \hat{}\,].[nil](E1Id, [K_{e_1}^s]) \\
Escrow2 &\equiv [\{id?, auth?, CO\}_{K_{e_2}^s} \rightarrow \{id, K_{c_2}^s\}_{K_{e_2}^s} \hat{}\,].[nil](E2Id, [K_{e_2}^s])
\end{aligned}
$$

Figure 3. Formal model of Clipper protocol.

and to receive the first half of *Phone*'s unit key (stored in the wildcard $kc_1?$). Similarly, the second sequence is directed at *Escrow*2 to receive the second half of *Phone*'s unit key (stored in $kc_2?$) Since no fresh names are used, $lstn = [nil]$ for the current sequence.

The definitions of *Escrow*1 and *Escrow*2 are similar to each other. *Escrow*1 is defined by $cseq(E1Id, [K_{e_1}^s])$ where $K_{e_1}^s$ is used to communicate with *Police*. *Escrow*1's *cseq* contains $\{id?, auth?, CO\}_{K_{e_1}^s}$ to receive information from *Police* and the message $\{id, K_{c_1}^s\}_{K_{e_1}^s}$ to send one-half of *Phone*'s unit key to *Police*. The pattern $\{id?, auth?, CO\}_{K_{e_1}^s}$ exposed by *Escrow*1 ensures that *Police* submits a verifiable (id, escrow authenticator, court order) tuple corresponding to *Phone*.

4. PROTOCOL SIMULATION

Most techniques for formally modeling protocols only consider the messages exchanged by principals. We adopt an integrated approach that models messages and principal behavior. Principals are formally modeled as concurrent agents that exchange complex messages and reduce to simpler forms. A virtual machine has been designed to simulate protocols by applying inference rules defined for agent communication and reduction [7]. This permits the comprehensive simulation of protocols – essential to their analysis and verification.

4.1. INFERENCE RULES FOR AGENT BEHAVIOR

Inference rules governing agent communication and reduction provide an unambiguous semantics for simulating agent behavior. Actions defined for agents include communication, reduction and binding.

Definition 4.1: Agent communication and reduction ($\Longrightarrow$) are defined by the following inference rules. Communication offers are denoted by $\xrightarrow{\alpha}$, where α is m (input) or $\bar{m}$ (output):

$$\textbf{In}: \frac{m \sim p}{[p \rightarrow seq].[lstn] \diamond cseq(id, lstv) \xrightarrow{m} [seq].[lstn] \diamond cseq\{m/p\}(id, lstv \cup m)}$$

$$\textbf{Out}: \frac{}{[m\hat{\ }seq].[lstn] \diamond cseq(id, lstv) \xrightarrow{\bar{m}} [seq].[lstn \cup fresh(m)] \diamond cseq(id, lstv \cup m)}$$

$$\textbf{Comm}: \frac{a \xrightarrow{\bar{m}} a',\ b \xrightarrow{m} b'}{a \ \&\ b \Longrightarrow a' \ \&\ b'}$$

The **In** rule defines the semantics for the receipt of a message using a pattern. The precondition $m \sim p$ specifies that the message m must match the pattern p exposed by agent (id, $lstv$) with communication sequence $[p \rightarrow seq].[lstn] \diamond cseq(id, lstv)$. The postcondition states that after the message is accepted, the agent reduces to $[seq].[lstn] \diamond cseq\{m/p\}(id, lstv \cup m)$. All free ocurrences of wildcards in p are replaced by the corresponding values in m in the remaining sequences of messages and/or patterns; this is specified by $[seq].[lstn] \diamond cseq\{m/p\}$. The agent's $lstv$ is updated with the message that has just been accepted. The new list of values is $lstv \cup m$ ($\cup$ denotes concatenation).

The **Out** rule has no preconditions. On offering message m, the communication sequence $[m\hat{\ }seq].[lstn] \diamond cseq$ of agent (id, $lstv$) reduces to $[seq].[lstn \cup fresh(m)] \diamond cseq$. The list of names $lstn$ associated with the remaining sequence of messages and/or patterns seq is updated with the set of fresh names in m ($fresh(m)$); this is expressed by $lstn \cup fresh(m)$. Similarly, the list of values $lstv$ held by the agent is updated with the offered message to produce $lstv \cup m$.

Comm governs agent reduction. Two preconditions must hold for $a \ \&\ b$, the concurrent composition of agents a and b, to reduce to $a' \ \&\ b'$ after communicating message m. First, agent a must be able to reduce to agent a' with output $\bar{m}$. Second, agent b must be able to reduce to agent b' with input m.

4.2. CLIPPER PROTOCOL SIMULATION

We illustrate the simulation of the Clipper protocol in Figure 2 by presenting the agent reductions for the first step. The agent definitions in Figure 3 serve as the starting point for the simulation.

Step 1 implements the LEAF Transmission. *Phone* outputs the LEAF as: $\{\{K_s^s\}_{K_{c_1}^s : K_{c_2}^s}, ID, AUTH\}_{K_f^s}$. *Police* exposes $\{ekey?, id?, auth?\}_{K_f^s}$.

Note that *Police* knows the Clipper family key K_f^s used to encrypt the LEAF, i.e., $K_f^s \in lstv$ of *Police*. The message and pattern match according to Definitions 2.4 and 2.5. Using **Comm** and chaining to **Out** for *Phone* and **In** for *Police*, the agents reduce to:

$$
\begin{aligned}
Phone &\equiv [\{M\}_{K_s^s}\hat{}\,].[nil](PhoneId, [K_s^s, K_{c_1}^s : K_{c_2}^s, K_f^s, \{\{K_s^s\}_{K_{c_1}^s : K_{c_2}^s}, ID, AUTH\}_{K_f^s}]) \\
Police &\equiv [emsg? \rightarrow].[nil] \diamond [\{ID, AUTH, CO\}_{K_{e_1}^s}\hat{}\{ID, kc_1?\}_{K_{e_1}^s} \rightarrow].[nil] \diamond \\
&\quad [\{ID, AUTH, CO\}_{K_{e_2}^s}\hat{}\{ID, kc_2?\}_{K_{e_2}^s} \rightarrow].[nil] \\
&\quad (PoliceId, [K_f^s, K_{e_1}^s, K_{e_2}^s, \{\{K_s^s\}_{K_{c_1}^s : K_{c_2}^s}, ID, AUTH\}_{K_f^s}])
\end{aligned}
$$

Note that $\{K_s^s\}_{K_{c_1}^s : K_{c_2}^s}$, ID and $AUTH$ are bound to *Police*'s wildcards *ekey?*, *id?* and *auth?*, respectively. Furthermore, the lists *lstv* of *Phone* and *Police* are updated to include $\{\{K_s^s\}_{K_{c_1}^s : K_{c_2}^s}, ID, AUTH\}_{K_f^s}$.

The remaining steps proceed similarly. Two communicating agents always reduce according to the **Comm** rule which requires **Out** to be applied to the sender and **In** to be applied to the receiver. When no further communication is possible the protocol run is complete.

5. PROTOCOL ANALYSIS

The agent inference rules in Section 4 formalize agent behavior, i.e., how agents exchange messages and evolve. To analyze protocols, it is also necessary to specify how agents can infer new information from exchanged messages. Inference rules are required for reasoning about the information held by agents, the freshness of the information, and whether or not agents can communicate. This section specifies inference rules for messages and illustrates their application in the Clipper example.

5.1. INFERENCE RULES FOR AGENT KNOWLEDGE

The rules in Definition 5.1 are used to determine: (i) what an agent knows, (ii) what it can infer, and (iii) what messages it can produce.

<u>**Definition 5.1:**</u> The inference rules **Knows**, **Extract** and **Construct** are defined by:

$$
\textbf{Knows}: \frac{v \in lstv}{Name(cseq(id, lstv)) \text{ knows } v}
$$

$$
\textbf{Extract}: \frac{\{v_1, ..., v_j\}_{k1} \in lstv,\ k_2 \in lstv,\ k_1 \overset{K}{\sim} k_2}{cseq(id, lstv) \equiv cseq(id, lstv \cup v_1 ... \cup v_j)}
$$

$$\textbf{Construct}: \frac{v_i(i = 1..j) \in lstv, \ k \in lstv}{cseq(id, lstv) \equiv cseq(id, lstv \cup \{v_1, ..., v_j\}_k)}$$

The **Knows** rule expresses predicates of the form "agent *id* knows value v;" this is written as "*id* knows v." This predicate is true only if $v \in lstv$ or if v can be derived using the **Extract** and **Construct** rules. The function $Name(A)$ returns the *id* of an agent A from the agent description, i.e., $Name(cseq(id, lstv)) = id$.

The **Extract** rule helps extract the components of a message held by an agent in its $lstv$. The list $lstv$ is augmented with the extracted components according to the rule conclusion. For example, if an agent holds the encrypted message $\{X\}_{K_w^s}$ and the key K_w^s in $lstv$, then the agent can obtain X and, therefore, X is added to $lstv$. Note that $\cup$ denotes the concatenation of a value list and a value.

Construct creates new values from values held in $lstv$; these new values are added to $lstv$. For example, if an agent's $lstv$ holds the values X, Y and Z, and the key K_w^s, then it can construct the encrypted message $\{X, Y, Z\}_{K_w^s}$; this encrypted message is added to the agent's $lstv$. Altering $lstv$ using **Extract** and **Construct** does not change agent behavior, only what the agent knows.

Variations of **Extract**, **Construct** and **Knows** are used in the GNY logic [5] as the "Being-Told" and "Possession" rules.

5.2. CLIPPER PROTOCOL ANALYSIS

The Clipper protocol in Figures 2 and 3 is used to illustrate the application of the message inference rules. We prove that at the end of the protocol, the *Police* agent "knows" the message M that is encrypted as $\{M\}_{K_s^s}$ and output by *Phone* in Step 2. The configuration of the *Police* agent after the protocol is completed serves as the starting point for the analysis. Since the *Police*'s knowledge ($lstv$) is of special importance, the analysis focuses on it.

$$[\underbrace{K_f^s}_{(4)}, \underbrace{K_{e_1}^s}_{(7)}, \underbrace{K_{e_2}^s}_{(8)}, \underbrace{\{\underbrace{\{K_s^s\}_{K_{c_1}^s : K_{c_2}^s}}_{(2)}, ID, AUTH\}_{K_f^s}}_{(3)}, \underbrace{\{M\}_{K_s^s}}_{(1)}, \{ID, AUTH, CO\}_{K_{e_1}^s},$$

$$\{ID, AUTH, CO\}_{K_{e_2}^s}, \underbrace{\{ID, K_{c_1}^s\}_{K_{e_1}^s}}_{(5)}, \underbrace{\{ID, K_{c_2}^s\}_{K_{e_2}^s}}_{(6)}]$$

To **Extract** M from (1), *Police* must know K_s^s which can be **Extract**ed from (2). To do so, *Police* must **Extract** (2) from (3) requiring knowledge of K_f^s (4), $K_{c_1}^s$ and $K_{c_2}^s$. The latter two must be **Extract**ed from (5) and (6), requiring *Police* to know $K_{e_1}^s$ (7) and $K_{e_2}^s$ (8).

Since *Police* **Knows** (4), (7) and (8) ($K_f^s, K_{e_1}^s, K_{e_2}^s \in lstv_{Police}$), the **Extract**-rule can be applied several times and finally $M \in lstv_{Police}$. This completes the proof of "*PoliceId* knows M."

6. AUTOMATING PROOFS

The inference rules defined in the previous sections provide the foundation for verification. A significant advantage is that the rules governing agent communication and reduction (used for simulation) can be integrated with the inference rules for messages (used for analysis) to reason about the properties of protocols and participating agents.

Proofs are automated using a translation (mechanization) [4] of the agent reduction and message inference rules into Higher Order Logic (HOL) [6], an interactive theorem proving environment. A HOL session results in a *theory* – an object containing sets of types, constants, definitions, axioms and theorems (logical consequences of the definitions and axioms). As new theorems are proved, they are added to the theory and may be used to develop additional results. Only well-formed theories can be constructed because formal proofs are required for all new theorems.

Automating proofs in HOL involves incorporating type definitions, function definitions, inference rules, tactics, and conversions.

Four types are defined in the HOL Protocol Theory: *key*, *value*, *message* and *pattern*, the last three being mutually recursive.

Then, functions are implemented to manipulate the specified types. E.g., functions for matching keys and matching messages and patterns, and the *Name* function for obtaining an agent's *id*.

Next, inference rules are defined for reasoning about agent behavior and knowledge (**In**, **Out**, **Comm**, **Knows**, etc.). This implements a HOL theory supporting basic proofs via manual rule application.

Tactics and conversions are required to automate proofs. A tactic tranforms a goal into an equivalent goal that is easier to prove. Tactics are introduced to selectively apply the inference rules governing agent behavior and knowledge to facilitate theorem proving.

The final step is to create conversions for transforming propositions into theorems. A conversion must establish the truth value for every expression of the form it is designed to handle. Although it is not feasible to develop conversions for all types of propositions, their introduction, even to a limited degree, can facilitate the automation of proofs.

7. CONCLUSIONS

The integration of logic and process calculus provides a powerful framework for simulating and analyzing cryptographic protocols. The approach advances logic techniques by not requiring protocols to be idealized before analysis. It improves on process calculi by permitting the exhaustive modeling of messages and principals. Novel features include an expressive message passing semantics, sophisticated modeling of concurrency, and seamless integration of inference rules for agent behavior and knowledge. Furthermore, no assumptions are made about the honesty of communicating agents. This facilitates the analysis of cryptographic protocols in open, potentially hostile environments.

References

[1] Abadi, M. and Cardelli, L. (1995) An imperative object calculus. *Proceedings of the Conference on Theory and Practice of Software*, 471-485.

[2] Abadi, M. and Gordon D. (1997) Reasoning about cryptographic protocols in the Spi calculus. *Proceedings of the Fourth ACM Conference on Computer and Communications Security,*, 36-47.

[3] Burrows, M., Abadi, M. and Needham, R. (1990) A logic of authentication. *ACM Transactions on Computer Systems*, **8(1)**, 18-36.

[4] Galiasso, P. (1998) *Mechanization of ROC in Higher Order Logic.* M.S. Thesis, Computer Science Department, University of Tulsa, Tulsa, Oklahoma.

[5] Gong, L., Needham, R. and Yahalom, R. (1990) Reasoning about belief in cryptographic protocols. *Proceedings of the IEEE Symposium on Research in Security and Privacy*, 234-248.

[6] Gordon, M. and Melham, T. (1993) *Introduction to Higher Order Logic (HOL).* Cambridge University Press, Cambridge, U.K.

[7] Hale, J., Threet, J. and Shenoi, S. (1997) A framework for high assurance security of distributed objects, in *Database Security, X: Status and Prospects* (eds. P. Samarati and R. Sandhu), Chapman and Hall, London, 101-119.

[8] Lowe G. (1995) An attack on the Needham-Schroeder public key authentication protocol. *Information Processing Letters*, **56(3)**, 131-133.

[9] Lowe G. (1996) Some new attacks upon security protocols. *Proceedings of the Ninth IEEE Computer Security Foundations Workshop*.

[10] Melham, T. (1992) A mechanized theory of the π-calculus in HOL. Technical Report 244, University of Cambridge Computer Laboratory, Cambridge, U.K.

[11] Milner, R. (1989) *Communication and Concurrency*. Prentice-Hall, New York.

[12] Milner, R., Parrow, J. and Walker, D. (1989) A calculus of mobile processes. Report ECS-LFCS-89-85&86, University of Edinburgh, Edinburgh, U.K.

[13] Pfleeger, C. (1997) *Security in Computing*. Prentice Hall, Upper Saddle River, New Jersey.

[14] Schneier, B. (1996) *Applied Cryptography*. John Wiley, New York.

[15] Syverson, P. and van Oorschot, P. (1994) On unifying some cryptographic protocol logics, *Proceedings of the IEEE Symposium on Research in Security and Privacy*, 165-177

CHAPTER 9
AUTHENTIC THIRD-PARTY DATA PUBLICATION

Premkumar Devanbu, Michael Gertz, Charles Martel
Department of Computer Science, University of California, Davis, CA 95616
{devanbu|gertz|martel}@cs.ucdavis.edu

Stuart G. Stubblebine
CertCo, 55 Broad Street, New York, NY 10004
stuart@stubblebine.com

Abstract Integrity critical databases, such as financial data used in high-value decisions, are frequently published over the Internet. Publishers of such data must satisfy the integrity, authenticity, and non-repudiation requirements of clients. Providing this protection over public networks is costly.

This is partly because building and running secure systems is hard. In practice, large systems can not be verified to be secure and are frequently penetrated. The consequences of a system intrusion at the data publisher can be severe. This is further complicated by data and server replication to satisfy availability and scalability requirements.

We aim to *reduce the trust required* of the publisher of large, infrequently updated databases. To do this, we separate the roles of owner and publisher. With a few trusted digital signatures from the owner, an untrusted publisher can use techniques based on Merkle hash trees to provide authenticity and non-repudiation of the answer to a database query. We *do not* require a key to be held in an on-line system, thus reducing the impact of system penetrations. By allowing untrusted publishers, we also allow more scalable publication of large databases.

1. INTRODUCTION

Consider an Internet financial-data warehouse, with historical data about securities such as stocks and bonds, that is used by businesses and individuals to make important investment decisions. The *owner* (or creator) of such a database might be a rating/analysis service (such as Standard & Poors), or a government agency. The owner's data might be needed at high rates, for example by the user's investment tools. We focus our attention on data which changes infrequently and needs to be delivered promptly, reliably and accurately.

One approach to this problem is for the owner of the information to digitally sign the answers to clients' queries, using a private signing key, sk_O. This signature is verified using the corresponding public key, pk_O. Based on the signature, a client can be sure that the answer comes from the owner, and that the owner can't claim otherwise. However, there are several issues here. First, the owner of the data may be unwilling or unable to provide a reliable and efficient database service to handle the needed data rates. Second, the owner needs to maintain a high level of physical security and system security to defend against attacks. This has to be done to protect the signing key, sk_O, which must be resident at the server at all times to sign outgoing data. In practice, large software systems have vulnerabilities, and keeping secret information on a publicly-accessible system is always risky. Using special hardware devices to protect the signing key will help, as would emerging cryptographic techniques like "threshold cryptography," but these methods do not fully solve the system-vulnerability problem, and can be too expensive in our domain, both computationally and financially.

A more scalable approach uses trusted third-party *publishers* in conjunction with a key management mechanism which allows a certified signing key of a publisher to speak for the owner (see also [3]). The database (or database updates) is provided securely to the publisher, who responds to client queries by signing them with it's own (certified) signing key, sk_P. Presumably, the market for useful databases will motivate publishers to provide this service, unburdening database owners of the need to do so. The owner simply needs to sign the data after each update and distribute it to the publisher. As demand increases, more publishers will emerge, or more capable ones, making this approach inherently scalable. But the approach still suffers from the problem and expense of trying to maintain a secure system accessible from the Internet. Furthermore, the client might worry that a publisher engages in deception. She would have to believe that her publisher was both competent and careful with site administration and physical access to the database. She might worry about the private signing-key of the publisher, which is again vulnerable to attacks. To gain trust, the publisher must adopt meticulous administrative practices, at far greater cost. The need for trusted publishers would also increase the reliance on brand-names, which would limit market competition.

In a summary of fundamental problems for electronic commerce [10], Tygar asks "How can we protect re-sold or re-distributed information ... ?" We present a solution to this problem in the context of relational databases.

2. BASIC APPROACH

We allow an **untrusted** *publisher* to provide a **verification-object** $\mathcal{VO}$ to a *client* to verify an answer to its database query. The client can use the $\mathcal{VO}$ to gain assurance that the answer is just what the database *owner* would have provided. The verification-object is based on a **summary-signature** that the owner periodically distributes to the publisher (Figure 1).

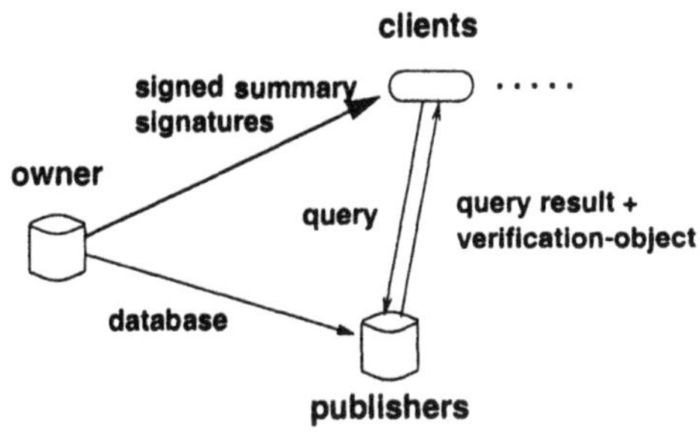

Figure 1. We partition the role of information provider into *owner* and *publisher*. The owner provides database updates to the publisher. The publisher is untrusted. The *client* makes inquiries to the publisher. Its gets responses which can be verified using a returned *verification-object*. Superscripts denote keys known to that party. Only sk_O is secret. The client must be sure of the binding of pk_O to the owner.

The summary-signature is a bottom-up hash computed recursively over B-tree type indexes for the entire set of tuples in each relation of the owner's database, signed with sk_O. Answers to queries are various combinations of subsets of these relations. Given a query, the publisher computes the answer. To show that an answer is correct the publisher constructs a verification-object using the same B-tree that the owner had used to compute the summary-signature. This verification-object validates an answer by providing an unforgeable "proof" which links the answer to the summary-signature. Our approach has several features:

1 Besides its own security, a client needs only trust the key of the owner. The owner only needs to distribute the summary-signature during database updates. So, the owner's private key can be maintained in an "off-line" machine, isolated from network-based attacks. The key itself can be ensconced in a hardware token, which is used only to sign a single hash during updates.

2 Clients need not trust the publishers, nor their keys. In particular, if a particular publisher were compromised, the result would *only* be a loss of service at that publisher.

3 In all our techniques, the verification-object is of size linear in the size of the answer to a query, and logarithmic in the size of the database.

4 The verification-object guarantees that the answer is correct, without any extra or missing tuples.

5 In all of our techniques, the overheads for computing the summary-signature, the $\mathcal{VO}$, and for checking the $\mathcal{VO}$ are reasonable.

6 The approach offers far greater survivability. Publishers can be replicated without coordination, and the loss of one publisher does not degrade security and need not degrade availability.

A correct answer and verification-object will always be accepted by the client. An incorrect answer and verification-object will almost always be rejected, since our techniques make it computationally infeasible to forge a correct verification-object for an incorrect answer. Overall, the approach nicely simplifies the operational security requirements for both owners and publishers.

3. MERKLE HASH TREES

We describe the computation of a Merkle Hash Tree [6] for a relation r with m tuples and relation schema $R = \langle A_1, \ldots, A_n \rangle$. A more complete description can be found in [4]. Assume that $\mathcal{A} = \langle A_i, \ldots, A_k \rangle$ is a list of attributes from $schema(R)$. A Merkle Hash Tree, denoted by $MHT(r, \mathcal{A})$, is a balanced binary tree whose leaves are associated with the tuples of r. Each node in the tree has a value computed using a collision-resistant hash function h:

1 First, compute the *tuple hash* h_t for each tuple $t \in r$, thus

$$h_t(t) \;=\; h(h(t.A_1) \;||\; \ldots \;||\; h(t.A_n))$$

The tuple hash (by the collision resistance of the hash function) is a "nearly unique" tuple identifier. We also assume distinct "boundary tuples" t_0, t_{m+1} with artificial attribute values chosen to be smaller (larger) than any real tuple. These are associated with the left (right) most leaves in the tree.

2 Next, compute the Merkle hash tree for relation r. We assume that r is sorted by the values of $\mathcal{A}$ so that for two distinct tuples $t_{i-1}, t_i \in r$, $t_{i-1}.\mathcal{A} \leq t_i.\mathcal{A}$. Any total order over r based on $\mathcal{A}$ will work. We now describe how to compute $V(u)$ the value associated with a node u of $MHT(r, \mathcal{A})$. Let u_i be the leaf associated with t_i.

Leaf-node u_i : $V(u_i) = h_t(t_i)$

Internal node u : $V(u) = h(V(w) \,||\, V(x))$

where w, x are the children of u. We also refer to w, x as *hash siblings.*

The value of the root is the "root hash" of the Merkle tree. This construction easily generalizes to a higher branching factor $K > 2$, such as in a B^+-tree; however, for our presentation here we use binary trees. If the *owner* and the *publisher* build a MHT around index structures that are used in query evaluation, then constructing a $\mathcal{VO}$ is a minor overhead over the query evaluation process itself.

Note that (by the cryptographic assumption of a collision-resistant hash function) if the correct value of the *parent* is known to the client, it is hard for the publisher to forge the value of its children.

Definition 1 (Hash Path)

For a leaf node u_i in $MHT(r, \mathcal{A})$ the nodes necessary to compute the hash path up to the root hash is denoted as $path(t_i)$. Such a hash path always has the length d, the depth of node u_i, $d \leq \lceil \log(m+2) \rceil$. With t_i and the values of siblings of the nodes on the path we can recompute the value at the root. Hash paths can also be provided for non-leaf nodes.

The d values of the siblings of $path(t_i)$ constitute the $\mathcal{VO}$ showing that tuple t_i is actually in the relation. Indeed any interior node within the hash tree can be authenticated by giving a path to the root. Hash paths show that tuples actually exist in a relation; to show that set of tuples is complete, we need to show boundaries. Any non-empty contiguous sequence $q = \langle t_i, \ldots, t_j \rangle$ of leaf nodes in a Merkle Hash Tree $MHT(r, \mathcal{A})$ uses t_{i-1} and t_{j+1} as its *boundary tuples.*

Any non-empty contiguous sequence $q = \langle t_i, \ldots, t_j \rangle$ of leaf nodes in a Merkle Hash Tree $MHT(r, \mathcal{A})$ has a lowest common ancestor $LCA(q)$. This situation is illustrated in Figure 2. Given $LCA(q)$, one can show a hash path $path(LCA(q))$ to the authenticated root hash value. After this is done, (shorter) hash paths from its boundary tuples t_{i-1} and t_{j+1} to $LCA(q)$ and the values of $t_i, \ldots, t_j$ allow us to compute $V(LCA(q))$. We can then compute the root hash using the values of the siblings of $path(LCA(q))$. This lets us verify of that $t_{i-1}, \ldots, t_{j+1}$ are associated with contiguous leaves in our tree.

We finally define desirable properties of the answer set q returned by *publisher*, in terms of the correct answer that would have been returned by *owner*.

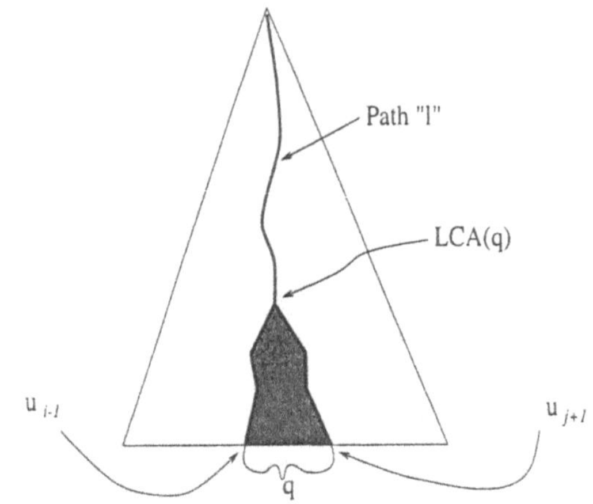

Figure 2. A Merkle tree, with a contiguous subrange $q = \langle t_i, \ldots, t_j \rangle$, with a least common ancestor LCA(q), and upper and lower bounds. Note verifiable hash path "l" from LCA(q) to the root, and the proximity subtrees (thick lines) for the "near miss" tuples u_{i-1} and u_{j+1} which show that q is complete.

Definition 2 *The answer given by* publisher *to a query q is* inclusive *if it contains only the tuples that would have been returned by* owner, *and is* complete *if it contains all the tuples that would have been returned by* owner.

4. BASE LEVEL RELATIONAL QUERIES

In this section we outline the computation of $\mathcal{VO}$ for answers to basic relational queries. We illustrate the basic idea behind our approach for selection and projection queries in Section 4.1 and 4.2, respectively. Slightly more complex types of queries (join queries) and set operators are discussed in Sections 4.3 and 4.4.

4.1. SELECTIONS

Assume a selection query $\sigma_{A_i \Theta c}(r)$ (c $\equiv$ constant) that asks for tuples with attribute values for A_i in a specified range. Assuming that the tree $MHT(r, A_i)$ has been constructed, we can provide compact $\mathcal{VO}$s for the answer q to a query. We consider two cases: when $q = \{\}$, and otherwise. If $q \neq \{\}$, assume a set of answer tuples $t_i, t_{i+1}, \ldots, t_j$ which build a contiguous sequence of leaf nodes in $MHT(r, A_i)$. We simply include a couple of boundary tuples and return the set $t_{i-1}, \ldots, t_{j+1}$, along with the hash paths to t_{i-1} and t_{j+1}. If q is empty, just the boundary tuples are returned. In either case, the size of the $\mathcal{VO}$ is $O(\mid q \mid + \log_2 \mid r \mid)$.

In [4] we present a formal proof that our construction $\mathcal{VO}$s for selection queries is secure:

Lemma 3 *If* publisher *cannot engineer collisions on the hash function or forge signatures on the root hash value, then if* client *computes the right authenticated root hash value using the $\mathcal{VO}$ and the answer provided for* selection *queries, then the answer is indeed complete and inclusive.*

4.2. PROJECTIONS

For queries of the pattern $\pi_{\mathcal{A}}(r), \mathcal{A} \subset schema(R)$, the projection operator eliminates some attributes of the tuples in the relation r, and then eliminates duplicates from the set of shortened tuples, yielding the final answer q. A user can choose many different ways to project from a relation R; if this choice is dynamic, it may be best to leave the projection to the *client*. However, the *client* then gets a potentially large intermediate result $\mathcal{I}$; so the $\mathcal{VO}$ will be linear in size $\mid \mathcal{I} \mid$, rather than in the smaller final result $\mid q \mid$. We note that we can, if necessary, mask some of the attributes from the *client*; with just the hash of those attributes in each tuple, the *client* can compute the tuple hash.

Consider, however, an often-used projection $\pi_{\mathcal{A}}(r)$ which projects onto attributes where duplicate elimination will remove numerous tuples. Given the pre-projection tuple set, the *client* would have to do all this work. Now, suppose we have a Merkle tree $MHT(r, \mathcal{A})$, *i.e.*, we assume that the sets of retained attribute values can be mapped to single values with an applicable total order. In this case, we can provide a $\mathcal{VO}$ for the projection step that is linear in the size of the projected result q.

Each tuple t in the result set q may arise from a set $S(t) \subseteq r$ with tuples having identical values for the projected attribute(s) $\mathcal{A}$. We must show that the set q is inclusive and complete:

1 To prove $t \in q$, we show the hash path from *any* witness tuple $y \in S(t) \subseteq r$ to the Merkle Root. However, "boundary" tuples make better witnesses, as we describe next.

2 To show that there are no tuples missing, say between t and $t', (t, t' \in q)$, we just show that $S(t), S(t'), \subseteq r$ are contiguous in the sorted order. Hash paths from two "boundary" tuples $y \in S(t)$ and $x \in S(t')$ that occur next to each other in the Merkle tree can do this.

We observe that both the above bits of evidence are provided by displaying at most $2 \mid q \mid$ hash paths, each of length $\lceil \log_2 r \rceil$. This meets our constraint that the size of the verification object be bounded by $O(\mid q \mid \log_2 \mid r \mid)$.

Constructing Merkle trees to provide compact $\mathcal{VO}$s for duplicate elimination with every possible projection might be undesirable. We might construct trees for only highly selective, common projection attributes, and leave the other duplicate eliminations to the client.

4.3. JOINS

Joins between two or more relations, specially equi-joins where relations are combined based on primary key – foreign key dependencies, are very common. We focus on pairwise joins of the pattern $r \bowtie_C s$ where C is a condition on join attributes of the pattern $A_R \Theta A_S$, $A_R \in schema(R), A_S \in schema(S), \Theta \in \{=, <, >\}$. For Θ being the equality predicate, we obtain the so-called equi-join. We show 3 different approaches, for different situations.

Given a query of the pattern $r \bowtie_C s$, one structure that supports computation of very compact $\mathcal{VO}$s for the query result is based on the materialization (i.e., the physical storage) of the Cartesian Product $r \times s$. This structure supports the three types of joins, which can all be formulated in terms of basic relational algebra operators, i.e., $r \bowtie_{A_R \Theta A_S} s \equiv \sigma_{A_R \Theta A_S}(r \times s)$. Assume $m =\mid r \mid, n =\mid s \mid$. The verification structure for $r \bowtie_C s$ queries is constructed by sorting the Cartesian Product according to the *difference* between the values for A_R and A_S, assuming such an operation can be defined, at least in terms of "positive", "none" or "negative". This yields three "groups" of leaf nodes in the Merkle Tree: (1) nodes for $t.A_R - u.A_S$ for two tuples $t \in r, u \in s$ is 0, thus supporting equi-joins, (2) nodes where the difference is positive, for the predicate $>$, and (3) nodes where the difference is negative, for the predicate $<$. If only simple Θ joins, with $\Theta \equiv =, >$ *or* $<$ are desired, there is no need to construct binary Merkle trees over the entire cross product—we can just group the tuples in $R \times S$ into the three groups, hash each group in its entirely, and append the three hashes to get the root hash. In this case, the $\mathcal{VO}$s for the three basic Θ queries would consist only of 2 hash values!

For equi-join queries, an optimized structure, presented briefly below, can be used. Rather than the full Cartesian Product $r \times s$, we materialize the *Full Outer Join* r ⟗ s which pads tuples for which no matching tuples in the other relation exist with null values (see, e.g., [2, 8]). The result tuples obtained by the full outer-join operator again can be grouped into three classes: (1) those tuples $tu, t \in r, u \in s$, for which the join condition holds, (2) tuples from r for which no matching tuples in s exist, and (3) tuples from s for which no matching tuples in r exist. Constructing a $\mathcal{VO}$ for the result of query of the pattern $r \bowtie_{A_R \Theta A_S} s$ then can be done in the same fashion as outlined above.

Suppose R and S have B-tree indices over the join attributes, and these trees have been Merkle-hashed; also suppose, without loss of generality, that of the two relations, r has the smaller number of distinct values, say r^d, and that the size of the answer is q. We can now provide larger $\mathcal{VO}$s of size $O(r^d \log n + r^d \log m + \mid q \mid)$ in the worst case[1]. This is done by doing a "verified" merge of the leaves of the two index trees. Whenever the join attributes have the right θ relation, witness hash paths in the trees for R and S are provided to show inclusiveness of the resulting answer tuples; when tuples in r or s are skipped during the merge, we provide a pair of proximity subtrees in R or S respectively to justify the length of the skip. This conventional approach to joins gives rise to larger $\mathcal{VO}$s than the approach described above, but at reduced costs for *publisher* and *owner.*

4.4. SET OPERATIONS

Consider set operations over relations u and v, which may be intermediate query results. u and v may be subsets of some relations r and s respectively, which are each sorted (possibly on different attributes) and have its own Merkle tree $MHT(r, \mathcal{A})$ and $MHT(s, \mathcal{A}')$, the root of which is signed as usual. We consider unions and intersections.

Union. In this case, the answer set is $q = u \cup v$. The *client* is given $\mathcal{VO}$s for u and v, along with $\mathcal{VO}$s for both; *client* verifies both $\mathcal{VO}$s, and computes $u \cup v$. This can be done in $O(u + v)$ using a hash merge. Since $\mid q \mid$ is $O(\mid u \mid + \mid v \mid)$, the overall $\mathcal{VO}$, and the time required to compute and verify the answer, are linear in the size of the answer.

Intersection. The approach for union, however, does not produce compact $\mathcal{VO}$s for set intersection. Suppose $q = u \cap v$ where u and v are as before: note that often $\mid q \mid$ could be much smaller than $\mid u \mid + \mid v \mid$. Thus, sending the $\mathcal{VO}$s for u and v and letting the *client* compute the final result could be a lot of extra work. We would like a $\mathcal{VO}$ of size $O(\mid q \mid)$. If Merkle trees exist for u and v, we can do inclusiveness in $O(\mid q \mid)$: *publisher* can build a $\mathcal{VO}$ for q with $O(\mid q \mid)$ verification paths, showing elements of q belong to both u and v. Completeness is harder. One can pick the smaller set (say u) and for each element in $u - q$, construct a $\mathcal{VO}$ show that it is not in v. In general, if u and v are intermediate results not occurring contiguously in the same Merkle

---

[1]While we can construct pathological cases that require $\mathcal{VO}$s of this size, practical cases may often be better, being closer to $O(q \log n + q \log m)$. Further empirical study is needed.

tree, such a $\mathcal{VO}$ is linear in the size of the smaller set (say u). A similar problem occurs with set differences $u - v$.

We have not solved the general problem of constructing $\mathcal{VO}$'s linear in the size of the result for intersections and set differences. Indeed, the question remains as to whether (in general) linear-size $\mathcal{VO}$s *can* even be constructed for these objects. However, we have developed an approach to constructing linear-size $\mathcal{VO}$s for a common type of intersection, *range query*, for example, a selection query where the age and salary fall in specified ranges. For these, we use a data structure drawn from computational geometry called a *multi-dimensional range tree.* This also supports set differences over range queries on several attributes.

In d-dimensional computational geometry, when one is dealing with sets of points in d-space, one could ask a d-space range query. Consider a spatial interval $(< x_1^1, x_2^1 > \ldots < x_1^d, x_2^d >)$; this represents an axis-aligned rectilinear solid in d-space. A query could ask for the points that occur within this solid. Such problems are solved efficiently in computational geometry using so-called *Range Trees* (See [5], Chapter 5). We draw an analogy between this problem and a query of the form

$$\sigma_{c_1^1 < A_1 < c_1^2}(r) \bigcap \cdots \bigcap \sigma_{c_d^1 < A_d < c_d^2}(r)$$

where $\{A_1, \ldots A_d\} \subseteq schema(R)$. We use the multi-dimensional range tree (*mdrt*) data structure to solve such queries and provide compact verification objects. For brevity, we omit the full details of our approach. However, in [4], we show how to construct $\mathcal{VO}$s for "d"-way range queries such as the ones shown above. We also argue that the size of these $\mathcal{VO}$s, for a relation with size n, is $O(\mid q \mid + \log^d n)$. The *mdrt* itself uses $O(n \log^{d-1} n)$ space and can also be constructed in time $O(n \log^{d-1} n)$. While the data structure arises out of computational geometry, it can be used with any domain that has enough structure to admit a total order. Full details are discussed in [4]

5. CONCLUSIONS AND FUTURE RESEARCH

We have explored the problem of authentic third party data publication. In particular, we have developed several techniques that allow untrusted third parties to provide evidence of *inclusive* and *complete* query evaluation to clients without using public-key signatures. In addition, the evidence provided is linear in the size of the query answers, and can be checked in linear time. Our techniques can involve the construction of complex data structures, but the cost of this construction is amortized over more efficient query evaluation, as well as the production of compact verification objects. Such pre-computation of views and indexing structures are not uncommon in data warehousing applications.

We now examine some pragmatic considerations in using our approach, as well as related work and future research.

Query processing flexibility. What queries can be handled? A typical SQL "**select** ... **from** ... **where** ..." can be thought of one or more joins, followed by a (combined) selection, followed by a projection. A multi-dimensional range tree can be used for both efficient evaluation and construction of compact $\mathcal{VO}$s for such queries. Specifically, consider a query that involves the join of two relations R and S, followed by a series of selections and a final projection. Let's assume a Theta-join over attribute A_1 (occurring in both relations), followed by selections on attributes A_2 and A_3, and a final projection on several attributes, jointly represented by A_4. Full details are deferred to [4]. However, to summarize briefly: such a query can be evaluated by constructing a mdrt, beginning with the join attributes, followed by trees for each selection attribute, and perhaps finishing with a tree for some selective projection attributes.

Conventions. It is important to note that all interested parties: *owner*, *publisher* and *client*, share a consistent schema for the databases being published. In addition there needs to be secure binding between the schema, the queries and the query evaluation process over the constructed Merkle trees. A convention to include this information within the hash trees needs to be established. All parties also need to agree on the data structures used for the $\mathcal{VO}$. It is also important that the *publisher* and the *client* agree upon the format in which the $\mathcal{VO}$ together with the query result is encoded and transmitted. Tagged data streams such as XML provide an attractive option.

Recent Query Evaluations. Verifiers must verify that query evaluation is due to an "adequately recent" snapshot of the database and not an old version. We assume the technique of recent-secure authentication [9] for solving this problem. Risk takers (e.g., organizations relying on the accuracy of the data) specify freshness policies on how fresh the database must be. The digital signatures over the database include a timestamp of the last update as well as other versioning information. Clients interpret the timestamps and verify the database is adequately recent with respect to their freshness policies.

Query flexibility. For efficient verification of query answering, we make use of different trees over sorted tuple sets. Without such trees, our approach cannot provide small verification objects. This points to a limitation of our approach—only queries for which Merkle trees have been pre-computed can be evaluated with compact verification objects. Our approach cannot support arbitrary interactive querying with compact verification objects. Arbitrary interactive querying, however, is *quite rare* in the presence of fixed applications at *client* sites. In practice, however, data-intensive applications make use of a fixed set of queries. These queries can still make use of parameters entered by a user and which are typically used in selection conditions. Our approach is compatible with such applications. Essentially, client applications commit *a priori* the queries they wish to execute; the owner and the publisher then pre-compute the required Merkle hash trees to produce short verification objects. While our approach cannot provide compact verification objects in the context of arbitrary interactive database querying, it is quite compatible with the widely-used practice of embedding pre-determined (and parameterizable) queries within data-intensive applications.

References

[1] M. Bellare. Practice-oriented Provable Security. In G. Davida E. Okamoto and M. Mambo (eds.), *Proceedings of First International Workshop on Information Security (ISW 97)*, LNCS 1396, Springer Verlag, 1997.

[2] C.J. Date. An Introduction to Database Systems, Addison-Wesley, 1999.

[3] P. Devanbu and S.G. Stubblebine. Software Engineering for Security: a roadmap. In *The Future of Software Engineering*, Special volume published in conjunction with ICSE 2000, ACM Press, 2000.

[4] P. Devanbu, M. Gertz, C. Martel, and S.G¿ Stubblebine. Authentic Third-party Data Publication. Technical Report, `www.db.cs.ucdavis.edu/publications/DGMOO.ps`, 2000.

[5] M. D. Berg , M. V. Kreveld, M. Overmars and O. Schwarzkopf. *Computational Geometry.* Springer-Verlag, New York, 2000.

[6] R.C. Merkle. A Certified Digital Signature. In *Advances in Cryptology (Crypto '89)*, LNCS Vol. 435, Springer Verlag, 218–238, 1989.

[7] M. Naor, K. Nissim. Certificate Revocation and Certificate Update. *Proceedings of the 7th USENIX Security Symposium*, 1998.

[8] A. Silberschatz, H. Korth, S. Sudarshan. Database System Concepts, (3rd edition), McGraw-Hill, 1997.

[9] S. G. Stubblebine. Recent-secure authentication: Enforcing Revocations in distributed systems. IEEE Computer Society Symp. on Security and Privacy, 1995.

[10] J. D. Tygar Open Problems in Electronic Commerce. In *Proc. SIGACT-SIGMOD-SIGART Symp. on Principles of Database Systems*, ACM, 101, 1999.

CHAPTER 10

Protecting File Systems Against Corruption Using Checksums[1]

Daniel Barbará, Rajni Goel, and Sushil Jajodia

Abstract: We consider the problem of malicious attacks that lead to corruption of files in a file system. A typical method to detect such corruption is to compute signatures of all the files and store these signatures in a secure place. A malicious modification of a file can be detected by verifying the signature. This method, however, has the weakness that it cannot detect an attacker who has access to some of the files and the signatures (but not the signing transformation) and who replaces some of the files by their old versions and the corresponding signatures by the signatures of the old versions.

In this paper, we present a technique called Check2 that also relies on signatures for detecting corruption of files. The novel feature of our approach is that we compute additional levels of signatures to guarantee that any change of a file and the corresponding signature will require an attacker to perform a very lengthy chain of precise changes to successfully complete the corruption in an undetected manner. If an attacker fails to complete all the required changes, check2 can be used to pinpoint which files have been corrupted. Two alternative ways of implementing Check2 are offered, the first using a deterministic way of combining signatures and the second using a randomized scheme. Our results show that the overhead added to the system is minimal.

Key words: Security, data corruption, integrity

[1] This work was supported by the Air Force Research Laboratory/Rome under the contract F30602-98-C-0264.

1. INTRODUCTION

A file system may be a target of an attack that aims to disrupt its correct functioning so that the files containing user data, applications, or system executables become degraded and dysfunctional. To date, information security systems focus on preventing attacks, though experience has indicated that prevention is not completely successful. Our aim is to formulate a defence mechanism that is effective against an attacker who penetrates the prevention system, or an insider attacker. A legitimate user misusing the system within his or her access domain, or attackers having sniffed passwords thus appearing as authorized users could pose the insider threat. Access controls or encryption technologies do not stop this kind of file data corruption. In this paper we describe a technique called *Check2* that is designed to detect malicious changes to a file system. *Check2* provides a protection layer by creating a chain of obstacles that protect a file system from unauthorized malicious modifications, deletions or additions.

Existing integrity and intrusion detection tools assist the users and administrators in monitoring and detecting changes in individual files. To date, integrity-checking tools identify and notify security officials about any changed, deleted or added files, after the occurrence. Established approaches identify corruption using statistical or pattern matching techniques, or by comparing replicated copies of files' contents. Some [3] use securely stored signatures (usually a message digest) to identify an alteration to a single file. The functionality of integrity checking tools, such as Tripwire, relies on the tamper proof security of these signatures. But, this intrusion security system is susceptible to penetration by an attacker who has managed to gain access to the signatures. This well-equipped intruder *directly alters* the stored file signature to coincide with his or her malicious changes to a file. To detect such attacks, the latest release of Tripwire signs the database of signatures with a single signature [8]. In Tripwire, if an intruder gains write access to stored file signatures, he or she can then be successful in corrupting the system by completing one extra signature change. We propose to further complicate the situation for an attacker who gains write access to the checksums, which can be of concern in particular when the attacker tries to restore an old version of a file for which the correct signature had been observed.

Our proposed technique, *Check2,* operates on the file system as one entity; each file alteration produces a set of reactions throughout the file system. These reactions appear as modifications in some pre-calculated values involving the contents of the files. The algorithm utilizes unique combinations (subsets) of the set of file signatures to compute a second and a third level signature. Each level is recomputed upon any change to a file.

To significantly increase the workload of the intruder, each file change triggers numerous changes in these higher-level signatures. When damaging a single file, the intruder is accountable of updating each of these other signatures and/or files for the system validation. Accumulating a *stock*, a databank of old versions of valid files and matching signatures and identifying the string of signatures to replace is part of the intruder's battle. We aim to make this *stock* too large to collect and the chain of reactions nearly impossible to calculate and unrepeatable. The availability of high-speed processors results in low maintenance costs for *Check2* (the extra cost is primarily computation time of extra signatures).

Check2 has one additional very desirable property: If the intruder fails to complete all this work, the system is able to identify the files that have been corrupted, so that the security officer can take proper action (presumably by restoring them to the proper versions, safely stored elsewhere).

We present two strategies for *Check2*. Both use techniques that have been utilized previously to solve other problems (viz., file comparison and mutual exclusion) [2]. From the set of file signatures, the *Check2* algorithm utilizes either a randomized or deterministic procedure to produce a set of subsets. In the randomized algorithm, each file signature appears exactly once in one of the subsets. The deterministic strategy derives the subsets where each file signature appears in more than one subset, which abides by the parities non-null intersection property. In this strategy, the system further calculates a third level of signatures using the same algorithm except using the set of second level signatures in place of the file signatures. Furthermore, the assumption is that authentic changes to the file system occur occasionally. Although *Check2* produces extra system expenses of calculating signature values beyond the existing file signatures upon each update in the system, our empirical results, using the MD5 [6] signature algorithm, show that this cost is extremely low. Moreover, this cost is incurred only occasionally, and it is well justified by the chain of copying and the enormous data bank the intruder must accumulate in order to complete a single file corruption.

We begin in Section 2 by presenting a motivating example. In Section 3, we present our deterministic and randomized techniques. Finally in section 4, we offer some conclusions and future directions.

2. MOTIVATING EXAMPLE

To illustrate, Figure 1 displays a simplified application file system with seven files C1, C2, ..., to C7. Each column i represents a file name, its content, and its signature value, Ck^{1}_{i}.

	C_1	C_2	C_3	C_4	C_5	C_6	C_7
Contents	⊗®	©	Δ	♦	∇	•	
	Ck^1_1	Ck^1_2	Ck^1_3	Ck^1_4	Ck^1_5	C^1k_6	C^1k_7

Figure 1. An example of a signature protected file system. The symbols indicate different contents, and these in turn determine the signatures

The system utilizes a trusted and secret one way hashing function f (in reality the function is not the "trusted" part, rather the function will be driven by a trusted, presumably inviolable key that is likely to be stored in a safe place), to compute a checksum value [6,7] involving the contents of each file: $f(\#) = Ck^l_i$. Here "#"represents the contents of the file i (i.e., one of the symbols in {⊗,®,©,Δ,♦,∇,•}). In this paper we use the term signature in a general manner: a fixed-size "fingerprint" generated by a one-way hashing function on any set of data. These checksums are stored in a highly secure database, where the value automatically is recalculated when a file contents changes. When an unauthorized user corrupts a file item, the stored signature will no longer be valid, thus indicating intrusive behavior.

Now, consider a scenario in which the software application new release is to be installed. Some files have been altered from a prior version. The process of installing these new releases of information consists of securing the validity of many separate files. Since each of these files is protected by one signature whose value is unlikely to be calculated by an intruder, a malicious altering appears improbable.

Unfortunately, one may circumvent this protection. A legitimate system user (or an intruder who has broken into the system) may have extensive knowledge of the layout of the file information storage and security system. This intruder tracks previous versions of the software and collects copies of the files and associated signatures. Having *accumulated* previous copies of numerous combinations of the valid file versions with the corresponding matching checksums associated to them, he or she can compromise the integrity of the file system as follows. He replaces a current new version of a file by *copying* over it an entire *old valid file, and* copy the matching signature into the database. If the system performs a checksum validation on this block, it will not discover any anomaly in the file data. In our example above, an intruder has copies of the files of the system at time t_0 as it is in Figure 1. After several updates and/or new releases take place, the state of the file system at time t_1 is as shown in Figure 2:

	C_1	C_2	C_3	C_4	C_5	C_6	C_7
Contents	⬀	⊙	⊖	←	⌖	Ξ	⟩
	$Ck^1_{1'}$	$Ck^1_{2'}$	$Ck^1_{3'}$	$Ck^1_{4'}$	$Ck^1_{5'}$	$Ck^1_{6'}$	$Ck^1_{7'}$

Figure 2. The file system of Figure 1 after a new release

To maliciously modify file C_3 back to the content at t_0, the attacker replaces the current column 3 in figure *2*, with a *copy* of the previous contents, column 3 in figure 1 (checksum changed in the database), resulting on the status shown in Figure 3. File corruption has been successfully completed.

	C_1	C_2	C_3	C_4	C_5	C_6	C_7
Contents	⬀	⊙	©	←	⌖	Ξ	}
	$Ck^1_{1'}$	$Ck^1_{2'}$	Ck^1_3	$Ck^1_{4'}$	$Ck^1_{5'}$	$Ck^1_{6'}$	$Ck^1_{7'}$

Figure 3. The corrupted file system

To detect this attack, we propose a technique that employs a second set of checksums. The system determines subsets of the file signatures and applies a predetermined one way hashing function, *g*, on the contents of each subset, as in figure 4. These *2nd level signatures*, Ck^2_i , are also stored in a secure database.

$$Ck^2_1 = g(Ck^1_{1'},Ck^1_{2'},Ck^1_{3'}) \quad Ck^2_2 = g(Ck^1_{1'},Ck^1_{4'},Ck^1_{5'}) \quad Ck^2_3 = g(Ck^1_{1'},Ck^1_{6'},Ck^1_{7'})$$
$$Ck^2_4 = g(Ck^1_{2'},Ck^1_{4'},Ck^1_{6'}) \quad Ck^2_5 = g(Ck^1_{2'},Ck^1_{5'},Ck^1_{7'}) \quad Ck^2_6 = g(Ck^1_{3'},Ck^1_{4'},Ck^1_{7'})$$
$$Ck^2_7 = g(Ck^1_{3'},Ck^1_{5'},Ck^1_{6'})$$

Figure 4. Possible subsets of example system to link the seven file signatures of revised files with 2nd level signatures

With this layer of signatures, when the intruder copies signature Ck^1_3 to match the old copy of the file 3, all second level signatures involving Ck^1_3 in their calculations must also be replaced, namely Ck^2_1, Ck^2_2, *and* Ck^2_3. In order to successfully complete this, two conditions must have occurred. First, at some prior time, the system must have been in such a state where $Ck^2_1 = g(Ck^1_{1'},Ck^1_{2'},Ck^1_3)$, $Ck^2_6 = g(Ck^1_3,Ck^1_{4'},Ck^1_{7'})$, and $Ck^2_7 = g(Ck^1_3,Ck^1_{5'},Ck^1_{6'})$; implying that files 1,2,4,5,6, and 7 contained contents as in Figure 2, and file 3 has contents as in Figure 1. Second, the intruder copied the signatures at that instance into his *stock*. Now, not only must the attacker consistently track prior behavior of the system, store and make the 3 extra signature copies, but also track any other file modifications that occur concurrently in the system during the copying process.

Furthermore, if the intruder fails to change all these files properly and simply performs the change shown in Figure 3, the security administrator will be notified of the anomaly and will be able to track the exact file that was modified. Noting which three 2nd level signatures changed and calculating the intersection of the subsets of the file signatures from which each was computed, only one file, precisely C_3, can be diagnosed as the corrupted file. Moreover, this design is flexible and scalable with the file system size.

3. OUR TECHNIQUE

We consider a file system S that is composed of N files: F_1, F_2, ...,F_N, denoted by S = [F_1, F_2,...,F_N]. Since each file size may be quite large, we first compute a concise representation, called a *signature* or *check sum,* of each file F_i: $S1_i = Ck^1(F_i)$. The *signature* has a fixed length of b bits, for some integer b, and is computed by some one-way hash function. It is stored in a secure database elsewhere. Before a change to a file is saved, the system computes and validates the *signature* value for the updated file. An intruder copying an old version file, F'_i, in place of one current file, F_i, will also need to manually replace the signature of F'_i with the correct match, since during this type of intrusion, the system would not automatically compute values.

Generating signatures may require more computation, though little time is necessary for this and it requires less storage than storing a copy of the entire file. Also, two different pages may have the same signature. The probability of this happening is proportional to 2^{-b}. Moreover, it is computationally infeasible to produce two messages having the same message digest, or to produce any message having a given pre-specified target signature [6].

The system responds to any file alteration by computing the *2nd level signatures*, which utilizes a non-reversible, trusted and secret hash function, (again, the key to the function is unattainable, thus 'trusted'), on a combination of a selection of the file signatures, *Ck_i^1's*. Thus since it is unlikely that an intruder accesses the ability of compute the signatures, copying valid values is the avenue of corruption. *Check2* computes a maximum of N second level signatures; each is a function of a subset of the N file signatures: $Ck^2_j = Ck(Ck^1_1, Ck^1_2 \ldots Ck^1_i)$ where $1 \le i, j \le N$

Each checksum, Ck^1j, is integrated with $(i - 1)$ other file signatures to compute another signature. We propose two algorithms to determine the elements of these subsets. One is a deterministic approach, using methodology proposed by Albert and Sandler [1]. The other is a randomized strategy that has been previously used to compare file copies in [2].

3.1 Deterministic Signatures

Consider the N files (objects) in our system; from the contents of each, the system generates a set, *A*, containing N elements, each a file signature Ck (F_i), $1 \le i \le N$. A set of subsets of *A* will have at most 2^N elements. We shall not be concerned with every collection of subsets of the set *A*, but rather with those sets which satisfy the specific properties, defined later in this section.

The elements of each subset form the combination onto which the secret and trusted function is applied to calculate the set of *2nd level signatures.*

The goal is to produce subsets, S_i, which satisfy a pairwise non-null intersection property: $S_i \cap S_j \neq \emptyset$, for any combination i and j where $1 \leq i, j \leq N$. The fundamental idea of such sets stems from the Sperner sets theorem, which provides existence of sets that follow the properties stated. This provides assurance that when a change occurs in all the elements used in the calculation of one signature (**Ck^2j**), it directly relates to changes every other 2nd level signature. Each file signature appears in more than one subset and there exists at least one common node between a pair of S_i and S_j. In essence, viewing all the signatures as nodes in a hyperplane, each file signature node will be connected to every other signature node in the system.

Following are properties that the second level subsets satisfy. They mimic the same structure as used by Maekawa [5] to create mutual exclusion in decentralized systems.

- At least one common element between a pair of subsets, S_i and S_j
- $| S_i | = K$ for any i
- Any j is contained in the D S_i 's where $1 \leq i,j \leq N$. (i.e., D is the number of subsets in which each element appears, number of duplications of each distinct element)

Each member of $| S_i |$ can be contained in D-1 other subsets, and the maximum number of subsets that satisfy the intersection property is (D - 1)K+1, where K is the size of the subset. It is shown in [5] that K and D are such that K=D, and that N and K are related as follows

$$N = K(K - 1) + 1 \quad \textbf{(1)}$$

As described in [1], such a system of subsets is perceived as a projective plane of N points with properties equating to the conditions stated above. There exists a finite projective plane of order k if k is a power p^m of a prime p. This finite projective plane has k(k+1) +1 unique points. Hence in our technique for creating subsets S_i 's (considering K(K-1)+1 vs. k(k+1)+1) a set of S_i 's for the N files exists if (K-1) is a power of a prime. For other values of k, the system can still create a set of S_i 's by relaxing conditions that each subset having same number of elements K, as well as relaxing the property that each file signature must appear in K-1 subsets. As Maekawa [5] also concludes, $K = \sqrt{N}$, with some fractional error.

Figure 5 illustrates an example for a file size of 13, where **$S2_i$** represents the checksums using the subset S_i. The change of one file triggers K 2nd level signature changes and if all K files of any subset are altered simultaneously, then all N second level signatures change.

N=13, K=4 S_1 = {1,2,3,4} = $\boldsymbol{S2_1}$ S_5 = {1,5,6,7} = $\boldsymbol{S2_5}$
S_8 = {1,8,9,10}= $\boldsymbol{S2_8}$ S_{11}= {1,11,12,13}}= $\boldsymbol{S2_{11}}$
S_2= {2,5,8,11}}= $\boldsymbol{S2_2}$ S_6 = {2,6,9,12}}= $\boldsymbol{S2_6}$
S_7 = {2,7,10,13}}= $\boldsymbol{S2}$ S_{10} = {3,5,10,12}}= $\boldsymbol{S2_{10}}$
S_3= {3,6,8,13}}= $\boldsymbol{S2_3}$ S_9 = {3,7,9,11}}= $\boldsymbol{S2_9}$
S_{13} = {4,5,9,13}}= $\boldsymbol{S2_{13}}$ S_4= {4,6,10,11}}= $\boldsymbol{S2_4}$
S_{12} = {4,7,8, 12}= $\boldsymbol{S2_{12}}$

Figure 5. 2nd level signature sets using combinations of file signatures 1-13. The intersection of any two combinations is nonempty

When the values of N cannot be expressed as K(K -1) + 1, the subsets are built making one of the following corrections [5]:

- Pad the file signature set with extra duplicate values, i.e., increase the value of the N until N can be expressed as K(K-1) + 1.
- Create degenerated (nonequivalent number of elements) sets of S_i 's by temporarily assuming enough elements exist so that N = K(K -1) + 1.

The same process is repeated to construct the elements of a *3rd level of signatures* for added protection. These third level signatures are each calculated using the set of second level signatures, $\boldsymbol{Ck^2i}$. The domain for the hash functions calculating third layer signatures are the elements of the set of $\mathbf{Ck^2_i}$, from which the system generates the subsets, abiding by the above stated properties, for the 3rd level. The system stores the N, or possibly more if N can not be expressed as N = K(K-1)+1, third level signatures. With the inclusion of this level, one file change causes all 3rd level signatures to change. If only the contents of one file change, exactly (N + K) unique signatures automatically change.

3.1.1 Diagnosis of deterministic signatures.

The structured design of the second and third level checksum produces a set percentage of increase in system calculations during an authorized file update. But, it forces an internal intruder to track and copy a precise chain of signatures. With the predetermined subset algorithm, when *one* authorized file changes, *Check2* generally recomputed the **K** 2nd and **N** 3rd level signatures; this causes the system to do at most N + K calculations. If N $\neq$ K(K-1) + 1, then these quantities will be larger because of the increase in the value of K, as displayed earlier above in **(2)**. For the intruder to incur this minimum copying cost, he/she must collect a *stock* of 1st, 2nd and 3rd level signature values, corresponding to the appropriate files. Because all file signature nodes are interleaved in the subsets, this *stock* must include every variation of any previously occurring state of file contents of the entire system. The general (assuming N can be expressed as K(K-1) +1), the combined cost includes collecting all the stock, making K signature copies at the 2nd level, and N signature copies at the 3rd level, thus the cost of copying becomes **K + N.**

In a crude analysis, it is possible that just one state of the system is captured by the malicious user. For that one instance, this malicious user copies all file contents, their file signatures, 2nd level and 3rd level signatures of that one state into his/her *stock* and then copy over the entire system and signatures. But, with such drastic and noticeable changes, the security administrator would immediately flag such modifications.

Furthermore, the system is able to determine exactly which file is corrupted. This is achieved by calculating the intersection of the K second level subsets. These K subsets are those used in computing the 2nd level signatures that were affected by a particular file modification. The system captures the file signature, Ck^1_i, which is common in these K subsets causing the 2nd level signature to change. The file corresponding to this file signature is which has been modified.

3.2 Randomized Subsets

The randomized technique produces the subsets of the set of file signatures by using a pseudorandom generating algorithm. This strategy uses a notion of creating subsets whose elements are randomly determined each time the *Check2* is executed. This schema avoids malicious tampering, since the system is programmed to randomly change the sets frequently by using a new seed for the pseudorandom generator. Again, for each of the N files, we compute a checksum: $CK^1_i = Ck(F_i)$.

The system's security administrators decide on the number of subsets, m (m<N), $S_1, S_2, \ldots S_m$, where each set $S_i \subseteq \{CK^1_1, CK^1_2, \ldots CK^1_N\}$. That is, each subset is made up of a number of first-level checksums. The composition of these subsets is decided in a randomized way (there are actually many strategies to achieve this, and we will illustrate one later in the paper). Each subset m may not necessarily have the same number of first-level checksums. The signature for the i-th subset is constructed as the hash or Exclusive OR of the first-level checksums in S_i. This combined signature is the *2nd level Signature*, Ck^2_i. If the original signature has b bits, the combined signature will also have b bits. When a file, F_i, is altered, the system generates the 2nd level signatures, compares them to the stored signatures (which were computed using the same random sets) and with authorization, automatically changes those signatures that utilize F_i in its computation.

This algorithm allows varying levels of security. The number of second level signatures is variable, unlike in the deterministic approach, where each 2nd signature is a function of K signatures. The number, m, of 2nd level signatures is directly proportional to the level of security the administration wishes for the system. The more of 2nd level signatures computed, and higher the security because the larger the *stock* necessary to make a valid copy. By frequently recreating new a set of randomized subsets from the set of N file signatures, there is an extremely low probability that the intruder has acquired an exact copy with which to corrupt.

Once *m* is established, at the initialization of the algorithm, using a pseudorandom number generator and a strategy to decide membership, we can assign first-level checksums into the *m* subsets. At any update or alteration of a file, the 2nd level signatures are recomputed and stored and at times. Moreover, the system may randomly redistribute the N signatures by applying again the pseudorandom generator and the strategy to the set of files.

There are many strategies to randomly combine first-level signatures into the second level signatures. A few of them are described and analyzed in the context of the file comparison problem in [2].

To illustrate this, we include here one of their algorithms, called *Innocents*. In this strategy, each first-level checksum is included in a set *Si*, with probability *1/f*, where *f* is a parameter of the algorithm. In the original strategy, *f* meant the number of pages on the file that the algorithm was designed to diagnose as being different in the two copies; in our technique it represents the number of corrupted files that we are set to detect. Due to the randomness of the algorithm, there is a 2^{-m} probability of a page being left out of all second-level signature subsets. To resolve this issue, after the random subsets have been chosen, the system checks whether every file has been included in a subset. If it is not the case, it adds an additional set that includes all files that have been left out.

Recall that the *stock* only contains old file copies and corresponding signatures. In this approach, two exact same file systems may have a different set of second level signatures. For a file F_1, the attacker's copy of a 2nd level signature in his or her *stock* from time t_o may not be the same signature that is generated at time t_1. In the randomized approach, the probability that the randomized distribution for the 2nd level combined signatures corresponds to the copy in the intruder's *stock* is $1/(m^N)$. This does not reflect any modifications to system files from the time of the old copy. Thus, it is very unlikely the intruder process the correct signatures, which the system would validate.

3.2.1 Diagnosis of probabilistic techniques.

Figure 6 shows the algorithm that diagnoses corruption in a file system protected by the *Innocents* technique. This algorithm can be run periodically in order to alert the security officer from possible corruption in one or more of the files. The algorithm proceeds as follows. First it computes all the subset's signatures and creates a syndrome matrix of elements (one per subset) whose values can be 0 or 1, according to whether the signature of the subset matches the stored signature or not. Once this matrix is built, the algorithm examines those subsets whose signature matched and puts the number of the files included in the subset in a set *T*. At the end, *T* will contain the "innocent" files, i.e., those presumably uncorrupted. The complement of that set is the set of files that might have been corrupted.

In diagnosing corrupted files by probabilistic means, one has to take into account the possibility of false diagnosis. There are two ways in which a false diagnose can happen: an uncorrupted file may be diagnosed as corrupted (false positive), or a corrupted file may fail to be diagnosed as corrupted (false negative). Fortunately, the probability for both of these events can be made arbitrarily low by setting the algorithm parameters (m,b,f) properly.

Create syndrome matrix with elements
    $\alpha_i=0$ *if the second-level signature of subset i matches the one stored.*
        1 otherwise.
  $T = \varnothing$
  For $i = 1$ *to* m
    If $\alpha_i = 0$
      Then
        For $j = 1$ *to* n *if* CK^1j *is in Si then*
          $T = T \cup \{j\}$
  $T = S - \{T\}$

Figure 6. Probablistic diagnosing algorithms for Innocents

In [2], the analysis of the probabilities for the false positive and false negative diagnoses is presented. We only repeat the results here. The probability of a false positive event can be made less than δ (which can be fixed by the security officer) by insuring that the inequality in Equation 3 is true.

$$b \geq \log(m) + \log(f) + \log(2/\delta) \qquad \textbf{(3)}$$

Equation 3 establishes a lower bound for the number of bits in the signature in order to guarantee that the probability of false positive diagnosis is less that δ.

On the other hand, the probability of a false negative will be bounded by δ if the number of subsets m is such that the inequality in Equation 4 is true.

$$m \geq 4f\,(\ln(n-f) + \ln(2/\delta)) \qquad \textbf{(4)}$$

For instance, selecting $m = 500, f = 10$, $b > 7$, and for a system with 100 files, we would achieve an upper bound for the false diagnosis of 2^{-10} (or 0.00097).

4. CONCLUSIONS AND FUTURE DIRECTIONS

The file corruption addressed by our analysis involves copying of files by intruders who gain write access to a file system protected by signatures. We have presented *Check2,* a technique to protect a set of files against corruption by insider intruders (or individuals who impersonate authorized users). The system has two very desirable properties. First, it forces a potential intruder to track and perform a string of precise changes, if he or she wants to remain undetected. Secondly, if the attack is not performed properly, *Check2* is able to pinpoint the corrupted pages to the security officer.

The foundation of *Check2* is based on computing checksums for each file, as other techniques such as Tripwire currently use. However, our technique contributes the usage of two or more levels of signatures, combining file signatures with a deterministic or probabilistic schema, in order to increase the work of intruder. This includes calculating the exact lengthy chain of alterations and successfully implementing the changes in a dynamic real-time situation. In either strategy, an additional cost of copying the actual contents of extra *files*, other than the corrupted file can be integrated into each technique.

REFERENCES

[1] Albert, A.A and Sandler, R. An Introduction to Finite Projective Planes. Holt, Rinehart, and Winston, New York, 1968.

[2] Barbara, Daniel and Lipton, Richard, J. A class on randomized strategies for low-cost comparison of file copies. IEEE Trans. Parallel and Distributed Systems, Vol. 2, No. 2, April 1991, pages 160-170.

[3] Kim, Gene. H., Spafford, Eugene, H., The design and implementation of Tripwire: A file system integrity checker. Proc. 2nd ACM Conference on Computer and Communications Security, 1994.

[4] Kim, Gene. H., Spafford, Eugene, H., Experiences with Tripwire: Using integrity checkers for intrusion detection. Systems Administration, Networking and Security Conference III. Usenix 1994.

[5] Maekawa, Mamoru. A √N algorithm for mutual exclusion in decentralized systems. ACM Transaction on Computer Systems, Vol. 3, No. 2, May 1985, Pages 145-159.

[6] MD5 Message - Digest Algorithm, MIT Laboratory for Computer Science and RSA Data Security, April 1992.

[7] Merkle, R. C., A Fast Software One-way Hash Function. Journal of Cryptology,3(1):43-58, 1990.

[8] Website: www.tripwiresecurity.com/vs.html as seen in January 2000.

CHAPTER 11

Web Security and Privacy

Panel 1

Bhavani Thuraisingham
MITRE Corporation, Bedford MA, USA

Abstract: This panel discussed various issues on web security and privacy including XML security, data mining for intrusion detection, and various other aspects including e-commerce security.

1. INTRODUCTION

The panel consisted of the following researchers.

* E. Bertino, University of Milan
* E. Damiani, George Mason University and University of Milan
* Kristin Nauta, SAS Institute
* Sushil Jajodia, George Mason University

The panel discusses essentially summarized the papers and research by the authors presented mainly at the conference. In section 2 we summarize the discussions and in section 3 we discuss future directions.

2. Panel Content

Bertino and Damiani discussed XML security. In particular, Berino's discussion focussed on the paper she and co-author presented on access control for XML. This was followed by Damiani's discussion on standards work for XML. The panel also discussed the W3C work on XML security and where one could get more information.

Nauta discussed summarized essentially her keynote presentation that was to follow. This was on using intrusion detection techniques for intrusion detection. This is a subject of much interest to the group these days and Nauta presented various techniques they were applying. Jajodia provided his views on e-commerce security as well as integrity. E-commerce security is also getting a lot of attention when we discuss web security.

Thuraisingham concluded the panel with privacy issues. The same question that she has been repeating at various IFIP keynote presentations and panels in 1996, 1997 and 1998 were repeated. While data mining helps intrusion detection it does invade into the privacy of people. What can we do about it? There were no solution, but interesting discussions.

The audience was very active and asked many questions on all aspects covered by the panelists including XML security, data mining for intrusion detection and e-commerce security. It was also mentioned that we need a research agenda for web and e-commerce security.

3. Future Directions

As suggested by the audience, we need a research agenda. IFIP 11.3 is in a good position to draft the agenda for web security. There is a lot of work that is being done outside. WE need to survey what is being done and then formulate a research plan. While data mining shows much promise, we are still not sure what to do about privacy issues. Some say that there are no technical solutions and that we need legal solutions. We still need to investigate this area and hopefully in years to come we can come to some acceptable solution. Everyone was convinced that we security is one of the critical areas in computer science research today.

CHAPTER 12

Coordinating Policy for Federated Applications

Keynote II

Ken Moody
University of Cambridge Computer Laboratory
New Museum Site, Pembroke Street
Cambridge CB2 3QG, UK
km@cl.cam.ac.uk

Abstract At the start of its present term of office in 1997 the UK government published a planning document promising ubiquitous access to Electronic Health Records (EHRs) held within the National Health Service (NHS). If such access is to become a reality then it is essential to guarantee confidentiality, since otherwise the media and the privacy vigilantes will prevent deployment. Among the rights included in the Patients' Charter is a promise that each individual may determine who may access their health records and in what circumstances, and that every access made shall be logged. In October 1999 the Cambridge Computer Laboratory's Opera group joined a consortium within the Eastern Regional Health Authority to propose an experimental architecture that included access control. Policy governing access to a particular set of records is derived from many high-level sources, and must be updated when any of these sources change. We outline an architecture to achieve this, within the framework of access control policy for EHRs. The problems of coordinating policy arise in many applications that span management regimes, and the techniques outlined are more generally relevant. This is work in progress.

1. Introduction

The thrust of the Opera group in the Computer Laboratory has been to develop a Middleware architecture in which individual services retain autonomy. Key components are the Cambridge Event Architecture (CEA) [8], which offers support for generic registration and notification of events, and the role-based access control model Oasis [5]. These components are interdependent. An overview of the work of the Opera group can be found in [1].

It is one thing to propose an architecture for distributed applications, quite another to evaluate such an architecture realistically. In Oasis role names are defined and policies expressed on a service-by-service basis, so providing for independent management of the individual services involved. It is therefore possible to deploy policy while respecting the autonomy of management domains, enabling complex wide-area applications to evolve without fine-grained coordination. In April 1999 members of the Opera group visited the Information Authority of the UK National Health Service (NHS), and the group has since developed a detailed architecture to support ubiquitous access to EHRs, including role-based access control. We have learnt a lot from carrying out the design, but we should learn a lot more by testing it in practice.

2. Electronic Health Records: a Federated Management Problem

The UK NHS has been underfunded over a long period, and is recognized as being in crisis. The Labour government that took office in 1997 made reviving the NHS one of its prime goals [12]. [13] outlined an implementation strategy intended to lead progressively to the integrated storage of health data, with access from all health care points. The strategy was based on bottom-up deployment, and there was no clear explanation of the mechanisms that would ensure compatibility across the country as a whole. The Opera group joined a consortium (EREHRC) formed by health care providers within the Eastern Region, coordinated by the Clinical and Biomedical Computing Unit (part of the University of Cambridge), based at Addenbrooke's Hospital. The EREHRC included health professionals and academics based within the region and from outside, among them Jane Grimson of Trinity College, Dublin, who led the European Community *Synapses* project [10]. In November 1999 the EREHRC submitted a proposal to the NHS for a "pan-community demonstrator", focussing on what we see as the main obstacles to the introduction of EHRs: heterogeneity, local autonomy, and above all continuing evolution - of hardware and software, management structures, and medical practice and taxonomy.

The EREHRC proposal contained a separate technical appendix developed by the Opera group, together with a sabbatical visitor, John Hine, from the Victoria University of Wellington, New Zealand. Specific proposals for a certificate authority suitable for supporting Oasis in a health care environment are described in [6]. An overview of the architecture is given in Figure 1.

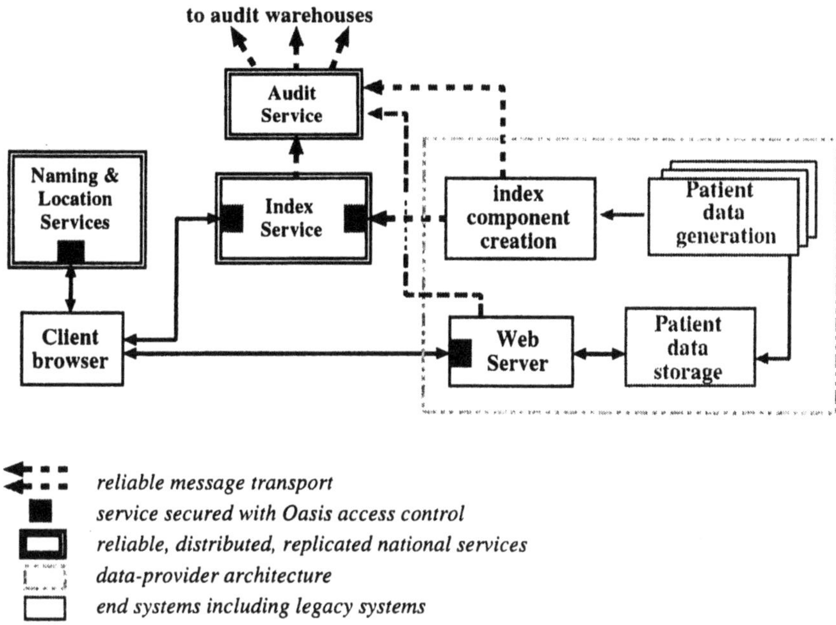

Figure 1. An Architecture for an Electronic Health Record Service

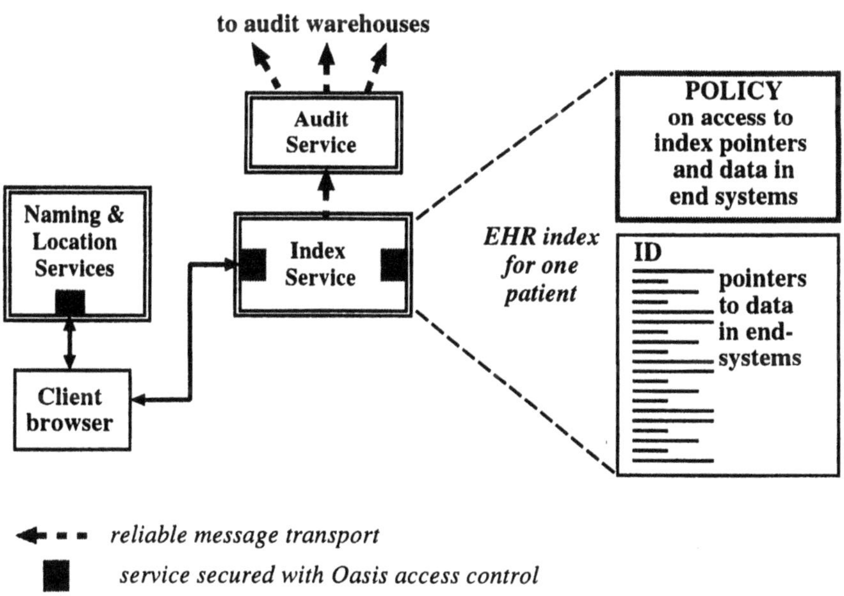

Figure 2. The Virtual Health Record (Index) Service

A crucial feature of the design is the use of virtual health records [3, 4], essentially index items structured according to a medical ontology. Each such item contains references to all the patient records relating to a given individual, see Figure 2. By law every access to an individual's EHR must be recorded, and we provide an audit trail asynchronously, noting the principal reading the data, and the context. This context must include information sufficient to identify the policy regime that was current at the time of access, together with the credentials presented by the principal in order to establish the right to access the data.

NHS thinking at that time was based on solutions involving a centralised database, and the proposal was not funded. Public opinion has remained critical of the NHS, and after wide consultation the Labour government presented a new national plan for the health service in July 2000 [14]. There is little emphasis on ubiquitous access to EHRs, and the implementation strategy introduced in [13] has been quietly forgotten.

3. The requirements for managing access control policy

Access to an individual's EHR is regulated in a variety of ways. In particular, EHRs must be identified, and they contain personal data; EHRs are therefore subject to Data Protection legislation, as enacted in both the UK and European parliaments. The Health Service is administered independently in England, Wales, Scotland and Northern Ireland, and each province has established its own Patient's Charter [11]. Amongst other things, each charter makes explicit each patient's right to determine who may access their health records. Health authorities will express policies in terms of the role and seniority of their staff, and the nature of the data that is to be accessed or service that is to be managed. Specialist departments will recognize professional skills in addition to seniority. All of these sources of policy must be respected when generating procedures (Java classes, in our case) to implement the access control guards on databases which contain patient records. For each high-level source non-specialists should be able to express policy intuitively, in a language appropriate to the context. The large scale of an application such as the NHS means that guards on the individual databases must be generated automatically. Audit records must identify the policy regime under which each access has been authorised.

4. Oasis Role-Based Access Control

In Oasis each named role is associated with a particular service. A service that administers roles is responsible for authenticating its clients.

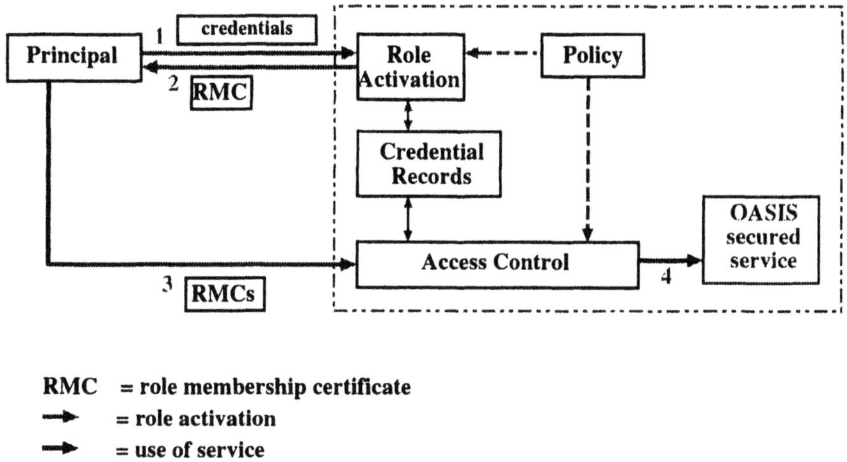

Figure 3. A service secured by Oasis access control

Rights to access a service are derived from membership of roles, either of the service itself or of other services. Figure 3 shows a service secured by Oasis access control. Policy is checked both on role activation and when the service is used.

A client becomes authenticated in a particular role by presenting credentials that enable the service to **prove** that the client conforms to its policy for activating that role, see [9] which describes the formal model. The credentials presented can include parameters that are checked during role activation. The client is then issued with a role membership certificate (RMC). The RMC may include parameters derived from the credentials that identify aspects of the client, for example a local user identifier may be copied from a log-in certificate; a digital signature is generated to protect the parameter values and to ensure that the certificate is useless if stolen.

Services authorise clients by specifying the privileges associated with each role. The policy may require parameter values to satisfy constraints which must be checked whenever access is attempted.

Role-based access control (RBAC) has a number of advantages. Permissions are expressed in terms of roles that may be adopted by principals. The policy governing role activation is decoupled from the rights associated with each role, which may be modified at a generic level. This leads to essentially scalable policy management, and incidentally enables secure access by anonymous principals, should this be desired.

A crucial practical advantage of making roles specific to a service is that each service may specify its own policy for both role activation and access control. In an environment such as a hospital it is likely that a central registry service will act as the sole certificate issuing authority [6], with individual hospital departments granting access on the basis of the RMCs that have been issued. Policy within each hospital will determine role membership hospital wide; once an appropriate policy has been expressed, any departmental service can control access on the basis of the RMCs issued by the central registry service. In this way both hospitals and individual departments can be managed independently; Oasis access control can thus be deployed incrementally. This is vital in any application that comprises a federation of independent partners.

5. Expressing and enforcing policy

In the NHS application access control must respect both individual preference and hospital policy. The former is determined at the index service, the latter by guards established at each departmental patient record service. A student on the MPhil course in Computer Speech and Language Processing has defined a simple formal language for policy expression [7, 2]. Successive translations generate Higher Order Logic, First Order Predicate Calculus (FOPC), and finally target languages specific to both Role Activation and Method Invocation (including data access). Basic RBAC will not handle the negative permissions that patients may require, but in Oasis role activation conditions can also include environmental constraints [9]. Examples of such constraints are to check on the time of day, or to evaluate a predicate in a local database. Since parameters such as a local user identifier may be set during role activation it is possible to handle patient preferences by consulting a list of exceptions in some appropriate database.

The use of environmental constraints makes it possible to define generic policies that can be tailored to each particular context. We are at present setting up mappings between the names of predicates which express environmental constraints and the names of database relations. For example, a software package for primary health care can specify default policy using role-based access control. Any exceptions requested by individual patients can be handled by consulting a locally maintained database, provided that names are handled consistently from practice to practice. Additional policy expression languages will be needed, but they will also generate FOPC. It is vital to establish a common target representation in order to check the overall consistency of policies.

6. Managing change

The high bandwidth and reliability of modern communications make it inevitable that applications will be federated across a wide area, with individual management domains interacting subject to a high-level regulatory framework. In the NHS application each of the four home countries has its own Patient's Charter, and the access control policy effective when health care is delivered must take account of the appropriate version. Throughout the UK any policy must respect the provisions of the Data Protection Act.

For the NHS EHR application we have implemented active database support that should help us to automate policy deployment. The policy effective at a health care point may derive from a number of sources; national law, regulatory frameworks such as the Patient's Charter, local health authority access control policy and individual patient preference. Any inconsistencies must be identified and resolved before deployment. We are storing each such policy in an object-relational database, setting triggers to alert all sites dependent on it whenever a change occurs. What action is taken will vary from site to site. If no inconsistency results then it should be possible to deploy a modified policy automatically, otherwise local management must decide how to resolve the conflict. Many problems remain to be solved before automatic enforcement of expressed policy can become a reality.

7. Risks of automated policy enforcement

An essential feature of the EREHRC architecture is that change can be managed locally, with national decisions being implemented on a time scale that is feasible within each environment. Policy is only one of many sources of change. The structure of EHRs must be modified in the light of medical research; advances in genetics are now threatening the simplistic view of individual patient preference, as genetic counsellors are confronted more and more frequently with differences of opinion between siblings - the sister wishes to know the result of a test, but the brother does not. This raises a dilemma. As the scale of electronic health data increases it will become essential to automate the capture of both data and policy, yet the computer is insensitive at best in matters such as ethics.

Business to business dealings between multinationals are subject to even worse problems; not only must contracts be interpreted within a variety of legal frameworks, but any disputes arising may be subject to multiple jurisdictions. In such a world there is a real danger of unstable behaviour, with a consequent threat to secure economic growth.

Acknowledgements

We acknowledge EPSRC's support for the continuation of this work under GR /N35786 "Access Control Policy Management".

References

[1] Bacon, J., Moody, K., Bates, J., Hayton, R., Ma, C., McNeil, A., Seidel, O., and Spiteri, M.: Generic Support for Asynchronous, Secure Distributed Applications. IEEE Computer Vol. 33(3), 68–76, March 2000

[2] Bacon, J., Lloyd, M and Moody, K.: Translating role-based access control policy within context. To appear in Policy 2001, Workshop on Policies for Distributed Systems and Networks, Bristol, UK, January 2001. Lecture Notes in Computer Science 1995, Springer-Verlag, Berlin, Heidelberg and New York, 105–117, 2001

[3] Grimson, J., Felton, E., Stephens, G., Grimson, W. and Berry, D.: Interoperability issues in sharing electronic healthcare records - the Synapses approach. Proceedings of Third IEEE International Conference on Engineering of Complex Computer Systems, IEEE CS Press, Los Alamitos, Calif., 180–185, 1997

[4] Grimson, J., Grimson, W., Berry, D., Kalra, D., Toussaint, P. and Weier, O.: A CORBA-based integration of distributed electronic healthcare records using the Synapses approach. Special Issue of IEEE Transactions on Information Technology in Biomedicine on EMERGING HEALTH TELEMATICS APPLICATIONS IN EUROPE, Vol.2, No.3, IEEE CS Press, Los Alamitos, Calif., 1998

[5] Hayton, R., Bacon, J. and Moody, K.: OASIS: Access Control in an Open, Distributed Environment. Proceedings IEEE Symposium on Security and Privacy. IEEE CS Press, Los Alamitos, Calif., 3–14, 1998

[6] Hine, J.H., Yao, W., Bacon, J. and Moody, K.: An Architecture for Distributed OASIS Services. Proceedings Middleware 2000, Lecture Notes in Computer Science, 1795. Springer-Verlag, Berlin, Heidelberg and New York, 107–123, 2000

[7] Lloyd, M.: Conversion of NHS Access Control Policy to Formal Logic. MPhil in Computer Speech and Language Processing, University of Cambridge, 2000

[8] Ma, C., and Bacon, J.: COBEA: A CORBA-based Event Architecture. In Proceedings of the 4th Conference on Object-Oriented Technologies and Systems (COOTS-98), USENIX Association, Berkeley, 117–132, April 1998

[9] W. Yao, K. Moody, J. Bacon. A Model of OASIS Role-Based Access Control and its Support for Active Security. In *Proceedings, Sixth ACM Symposium on Access Control Models and Technologies (SACMAT)*, Chantilly, VA, May 2001

[10] Synapses Project Deliverables, Trinity College, Dublin see http://www.cs.tcd.ie/synapses/public/html/projectdeliverables.html

[11] The Patients's Charter (for England), January 1997 see http://www.doh.gov.uk/pcharter/patientc.htm

[12] UK Government White Paper, "The New NHS: Modern, Dependable", December 1997, see http://www.doh.gov.uk/nnhsind.htm

[13] UK Government White Paper, "Information for Health", September 1998, see http://www.doh.gov.uk/nhsexipu/strategy/index.htm

[14] UK Government White Paper, "The NHS Plan - A Plan for Investment, A Plan for Reform", July 2000, see http://www.nhs.uk/nationalplan/

CHAPTER 13

Integrating Multilevel Security Policies in Multilevel Federated Database Systems

Marta Oliva[1] and Fèlix Saltor[2]

[1]Dept. Informàtica i Enginyeria Industrial, Universitat de Lleida, C. Jaume II, 69, E-25001 Lleida (Catalonia).

[2]Dept. Llenguatges i Sistemes Informàtics, Universitat Politècnica de Catalunya, Campus Nord-Mòdul C5, Jordi Girona Salgado, 1-3, E-08034 Barcelona (Catalonia).

Key words: Multilevel security, integration, interoperation, federated DBMS.

Abstract: This paper describes a multilevel security policies integration methodology to endow tightly coupled federated database systems with a multilevel security system. The proposal is based on a schema integration process. It obtains, in a semi-automatic form, the ordered set of classification levels for the multilevel security system of the federation, and the translation functions between each ordered set belonging to each component database and the federated ordered set as well. The proposed methodology also includes a way to solve the problem of classification of the components of the Federated Schema generated during the integration process.

1. INTRODUCTION

The growing need for information sharing, among independent entities which have their own database systems, is often solved by a *Federated DataBase System* (FDBS) ([SL90]). There are different aspects to take into account when building and operating such a FDBS: one of them is data protection.

Although the independent entities, named *Component DataBases* (CDBs), have their own access control mechanisms (based on *Discretionary Access Control* (DAC) or *Mandatory Access Control* (MAC)), accesses to the federated system need take into account not only security features of CDBs, but also security features of the federation ([Per93]). The mechanism used by our FDBS to protect data, and more particularly to allow or forbid access, is *MultiLevel Security* (MLS, [BL75]), because its own operation not only helps to control access but also to control information flow.

A FDBS can be *tightly coupled* or *loosely coupled* ([SL90]). Since we deal with strict access control policies, such as MLS, we assume tightly coupled FDBSs only, with administrators at the federated level. We present a methodology of integration of security policies to be used in building tightly coupled federated systems by MLS-CDBs integration.

The main concepts and notation used in this paper to describe the methodology can be found in section 2. Section 3 presents the principal characteristics of the schema integration methodology, upon which our methodology of integration of MLS systems is based. The core of the paper is in section 4 and contains the development of the proposed methodology. The paper ends with a comparison with other research and conclusions in section 5.

2. MAIN CONCEPTS AND NOTATION

A MLS system assigns a *clearance level* to each subject and a *confidentiality level* to each object. Levels assigned to subjects and objects should belong to either a partial or linear (total) ordered set, or a lattice of classification levels (or labels). At this stage we assume that every system uses a linear ordered set. The natural manner to represent an ordered set is through a *Hasse diagram* ([SM77]). The cardinality of an ordered set is the number of elements that are members of the set of classification levels.

When a FDBS is built it is necessary to take into account that although different preexistent CDBs have a MLS system, it is impossible to presume that their ordered sets of classification levels could coincide neither on the number of levels (cardinality), nor on confidentiality meaning ([MLTS92, DJ94]). That is why it is essential to have a mechanism that helps in obtaining the ordered set of the federation MLS system itself (from now on we will call it *Federated Ordered Set (FOS)*).

As accesses at the federated level are subject to the mechanisms that CDBs have to protect data, the FOS of classification levels must take into account the preexistent ordered sets. So the CDBs integration process has to make an integration process of ordered sets of classification levels of distinct preexistent MLS systems.

As an integration of ordered sets of classification levels we understand the process needed to deduce the equivalence among classification levels belonging to different ordered sets. It is important to note that it is possible that a level member of a specific ordered set does not coincide with any levels belonging to whichever of the remainder ordered sets to integrate.

Taking into account that classifications at the component level must be maintained at the federated level, the conclusion is that the FOS needs to have at least the same number of classification levels as the ordered set having the biggest number of classification levels of all ordered sets. Moreover, in the worst case it is possible that the FOS has as many classification levels as the sum of all ordered set cardinalities, due to the possibility of lack of any equivalence among classification levels of distinct ordered sets.

Given $(S_i, \leq_i)$, $i = 1,\ldots,N$, the ordered sets of the N preexisting CDBs, each S_i represents the set of classification levels of its correspondent CDB, and each $\leq_i$ is a binary relation that defines the order among elements of S_i. Through integration process of ordered sets, we obtain a new ordered set $(S_F, \leq_F)$ (FOS) where S_F is the set of classification levels of the federated MLS system and $\leq_F$ is the binary relation that indicates the order among elements of S_F. The cardinality of S_F ($| S_F |$) is bounded by the cardinalities of S_i ($| S_i |$):

$$| S_k | \leq | S_F | \leq (\Sigma^{N}_{i=1} | S_i |) \quad \text{where } | S_k | \geq | S_i | \ \forall\, i = 1,\ldots,N$$

depending on the quantity of classification levels from an ordered set that coincide with any classification level of another ordered set.

With the help of the integration process the FOS $(S_F, \leq_F)$ is obtained, and also the translation functions $(f_i, i=1,\ldots,N)$. A translation function allow us to translate each classification level from an ordered set to the FOS with the preservation of the order from original ordered set:

$$x, y \in S_i \quad x \leq_i y \quad \Leftrightarrow \quad f_i(x) \leq_F f_i(y)$$

3. THE SCHEMA INTEGRATION METHODOLOGY

[GSSC95] describes a schema integration methodology based on BLOOM (BarceLona Object Oriented Model, [CSGS94]) that allows obtaining a *Federated Schema* (according [SL90], [ROSC97]). The BLOOM data model is used because it is a semantically rich model (it has distinct kinds of specializations and aggregations) capable of expressing not only semantics already expressed in local schemas, but also additional semantics very useful for integration tasks. The schema integration methodology is divided into three phases:

- *Semantic Enrichment*: enriches semantically local schemas of the CDBs, which were expressed by some traditional models. It starts with a step of knowledge acquisition and then local schemas augmented with the knowledge previously discovered are converted into rich Component Schemas expressed in our Canonical Data Model (CDM, [SL90]) BLOOM.
- *Detection*: identifies semantically related objects (that belong to different CDBs), through a comparison process guided by a strategy. The strategy operates at two levels: at the coarse level the strategy identifies pairs of specializations to be compared, taking into account the generalization dimension, and at the fine level the strategy identifies pairs of classes to be compared based in the aggregation dimension. Later, a criterion, based on aggregation dimension too, is used to yield a degree of similarity between the pair of classes.
- *Resolution*: integrates the BLOOM schemas of the CDBs after identification of semantically related objects using a *discriminated generalization*. In this variant of generalization, the description of the superclass inherits upwards the description of its subclasses (it takes the union of their abstractions), and each object of a subclass, seen as a member of the superclass, has a discriminant attribute. The discriminant attribute is used for integration purposes and it takes as value the name of the database where it comes from.

4. THE SECURITY POLICIES INTEGRATION METHODOLOGY

Our security policies integration methodology complements the schema integration methodology presented in the previous section, in such a way to allow us to get:

- the FOS
- the translation functions between ordered sets
- the classification of the Federated Schema, which is a result of integration process, according to the obtained FOS.

Our methodology produces, in a semi-automatic form, a FOS that only needs to be validated by the federated system administrator, to be used as the ordered set of the MLS system of the federation. If the ordered set does not get the administrator's validation, the integration process would generate a new FOS proposal in order to be validated by the administrator. Validation can be total or partial; so from a partial validation new proposals can be generated until total validation is obtained. This is because when different ordered sets are integrated there are distinct combinations that can be used as FOS.

The analysis and validation of all possible combinations among classification levels of distinct ordered sets would require lots of administrator's effort. To reduce the number of combinations to analyze by the administrator, our integration process takes advantage of the information related to the data classification stored in *Export Schemas* (according to [SL90, ROSC97]), as well as the information obtained by schema integration process.

Although it is also necessary to complement the semantic enrichment phase to reach a complete integration of CDBs, this paper focuses on the two last phases of schema integration methodology. Particularly, the detection phase, properly complemented, yields the FOS and the translation functions (thanks to the validation of the administrator). Besides, after complementing the resolution phase, this will allow classifying the components of the Federated Schema.

4.1 Detection phase

The detection phase of the schema integration methodology (presented in section 3) produces semantic relationships between components of different Export Schemas. Semantic relationships are expressed by *semantic assertions* and there are two kinds:

a) equivalence assertion (*Equivalence Semantic Relationship, E-SR*): the two classes represent equivalent concepts
b) specialization assertion (*Specialization Semantic Relationship, S-SR*): one class represents a superconcept of the concept represented by the other class.

Figure 1 introduces a simple example that allows remembering the operation of the schema integration methodology, and then it is used to illustrate our security policies integration methodology.

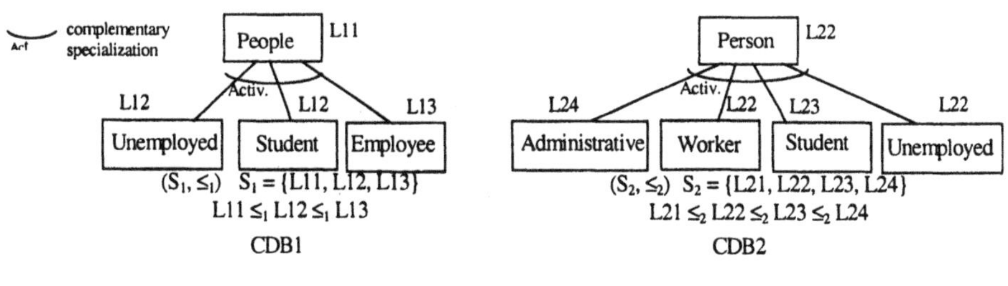

Figure 1. CDB1 and CDB2

Specifically, figure 1 describes the Export Schemas of CDB1 and CDB2, their ordered sets of classification levels, and also the classification of each component of the schemas as well.

The five semantic assertions obtained by means of the detection phase of schema integration methodology are shown in figure 2.

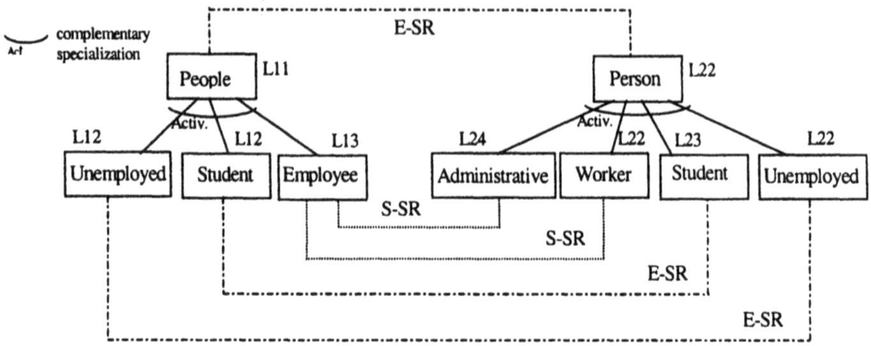

Figure 2. Obtained assertions by detection phase

The ordered set integration process uses the information of the semantic assertions. So, with the initial information of ordered sets of CDBs to integrate and assertions obtained by detection phase, the proposal of a FOS is originated in order to let administrator validate it.

Taking into account the hypothesis of homogeneous integration (CDBs belong to the same universe of discourse) it is logical to presume that interest in information privacy will be similar. For that:

1. in an E-SR it is assumed that classification levels of classes which are considered equivalent concepts, are equivalent classification levels.
2. in an S-SR it is assumed that the classification level of the superconcept is ≤ than the classification level of the concept (according to [ML92, IGQ94] a concept always has to be classified at a level ≥ than the superconcept, because concept needs to inherit superconcept characteristics).

For the analysis and representation of all information, needed by the ordered set integration process, a multiple directed graph (digraph ([SM77]) where multiple arcs are allowed between two vertices, *multidigraph*) is used. The multidigraph is built from Hasse diagrams, which define initial ordered sets to integrate, and necessary arcs corresponding to different assertions obtained by detection phase. The source and target of each arc belong to distinct ordered sets. The representation of each semantic assertion is the following:

1. for each E-SR an arc from the classification level of a class to the classification level of the other class is added to the multidigraph; and also the inverse arc.
2. for each S-SR an arc from the classification level of the superconcept to the classification level of the concept is added to the multidigraph.

It is important to note that all assertions are taken into account, although they seem redundant or produce conflicts, without any verification. The reason for this is to ensure the use of the greater quantity of information, because the feasibility study of each arc, originated from semantic assertions, before its addition to the multidigraph, could produce a final multidigraph with less quantity of information. Each arc produces some conflict depending on the other arcs of the multidigraph, so if the multidigraph is not complete the decision whether to add or to remove an arc could affect further inclusions or removals of other arcs.

According to the example introduced in figures 1 and 2, from the Hasse diagrams of ordered sets (S_1, $\leq_1$), (S_2, $\leq_2$), and arcs needed to represent assertions (E-SR, People-Person), (E-SR, Unemployed-Unemployed), (E-SR, Student-Student), (S-SR, Employee-Administrative) and (S-SR, Employee-Worker) the multidigraph shown in figure 3 is obtained.

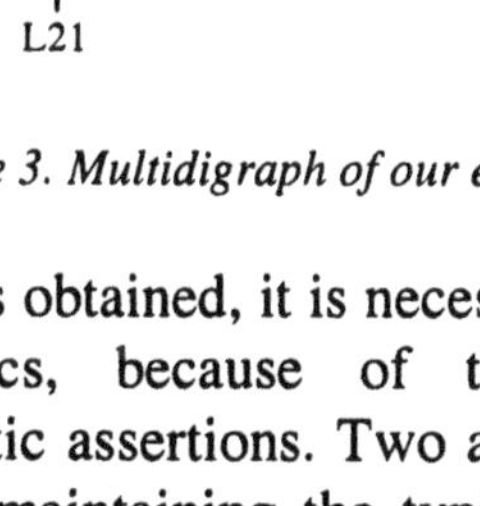

Figure 3. Multidigraph of our example

Once the multidigraph is obtained, it is necessary to analyze it to identify possible incompatible arcs, because of the incorporation of arcs corresponding to all semantic assertions. Two arcs are incompatible if their existence does not permit maintaining the typical characteristics of initial ordered sets. Because an arc can be incompatible with different arcs, and at the same time these arcs can be incompatible with others, it is necessary to use a mechanism to determine which is the more incompatible arc. As a mechanism we use a *penalization* system based on the detection of cycles with more than two participant vertices.

Figures 4 (a) and (b) show the two kinds of cycles that can be detected in a multidigraph. Every arc involved in a cycle has to be penalized. An arc must accumulate as many penalizations as cycles in which it is involved.

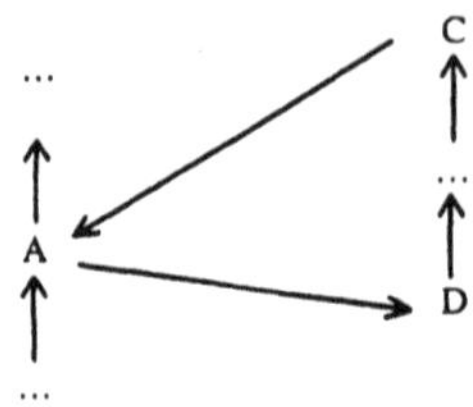

Figure 4. (a) Cycle

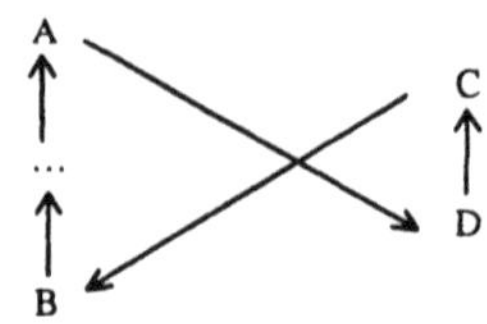

Figure 4. (b) Crossed cycle

Particularly, in the multidigraph of our example, there are the cycles: L11-L12-L22-L11, L12-L13-L22-L12, L11-L12-L13-L22-L11, L22-L23-L12-L22, and L13-L22-L23-L12-L13.

To obtain the FOS from the multidigraph it is necessary to do the following steps:

1. To remove, iteratively, the more penalized arc from the multidigraph. The elimination of an arc implies the updating of the penalization of other arcs that were affected by the existence of the eliminated arc.
2. To replace cycles that have two participant vertices, belonging to different ordered sets, by only one vertex. Two vertices participate in a cycle if $\exists((v1, v2) \wedge (v2, v1))$ where $v1 \in S_i$, $v2 \in S_j$, $i \neq j$.
3. To convert the multidigraph obtained into an ordered set.

After calculating the corresponding penalizations of distinct arcs of the multidigraph shown in figure 3, we obtain the next penalizations: (L22, L12) has 1 penalization, (L22, L11), (L12, L22), (L23, L12) have 2 penalizations and (L13, L22) has 3 penalizations. The arc which must be deleted is (L13, L22), because it is the arc with larger penalization. When arc (L13, L22) is deleted then the penalizations of others arcs change to the penalizations: (L22, L11), (L23, L12) have 1 penalization and (L12, L22) has 2. This time, the arc more penalized is (L12, L22), and after removing it the remaining arcs do not have any penalization. So, the resultant multidigraph is that is in figure 5.

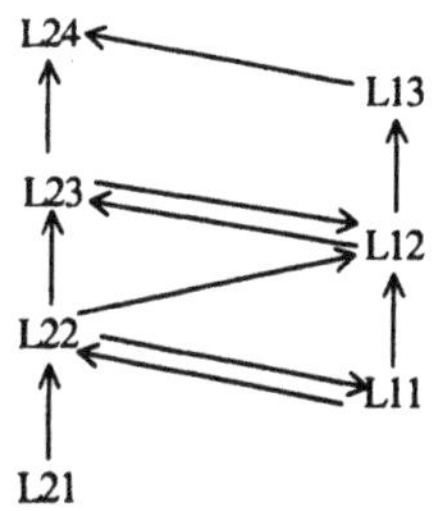

Figure 5. Resultant multidigraph

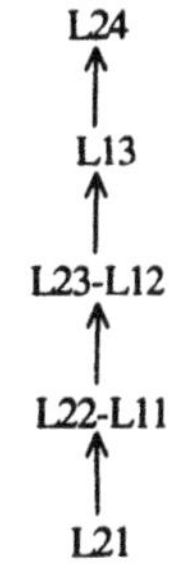

Figure 6. Final digraph

After replacing vertices involved in a cycle by only one vertex, the digraph shown in figure 6 is obtained. It is important to note that arc (L23-L12, L24) is not necessary because they are deduced from the final digraph. So, the obtained digraph defines the FOS to be used by MLS security system of the federation (if it is validated by the administrator), where S_F = {L21, L22-L11, L23-L12, L13, L24}, $|S_F| = 5$ y $\leq_F$ = {(L21, L22-L11), (L22-L11, L23-L12), (L23-L12, L13), (L13, L24)}.

The translation functions f_1 and f_2 obtained through the application of the methodology are defined as:

f_1(L11) = L22-L11, f_1(L12) = L23-L12, f_1(L13) = L13

f_2(L21) = L21, f_2(L22) = L22-L11, f_2(L23) = L23-L12, f_2(L24) = L24

To finalize the CDBs integration process it is necessary to solve the classification of the components of the integrated schemas, taking into account the classifications of the components of the initial schemas and the FOS of classification levels as well as the translation functions obtained. This resolution of classifications has to be carried out by the complemented resolution phase of the schema integration methodology.

4.2 Resolution phase

The resolution phase of the schema integration methodology gets the Federated Schema after the integration of the Export Schemas of the CDBs. By use of the discriminant generalization similar classes are integrated whenever specializations to which they belong are similar too.

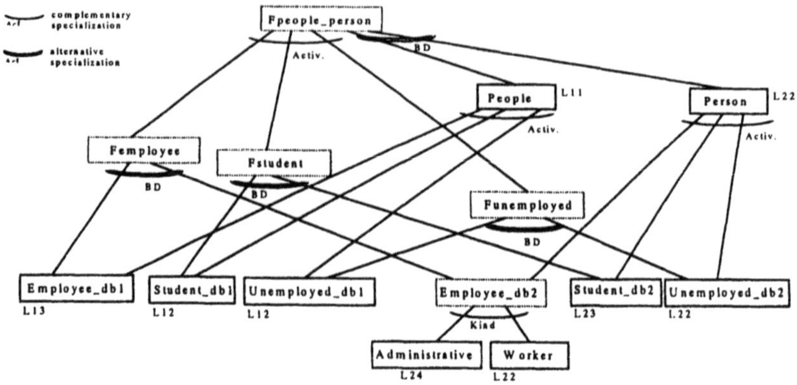

Figure 7. Federated Schema

Taking up again the example in figures 1 and 2, after the resolution phase, the resultant Federated Schema corresponds with the schema shown in figure 7. The class `Employee_db2` has been created as a conformation of CDB1 and CDB2. At the moment, in this schema only the classification of the components of the initial schemas appears.

To classify the Federated Schema taking into account the FOS, it is necessary to perform the following steps:

1. To update the original classifications of Federated Schema components, which already appear in Export Schemas, applying the translation functions obtained in the detection phase.
2. To classify components that were originated by the use of the discriminant generalization, taking into account these conditions:
   a) if the classification levels of all subclasses are the same then the superclass is classified at the same level of the subclasses.
   b) if subclasses are classified at different levels then the superclass is classified at the least confidential level where subclasses are classified.
   c) it is important to note, as a special property of the discriminant generalization, that when a superclass inherits upwards the union of the abstractions of all its subclasses, a multilevel classified superclass is obtained, although classes of CDBs were not multilevel classified. If an abstraction only appears in a subclass then its original classification level is maintained (with the corresponding translation). Otherwise, an abstraction that appears in several subclasses will be upward inherited depending on its semantics. If classification levels of the subclass abstractions are distinct then abstractions are semantically different, so they will be upward inherited as different abstractions (maintaining its classification).

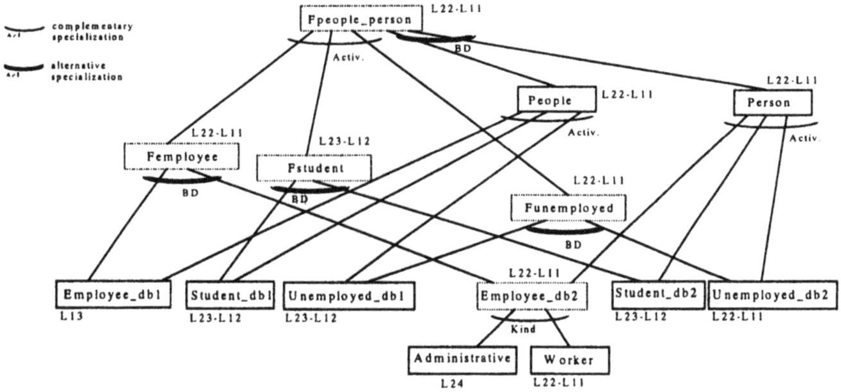

Figure 8. Classified Federated Schema

Figure 8 shows the final result of resolution phase of our security policies integration methodology, where it is possible to see the Federated Schema totally classified according to the FOS.

Although our integration process takes into account only two ordered sets, the integration of a large number of initial ordered sets is done by repeating the same integration process in pairs. The strategy consists in using a ladder integration sequence starting with two ordered sets of the highest cardinality, or two of the larger cardinality, and later, the process is repeated using the FOD obtained from the previous process and one of the larger cardinality among remaining ordered sets ([OS00]).

According to [GQ96], a federated/interoperable system has to comply with the following principles:

1. Principle of autonomy: any access permitted within an individual system must be also permitted under secure interoperation.
2. Principle of security: any access not permitted within an individual system must be also denied under secure interoperation.

Let's see, by an example, how both principles are fulfilled if FDBS uses the classified Federated Schema shown in figure 8. Remembering another time the CDBs introduced in figure 1, a user of the CDB1 having the clearance level L11 can only access class `People`. If the same user, having the same clearance level, was a user of the federation, after applying the corresponding translation function the equivalent clearance level obtained is level L22-L11. So, through the federated system this user can also only access the class `People` (from CDB1). Besides, the same user can access the information of the federation related to `Fpeople_person`, `Femployee`, `Funemployed`, `Person`, `Unemployed_db2`, `Employee_db2`, and `Worker`.

5. COMPARISON WITH OTHER RESEARCH AND CONCLUSIONS

Our security policies integration process methodology allows us to integrate, in a semi-automatic form, different CDBs taking into account data protection. This data protection aspect is only slightly studied in the federated system field. The process of the methodology presented in this paper integrates CDBs that have MLS as security systems, but the main difference with the proposal presented in [IGQ94] is that the integration is performed although ordered sets of classification levels of different systems do not coincide. Besides, as in [IGQ94], the proposed methodology complements a schema integration methodology, so it can offer a very important support to the administrator of a federated system; contrary to the proposals presented in [GQ96, BSS96] where an administrator, or somebody else, has to establish mappings between distinct ordered sets.

References

[BSS96] P.A. Bonatti, M.L. Sapino and V.S. Subrahmanian. Merging Heterogeneous Security Orderings. In E. Bertino, G. Kurth, H. Martella and E. Montolivo, editors, *Computer Security - ESORICS 96 (4th European Symposium on Research in Computer Security, Rome, Italy, September 25-27, 1996, Proceedings)*, volume 1146 of LNCS, pages 183-197, Springer-Verlag, 1996.

[BL75] D.E. Bell and L.J. LaPadula. Secure computer systems: Unified exposition and multics interpretation. Technical Report MTR-2997, (AY/W 020 445), The MITRE Corporation, Bedford, MA, Jul 1975.

[CSGS94] M. Castellanos, F. Saltor and M. García-Solaco: A Canonical Data Model for the Interoperability among Object-Oriented and Relational Databases. In Özsu, Dayal and Valduriez (eds), *Distributed Object Management*, pages 309-314, Morgan Kaufmann,1994.

[DJ94] K.R. Dittrich and D. Jonscher. Current Trends in Database Technology and Their Impact on Security Concepts. In J. Biskup, M. Mongersten and C.E. Landwehr (eds), *Database Security VIII (A-60)*,. Elsevier Science B.V. (North Holland) IFIP, pages 11-33, 1994.

[GQ96] L. Gong and X. Qian. Computational Issues in Secure Interoperation. *IEEE Transactions on Software Engineering*, 22(1):43-51, January 1996.

[GSSC95] M. García-Solaco, F. Saltor and M. Castellanos. A Structure Based Schema Integration Methodology. In *Proc. 11th Int. Conference on Data Engineering*, Taipei. IEEE-CS Press, 1995.

[IGQ94] N.B. Idris, W.A. Gray and M.A. Qutaishat. Integration of Secrecy Features in a Federated Database Environment. In T.F. Keefe and C.E. Landwehr, editors, *Database Security VII (A-47)*, pages 89-109. Elsevier Science B.V. (North-Holland) IFIP, 1994.

[ML92] J.K. Millen and T.F. Lunt. Security for Object-Oriented Database Systems. In *Proceedings of the IEEE Computer Society Symposium on Research in Security and Privacy*, Oakland, California, pages 260-272, May, 1992.

[MLTS92] M. Morgenstern, T. Lunt, B. Thuraisingham and D. Spooner. Security issues in federated database systems: panel contributions. In C.E. Landwehr and S. Jajodia, editors,

Database Security V (A-6): Status and Prospects, pages 131-148. Elsevier Science B.V. (North Holland) IFIP, 1992.

[OS00] M. Oliva & F. Saltor. Integrating Multilevel Security Policies in Multilevel Federated Database Systems. In *Proc. 14th Annual IFIP WG 11.3 Working Conference on Database Security*, Schoorl, The Netherlands, August 21-23, 2000.

[Per93] G. Pernul. Canonical Security Modeling for Federated Databases. In D.K. Hsiao, E.J. Neuhold, and R. Sacks-Davis, editors, *Interoperable Database Systems (DS-5) (A-25)*, pages 207-222. Elsevier Science Publishers B.V. (North-holland) IFIP, 1993

[ROSC97] M.E. Rodríguez, M. Oliva, F. Saltor and B. Campderrich. On Schema and Functional Architectures for Multilevel Secure and Multiuser Model Federated DB Systems. In S. Conrad, W. Hasselbring, A. Heuer, G. Saake, editors, *Proceedings of the International CAiSE'97 Workshop on Engineering Federated Database Systems* (EFDBS'97, Barcelona), Otto-von-Guericke-Universität Magdeburg, Fakultät für Informatik, preprint Nr. 6, pages 93-104, 1997.

[SL90] A.P. Sheth and J.A. Larson. Federated Database Systems for Managing Distributed, Heterogeneous, and Autonomous Databases. *ACM Computing Surveys*, 22(3):183-236, September 1990.

[SM77] D.F. Stanat and D.F. McAllister. *Discrete Mathematics in Computer Science*. Prentice-Hall International Editions, 1977.

CHAPTER 14

Wrappers - A Mechanism to Support State-Based Authorization in Web Applications

Martin S Olivier
Computer Science, Rand Afrikaans University, PO Box 524, Auckland Park, 2006, South Africa
molivier@rkw.rau.ac.za

Ehud Gudes
Mathematics and Computer Science, Ben-Gurion University, Beer-Sheva, 84105, Israel
ehud@cs.bgu.ac.il

Abstract The first premise of this paper is that security should ultimately be associated with an application because application semantics have a direct influence on proper protection. The second premise is that applications are generally too complex to be trusted to implement security as specified by the given security policy. These problems are aggravated if the application operates over normal time and space constraints: The best example of such applications is workflow systems where various actors — possibly from multiple organisations — interact on long transactions to complete a given task.

The solution presented in this paper is an approach referred to as wrappers: a wrapper is a simple program that has enough knowledge about a specific application's potential states and the actions that are permissible in each state. Using this knowledge, it is able to filter requests that should not reach an application at a given point. It is important to note that wrappers are not intended to subsume the security functionality of an application, but serve as an additional check.

The paper presents its concepts in a World-wide Web environment that renders it immediately useful.

1. Introduction

It is generally accepted that security should ideally be based on the concerned application: Only when the application logic is considered, is it possible to precisely determine security-related concerns such as the need-to-know or context sensitive security requirements. Such requirements have most notably been expressed in the workflow context where, for example, someone's authorisation to modify a given document depends on the current state of the workflow process.

Such context-dependent security measures are clearly not restricted to workflow systems. Applications in general exhibit this requirement. As a simple example note that in almost any sensitive application it should not be possible to do any processing before proper user authentication has been performed. Although such a simple requirement seems obvious, it is a generally accepted fact that many complex applications do contain backdoors that enable the developer access to the system without going through the normal authentication procedure [9]. Many forms of attack will also deviate from normal application flow of logic. One well-known attack is to overflow buffers on the stack and so take control of the system. This form of attack was, amongst others, used in the Internet worm [9] and was again recently exposed as vulnerabilities in well-known Microsoft and Netscape products [4].

It is our contention that application-layer security should be part of the design process of any major application and that an appropriate security model should be implemented as part of the application development process. It is, however, a fact that real-world applications are complex by nature and that it is very hard to ensure their correctness in general, and the implementation of their security features in particular. Add to this the fact that application designers are often not security experts and that weak methods are often employed to protect the system (in addition to the fact that the system is complex to protect), concern is indeed warranted.

The option that interests us in the current paper is the possibility to place a 'wrapper' around the application such that the user interface falls outside the wrapper and all communication between the user interface and the application has to occur via this wrapper. In some senses this wrapper is similar to a firewall that protects the internal network of an organisation from the untrusted external network. The wrapper is, however, fundamentally different from a firewall since it is intended to wrap a specific application, possibly even on a single host without any notion of networking.

Such a wrapper is obviously a much smaller system since it does not implement the application logic, but simply forms an additional security layer. Since the wrapper is much simpler, it is much easier to verify that it does indeed implement the required security policies and therefore much easier to trust. In addition, since the primary concern of the wrapper is security, it is natural that it may be developed by security experts rather than application experts that may mean that common pitfalls will be avoided.

Although not the only (or necessarily the best) way to separate the application from its user interface, we shall use a Web browser as the user interface component and HTTP as the communication protocol.

This paper is structured as follows. Section 2 contains background material about HTTP. Section 3 gives an overview of the approach that we present. Section 4 discusses implementation issues associated with our approach. Section

5 compares our approach to existing approaches while section 6 concludes the paper.

2. Background

This paper assumes knowledge of the HTTP protocol. We therefore give a very brief introduction to this protocol. Readers interested in a more detailed treatment are referred to RFC 2616 [8].

The HTTP protocol is used to connect a client (typically a Web browser) to a Web server. It establishes this connection using the TCP/IP protocol suite.

The primary request sent by a browser is a GET request. It may be formulated in a number of ways but the following is typical when programs are to be executed:

```
GET /cgi-bin/program.cgi?param1=val1&param2=val2 HTTP/1.1
HOST: server.domain
```

The requested program is then executed and its output is sent to the browser. The program has a standard mechanism to access the values of parameters sent to it (such as `param1` and `param2` in the example above). The output of the program is typically encoded in HTML and rendered by the browser.

HTTP is a stateless protocol where each request sent from the browser is replied to by the server and then 'forgotten' — ie it does not influence further operation of the protocol. Two mechanisms are typically used to add state information when required. Firstly, cookies may be used. Cookies are short files written to the disk of the client machine; the values of these files can be obtained during subsequent requests and used to establish the current state of a longer interaction. The second mechanism that is commonly used is a session identifier. When a 'session' is initiated, the server sends some unique identifier along with its response such that the identifier will be sent back to it with a subsequent request. This identifier is then passed to and fro between the client and server and used to keep track of the session state.

3. State-based security checking

The application wrapper proposed in this paper is intended to form a layer between the application and the user interface such that the wrapper contains enough information to verify state-based access controls. However, to be useful, it is essential that the wrapper (1) is simple enough that it potentially has a much higher level of trust than the application; and (2) does not have access to any application data, so that if the wrapper is somehow compromised, the attacker has gained very little.

The first goal will be reached by showing that it is possible to produce a generic wrapper that may be configured for any application. Furthermore, it will be shown that this can indeed be done without giving this wrapper access to sensitive information.

To accomplish this consider the data that is required by the wrapper. We will assume that the user interface is a thin client that contains no application specific logic. Requests are passed from this client, through the wrapper to the application, which is implemented as a server. Responses are returned along the same route in the opposite direction.

3.1. Wrappers and Firewalls

Note that wrappers are similar in many ways to application gateway firewalls. Wrappers are, however, (1) intended for a more general class of applications than the services to which application gateways have traditionally been applied, and (2) wrappers are not intended as a defence between an organisation's network and the outside world, but all accesses to a wrapped application are forced to go via its wrapper — even from the most trusted machines on a local network.

3.2. Basic access control

In order to keep the wrapper as simple as possible, we will assume that it is not concerned with authentication: The user is expected to obtain a 'ticket' from an authentication server and present it with every request relayed by the wrapper. For simplicity we will assume that roles are used. Therefore, it is assumed that every request will consist of a (certified) role r and the action q to be performed. How the role will be 'certified' is not important for the discussion of the concept and an explanation of such certification will be delayed until section 4. For the current discussion it is only necessary to assume that an unauthorised user (ie someone who is not authorised to operate in role r) will not be able to obtain such a certification.

If the wrapper has access to a table that contains all valid (role, action) pairs, it is simple for the wrapper to enforce the required checking.

3.3. The single-session case

More challenging than simple access control (and more relevant to the current paper) is enforcement of state-based access control. State-based access controls are useful whenever a partial ordering of actions exist in which they have to be performed. (Consider the example where a customer is expected to supply credit card details *before* being allowed to download software purchased online.)

The set of requests may be purely sequential or may represent a complex partial order set of requests such as is customary in workflow applications (see for example [1]).

The essential question that the wrapper needs to be able to answer is, is some request t valid if it follows a series of requests $t_1, t_2, t_3, \ldots, t_n$? This is, amongst others, a well-known problem addressed by formal languages: given two sentential forms T_1 and T_2 is it possible to derive T_2 from T_1, ie $T_1 \Rightarrow T_2$? Using a grammar for state-based authorisation has been dicussed in detail by Biskup and Eckert [2]. That paper also describes the translation of such specifications to finite automata, that are used by *monitors* to enforce the specifications.

It is obvious that most existing online applications have a very simple state-based security requirement, such as login must precede any further interaction with the application and payment must precede download of purchased items (assuming an online shop that sells 'soft' goods). The grammar based approach has the potential to specify policies such as allow no further interaction from a customer during the current session who has three times specified credit card details that were not accepted by the bank; this may, for example be specified using a grammar such as

$$\begin{array}{lll} \Sigma & \rightarrow & lXPY \\ P & \rightarrow & c|c'c|c'c'c|c'c'c'F \end{array} \quad \text{where} \begin{cases} l \text{ is the login request} \\ X \text{ is any pre-payment request} \\ Y \text{ is the downloading of purchased item} \\ P \text{ is the payment request} \\ c \text{ is an accepted credit card specification} \\ c' \text{ is a denied credit card specification, and} \\ F \text{ is any request that is still allowed after failing} \\ \text{credit card verification, such as logoff} \end{cases}$$

Exactly how a wrapper knows that credit card verification has failed will be discussed below. It is clear from the specification above that 'payment' only succeeds if credit card verification occurs within three attempts.

The example above illustrates a crucial requirement of wrappers: it is essential to keep the wrapper synchronised with the application. Since the wrapper is explicitly barred from accessing application data, a wrapper may allow an operation that is denied by the application. Therefore the wrapper needs to be able to monitor responses from the application to the client. The wrapper now proceeds as depicted in figure 1.

3.4. The multi-session case

Thus far we have only considered 'transactions' that occur within a single session. The ultimate challenge is to handle 'long transactions' that span multiple sessions (and that are potentially executed by more than one user). This scenario is typical of workflow applications where one user submits a claim during one session. During a subsequent session an approver works sequentially through submitted claims and either approves or denies them. Finally, during a third session, the cashier looks at approved claims and issues cheques.

In order to handle long transactions it becomes necessary to associate a transaction identifier t with each long transaction. It is obviously necessary to set and modify t when required: consider the approver who looks at one transaction after the other — each time a different transaction is involved, and

```
while (true)
  acceptrequest(ρ_i) with ρ_i = (r_i, q_i)
  if q_i is not acceptable in current state or r_i is not allowed to request q_i then
    send 'reject' to client
  else
    send ρ_i to application
    receive response a from application
    if a.success then
      append q_i to log // state successfully exited
      enter new state based on q_i
    else
      append q'_i to log // alternative state used
      if q'_i is not acceptable in current state then
        send 'reject' to client; send 'abort' to application
      else
        enter new state based on q'_i
```

Figure 1. Pseudocode for wrapper

whether the transaction is a candidate for approval depends on the state of the particular transaction. Obtaining t may be accomplished by identifying all requests (to the wrapper) which may lead to an updated value of t; t may be extracted from a parameter that accompanies a request and/or determined from the response $a.transaction$ that the algorithm above is now expected to return.

An interesting point to note is that a user's behaviour may now be governed by two distinct state-oriented policies. To illustrate, consider the familiar claim example. When the client logs onto the claim system, the system may assign a transaction identifier to this specific claim. From this point on the actions of the client are governed by the rules for claim submission. Suppose that the client completes submission of the claim, is the client now permitted to look at the status of another claim during the same session? This is clearly a session-state issue rather than a transaction-state issue.

We propose the following solution. Firstly, rules for transactions are specified. For the claim example this may involve specifying the sequence for submitting and subsequently approving the claim, until it is eventually settled. Different 'sessions' may then be identified. For this example a 'client session' may, for example, be specified as a session initiated by a client login request, which may then be followed by a request to initiate submission or a status request. The submission or status request is governed by the rules for the transaction, rather than the session. Consider

$$\begin{array}{rcl} \Sigma & \rightarrow & m_c T_c \\ T_c & \rightarrow & c \oplus | s \oplus \end{array} \quad \text{where} \left\{ \begin{array}{l} m_c \text{ is a client menu request} \\ T_c \text{ is a client transaction} \\ c \text{ is the first step of a claim submission} \\ s \text{ is the first step of a status query; and} \\ \oplus \text{ is discussed below} \end{array} \right.$$

$\oplus$ is used in the specification above to indicate that the preceding request (c or

s) is the start of a sequence that will be governed by a transaction specification. This implies that a transaction has to be identified by c and s.

Note that it is simple to modify the session specification to $\Sigma \rightarrow m_c T_c^*$ or even $\Sigma \rightarrow (m_c T_c)^*$ to express different policies.

At this point it becomes necessary to consider ordinary transactions. Consider an on-line banking application where a client selects an account from which money is to be transferred with one request and an account to which the money should be transferred with a subsequent request. If the session fails at this point, it is unlikely that the application will allow the client to continue from this point at a (significantly) later stage: The basic actions are likely to be grouped into a transaction that are to be executed as a unit. The question is whether the wrapper needs to be aware of such transactions. We argue that it is not the case, as long as the wrapper knows where a new session is allowed to start: In the case of the banking example, a session is allowed to start at the first account selection and nowhere else. We foresee that session specifications will often be used merely to indicate such possible starting points.

Note that the rules for transaction state access control will typically not be provided as a grammar by the security officer, but may be automatically derived from the workflow specification.

4. Implementation

The use of the Web as a means to implement various applications has increased tremendously over the last number of years. In addition, the separation between user interface (in a browser) and an application server (as required by our approach) is indeed present in the Web environment.

4.1. Filtering messages

It is relatively simple to write a wrapper that relays (filters) requests between the client and application as required for wrappers.

To illustrate the operation of a wrapper in the Web environment, consider the claim example again. The specification in figure 2 is not intended as an illustration of a specification language, but rather to make some of the issues previously discussed more concrete.

Lines beginning with a hash (#) are intended as comments. The initial section of the configuration specifies all messages (or requests), along with the parameters that are employed. The *role* parameter is implicit in all messages and not shown. It will be discussed below.

When a parameter is marked with an asterisk (such as `transaction*` with `view-a-claim`), it means that this value is not directly provided by the user, but is typically retrieved from a response to a previous message. In the example case `view-a-claim` is preceded by a `view-claims` message. The intention is that

```
MESSAGES
# Messages for claiming
  client-welcome         ()
  view-form              (session, transaction*)
  submit-claim           (session, transaction, incident, amount)
# Messages for approval
  admin-welcome          ()
  view-claims            (session)
  view-a-claim           (session, transaction*)
  approve-claim          (session, transaction)
  deny-claim             (session, transaction)
# Messages for payment
  view-approved-claims   (session)
  view-an-approved-claim (session, transaction*)
  issue-cheque           (session, transaction)

TRANSACTIONS
             -> Submission Approval Payment
  Submission -> view-form submit-claim
  Approval   -> view-a-claim { approve-claim | deny-claim end }
  Payment    -> view-an-approved-claim issue cheque end

SESSIONS
# Claim session
    -> client-welcome view-form...
# Approval session
    -> admin-welcome { view-claims view-a-claim... }*
# Payment session
    -> admin-welcome { view-approved-claims view-an-approved-claim... }*
```

Figure 2. Illustrative wrapper specification

the response to the `view-claims` message is a list of claims ready for approval, together with their associated (long) transaction identifiers. Therefore, when the user clicks on a particular claim, the form is composed so that the 'selected' transaction identifier is sent as a parameter with the `view-a-claim` message.

We assume that the selected names of messages are clear enough for the reader to interpret. However, keep in mind that the names refer to messages, not screens. Therefore an approver may look at a screen of claims ready for approval; when the approver clicks on one such claim, the `view-a-claim` request is sent and this is followed by a screen with claim details. On this screen the approver may click on approve or deny

The transaction rules should also be self-explanatory for this simple example. Note that this specification is rather inflexible and that more flexibility will be required for real-world applications. We contend that our approach is capable

eavesdropper. A similar argument shows that it cannot be misappropriated between the user and the wrapper or the wrapper and the application if encryption is used. It is obviously simple for the wrapper (and the application) to verify the authenticity of the role identifier by using the authentication server's public key. Note that this approach presents a simplified version of *secure cookies* as presented by Park *et al* [13], but avoids the use of cookies.

4.3. Wrapper and Application Relationship

A major issue in the proposed scheme is the extraction of the state based behaviour from the application in order to specify it precisely for the wrapper. If one uses an external tool for such specification one runs the danger of creating inconsistencies between the application and the wrapper, and maintaining the wrapper specifications in case the application changes. An automatic or semi-automatic tool is much more desirable.

Let us assume that the application consists of a set of CGI scripts. There are several alternatives to generate the state-role/action sequences. Usually, such CGI scripts are very simple and as was explained above retrieve commands sent to them using GET or POST using some explicit mechanism. The semi-automatic scheme we propose involves the insertion, *by the application developer* statements which specify the desired role for each such GET/POST. In addition the application developer can insert statements that assert that some condition has been met (eg `assert user_logged_on`) in some scripts where this condition has indeed been met and state that the condition is required to execute other scripts (eg `require user_logged_on`). (Such statements may be handled by a pre-processor.) Then a simple program-flow analyzer can generate all the possible sequences of action/role pairs. Later on the application developer will need to maintain only such CGI scripts.

Another possibility is to write a simple parser which will scan the CGI scripts and for each GET/POST it finds will inquire the application developer for the relevant role/action pair. Then the generation of possible sequences will be done as mentioned before. Yet, another possibility is to develop a high-level tool for specifying states and actions (similar to State-charts [10] or Petri-nets [1]) and from that tool to *automatically* generate both the state-based sequences and skeletons for the CGI scripts required by the application.

5. Comparison with other work

The Wrappers idea is related to several other works which appeared in recent years. The idea of extracting security policies from an application and enforce and maintain them separately has appeared before. In [11] it is argued that in a distributed object environment, one cannot leave the security enforcement to monolithic components such as DBMSs. Since usually in such systems requests go through mediators or brokers like CORBA or DCOM we should associate security enforcement with these mediators. [11] is very general and does not go into the details of what kind of authorization should be handled by the brokers and what should remain with the application or DBMS.

Our work differs from that of Biskup and Eckert cited earlier [2] since (1) a greater emphasis is placed on isolation of the wrapper; (2) transactions where multiple subjects cooperate are considered; and (3) it is set in the Web context.

The DOK system for federated databases proposed by Tari [15] has a complex structure of agents enforcing security on behalf of the individual application or local DBMS (he even uses the term "Wrapper" but for translating global to local requests only). Our wrapper on the other hand is quite simple but has a focused goal — providing state-based security for Web-based applications. Therefore, issues such as translating queries are not handled by it.

The TIHI project by Wiederhold *et al* [16] is quite close to our ideas. It uses an object called "Security Mediator" for enforcing the security policies of a Web-based medical application. It is also implemented using CGI scripts. It is however, application specific, and not generic like our wrapper. It also handles all authorization and not only the state-based.

Another paper on Role-based security by Demurjian *et al* [6] is also related to our work. They suggest the concept of an OSA (Object Security Officer) which separates an object from the outside world like a firewall. However their OSA is linked to the application object much tighter than our wrapper, since it invokes the object methods directly.

Finally, in our own work on workflow security [7, 12] we showed how we can specify and enforce history and dynamic authorization rules. All the authorization is done by the workflow security administrator object. Thus it is tightly coupled with the workflow specification. Again, the Wrapper idea here is not as tightly coupled with the application. It must be synchronized with it with respect to the major states and roles but it still leaves data dependent and dynamic authorization checks to the application.

6. Conclusion

This paper has presented an approach to reinforce application security in an environment such as the Web by introducing another layer of defence between the firewall and the application itself. It is important to remember that this layer is not intended to remove any responsibility from either the firewall or the application, but rather provide additional security.

It has been demonstrated that the concept is indeed simple — a requirement for trust — and can be based on a simple configuration approach. The paper has not investigated suitable specification approaches in any detail but merely posited that it should be possible to either specify the wrapper's behaviour manually for a simple application (such as many current online stores) or to create a tool that will automatically derive a specification from others such as those used for workflow systems in general. This remains to be verified.

Further, exactly how the specification is converted to a wrapper has not been considered in detail in this paper. Much work has been done over many years to generate parsers for arbitrary grammars and this should therefore be simple.

References

[1] V Atluri and WK Huang, "An extended petri net model for supporting workflow in a multilevel secure environment," in P Samarati and RS Sandhu, *Database Security X: Status and Prospects*, Chapman & Hall, 1997, pp. 240–258.

[2] J Biskup and C Eckert, "About the Enforcement of State Dependent Security Specifications," in TF Keefe and CE Landwehr (eds), *Database Security VII*, Elsevier, 1994, 3–17

[3] F Casati, S Ceri, B Pernici, G Pozz, "Conceptual Modelling of Workflows" *Proc. of the Object-oriented and Entity-Relationship Conf.*, Australia, 1995.

[4] CERT, *Buffer Overflow in MIME-aware Mail and News Clients*, CERT Advisory CA-98.10, 1998

[5] W Ford and MS Baum, Secure Electronic Commerce: Building the Infrastructure for Digital Signatures and Encryption, Prentice Hall, 1997

[6] SA Demurjian, TC Ting and M Saba, "Agent approaches to enforce Role-based security in distributed and web-based computing," Proceedings IFIP WG 11.3 Workshop on Database Security, Seattle, Washington, 1999, pp. 65-77.

[7] E Gudes, MS Olivier and RP van de Riet, "Modelling, Specifying and implementing workflow security in Cyberspace", Journal of Computer Security, *Journal of Computer Security*, 7, 4, 287–315, 1999

[8] R Fielding, J Gettys, J Mogul, H Frystyk, L Masinter, P Leach, T Berners-Lee, *Hypertext Transfer Protocol – HTTP/1.1.* RFC 2616, Internet Society

[9] S Garfinkel and G Spafford, *Practical Unix & Internet Security, 2nd ed,* O'Reilly, 1996

[10] D Harel and M Politi, *Modeling Reactive Systems with Statecharts: the STATEMATE Approach,* McGraw-Hill, 1998

[11] CD McCollum, DB Faatz, WR Herndon, EJ Sebes, RK Thomas, "Distributed object technologies databases and security", proceedings IFIP WG 11.3 Workshop on Database Security, Lake Tahoe, Ca. 1997, pp. 17–33.

[12] MS Olivier, RP van de Riet and E Gudes "Specifying Application-level Security in Workflow Systems," in R Wagner (ed), *Proceedings of the Ninth International Workshop on Security of Data Intensive Applications (DEXA 98)*, 346–351, IEEE, 1998

[13] J Park, R Sandhu and S Ghanta, "RBAC on the Web by secure cookies," Proceedings IFIP WG 11.3 Workshop on Database Security, Seattle, Washington, 1999, pp. 41-54.

[14] LD Stein, *Web Security: A Step-by-Step Reference Guide*, Addison-Wesley, 1998

[15] Z Tari, "Designing security agents for the DOK federated system," Proceedings IFIP WG 11.3 Workshop on Database Security, Lake Tahoe, Ca. 1997, pp. 35-59

[16] G Wiederhold, M Billelo and C Donahue,, "Web implementation of a security mediator for medical databases," Proceedings IFIP WG 11.3 Workshop on Database Security, Lake Tahoe, Ca. 1997, pp. 60-72.

CHAPTER 15

An Integrated Framework for Database Privacy Protection

LiWu Chang and Ira S. Moskowitz
Center for High Assurance Computer Systems, Naval Research Laboratory, Washington, DC

Key words: database inference, Bayesian network, similarity measure, information reduction, restoration

Abstract: One of the central objectives of studying database privacy protection is to protect sensitive information held in a database from being inferred by a generic database user. In this paper, we present a framework to assist in the formal analysis of the database inference problem. The framework is based on an association network which is composed of a similarity measure and a Bayesian network model.

1. INTRODUCTION

As the information explosion has grown, so has the trend of data sharing and information exchange also grown. Accordingly, privacy concerns have reached a critical level [13]. In his report [1], Anderson stated that the combination of birth date and post code (zip code) with data from a health database is sufficient to identify 98% of the UK population! It is certainly a concern for the Icelandic patients' database [11]. Many existing efforts (e.g., [10][11]) have been geared towards the hiding of stored data items and access control. It has been shown that even if the sensitive personal information is hidden, it can be derived from publicly accessible data by means of inference [2][5][14][15][16][17][21][22]. Denning [6] categorized several different types of attacks and analyzed the protection methods where query returns are statistical quantities (e.g., mean, variance). Hinke's work on deterministically chained related attributes shows how the information can be obtained from non-obvious links [9]. Duncan [5][22] presented cell suppression techniques where the marginal probability distributions are preserved by disturbing the probability mass of component variables. Sweeney's work applies the aggregation operation to the merge of the attribute values [20].

We wish to put the inference problem upon a firm theoretical foundation. The main contribution of this paper is to categorize and discuss inference from different perspectives and represent those different views in a coherent framework. Among the above mentioned approaches, ours and [5] are similar in that both attempt to minimize the information loss for a database user. The difference is that our protection method evaluates values of each data item. At the core of our model a structured representation of probabilistic dependency among attributes is adopted.

Summarizing from previous work, we envision two perspectives of inference characterized by attribute properties. One perspective is about the probabilistic correlation among attributes. A complimentary perspective is that of individuality which emphasizes the uniqueness of each individual data item. For the former, a *Bayesian network* [18] can be used to model correlation relationships among attributes. Let attributes whose information we wish to protect be the *target attributes*. Based on this model, one can evaluate the potential impact that impinges upon a target attribute from information about other attributes, and decide the pertinent protection strategies accordingly. Although the probabilistic method is useful in describing the likelihood of the occurrence of an attribute value, it may be ineffective for identifying which attribute value is unique to a data item. This uniqueness can be deemed as the individuality of a data item. To protect such an attribute value, it is necessary to determine whether other attribute values, or their combinations, provide the same amount of information as the special one does to the data item. Thus, the identification of individuality is separate from the probabilistic correlation analysis. The proposed framework is the first to integrate these two perspectives.

2. POLICY

We use data modification to ensure high privacy protection. Our concerns are that a user (authorized for limited data access) might be able to combine his/her information with other users, or to simply generate inferences on his/her own, to glean knowledge about data that they should not have access to. Of course we are not concerned with the data originator learning this information. Our privacy policy can be phrased as follows:

- No sensitive information can be inferred from publicly released data.

- No false information is added to the database to increase privacy protection.

Of course we are still allowing ourselves to hide data to increase privacy protection --- we are only disallowing erroneous data. Since protection always involves a certain level of modification to the data, some statistical properties of a database will inevitably be affected --- this is good for privacy concerns but bad for functionality. Our proposed model will incorporate dynamic changes as a result of new attributes being added and new data being collected.

3. INFERENCE

What information needs to be protected in a database? Consider the example medical database as shown in Table 1, where attributes "address", "age" and "occupation" are the basic personal information, and "hepatitis", "mental depression", "AIDS" and "thyroid (function)" are the personal medical records. It is certain information about the unique user identification number "uid" that we wish to protect (AIDS, suicide, etc.). Our proposed model (referred to as an *association network*) is composed of two components. One component is based on the probabilistic causal network model. The other component describes the functional dependency or the similarity relationships.

Table 1: Data set

uid	addr	age	occup	hepatitis	mental depr.	AIDS	thyroid
1	FC1	67	md	n	norm	N	n
2	Al1	83	mil	y	dep	N	1
3	TC1	43	lwy	y	dep	Y	1
4	An1	19	aca	y	dep	Y	1
5	WA1	54	pol	y	dep	N	n
6	Al2	28	con	n	norm	N	n
7	Re1	34	lwy	y	norm	N	n
8	An2	32	con	y	dep	Y	1
9	FC1	39	aca	y	dep	Y	1
10	FC2	44	pol	n	norm	N	n
11	WA2	66	mil	n	dep	N	1
12	An1	23	md	y	norm	N	n
13	TC2	34	con	n	norm	N	n
14	WA3	50	pol	y	dep	Y	1

15	Re2	28	con	n	dep	N	l
16	WA4	47	lwy	n	norm	N	n
17	An3	92	aca	n	dep	N	l
18	Re2	28	lwy	y	dep	Y	n
19	TC3	49	mil	n	dep	N	l
20	Al3	32	aca	y	norm	N	n

3.1 Identification of Similar Attributes

To prevent inference attacks, information such as a person's name should automatically be removed from the database. However, the removal of the name attribute is hardly adequate. Other attributes, such as a person's address, may reveal essentially the same information and thus, should also be hidden from general users. Consider two attributes in a database and the natural relation given between their attribute values. If this relation is "close" to being a bijection then we say that the attributes are *similar*. In Table 2 we see the relation between "uid" and "address". If one "uid" corresponds to one "address" value, then "address" is congruent to "uid", this is not the case. However, the mapping between the two is almost a bijection so they are similar (only three addresses correspond to more than one uid, and in those cases they correspond to two uids). Intuitively, the less the spread of the frequency count shown in the table, the higher the similarity between the target and the candidate attributes.

Table 2: address vs. uid

	1	2	3	4	5	6	7	8	9	10	11	12	13	14	15	16	17	18	19	20
FC1	1								1											
Al1		1																		
TC1			1																	
An1				1								1								
WA1					1															
Al2						1														
Re1							1													
An2								1												
FC2										1										
WA2											1									
TC2													1							
WA3														1						
Re2															1			1		
An3																	1			
WA4																1				
TC3																			1	
Al3																				1

The criterion of determining which attributes are similar to the target attribute is quantified in terms of our information theoretical rule.

Definition 1. (Dispersion V)

$$V_i = -\sum_{j=1}^{N} Pr(t_j|c_i)\log(Pr(t_j|c_i)); \quad V = \left(\sum_{i=1}^{M} V_i\right)/M$$

where N and M stand for the number of attribute values of the target attribute T (with values t_j) and candidate attribute C (with values c_i), respectively. V_i is the dispersion measure of the ith attribute value of C, and V gives the total dispersion measure with normalization. A low V score is the selection criteria for similar. Similar attributes are the ones that we want to modify because they give us inference about the target attribute. In terms of the frequentist's view, we have $Pr(t_j|c_i)=n_{ij}/n_i$, where n_{ij} denotes the frequency count at the ith row and jth column, and n_i is the sum of the ith row. Note that the range of this dispersion measure is from 0 to $\log N$. The minimum occurs when only one entry in each row has a non-zero value. The maximum happens when the mass n_i is evenly distributed over ALL attribute values of T. Given that T="uid" the V-score for C="address" (Table 2) is 3/17=0.18. Note that if the V-score of a candidate attribute C is less than 1, then there exists V_i-scores of C that are equal to 0, for some i. Attribute values that correspond to low V_i-scores are subject to modification.

A candidate attribute can be a combination of several attributes. For instance, the combination of "address" and "mental depression" can uniquely identify each item in the Table 1. Figure 12 shows such a combination. The fact is that a merge of several attributes with high V-scores can yield a low V-score. Using V-scores an indicator, the proposed search evaluates possible combinations of different attributes until a bijection with the target attribute is reached, or a desired V-score is reached. Attributes or their combination with low V-scores are stored.

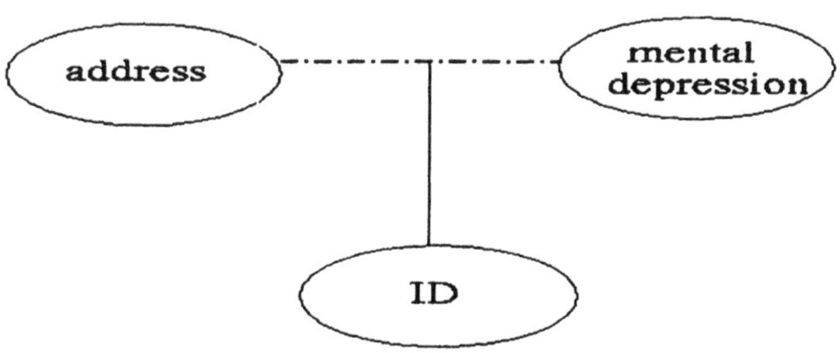

Figure 12: Example of Combination of Attributes. A node represents an attribute. The dashed line denotes the combination and the straight line denotes the similarity relationship.

3.2 Computation of Probabilistic Impact

The analysis of the probabilistic dependency is based on a Bayesian net representation ([8][18]). As shown in Figure 13, either "AIDS" or "thyroid" leads to "mental depression", while "hepatitis" and "mental depression" support the diagnosis of "AIDS". Thus, "AIDS" can be inferred from information about "hepatitis" and "mental depression". Note that attributes about a person's background are not included in this figure because of the low statistical significance due to their large sets of attribute values.

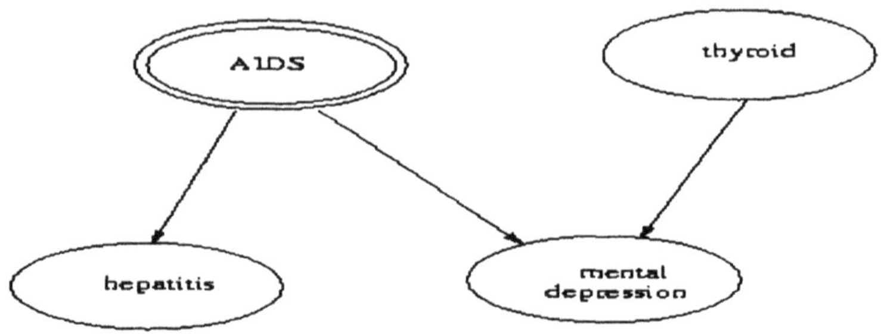

Figure 13: Architecture of a Bayesian network. An attribute is denoted by a node. An arrow indicates the probabilistic dependency between the two attributes. A double circle denotes information associated with the attribute is confidential.

As mentioned earlier, the combination of "address" and "mental depression" will lead to the identification of "uid". Thus, one may able to infer about whether a particular person contracts AIDS by joining together the information from Figure 12 and Figure 13. The joined network is shown in Figure 14. To prevent the potential association of "uid" and "AIDS", information, in particular, "mental depression" (since it contributes to both networks) must be reduced. To protect sensitive information, strategies of blocking and aggregation are used.

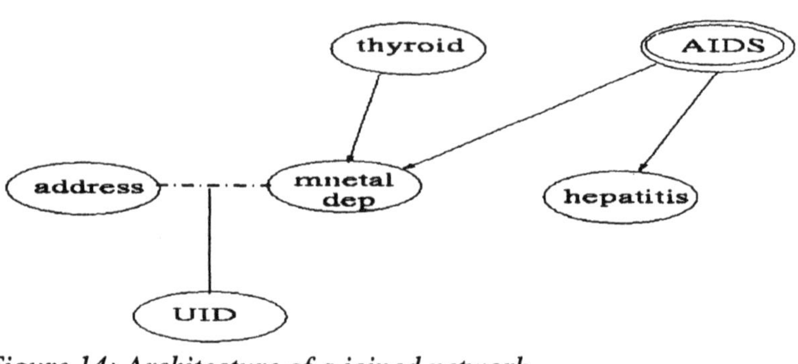

Figure 14: Architecture of a joined network

4. INFORMATION REDUCTION

In this paper, we consider the database modification strategies of blocking and merging. The purpose of modification is to mitigate database inference.

4.1 Reduction range

To give an objective quantitative description of the extent to which users are willing to tolerate the potential error induced from database modification, we invoke a quality index (QI) of a database. QI is generated during the data collection phase. It is represented as the logarithm (base 2) of the sample probability in our analysis:

Definition 2. (QI) $QI \equiv log(Pr(D|\boldsymbol{m}))$,

where D denotes the data set and $\boldsymbol{m}$ denotes a model. If $\boldsymbol{m}$ is a Bayesian network model **Bn** then QI will be log $Pr(D|\boldsymbol{Bn})$. QI is viewed as the lower bound of the level of tolerance, below which the validity of inference drawn from the modified database is in doubt. The operation range is defined in terms of the rate of change, γ.

Definition 3. (Ratio of Reduction)
$\gamma \equiv |QI\_\{original\} - QI\_\{modified\}| / |QI\_\{original\}|$

For instance, if the original QI is -60 and the QI of the modified database is -63, then the allowed rate of change, γ, is 5%. Our assumption is that the estimated inherent error in the original data and the tolerance measure of how much we are allowed to perturb the data are tied together in some underlying basic manner.

4.2 Blocking

The approach of blocking is implemented by replacing certain attribute values of some data items with a question mark --- this indicates total ignorance of the preference [2]. The set of attribute values that maximally change the posterior probability of the desired target value $Pr(T=tj|Dm,\boldsymbol{Bn})$, with respect to the modified database Dm and the given $\boldsymbol{Bn}$, are chosen for blocking. If the modification can cause drastic change to the present belief, it should be considered for hiding. The modification will stop when the change reaches beyond the specified γ.

Claim 1. The QI, $log(Pr(D|\boldsymbol{Bn}))$, is monotonically decreasing as more attribute values are blocked.

As an example, let the allowed rate of change γ be 3%. From Table 1, the 3% change of QI whose value changes from log(Pr(D|$\boldsymbol{Bn}$))=-38.85 to log(Pr(Dm|$\boldsymbol{Bn}$))=-40 can be best achieved by modifying
Data item 3: "hepatitis" = "y" as well as Data item 4: "mental depression" ="dep". The result of the released database is shown in Table 3. Since modification inevitably weakens the probabilistic dependency, it may lead to the change of network topology ***Bn***. Thus, the causal dependency of the target also needs to be re-evaluated.

Table 3: medical records released to generic users

hepatitis	n	y	?	y	y	n	y	y	y	n	n	y	n	y	n	n	n	y	n	y
mental	n	d	d	?	d	n	n	d	d	n	d	n	n	d	d	n	d	d	d	n
AIDS	?	?	?	?	?	?	?	?	?	?	?	?	?	?	?	?	?	?	?	?
thyroid	n	l	l	l	n	n	n	l	l	n	l	n	n	l	l	n	l	n	l	n

4.3 Aggregation

We apply an aggregation operation [17] for combining different values of an attribute of low *Vi*-score. Aggregation may be done according to the known taxonomic structure imposed on attribute values (e.g., home address with respect to zip code). One example is shown in Table 4, where home addresses of Table 1 are merged into larger districts lexicographically.

Table 4: merge of attribute values

	1	2	3	4	5	6	7	8	9	10	11	12	13	14	15	16	17	18	19	20
FC	1								1	1										
Al		1				1														1
TC			1										1						1	
An				1				1				1					1			
WA					1						1			1		1				
Re							1								1			1		

Aggregation amounts to the reduction of the complexity of a probability space spanned by attributes [7] and therefore, increases the statistical significance [4]. For the number of attribute values changing from 17 to 6, the threshold of the confidence region is given by a finite number that is 11.1 with the confidence level 0.95 based on chi-square estimation. In the absence of such structure, the concept clustering method with clustering criterion based on Pr(***Bn***|*Dm*) will be used as the selection criterion.

5. ASSOCIATION NETWORK

As discussed, different data analysis methods are used in light of the different statistical properties of attributes. We integrate the similarity relation and its related taxonomy structure [18] with probabilistic causal (Bayesian) to form what we call an association network as in Figure 15. It provides the basis for privacy protection analysis. We envision the following steps for generation.

- Conduct the similarity selection and Bayesian network induction. Attributes with low *V*-score will have their values be either aggregated to increase significance level or replaced with pseudo-code.
- Evaluate impact on target attributes from other attributes in association networks.
- Modify attribute values according to a calculated priority.
- After modification, (randomly) check if other combinations still violate the privacy protection criterion.

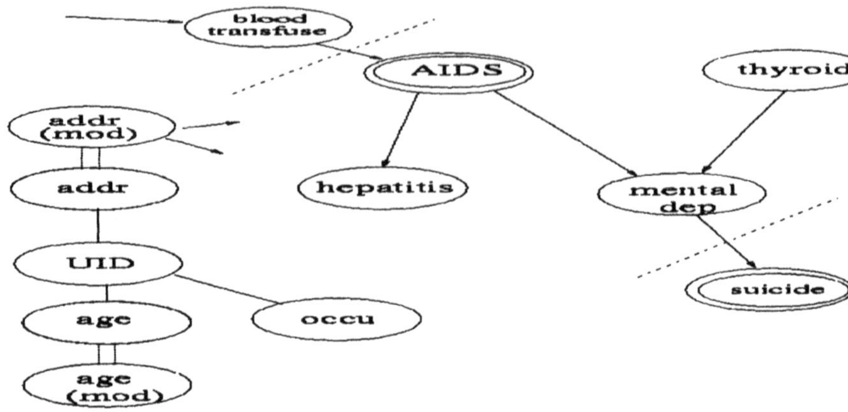

Figure 15: Association network model. The double-dashed line denotes an aggregated attribute. The aggregated attribute may have probabilistic dependency with other attributes. Attributes outside the dashed line are not included in the current database.

5.1 Restoration

It is possible to (partially) restore hidden attribute values if the information of the underlying Bayesian network structures of the database are known – this is the worst case to defend against. As in [2][8][12], the restoration approach primarily selects the set of instantiation **x** to the hidden values with respect to log Pr(*Dm*{**x**}|***Bn***) for *Dm.* With data of Table 3, one could obtain the values of "AIDS" shown in *Table 5.* Note that the two blockings (i.e., data items 3 and 4) are also correctly restored to their original states.

Table 5: restored medical records

hepatitis	n	y	y	y	y	n	y	y	y	n	n	y	n	y	N	n	n	y	n	y
mental	n	d	d	d	d	n	n	d	d	n	d	n	n	d	D	n	d	d	d	n
AIDS	n	y	y	y	n	n	n	y	y	n	y	n	n	y	Y	n	n	y	n	n
thyroid	n	l	l	l	n	n	n	l	l	n	l	n	n	l	L	n	l	n	l	n

Changes of the "AIDS" values occur in three places - a reasonably good guess, but a bad outcome for privacy protection. If the number of blockings increases to 4 with "mental depression" of data items 3, 8, 14 and 18 being blocked, the restoration is disrupted. The result is shown in Table 6, where changes in the restored values of "AIDS" increase to seven, a fairly random outcome. In general, to ensure no restoration, one needs to modify associated causes and evaluate their ramifications [3]. We will consider the combined strategy with respect to the constraint γ.

Table 6: restored from more blocking

hepatitis	n	y	y	y	y	n	y	y	y	n	n	y	n	y	N	n	n	y	n	y
mental	n	d	?	d	d	n	n	?	d	n	d	n	n	?	D	n	d	?	d	n
AIDS	n	y	n	y	n	n	n	n	y	n	y	n	n	n	Y	n	n	n	n	n
thyroid	n	l	l	l	n	n	n	l	l	n	l	n	n	l	L	n	l	n	l	n

5.2 Effectiveness Evaluation

The result of blocking will push the target probability toward the uniform distribution. In fact,

Claim 3. The entropy measure of T with $\Pr(T|Dm,\boldsymbol{Bn})$ is monotonically increasing w.r.t. blockings.

This property is in tune with our intuition that uniformity gives maximal entropy, while specificity gives minimal entropy. The evaluation of the effectiveness of modification in our framework is carried out by cross-validation over *Dm* where effectiveness is measured in terms of the error rate $Ucf(e,s)$ [19], meaning the chance of having e errors with s test data at the confidence level *cf*. For instance, in Table 3, with 3 misclassified test data and 7 test data, the predicted error rate, $Ucf(3,7)$, is 0.43 at cf=10%. The result means that if the error rate is high, the network model is unreliable and thus, the inference is mitigated.

6. CONCLUSION

Our results suggest that database privacy protection requires extensive evaluation and analysis of data relationships. Our model requires two-tier processing. First, a similarity analysis is carried out for examining similar attributes. The second tier is based on the probabilistic dependency analysis of attributes. Blocking and aggregation are used to prevent inference. Inference is analyzed with an association network, which consists of the probabilistic dependency structure, the taxonomy structure and the similarity measure. This provides a unified framework for database inference analysis.

Acknowledgements We thank the anonymous reviewers for their helpful comments and suggestions.

References

[1] Anderson, R. (1998) "http://www.cl.cam.ac.uk/simrja14/caldicott/caldicott.html".
[2] Chang, L. & Moskowitz, I. S. (1998) "Bayesian Methods Applied to the Database Inference Problem," Database Security XII (ed. Jajodia), pp. 237-251, Kluwer.
[3] Chang, L. & Moskowitz, I. S. (2001) "Analysis of Database Inference," in preparation.
[4] Cowan, G. (1998) "Statistical Data Analysis," Clarendon Press.
[5] Duncan, G. (1995) "Restricted Data versus Restricted Access,"In Seminar on New Directions in Statistical Methodology, OMB, pp 43-56.
[6] Denning, D. & Neumann, P. (1985) "Requirements and Model for IDES-A Real-Time Intrusion-Detection Expert System," # 83F83-01-00 CS SRI International.
[7] Freidman, J. (1996) "On Bias, Variance, 0&1 - Loss, and the Curse-of-Dimensionality,"Data Mining and Knowledge Discovery, 1, 55-77.
[8] Heckerman D. (1996) "Bayesian Networks for Knowledge Discovery," Advances in Knowledge Discovery and Data Mining, AAAI Press/MIT Press, pp. 273-305.
[9] Hinke, T., Delugach, H. & Wolf, R. (1997) "Protecting Databases from Inference Attack," Computers & Security, Vol. 16, No. 8, pp 687-708.
[10] HIPAA (1999) The Health Insurance Portability and Accountability Act seminar, NY.
[11] Iceland Database (1999) "http://www.decode.is/ppt/protection/index.htm".
[12] Kong, A., Liu, J. & Wong, W. (1994) "Sequential Imputation and Bayesian Missing Data Problems," Journal of ASA, Vol. 89, No. 425, pp 278-288.
[13] Lewis, P. (2000) book review "Losing Privacy in the Age of the Internet" (author Garfinkle) New York Times, Feb. 10, 2000.
[14] Lin, T.Y., Hinke, T.H., Marks, D.G., & Thuraisingham, B. (1996) "Security and Data Mining," Database Security Vol. 9: Status and Prospects, IFIP.
[15] Marks, D. "Inference in MLS Database Systems," IEEE Trans. KDE, V 8, # 1, pp46-55.
[16] Moskowitz, I. S. & Chang, L. (2000) "A Computational Intelligence Approach to the Database Inference Problem," Advances in Intelligent Systems: Theory and Applications (ed M. Mohammadian) IOS Press, 2000.
[17] Office of Management and Budget (1994) "Report on Statistical Disclosure Limitation Methodology," paper 22.
[18] Pearl, J. (1989) "Probabilistic Reasoning in Intelligent Systems," Morgan Kauffman.
[19] Quinlan, R. (1992) "C4.5", Morgan Kaufmann.
[20] Sweeney, L. (1997) "Maintaining anonymity when sharing medical data," MIT working paper, AIWP-WP344.
[21] Thuraisingham, B. (1998) "Data Mining: Technologies, Tools and Trends:, CRC Press.
[22] Zayatz, L. & Rowland, S. (1999) "Disclosure Limitation for American Factfinder," Census Bureau report (manuscript).

CHAPTER 16
DISCOVERY OF MULTI-LEVEL SECURITY POLICIES

Christina Yip Chung, Michael Gertz, Karl Levitt
Department of Computer Science, University of California, Davis, CA 95616, U.S.A.
{chungy|gertz|levitt}@cs.ucdavis.edu

Abstract With the increasing complexity and dynamics of database systems, it becomes more and more difficult for administrative personnel to identify, specify and enforce security policies that govern against the misuse of data. Often security policies are not known, too imprecise or simply have been disabled because of changing requirements.

Recently several proposals have been made to use data mining techniques to discover profiles and anomalous user behavior from audit logs. These approaches, however, are often too fine-grained in that they compute too many rules to be useful for an administrator in implementing appropriate security enforcing mechanisms.

In this paper we present a novel approach to discover security policies from audit logs. The approach is based on using multiple concept hierarchies that specify properties of objects and data at different levels of abstraction and thus can embed useful domain knowledge. A profiler, attached to the information system's auditing component, utilizes such concept hierarchies to compute profiles at different levels of granularity, guided by the administrator through the specification of an interestingness measure. The computed profiles can be translated into security policies and existing policies can be verified against the profiles.

1. INTRODUCTION

A major obstacle in securing todays information systems is not the lack of appropriate security mechanisms (see, e.g., [4] for an overview of access control models), but the lack of methods and concepts that allow security administrators to identify security policies. This is because in practice often only a very few policies are known at system design-time. Furthermore, at system run-time existing security policies typically need to be modified or new policies need to be added. In such cases, determining appropriate policy modifications is based on the normal behavior of users. What is needed are concepts and tools that help administrators in identifying security policies of interest and in verifying existing security policies.

Recently several proposals have been made to discover user profiles from audit logs (see, e.g., [2, 7, 6, 9, 12, 13, 14]). Profiles describe the normal behavior of users (groups) regarding the usage of the system and associated applications. Discovered profiles can be used to derive specifications of security enforcing mechanisms based on, e.g., an access control model. The ability to incorporate application specific domain knowledge is critical to the success and usability of these approaches. In [7, 6] we have shown how misuse detection, based on data mining techniques, can benefit from domain knowledge that is incorporated into applications associated with an information system. However, even these approaches turn out to generate too many fine-grained policies. Administrators typically do not want to deal with hundreds of closely related access patterns, but prefer a representation of access patterns at an abstract, more generalized level of description.

In this paper we describe an approach that tries to alleviate this shortcoming by discovering security policies at different levels of detail. The approach is applicable to database systems as well as Web-based information systems. We employ *concept hierarchies* [3] that describe properties (values) of data at different levels of granularity. Concepts modeled in such hierarchies build descriptive parts of user profiles and thus security policies at different levels of detail. Such hierarchies are either provided by the administrator (thus representing some kind of domain knowledge) or can be discovered from data using clustering techniques (see, e.g., [8, 10]). We propose an extension of the concept hierarchy framework in which we organize feature/value pairs (representing concepts) in trees. Our framework is more general than [11] in that it does not impose an arbitrary partial order on the attributes (concepts) in a concept hierarchy.

Our profiler is capable of considering multiple concept hierarchies in discovering profiles. Multiple concept hierarchies have been introduced in the data mining domain for deriving typical patterns of data at different levels of abstraction [3, 10, 11]. We extend the usage of multiple concept hierarchies by allowing different types of concepts in a single hierarchy. Depending on the security policies to discover or verify, the administrator can choose among (combinations of) concept hierarchies and abstract concepts (features) embedded in these hierarchies.

Finally, we introduce the notion of *interestingness measure* as an important means for administrators to guide the profile and policy discovery process. This measurement can be specified by the administrator depending on the type and granularity of policy she is interested in. Our approach provides a valuable tool for *security re-engineering* which utilizes audit logs generated by a database system at run-time.

2. CONCEPT HIERARCHIES

Concept hierarchies represent application specific domain knowledge about features of interest for the discovery of security policies. Starting from auditable features, a concept hierarchy can be developed bottom-up by the administrator or data clustering techniques.

In Section 2.1, we describe how concept hierarchies organize feature/value pairs in form of trees. In Section 2.2, we discuss a model to determine whether a given itemset, consisting of feature/value pairs, is of interest. Section 2.3 outlines the usage of concept hierarchies for generalizing itemsets.

2.1. PRELIMINARIES

Objects and data are conceptualized through feature/value pairs in which a feature is an object property and value is the value of the property. A feature/value pair is denoted by $\langle F = f \rangle$, meaning that the value of feature F is f. We use trees to model concept hierarchies organizing objects and data through feature/value pairs at different levels of abstraction. Each node in the tree corresponds to a feature/value pair. The root of the tree is a special node including all concepts.

While such a framework for a concept hierarchy is simple and intuitive, it captures many real world examples. It is worth mentioning that a concept hierarchy is not limited to only one type of feature. Features can be abstracted to other features. Figure 1 shows a concept hierarchy for the concept `time`, a feature that often is of interest in profiling.

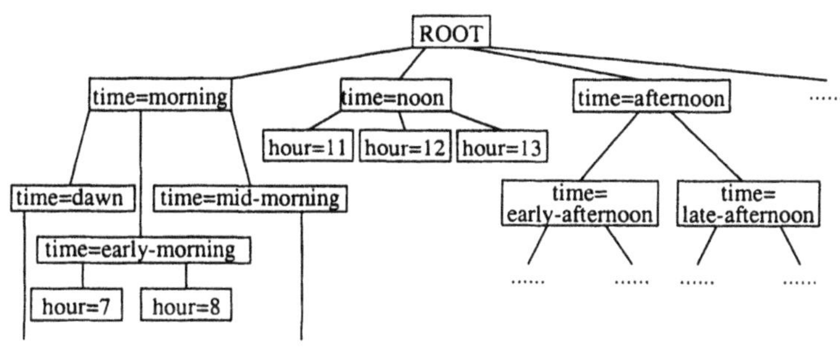

Figure 1. Concept Hierarchy on Time

Note that leaf nodes represent auditable features ("raw data" in the audit log), whereas inner nodes represent generalizations of these features at different levels. Formally, a concept hierarchy is a tree where nodes are labeled with feature/value pairs. A subtree with root $\langle F = f \rangle$, having n subtrees rooted with $\langle F_i = f_i \rangle, i = 1 \dots n$, is denoted by $T(F = f) := (\langle F = f \rangle, T(\langle F_1 = f_1 \rangle), \dots, T(\langle F_n = f_n \rangle))$.

Let $\mathcal{T}$ be a set of concept hierarchies. $Desc(n)$ denotes the set of nodes that are descendants of node n in $T \in \mathcal{T}$. The depth of a node n in T, denoted by $Depth(n, T)$, is the number of nodes on the path from the root to n. The depth of the root node is 0. The depth of T, denoted by $Depth(T)$, is the maximum depth of all nodes in the tree.

We say a feature/value pair $\langle F_i = f_i \rangle$ may be generalized to $\langle F_j = f_j \rangle$ with respect to a hierarchy T if $\langle F_j = f_j \rangle$ is an ancestor of $\langle F_i = f_i \rangle$ in T. Since F_j may be different from F_i, a feature may be generalized to another feature, e.g., a different type of concept, as indicated in Figure 1, where the feature `hour` has been generalized to the feature `time`.

2.2. INTERESTINGNESS MEASURE

For computing user profiles based on concept hierarchies, it is important to determine whether a set of feature/value pairs might be of interest, i.e., is likely to lead to useful information regarding the usage patterns an administrator is interested in. As a novelty to using concept hierarchies, we introduce the notion of *interestingness measure* to guide the discovery of interesting patterns in an audit session $Audit$ containing a set of itemsets. We consider four aspects, (1) *support*, (2) *depth*, (3) *distance*, and (4) *size* of itemsets describing sets of feature/value pairs.

(1) Support The support of an itemset gives a measure of how frequent that itemset occurs in an audit session. The higher the support of an itemset, the more regular is the pattern in the audit session. Let $Audit$ be an audit session and $I = \{\langle F_1 = f_1 \rangle, \ldots, \langle F_n = f_n \rangle\}$ an itemset. An itemset I' in $Audit$ *satisfies* I, denoted by $I \leq I'$, if

$\forall \langle F = f \rangle \in I : \exists \langle F' = f' \rangle \in I' : \langle F' = f' \rangle = \langle F = f \rangle$ **or** $\langle F = f \rangle \in Desc(\langle F' = f' \rangle)$.

The support of an itemset I in $Audit$, denoted by $Sup(I)$, is the number of itemsets in $Audit$ that satisfy I, normalized by the size of $Audit$:

$$Sup(I) := \frac{|\{I \mid I \leq I' \in Audit\}|}{|\, Audit \,|} \in \mathbb{R}[0,1]$$

(2) Depth We prefer feature/value pairs of lower level of abstraction since they are more specialized and convey more detailed information. This is captured by the depth of an itemset and describes the depths of its feature/value pairs in a set of concept hierarchies. Let $\mathcal{T}_{\langle F=f \rangle}$ be a set of concept hierarchies containing the feature/value pair $\langle F = f \rangle$. Then

$$Depth(\langle F = f \rangle) := \begin{cases} \frac{1}{|\mathcal{T}_{\langle F=f \rangle}|} \times \Sigma_{T \in \mathcal{T}_{\langle F=f \rangle}} \frac{Depth(\langle F=f \rangle, T)}{Depth(T)} & \text{if } \mathcal{T}_{\langle F=f \rangle} \neq \{\ \} \\ 1 & \text{otherwise} \end{cases}$$

Intuitively, the depth of a feature/value pair $\langle F = f \rangle$ is its average depth among all concept hierarchies that contain $\langle F = f \rangle$ as a node. The depth of an itemset I is the average depths of its feature/value pairs, i.e.

$$Depth(I) := \frac{1}{|I|} \times \Sigma_{\langle F=f \rangle \in I} Depth(\langle F = f \rangle), \quad \in \mathbb{R}[0,1]$$

(3) Distance We conjecture that usage patterns of users typically involve feature/value pairs that are semantically related. That is, users typically access information that is semantically related. Whether and how information is related is some kind of domain specific knowledge that often can be obtained from the information structures underlying the application, in particular the information schemas.

For example, in Web-based information systems, features such as IP address (called `src`), URL (`rsc`) of a requested page, and time of request (`time`) can often be organized into one or more hierarchies. For example, the feature/value pair ⟨`src` = `www.bases.mil`⟩ can be considered as the parent of the feature/value pair ⟨`src` = `www.ca.bases.mil`⟩ and so on.

The distance between two feature/value pairs can be defined based on their location in a concept hierarchy. Consider, for example, the feature/value pairs $\texttt{fv}_1 \equiv$ ⟨`rsc` = `/user/scott/doc`⟩, $\texttt{fv}_2 \equiv$ ⟨`rsc` = `/user/scott/schedule`⟩, and $\texttt{fv}_3 \equiv$ ⟨`rsc` = `/user/jones/reports`⟩. $\texttt{fv}_1$ and $\texttt{fv}_2$ are more related than $\texttt{fv}_1$ and $\texttt{fv}_3$ or $\texttt{fv}_2$ and $\texttt{fv}_3$ because $\texttt{fv}_1$ and $\texttt{fv}_2$ share a longer common path. Thus, the distance measure between two feature/value pairs in a concept hierarchy T can be defined as

$$Dist(\langle F = f \rangle, \langle F' = f' \rangle, T) := 1 - \frac{Depth(LCA(\langle F = f \rangle, \langle F' = f' \rangle, T))}{Depth(T)}$$

where the function $LCA(\langle F = f \rangle, \langle F' = f' \rangle, T)$ gives the least common ancestor of two nodes $\langle F = f \rangle$, $\langle F' = f' \rangle$ in a concept hierarchy T. The higher the depth of the least common ancestor of two feature/value pairs, the smaller is the distance measure, i.e. they are more related.

A similar notion of distance measure can be devised for queries against relations and attributes in relational databases (see [5]).

(4) Size We prefer itemsets that contain more feature/value pairs since they reveal correlated information between different feature/value pairs. This is reflected by the size component of the interestingness measure, i.e., the number of feature/value pairs the itemset I contains.

In sum, for the meaningful discovery of itemsets (and thus profiles and policies) we prefer itemsets that are more regular, more specialized, semantically closer and contain more feature/value pairs. Thus, the interestingness measure $M(I)$ of an itemset I should (1) increase with its support, depth, size and (2) decrease with its distance. A simple formulation of $M(I)$ that satisfies these criteria thus is

$$M(I) := (Sup(I) + Depth(I) + 1 - Dist(I) + Size(I)) \ / \ 4$$

2.3. GENERALIZATION

An important feature of using concept hierarchies in policy discovery is the usage of the abstraction mechanism embedded in the hierarchies. For example, using concept hierarchies, access patterns of user can be generalized to access patterns of user groups, accessed objects can be generalized to classes of objects, depending on their attribute values, and so on. A feature/value pair $\langle F = f \rangle$ in an itemset I can be *generalized* to $\langle F' = f' \rangle$ if it is replaced by $\langle F' = f' \rangle$ in the itemset I and $\langle F' = f' \rangle$ is an ancestor of $\langle F = f \rangle$ in some concept hierarchy. The support and depth components of the interestingness measure consider the effect of generalizing an itemset in all concept hierarchies. We incorporate multiple concept hierarchies into the discovery process by using the change of interestingness measure as a criteria to decide whether an itemset should be generalized.

There are two opposing forces in deciding whether $\langle F = f \rangle$ should be generalized to $\langle F' = f' \rangle$. On one hand, more general itemsets have higher support and hence a higher interestingness measure. On the other hand, it loses depth and hence drives down its interestingness measure.

Let I' be the generalized itemset of I after generalizing $\langle F = f \rangle$ to $\langle F' = f' \rangle$ with respect to some concept hierarchy. The change of interestingness measure is reflected by the change of its four components support, depth, distance, and size.

$$\Delta Sup(I \to I') := Sup(I') - Sup(I) \qquad \Delta Depth(I \to I') := Depth(I') - Depth(I)$$
$$\Delta Dist(I \to I') := Dist(I') - Dist(I) \qquad \Delta Size(I \to I') := Size(I') - Size(I)$$

The change of interestingness measure of I to I', denoted by $\Delta M(I \to I')$, then is defined as:

$$(\Delta Sup(I \to I') + \Delta Depth(I \to I') + \Delta Dist(I \to I') + \Delta Size(I \to I')) \ / \ 4$$

As a general guideline for the discovery of profiles, an itemset I should be generalized to an itemset I' if there is a gain in its change of interestingness, i.e. if $\Delta M(I \to I') > 0$.

3. ALGORITHM

In this section we outline the algorithm underlying the computation of itemsets using concept hierarchies in a profiler. In Section 3.1, we present the basic underlying data structures for managing itemsets. In Section 3.2, we describe the algorithm for computing interesting itemsets.

3.1. DATA STRUCTURES

The auditing component associated with a database system records audit data in an audit log implemented as relations in a database. Attributes of the audit log are the features audited and their values. Hence, a tuple in the audit log can be viewed as a set of feature/value pairs, called *itemset*, and a relation as a set of itemsets. Features to be audited by the system are determined by the administrator prior to the user-profiling and policy discovery. The administrator groups audit records into *audit sessions* based on security policy she is interested in. Each audit session consists of audit records sharing some property. For example, an audit session might contain all audit records that correspond to audited actions performed by a particular user. The profiler computes a profile for each audit session.

In the following, we assume the following relations for recording audit and features/value data. The relation **Audit(L1,l1,...,Ln,ln)** stores sets of feature/value pairs (itemsets). Each itemset corresponds to an audit record from an audit session. The relations **Lk(FIID,interest, sup, depth, dist, size, A1,a1,...,Ak,ak)** record itemsets $I = \{\langle \mathtt{A1} = \mathtt{a1}\rangle, ..., \langle \mathtt{Ak} = \mathtt{ak}\rangle\}$ up to size **k** and their interestingness measure (**interest**). Values for the attribute **interest** are based on the components **sup[port]**, **depth**, **dist[ance]** and **size** (see Section 2.2).

Relation F(FIID,A,v) stores all interesting itemsets discovered from tuples in relations L1 ... Ln. Finally, relation **FMaster(FIID,size, interest,sup,depth,dist)** stores the interestingness measure information about the itemsets in F. To relate itemsets in these two relations, each itemset is given a unique identifier, named FIID.

3.2. BASIC ALGORITHM

The method to compute interesting itemsets based on multiple concept hierarchies is divided into 6 steps, as described below

```
for k = 1 to n do (let n be the total number of features)
  Step 0: check if we need to continue
          if k>1 and Lk is empty then break end if
  Step 1: Generate & store itemsets of size k from itemsets of size k-1
          Lk <- generateItemsets(k)
  Step 2: Compute interestingness measure for each tuple in relation Lk
  Step 3: Generalize itemsets based on concept hierarchies
          for each feature/value pair afv in a set of hierarchies do
            generalizeToAFV(afv,Lk)
  Step 4: Delete non-interesting itemsets from Lk
  Step 5: Record interesting itemsets in relations F and FMaster
end do;
Step 6: Prune non-minimal itemsets
```

Readers are referred to [7] for more details regarding steps 2, 4, 5 and 6. Here we will only briefly describe Step 3, which extends our previous approach by generalizing itemsets in **Lk** for possible feature/value pairs in concept hierarchies. The order of applying **generalizeToAFV** to a feature/value pair **afv** is unspecified.

Procedure **generalizeToAFV(afv,Lk)** generalizes itemsets in **Lk** to feature/value pair **afv** (which stands for AncestorFeatureValue pair) if there is a gain in interestingness measure. First, all itemsets in **Lk** that consist of descendants of **afv** are copied to a temporary table **Lgen**. These feature/value pairs are replaced by their ancestor **afv** with the change in interestingness measure computed. Second, itemsets with a gain in interestingness measure are generalized in **Lk** by updating them according to **Lgen**. Since two or more feature/value pairs in an itemset may be generalized to **afv**, care is taken to remove redundant pairs from the generalized itemset. If **afv** is the root of the tree, the feature/value pair is dropped. Third, after **Lk** is generalized, there may be redundant itemsets which should be pruned. Redundant itemsets in **Lk** with **FIID** in **FIIDpair** are deleted except one itemset. If the feature/value pairs of an itemset are generalized to the root node, the itemset is empty and deleted. In our prototype profiler, all the above computations are performed on tables using SQL statements and stored procedures.

4. APPLICATION TO SECURITY

In this section, we describe a feasibility study on extending the profiler by concept hierarchies and compare its effectiveness with a profiler not employing concept hierarchies. We then give some guidelines on how to convert profiles to policies and their usage in detecting misuse. More details can be found in [5].

4.1. FEASIBILITY STUDY SETUP

We show the usefulness of our profiler, called *ProfilerCH* (CH stands for Concept Hierarchy), by running it over a web audit log gathered at an institution offering online courses. Further, we illustrate the difference of the profiles generated by using another profiler, called *ProfilerNoCH*, which is based on the same technique, but does not consider concept hierarchies. The web audit log records the access patterns of users over four consecutive days. We consider three features in the audit log, **src** (IP address of host requesting a web page), **rsc** (URL of requested page) and **hour** (time page has been requested, see also Fig. 1).

There are two audit sessions. The session **AuditSG** contains audit records whose feature **src** corresponds to the domain(s) ***.sg** and **rsc** to pages under `/course/*`. Another session `AuditUIUC` consists of records whose feature values for `src` satisfy `*.uiuc.edu` and values for `rsc` correspond to `/spep-95/*`. Due to space limitation, we only show the profile discovered by ProfilerCH for audit session `AuditSG`:

FIID	Interest	Sup	Depth	Dist	Size	A1	a1	A2	a2
2-10	0.51	1.00	0.21	1.00	2	rsc	/course/	src	sg
1-27	0.51	0.46	0.40	0.00	1	rsc	/course/plb1/rice/		
3-1	0.50	1.00	0.14	1.00	1	TIME	day		
2-1	0.47	0.79	0.21	1.00	2	rsc	/course/	TIME	day
2-21	0.47	0.79	0.21	1.00	2	src	sg	TIME	day
1-1	0.47	0.39	0.30	0.00	1	TIME	noon		
1-5	0.47	0.38	0.30	0.00	1	TIME	morning		
1-57	0.45	0.21	0.36	0.00	1	rsc	/course/plb1/tomato/		
2-25	0.43	0.54	0.26	1.00	2	rsc	/course/plb1/	TIME	day
1-11	0.43	0.14	0.36	0.00	1	rsc	/course/cant/current/		

4.2. DISCUSSION

We evaluate and compare the profilers based on the following criteria: (1) *Coverage*: Can the profiler discover criteria to group audit records into audit sessions? (2) *Simplicity*: How many itemsets are generated? (3) *Novelty*: Can the profiler discover new patterns which are not specified by the criteria that groups audit records into audit sessions?

Coverage ProfilerNoCH discovers that requests often come from `src=ce.singnet.com.sg` and `src=po.pacific.net.sg`. The other selection criteria (values for `rsc` are under `/course/*`) are also covered by those itemsets involving `rsc=/course/*`. However, the correlation that `rsc=/course/*` is accessed from `src=*.sg` is not discovered. This is because the data is sparse. Itemsets involving both `rsc` and `src` do not have high enough support and are pruned. This is, however, discovered by ProfilerCH as reflected in itemset 2-10. ProfilerCH discovers the selection criteria because data are aggregated into a higher level of abstraction based on the concept hierarchies. This makes the pattern more prominent and hence is discovered. In sum, both profilers can discover the patterns used to select the data, whereas ProfilerCH does a better job.

Simplicity There is a total of 74 itemsets discovered by ProfilerNoCH. Those patterns are represented by only 11 itemsets discovered by ProfilerCH, which is a significant reduction. The concise profile discovered by ProfilerCH helps the administrator in better understanding usage patterns of the user group `*.sg` (`singapore`).

Novelty ProfilerNoCH discovers patterns that were not expected, namely users from user group `singapore` often access pages at specific hours. Similarly, ProfilerCH discovers patterns that were unknown before. For example, the hours of access are often `TIME=noon`, morning (covered by `TIME=day`) and `TIME=midnight`. Hence, the administrator can add a new security policy stating that users from the group `singapore` are allowed to access the web pages during the aforementioned times. Alternatively, if someone from group `singapore` suddenly accesses the web pages at `hour=evening`, this may be not normal.

Further, ProfilerCH discovers that the resources that are most often accessed are actually `/course/plb1/[rice/tomato]` and `/course/cant/current/`. This can aid the administrator in refining the security policy that users from group `singapore` can access resources `/course/` to a finer detail. Other novel patterns discovered include that users from group `singapore` often access the web pages during day time (`TIME=day`) and that pages accessed are likely to be `/course/plb1/*`.

Inter-User Group Behavior The conjecture that users from different user groups exhibit different usage behavior is confirmed by comparing the profiles discovered by ProfilerCH on `AuditSG` and `AuditUIUC`. A comparison of the two profiles shows that users from group `uiuc` often access web pages during night (including midnight and late-night), afternoon and late-evening as opposed to day time by users from group `singapore`. This can be explained by the time zone difference between the US and Singapore.

4.3. MAPPING PROFILES TO POLICIES

We consider a policy to be an if-then statement describing a characteristic of a session, i.e., an interesting itemset in the profile. Here we describe how to map an interesting itemset to a policy.

The criteria that aggregates audit records into an audit session gives the precondition of the policy. Feature/value pairs in the interesting itemset are literals in the consequent combined by '`and`'s. A policy is refined in the following ways: (1) Care is taken to remove literals in the consequent that are logically implied by the precondition to avoid trivial true policies. (2) A policy is simplified by removing literals in the consequent that are descendants of some other literals in concept hierarchies. (3) A refined policy can be obtained by replacing literals in the precondition by those in the consequent that logically imply them. (4) Policies with the same precondition can be aggregated into a single policy by combining their consequents by '`or`'s. Based on these guidelines, we can derive the following policies for session `AuditSG`:

```
if src=*.sg and rsc=/course/* then rsc=/course/plb1/rice/*
        or rsc=/course/plb1/tomato/* or rsc=/course/cant/current/*
if src=*.sg and rsc=/course/* then TIME=day or TIME=midnight
if src=*.sg and rsc=/course/plb1/* then TIME=day
```

Anomalies can be detected by comparing the policies derived from a new session with the policies of the corresponding profile(s). A policy from a new session whose precondition matches some policies, but its consequent matches none of these policies is a violating policy. Violating policies represent behavior deviating from normal. A policy from a new session whose precondition matches none of the profile policies is a new policy. New policies signal new usage and a high ratio of violating and new policies in a new session indicates possible misuse of the system.

5. CONCLUSIONS AND FUTURE WORK

In this paper we presented an important practical extension to existing approaches for discovering user access patterns and security policies from audit logs associated with diverse types of information systems. We strongly believe that for todays complex databases and information systems, it is vital to employ sophisticated concepts and tools that help administrators in discovering and verifying security policies. Such tools and concepts will play a major role in security (re-)engineering as part of the administration of such complex systems.

We extended existing approaches to user profiling and policy discovery in several ways. We use concept hierarchies that allow administrators to embed domain specific knowledge at different levels of abstraction. The discovery of access patterns and security policies, based on data mining techniques, takes multiple such hierarchies into account, allowing to relate different concepts of interest in the search for interesting patterns. In particular, by introducing the notion of interestingness measure, which considers data semantics, the presented profiler is capable of discovering interesting data access patterns at the right level of abstraction. By considering multiple concept hierarchies describing different features at a time, more complex and non-trivial profiles and policies can be discovered.

We have presented a simple formulation of interestingness measure that satisfy certain criteria based on our experience with different types of audit logs and applications. One direction of future research is to explore other formulations of the interestingness measure, and also to incorporate other aspects of domain knowledge available from applications. Currently, the administrator is responsible for choosing relative weights of the components of the interestingness measure. It would be useful if the system can automatically adjust and fine tune the parameters. We demonstrated the effectiveness of our profiler by running it over a web server access log. We also outlined guidelines on how discovered profiles can be translated into policies.

We also plan to automate the translation of profiles to policies and enforcing mechanisms. For example, in case of relational database systems, profiles can be converted into either appropriate user roles (with associated profiles) or user/application-specific views on data.

References

[1] R. Agrawal and R. Srikant. Fast algorithms for mining association rules. In *Proceedings of the 20th VLDB Conference*, 487–499, Morgan Kaufmann, 1994.

[2] R. Bueschkes, M. Borning, D. Kesdogan. Transaction-based anomaly detection. In *Proc. of the Workshop on Intrusion Detection & Network Monitoring*, 1999.

[3] Y. Cai, N. Cercone, and J. Han. Attribute-oriented induction in relational databases. In *Knowledge Discovery in Databases*, 213–228. AAAI/MIT Press, 1991.

[4] S. Castano, M.G. Fugini, G. Martella, and P. Samarati. *Database Security*. Addison-Wesley, 1995.

[5] C.Y. Chung, M. Gertz, and K. Levitt. Discovery of multi-level security policies. Technical Report, Department of Computer Science, University of California, Davis, `http://www.db.cs.ucdavis.edu/publications/CGL00a.ps`

[6] C.Y. Chung, M. Gertz, and K. Levitt. DEMIDS: A misuse detection system for database systems. In *Third International IFIP TC-11 WG11.5 Working Conf. on Integrity and Internal Control in Information Systems*, 159–178, Kluwer, 1999.

[7] C.Y. Chung, M. Gertz, and K. Levitt. Misuse detection in database systems through user-profiling. In *2nd Int. Workshop on Recent Advances in Intrusion Detection (RAID'99)*, West Lafayette, Indiana, 1999.

[8] B. Everitt. *Cluster Analysis*. John Wiley & Sons - New York, 1973.

[9] T. Fawcett and F. Provost. Combining data mining and machine learning for effective user profiling. In *The Second International Conference on Knowledge Discovery and Data Mining (KDD-96)*, 8–13, 1996.

[10] J. Han and Y. Fu. Dynamic Generation and Refinement of Concept Hierarchies for Knowledge Discovery in Databases. *AAAI'94 Workshop on Knowledge Discovery in Databases*, 157–168, July 1994.

[11] J. Han and Y. Fu. Discovery of multiple-level association rules from large databases. *Proc. of Int. Conf. on Very Large Data Bases*, 420–431, 1995.

[12] W. Lee, S.J. Stolfo, and K.W. Mok. Mining audit data to build intrusion detection models. In *Proc. of the 14th International Conf. on Knowledge Discovery and Data Mining (KDD-98)*, 66–72. AAAI Press, 1998.

[13] R. Mukkamala, J. Gagnon, and S. Jajodia. Integrating data mining techniques with intrusion detection methods. In *Proc. XIII Annual IFIP WG 11.3 Working Conf. On Database Security*, Seattle, WA, July 1999.

[14] R.S. Silken. Application intrusion detection. Technical Report CS-99-17, University of Virginia, Computer Science Department, June 1999.

Chapter 17

PROTECTING DEDUCTIVE DATABASES FROM UNAUTHORIZED RETRIEVALS

Steve Barker

Abstract An approach is presented that addresses the problem of protecting deductive databases from unauthorized disclosures of the information they contain. Our treatment of this problem involves rewriting a database in a form that is guaranteed to allow users to access only the subset of the logical consequences of the database that they are authorized to see. Security requirements can be seamlessly added to the database, and decisions on the legitimacy of access requests can be made by using efficient computational methods for which attractive technical results exist. The approach enables the specification of security requirements to be exploited to help to improve the efficiency of query evaluation, and naturally extends to enable deductive databases to be protected against unauthorized update and revision requests.

1. INTRODUCTION

Little attention has thus far been given to the problem of securing the information contained in deductive databases. In part, this may have been due to the hitherto limited use that has been made of deductive databases in commercial environments. The practical value of deductive databases is, however, increasingly being recognized [13], and deductive databases are predicted to become increasingly important in the future [11]. For deductive databases to become significant in practice, the problem of protecting the information they contain must be addressed.

In [6] and [9], modal logics are considered for specifying the confidentiality of the information contained in a deductive database. However, the suggested approaches are not especially compatible with the methods of representation and computation that deductive databases typically employ. In contrast, our approach uses specifications of security that are consistent with the standard formulation of a deductive database as a *function-free normal clause theory* [10] and enables standard methods of computation to be exploited to protect deductive databases from unauthorized access requests. Due to space limitations, in this paper we only consider the protection of deductive databases from unauthorized read requests. The extensions required to protect a deductive database from unauthorized modifications are described in [4].

We use a *role-based access control (RBAC)* [14] policy to protect a deductive database. More specifically, we formulate security policies that are based on the $RBAC_1$ model described in [14]. That is, we consider $RBAC$ models that permit user and permission assignments on objects to be specified, and include role hierarchies. Amongst other attractions, we believe that the "high-level" nature of authorizations in $RBAC$ makes it more suitable for protecting deductive databases than the *discretionary access control (DAC)* policies that DBMSs have traditionally used to protect other types of database.

The rest of this paper is organized thus. In Section 2, some basic notions in deductive databases, theorem-proving and security are outlined. In Section 3, the representation of an $RBAC$ model as a clause form theory is discussed. Section 4 describes how a deductive database may be specified as being protected from unauthorized read requests. In Section 5, computational issues are considered. Finally, in Section 6, some conclusions are drawn and suggestions for further work are made.

2. PRELIMINARIES

A deductive database, D, consists of a finite set of ground atomic assertions (i.e., facts) and a finite set of deductive rules. The set of facts is referred to as the *extensional database (EDB)* and the deductive rules are referred to as the *intensional database (IDB)*.

To protect D from unauthorized disclosures of information, our approach is to express D in a form (defined below) that ensures that retrievals of information are only possible if the $RBAC_1$ security theory, that defines authorized accesses, permits the read access on D. Henceforth, we will refer to the secure form of D protected from unauthorized read requests as a read *protected database* and we denote an arbitrary read protected database by $D*$. To denote specific instances of D and $D*$, we use D_i and D_i*, respectively, where i is a natural number. We also use $S*$ to denote an arbitrary $RBAC_1$ security theory and S_i* to denote a specific instance of an $RBAC_1$ theory where i is a natural number. As we will see, theorem-proving techniques may be used on $D*$

$\cup$ $S*$ to determine whether or not a user's request to perform a read operation on $D*$ is authorized by $S*$ or not.

The protected databases and $RBAC_1$ security theories that we consider consist of a finite set of function-free *normal clauses* [10]. A normal clause takes the form: $H \leftarrow L1, L2, \ldots, Lm$. The *head* of the clause, H, is an *atom* and $L1, L2, \ldots, Lm$ is a conjunction of *literals* that constitutes the *body* of the clause. The conjunction of literals must be true (proved) in order for H to be true (proved). A literal is an atomic formula or its negation; in this context negation is *negation as failure* [10], and the negation of the atom A is denoted by *not* A. A clause with an empty body is an *assertion* or a *fact*.

Since we consider function-free theories, the only terms that appear in $D* \cup S*$ are constants and variables. Henceforth, we will denote the constants that appear in $D* \cup S*$ by symbols that appear in the lowercase in literals. The variables that appear in the literals in $D* \cup S*$ will be denoted by using uppercase symbols (possibly subscripted).

Since $D* \cup S*$ is expressed in normal clause logic, it follows that the *well-founded semantics* [16] may be used for the associated declarative semantics, and that *SLG-resolution* [8] may be used for the corresponding procedural semantics.

When SLG-resolution is used with the normal clause theory $D* \cup S*$, a *search forest* is constructed starting from the *SLG-tree* with its root node labeled by the *goal clause* $Q \leftarrow Q$ [8]. From the soundness and (search space) completeness of SLG-resolution (for flounder-free computations), Q is true in *WFM*($D* \cup S*$) (where *WFM*($D* \cup S*$) is the well-founded model of $D* \cup S*$) iff there is an SLG-derivation for $Q \leftarrow Q$ on $D* \cup S*$ that terminates with the answer clause $Q \leftarrow$. That is, $Q \in$ *WFM*($D* \cup S*$) iff the body of $Q \leftarrow Q$ is reduced to an empty set of literals. In contrast, Q is false in *WFM*($D* \cup S*$) iff all possible derivations of $Q \leftarrow Q$ either finitely fail or fail infinitely due to positive recursion; Q has an undefined truth value in all other cases. In the case where Q has an undefined truth value, SLG-resolution produces conditional answers of the form $Q \leftarrow \delta$ viz. Q is true if δ is true where δ is a nonempty set of *delayed* negative literals [8].

The soundness of SLG-resolution is important from a security perspective since it ensures that no unauthorized access request is permitted from an SLG-derivation on $D* \cup S*$; completeness is important since it implies that non-floundering SLG-resolution is sufficiently strong to ensure that no authorized access request is ever denied.

Given that the only terms that are included in $D* \cup S*$ are constants and variables, it follows that $D* \cup S*$ satisfies the *bounded-term-size property* [17]; SLG-resolution is guaranteed to terminate for theories that satisfy this property [8]. Moreover, SLG-resolution has polynomial time *data complexity* [17] for function-free normal theories [15].

We assume that a ***security administrator (SA)*** is responsible for specifying $D* \cup S*$. We also assume that a ***closed policy*** [7] is to be used for protecting a deductive database. It is, however, entirely straightforward to modify our approach to implement an *open policy* [7] or any number of hybrid (i.e., open/closed) policies for protected databases.

Whilst we recognize that the session concept [14] is an important aspect of RBAC, we will not consider role activation/deactivation in the discussion below. In the examples of the evaluation of access requests that we consider later, we simply assume that a user has active the set of roles that is necessary to read from a protected database. However, it should be noted that role activation/deactivation can be naturally accommodated in the approach we describe (see [5]).

3. $RBAC_1$ AS A LOGICAL THEORY

The minimum requirements of any *RBAC* model are that it provides means for specifying that users are assigned to roles and permissions to perform operations on database objects are associated with a role. The database objects to be protected in a deductive database are *n*-ary predicates.

The assignment of users and permissions to roles is represented in our approach by an *SA* including definitions of *ura(U,R)* and *rpa(R,P,O)* predicates in a clause form theory that represents an application-specific $RBAC_1$ security policy, an $RBAC_1$ theory.

In the *ura(U,R)* relation, the predicate name *ura* is shorthand for *user-role assignment*; instances of *ura* are used in an $RBAC_1$ theory to represent that user *U* is assigned to a role *R*. Similarly, *rpa(R,P,O)* stands for *role-permission assignment*; instances of *rpa* in an $RBAC_1$ theory are used to specify that the role *R* is assigned the permission to perform a *P* operation on a database object *O*. Since we only consider protection against unauthorized retrieval requests, *P=read* in this paper.

The *ura(U,R)* and *rpa(R,P,O)* relations are defined by a *SA* using normal clauses. For example, *ura(bob,r1)*← specifies that the user *Bob* is assigned to the role *r1*; *rpa(r1,read,q(V,Y,Z))*← $V \neq a$ specifies that role *r1* is assigned read permission on any instance of *q(V,Y,Z)* such that *V* is not equal to *a*; *rpa(R,read,r(X,Y))* ← specifies that all roles are permitted to read all instances of *r* (i.e., read access on *r* is publicly accessible); and *rpa(r1,read,s(a,Y,Z))*← $Z < 20$ specifies that the role *r1* has the read permission on instances of *s* such that the first argument of $s(V,Y,Z)$ is constrained to be *a* and *Z* values are less than 20.

Additional authorization rules can be straightforwardly specified by formulating *ura* or *rpa* definitions in terms of *ura*, *rpa*, *not ura* or *not rpa* conditions. Since constants and variables are used in their specification, *ura* and *rpa* definitions can be as specific or as general as is required.

In addition to user-role and permission-role assignments, role hierarchies are the other key component of $RBAC_1$. Role hierarchies are used to represent the idea that, unless constraints are imposed, "senior roles" (more powerful roles) inherit the (positive) permissions assigned to roles that are "junior" (less powerful) to them in a hierarchy (but not conversely). In cases where the unconstrained upward inheritance of positive permissions is not appropriate, only minor modifications of our representation of $RBAC_1$ are required to enforce alternative policies.

To represent an $RBAC_1$ role hierarchy, a *SA* uses ground instances of a binary relation to describe the pairs of roles that are involved in a "seniority" relationship in the partial order $(R,>)$ that represents a role hierarchy; R is a set of roles; and $>$ is a "senior to" relation.

In more formal terms, a role *R1* is *senior to* role *R2* in a role hierarchy, *RH*, iff there is a path from *R1* to *R2* in *RH* such that $R1 > R2$ holds in the partial order describing *RH*. The reflexive, antisymmetric and transitive *senior to* relation (i.e. $>$) may be defined in terms of an irreflexive and intransitive relation, "directly senior to". The *directly senior to* relation, denoted by $\rightarrow$, may be defined (since $>$ is not dense) in the following way (where $\wedge$ is logical 'and', $\neg$ is classical negation, and Ri ($i \in \{1,2,3\}$) is an arbitrary role):

$$\forall R1, R2\, [R1 \rightarrow R2 \text{ iff } R1 > R2 \wedge R1 \neq R2 \wedge \neg\exists R3[R1 > R3 \wedge R3 > R2 \wedge R1 \neq R3 \wedge R2 \neq R3]]$$

A *SA* uses ground instances of a binary *d-s* predicate in an $RBAC_1$ theory to record the pairs of roles that are involved in a "directly senior to" relationship. That is, the assertion $d\text{-}s(r_i,r_j)$ is used to record that role r_i is directly senior to the role r_j in an $RBAC_1$ role hierarchy.

The following set of clauses define the *senior to* relation (where '_' is an anonymous variable):

senior-to(R1,R1)←d-s(R1,_)
senior-to(R1,R1)←d-s(_,R1)
senior-to(R1,R2)←d-s(R1,R2)
senior-to(R1,R2)←d-s(R1,R3),senior-to(R3,R2)

The *senior-to* predicate is used in the definition of the *permitted* clause that follows:

permitted(U,read,O) $\leftarrow$ *ura(U,R1),senior-to(R1,R2),rpa(R2,read,O)*

The *permitted* clause expresses that a user *U* is authorized to perform the *read* operation on an object *O* if *U* is assigned to a role *R1* that is senior to the role *R2* in an $RBAC_1$ role hierarchy associated with the $RBAC_1$ theory, and *R2* has been assigned the *read* permission on *O*.

In implementations of our approach, *senior-to* should be stored as a *persistent relation* [1] that is recomputed only when changes are made to the set of *d-s* assertions in an $RBAC_1$ theory; it is not computed each time *permitted(U,read,O)* is evaluated.

The clauses defining *senior-to* are included in every instance of an $RBAC_1$ theory; the application-specific *d-s*, *ura* and *rpa* clauses define a particular instance of an $RBAC_1$ theory. For all "meaningful" $RBAC_1$ theories, the application-specific *d-s*, *ura*, and *rpa* clauses will be *acyclic* [2]. Although *senior-to* violates the acyclicity property, it is nevertheless negation-free. It follows therefore that any instance of an $RBAC_1$ theory is *locally stratified* and has a unique 2-valued *perfect model* [12] that coincides with the total well-founded model of the theory [8]. An important corollary of $RBAC_1$ theories being categorical and having a 2-valued model is that $RBAC_1$ theories define a consistent and unambiguous set of authorizations.

4. READ PROTECTED DATABASES

To see what is involved in protecting a deductive database *D* from unauthorized read requests, consider an *IDB* clause in *D* having the following general form:

$$H \leftarrow A1,\ldots,Am,\text{not } B1,\ldots,\text{not } Bn \qquad (m \geq 0,\ n \geq 0)$$

This type of clause is interpreted declaratively as stating that: *H* is true (or provable) in *D* iff $\forall Ai$ ($i \in \{1,..,m\}$) *Ai* is true (or provable) in *D* and $\forall Bj$ ($j \in \{1,..,n\}$) *Bj* is false (or not provable) in *D*.

When a clause defining *H* is to be included in the protected form, $D*$, of *D*, the required reading of the protected form of *H* is that: *H* is true (or provable) in $D*$ as far as a user *U* of $D*$ is concerned if $\forall Ai$ ($i \in \{1,..,m\}$) *Ai* is true in $D*$ and *U* is authorized (from $S*$) to know that *Ai* is true in $D*$ and $\forall Bj$ ($j \in \{1,..,n\}$) either *Bj* is not true (not provable) in $D*$ or U is not authorized (from $S*$) to know that Bj is true in $D*$. If U is not authorized to know that a literal C is true in $D*$ then we regard C as being false in $D*$ as far as U is concerned.

To define the read protection on H we use the following form of the *holds* predicate:

$$holds(U,read,H,D*,S*) \text{ iff } [S* \models permitted(U,read,H) \text{ and } D* \models H]$$

The $holds(U,read,H,D*,S*)$ definition expresses that U can read H (i.e., can know that H is true) from a protected database $D*$ iff U has the read permission on H from $S*$ and H is true in $D*$.

From the definition of *holds* we also have:

$$\neg holds(U,read,H,D*,S*) \text{ iff } [S* \not\models permitted(U,read,H) \text{ or } D* \not\models H]$$

This equivalence is consistent with our declarative reading of a read protected clause. That is, U cannot read H from $D*$ if U is not authorized to read H in $D*$ by $S*$ or if H is not true (provable) in $D*$.

Assuming that the 5-ary *holds* predicate is used with respect to a given instance of $D* \cup S*$ the read protected form of the *IDB* predicate H may be expressed in clausal form thus:

$$\begin{aligned} holds(U,read,H) \leftarrow\ & permitted(U,read,H), \\ & holds(U,read,A1),\ldots,holds(U,read,Am), \\ & not\ holds(U,read,B1),\ldots,not\ holds(U,read,Bn) \end{aligned}$$

That is, U reads H from $D*$ (i.e., U knows that H is true in $D*$) iff U is permitted to read H and for all Ai literals ($i \in \{1,..,m\}$), U is authorized to know that Ai is true in $D*$ and Ai is true in U's view of $D*$ and for all Bj ($j \in \{1,..,n\}$) Bj is either not in U's authorized view of $D*$ or Bj is false in $D*$.

The read protection for each of the predicates $A1,\ldots,Am,B1,\ldots,Bn$ that appears in the body of $holds(U,read,H)$ is defined in essentially the same way as that for H.

In the case of an n-ary *IDB* predicate I appearing in the body of $holds(U,read,H)$, the head of the read protected form of I in $D*$ will be $holds(U,read,I(t_1,t_2,\ldots,t_n))$ (where tj ($j=(1,..,n)$) is a term) and the body of the protected form of I will include a $permitted(U,read,I(t_1,t_2,\ldots,t_n))$ condition. The rest of the body of I in $D*$ will be a conjunction of $holds(U,read,Ak)$ or $not\ holds(U,read,Bl)$ conditions where Ak (Bl) is a positive (negative) literal appearing in the body of I in D.

In the case where the predicate to be protected in the body of *holds(U, read,H)* is an *n*-ary *EDB* relation, *E*, the head of the protected clause for *E* is $holds(U,read,E(X_1,..,X_n))$ and the body of this clause includes a $permitted(U,read,E(X_1,...,X_n))$ condition together with $E(X_1,...,X_n)$ itself. That is, for every *n*-ary *EDB* relation *E* the read protected form of *E* is:

$$holds(U,read,E(X_1,..,X_n)) \leftarrow permitted(U,read,E(X_1,..,X_n)),E(X_1,..,X_n)$$

The set of assertions that appear in the *EDB* of *D* do not change when *D* is rewritten in its protected form, $D*$. As such, to simplify the examples of protected databases that follow, we will omit assertions in $D*$.

Example 1 (The representation of a read protected databases)
Consider the database, $D_1=\{p(a,Y,Z) \leftarrow r(a,Y),s(Y,Z);\ r(a,Y) \leftarrow t(a,Y);\ r(b,Y) \leftarrow t(b,Y);\ t(a,b) \leftarrow;\ t(b,b) \leftarrow;\ s(b,10) \leftarrow\}$, where *s* and *t* are *EDB* relations and ';' separates clauses. The protected form of D_1, D_1*, is:

$$holds(U,read,p(a,Y,Z)) \leftarrow permitted(U,read,p(a,Y,Z)),$$
$$holds(U,read,r(a,Y)),holds(U,read,s(Y,Z))$$
$$holds(U,read,r(a,Y)) \leftarrow permitted(U,read,r(a,Y)),holds(U,read,t(a,Y))$$
$$holds(U,read,r(b,Y)) \leftarrow permitted(U,read,r(b,Y)),holds(U,read,t(b,Y))$$
$$holds(U,read,t(X,Y)) \leftarrow permitted(U,read,t(X,Y)),t(X,Y)$$
$$holds(U,read,s(Y,Z)) \leftarrow permitted(U,read,s(Y,Z)),s(Y,Z)$$

An example of an $RBAC_1$ security theory applicable to D_1* is:

$$S_1*=\{ura(bob,r1) \leftarrow;\ d\text{-}s(r1,r2) \leftarrow;\ rpa(r1,read,p(a,Y,Z)) \leftarrow Z < 20;$$
$$rpa(r2,read,r(a,Y)) \leftarrow;\ rpa(r1,read,s(Y,Z)) \leftarrow;\ rpa(r1,read,t(X,Y)) \leftarrow\}$$

5. COMPUTATIONAL ISSUES

Since $D* \cup S*$ is a function-free normal clause theory it follows that SLG-resolution may be used with $D* \cup S*$ to decide whether a user *U* has the read permission on an instance of an *n*-ary predicate $p(t1,t2,...,tn)$ in *D* (where t_j ($j=(1..n)$) is a term). To simplify the ensuing discussion we will assume that $D*$ is locally stratified. In this case, answer clauses generated by SLG-resolution will have an empty set of delayed literals. Our approach naturally extends to the case where $D*$ is not locally stratified and where answer clauses may not have a non-empty set of delayed literals.

In our approach, a query Q that includes *holds(U,read,p(t1,t2,...,tn))* (*not holds(U,read,p(t1,t2,...,tn))* literals may be directly posed by U and will be evaluated on $D* \cup S*$ iff U is authenticated to be the specifier of the *holds* (*not holds*) subgoals in Q. It follows from the discussion above that *holds(U,read,p(t1,t2,...,tn))* will be true in $D*$ iff *p(t1,t2,...,tn)* is true in D and U is authorized to know that *p(t1,t2,...,tn)* is true in D. If an SLG-tree with the root $Q \leftarrow Q$ where Q is *holds(U,read, p(t1,t2,...,tn))* terminates with $Q \leftarrow$ as an answer clause and Θ is an answer substitution then *p(t1,t2,...,tn)*Θ is true in D and U is authorized to know that *p(t1,t2,...,tn)*Θ is true in D by $S*$. If Q is *not holds(U,read,p(c1,c2,...,cn))* (where *ci* (i=(*1..n*)) is a constant to ensure *safe evaluation* [10]) and *holds(U,read,p(c1,c2,...,cn))*$\leftarrow$ is an answer clause by SLG-resolution on $D* \cup S*$ then U is authorized to know that *p(c1,c2,..,cn)* is true (provable) from $D* \cup S*$, *p(c1,c2,..,cn)* is true (provable) in D and *not holds(U,read,p(c1,c2,...,cn))* is *failed* by SLG-resolution. That is, $\neg$*p(c1,c2,...,cn)* is false in U's view of D since *p(c1,c2,...,cn)* is true in U's authorized view of $D*$. Conversely, if Q is *holds(U,read,p(t1, t2,...,tn))* and $Q \leftarrow Q$ is failed by SLG-resolution on $D* \cup S*$ then either *p(t1,t2,...,tn)* is false in D or U is not permitted to know that *p(t1,t2,...,tn)* is true in D; either way, *p(t1,t2,...,tn)* is false in D from U's perspective. If the evaluation of *not holds(U,read,p(c1,c2,...,cn))* succeeds by SLG-resolution then U is either not authorized to know that *p(c1,c2,...,cn)* is true in D from $D* \cup S*$ or *p(c1,c2,...,cn)* is false in D. In either case, $\neg$*p(c1,c2,...,cn)* is true in U's view of D.

Example 2 (Read Protection)
Suppose that Bob poses the query to retrieve all instances of p from D_1 in Example 1 and that S_1* (also from Example 1) is the $RBAC_1$ theory for D_1*. In this case, SLG-resolution produces the following set of answers: $\{X{=}a,\ Y{=}b,\ Z{=}10\}$. That is, only *p(a,b,10)* may be disclosed to Bob. Though $WFM(D_1) \models$ *p(b,b,10)*, *holds(bob,read,p(b,b,10))*$\leftarrow$ is not an answer clause by SLG-resolution since Bob is not authorized to know that *p(b,b,10)* is true in D_1. □

Query evaluation on $D* \cup S*$ may appear to be more expensive than on D since the clauses in $D*$ include additional *permitted* conditions. Moreover, $S*$ is part of the theory on which query evaluation is performed. However, the security information in $D* \cup S*$ has the effect of partitioning D into a number of subsets. An individual user can retrieve information from the one subset of $D*$ that $S*$ authorizes them to retrieve from. Hence, a user's queries are evaluated with respect to "their" subset of D, and since this subset is typically a smaller theory than D, a user's queries may be *more* efficiently performed on $D*$ than D. From a computational perspective, constants or restricting conditions (i.e., those involving comparison operators) from $S*$ may be introduced at an early stage in the evaluation of a user's query to constrain the search space of authorized solutions. Moreover, $S*$ may cause computations to fail early if a user has insufficient read permission to evaluate a query.

In all cases of failure of a goal clause, G, the user, U, receives a "no" response. From this, U cannot infer that $\neg G$ is true in the database D; G may have failed because U is not permitted to know that G is true in D.

Example 3 (Queries involving negation)
Consider the database, D_2={*p(X)←not q(X); q(b)←*}, where *q* is an *EBD* relation, protected by the security theory, S_2*, where:

S_2*={*ura(sue,r1)←; rpa(r1,read,p(X))←;*
rpa(r2,read,q(a))←; d-s(r1,r2)←}

For D_2* we have:

holds(U,read,p(X))←permitted(U,read,p(X)),not holds(U,read,q(X))
holds(U,read,q(X))←permitted(U,read,q(X)),q(X)

Now, suppose that Sue wishes to know whether *p(a)* is true in D_2. Since *holds(sue,read,p(a))←* may be generated from $D_2* \cup S_2*$ by SLG-resolution, Sue is permitted to know that *p(a)* is true in D_2. □

The next example shows that recursive databases require no special treatment to protect them from unauthorized disclosures of information.

Example 4 (Recursive query evaluation)
Consider the database, D_3={*q(X,Y)←r(X,Y); q(X,Y)←r(X,Z),q(Z,Y); r(a,b)←; r(b,c)←*}, where *r* is an *EDB* relation, and suppose that the security theory, S_3*, applies to D_3 where:

S_3*={*ura(jim,r1)←; rpa(r1,read,q(a,Y))←;*
rpa(r2,read,r(X,Y))←; d-s(r1,r2)←}

For D_3* we have:

$holds(U,read,q(X,Y)) \leftarrow permitted(U,read,q(X,Y)), holds(U,read,r(X,Y))$
$holds(U,read,q(X,Y)) \leftarrow permitted(U,read,q(X,Y)),$
$\quad holds(U,read,r(X,Z)), holds(U,read,q(Z,Y))$
$holds(U,read,r(X,Z)) \leftarrow permitted(U,read,r(X,Z)), r(X,Z)$

Now, suppose that Jim poses the query to list all instances of $q(X,Y)$ such that $X{=}a$. By SLG-resolution, with respect to $D_3* \cup S_3*$, the answer $Y{=}b$ is generated. It follows that only the answer $Y{=}b$ is revealed to Jim. Although $WFM(D_3) \models q(a,c)$ and Jim is permitted to see any instance of $q(X,Y)$ if $X{=}a$, for $q(a,c)$ to be disclosed to Jim, Jim must be permitted to know that both $WFM(D_3) \models q(a,b)$ and $WFM(D_3) \models q(b,c)$. However, since Jim does not have read access on $q(X,Y)$ where $X{=}b$ the fact that $WFM(D_3) \models q(a,c)$ cannot be divulged to him. □

6. CONCLUSIONS AND FURTHER WORK

By adopting the approach that we have described, it is possible to protect any normal deductive database from unauthorized reads of its data by specifying a user's access permissions in the same language that is ordinarily used to describe deductive databases. Moreover, no special methods of computation are required for query evaluation on read protected databases.

Our approach may be used to protect the information in databases defined in subsets of normal clause logic (e.g., relational databases), and may be used to protect the information contained in other types of "logic-based" databases (e.g., abductive databases). What is more, the approach enables *RBAC* to be directly represented in candidate deductive DBMSs (e.g., *XSB* [15]) without requiring any security-specific features.

In future work, we intend to investigate how our recent work on temporal *RBAC* [3] may be combined with the ideas presented here.

References

[1] Abiteboul, S., Hull, R., and Vianu, V., *Foundations of Databases*, Addison-Wesley, 1995.

[2] Apt, K., and Bezem, M., Acyclic Programs, *New Generation Computing*, 1990.

[3] Barker, S., Data Protection by Logic Programming, *1st International Conference on Computational Logic*, LNAI 1861, Springer, 2000.

[4] Barker, S., Secure Deductive Databases, *3rd International Workshop on Practical Applications of Declarative Languages (PADL'01)*, 2001.

[5] Barker, S., Access Control by Constraint Satisfaction, *To Appear.*

[6] Bonatti, P., Kraus, S., and Subrahmanian, V., Foundations of Secure Deductive Databases, *IEEE TKDE*, 7(3), 1995.

[7] Castano, S., Fugini, M., Martella, G., and Samarati, P., *Database Security*, Addison Wesley, 1995.

[8] Chen, W., and Warren, D., Tabled Evaluation with Delaying for General Logic Programs, *J. ACM*, 43(1), 1996.

[9] Cuppens, F., and Demolombe, R., A Modal Logical Framework for Security Policies, *ISMIS'97*, 1997.

[10] LLoyd, J., *Foundations of Logic Programming*, Springer, 1987.

[11] Minker, J., Logic and Databases: A 20 Year Retrospective, *1st I'nat. Workshop on Logic in Databases*, LNCS 1154, Springer, 1996.

[12] Przymusinski, T., Perfect Model Semantics, *Proc. 5th ICLP*, 1988.

[13] Ramakrishnan, R., *Applications of Logic Databases*, Kluwer, 1995.

[14] Sandhu, R., Coyne, E., Feinstein, H., and Youman, C., Role-Based Access Control Models, *IEEE Computer*, 1996.

[15] Sagonas, K., Swift, T., Warren, D., Freire, J., Rao. P., The XSB System, Version 2.0, Programmer's Manual, 1999.

[16] Van Gelder, A., Ross, K., and Schlipf, J., The Well-Founded Semantics for General Logic Programs, *J. ACM*, 38(3), 1991.

[17] Vardi, M., The Complexity of Query Languages, *ACM Symp. on the Theory of Computing*, May, 1982.

CHAPTER 18

Confidentiality vs Integrity in Secure Databases

Adrian Spalka and Armin B. Cremers
Department of Computer Science III, University of Bonn
Roemerstrasse 164, D-53117 Bonn, Germany
adrian@cs.uni-bonn.de

Key words: Databases, Security, Confidentiality, Integrity, Logic

Abstract: The problem of enforcing confidentiality in the presence of integrity constraints in secure and, in particular, in multi level databases is still open. To enforce confidentiality the majority of previous works either advocates a violation of integrity or proposes pragmatically its preservation or restoration. In this work we argue that there can never be a trade-off between these two properties for integrity is a fundamental quality of every database, ie also a secure one. Confidentiality always implies a kind of distortion of the open database. We introduce a formally sound method for its enforcement which relies on aliases, ie, additional tuples the only purpose of which is the preservation of integrity of both the open database and each distortion of it.

1. INTRODUCTION

The two, by far, most controversial issues in the field of secure and multi level databases are:

1. the handling of integrity constraints
2. the relationship of information at different security levels

The actual problems – and the failure to find a formally sound solution – can be best explained by observing the evolution from an open, flat database to a secure or multi level one.

In an open database the fact that a data set is the present database state implies that it satisfies the database's integrity constraints. Formally, integrity constraints represent invariant properties of any database state, ie, they play the role of boundary conditions which are as such given. From a practical viewpoint, a database is expected to be an image of some real-world section. A database state represents a snapshot of this section. The present state is said to be accurate if it truthfully describes the present situation in the section. Apart from the trivial case in which the real-world section is itself static, the database has no means for deciding the present state's accuracy. However, the database is very well able to separate all data sets into two groups: the nonsensical sets, ie those that cannot possibly be accurate, and the potentially accurate, ie the remaining ones. The separation criteria are the integrity constraints. Thus to have an open database with an invalid present state is an unmistakable indicator that the database is definitely not an image of the real-world section. If the integrity constraints are correctly specified, then the state is nonsensical and must be corrected. If the state is accurate, then the integrity constraints are erroneous and must be corrected. In any case, this unsatisfactory situation calls for a corrective action. This seems to be not so if this open database becomes a secure or multi level one.

An open database permits every transaction that leads to a valid state, there are no confidentiality demands and each user has unlimited powers. The integrity constraints' role is interpreted here as a voluntary protection against inadvertent mistakes. At the same time, integrity constraints provide an explanation to a user for a rejected transaction.

In a secure database, we assume that there is a global open database, which captures the open intended state of the world section, and a distorted local database for each user or group of users from which a part of the open state should be kept confidential. Spalka/Cremers (1999) show that a necessary precondition for the enforcement of confidentiality is the determination of a user's powers and an assessment of his assumed knowledge with respect to the database.

Given that a database comprises a signature, a set of integrity constraints and a state, there are at least three factors that can be manipulated in order to satisfy a confidentiality demand. A change in the signature yields a completely different database language, and a change in the integrity constraints affects a lot of database states. Even if successful, these means often incur a too radical distortion of a local database. The least obtrusive encroachment inserts and deletes single elements of the state. These locally distorted elements are called aliases for a confidentiality demand.

When a confidentiality demand is stated, the attempt to enforce it can threaten integrity at two points. Firstly, let us call it the static case, it can immediately violate the local database's integrity. Or secondly, this is the dynamic case, it leaves the local database in a valid state but the users with access to this database can perform a transaction that leaves this local database in a valid state but violates the integrity of the global database, ie, the user's transaction is rejected without a reason that is visible and comprehensible to this user. Given that the integrity of both the global and each local database must be preserved, our alias-based method examines the integrity constraints and the present state and determines if and how a confidentiality demand can be enforced. The distortion of a local database dictated by the confidentiality demand is a necessary one. The use of aliases – which can be both inserted or deleted of tuples – is an additional distortion, which is necessary to enforce a confidentiality demand and, at the same time, to preserve integrity of all databases.

In the static case our method picks the violated instances of the integrity constraints and attempts to modify the local state in such a way, that:

- the violated instance becomes satisfied again (preservation of integrity)
- the modification cannot be modified or deleted by the users of the local database (observation of the users' powers)
- the modification cannot be recognised by the users of the local database as a bogus one (observation of the users' assumed knowledge)

In the dynamic case our method picks the instances of the integrity constraints affected by the confidentiality demand and identifies those instances among them which, after a local user's authorised and valid transaction, remain satisfied in the local database but become violated in the global database, and attempts to modify the local state in such a way that such a transaction will be rejected.

Whenever aliases are needed to enforce a confidentiality demand but no suitable ones can be found, we reject it. The rejection is not a weakness of our method – it is in parallel to the real life situation, where some things can be kept secret and some not due to the person's knowledge and ability.

To make the identification of integrity constraints at threat (ie those that are or can become violated due to a confidentiality demand) tractable, we assume that they have been transformed from a closed formula into a set of normal clauses and possibly a set of rules, which needs to be included into the database state. Such a transformation is always possible[3].

Section 2 comprises quite a detailed and extensive discussion of previous works. The main result, our attempt to enforce confidentiality in the presence of integrity constraints, is presented in chapter 3. The conclusion comments on our approach and mentions some further steps.

2. PREVIOUS AND RELATED WORK

Most algebraic approaches to bring confidentiality in line with integrity are based on SeaView, a multi level relational data model introduced by

[3] Cf, eg, Cremers/Griefahn/Hinze (1994):69.

Denning et al (1987). The reason for classifying single attributes, according to the authors' opinion, is that an element, ie a tuple's attribute value, represents a fact[4] – from the viewpoint of logic a simply wrong statement[5]. In addition to it, a classification is also assigned to the whole relation scheme. The primary-key and the foreign-key constraints are taken to be the only integrity constraints. The authors note that: 'Functional dependencies correspond to real-world constraints; that is, they are not just a property of a particular relation instance'[6] and 'The requirements for consistency [at each security level] affect the integrity rules of the relational model, which are formulated as global constraints on an entire database.'[7] Yet their approach to the handling of multi level integrity does not account for these semantic facts. It relies on purely syntactical adjustments instead. In particular the decision to redefine a multi level relation's primary key as a combination of the standard relation's key and its classification is accompanied by semantic havoc.

Meadows/Jajodia (1987) speak of a conflict between database security and integrity because if there is an integrity constraint defined over data at more than one security level, then a user at a low security level can use accessible data and this constraint to infer information about data at a high security level. In the authors' view one can either upgrade the low data, ie, make them inaccessible to users at the low security level, or enforce the constraint only at the high security level, ie, sacrifice global integrity but preserve data availability.[8] W e believe that in the second case the low users could as well stop using the database at all. In their consideration of the primary-key constraint, the authors note that polyinstantiated objects can be a source of ambiguity.[9] But the question 'How do we provide guidelines to the user for choice of the best tuple?'[10] remains unanswered. In general, the proposals are made on the grounds of the opinion that

... the more likely it is that integrity can be restored in the future, the more acceptable it is to sacrifice integrity in the present.[11]

An opinion hardly targeted at semantic soundness.

Stachour (1988), Stachour (1989) and Haigh et al (1989) present LDV, an implementation approach of the multi level data model. Although the

[4] Denning et al (1987):220.

[5] A fact, ie a ground atomic formula, has a truth value, but an element is a term and as such has no truth value.

[6] Denning et al (1987):222.

[7] Denning et al (1987):221.

[8] Meadows/Jajodia (1987):95.

[9] In fact, they regard polyinstantiation as a means of reducing ambiguity and not as its origin. Cf Meadows/Jajodia (1987):92.

[10] Meadows/Jajodia (1987):93.

[11] Meadows/Jajodia (1987):98.

implementations of LDV and SeaView differ, the handling of polyinstantiation is the same – increased user flexibility is seen as the solution to semantic ambiguity.[12] In the LDV data model of Haigh/O'Brien/Thomsen (1990) security levels are assigned to tuples only. The authors recognise that '... if polyinstantiation is to be meaningful, it must be done in a manner consistent with the semantics of the database. The semantically significant entities in a relational database are tuples and relations'[13] This, admittedly, reduces ambiguity, yet does not eliminate it. The authors also claim that the enforcement of referential integrity and application integrity across access levels '... are problems for which no complete solution is possible'[14]. They suggest to '... establish quotas for each level and then enforce these quotas on a per level basis'[15]. Though possibly over-restrictive, this suggestion is semantically sound.

Gajnak (1988) investigates the adaptability of entity-relationship modelling to multi level security requirements. The author identifies three fundamental principles of multi level databases which must not be violated[16]. The important semantic determinacy principle states that '... factual dependencies should be non-ambiguous'[17]. This property is violated by SeaView's treatment of polyinstantiation. The author gives an example in which polyinstantiation can mean that: one database entry is an alias for another; a secret entry has been leaked; or the two entries refer to two real world objects. He concludes aptly that in this situation referential integrity as such must be ambiguous. Regrettably, the author's final advice – which we strongly support – that '... the determinacy principle should be supported directly by multilevel secure data models'[18] has been given little attention in the following years. Only Burns (1988) argues in direct support of Gajnak (1988) and presents some more examples illustrating the semantic inadequacy of SeaView's handling of polyinstantiation. She realises already that this '... automatic polyinstantiation is in direct conflict with ... the logical consistency of a database'[19].

Following her conviction that the loss of semantics can be as disastrous as the loss of confidentiality, Burns (1990a) undertakes an attempt to define a data model, the referential secrecy model, in which integrity is given the

[12] 'For flexibility, the user should be allowed to specify which tuples are to be filtered away from the response using time-oriented constructs and level-oriented constructs...' Stachour (1988):72.

[13] Haigh/O'Brien/Thomsen (1990):268.

[14] Haigh/O'Brien/Thomsen (1990):266.

[15] Haigh/O'Brien/Thomsen (1990):277.

[16] Gajnak (1988):189.

[17] Gajnak (1988):183.

[18] Gajnak (1988):189.

[19] Burns (1988):230.

same priority as confidentiality.[20] The ideas of this rather pragmatic approach are selective limitation of polyinstantiation and selective automatic upgrade of inserted tuples. While clearly not semantically sound, any solution limiting ambiguity should be regarded as an improvement. Burns (1990b) claims that '… the fundamental problem is that either the secrecy of the information within the database can be maintained, or the integrity of the database can be maintained, but not both simultaneously'[21]. While we strongly oppose this claim, we definitely sympathise with the author's opinion that 'Database integrity constraints are fundamentally invariant properties of the state of a database'[22] and with her conclusion that integrity must not be sacrificed. In a pragmatic manner, the author proposes to allow polyinstantiation and to audit it as an error so that the database administrator is able to correct it later.

Several suggestions for resolving the conflict between security and integrity are made in Maimone/Allen (1991). To prevent the duplicate existence of primary keys, the authors propose to prevent a user with a low access class from choosing a key existing at a high access class, eg, by partitioning the key space (a solution also proposed by Jajodia/Sandhu (1991)[23]) or by forcing the user to accept an application generated key – this amounts to a restriction of the database functionality. Referential integrity is not brought in accord with security but simply sacrificed[24]. To correct the resulting inconsistencies, a garbage collection procedure should at some time later remove the dangling tuples. The authors' proposal to replace value integrity constraints with triggers because they '… are procedural and event-based … [and] say nothing about the current or consistent state of the database'[25] is clearly opposed to any attempt at defining an unambiguous semantics of secure databases.

Sandhu/Jajodia (1993) deal also with referential integrity. This time the authors note that entity polyinstantiation, viz, the existence of two tuples with the same primary key value but different security levels, is responsible for the problem of referential ambiguity. Here one cannot properly determine which foreign key tuples correspond to which primary key tuples. In order to avoid it, the authors simply disallow this kind of polyinstantiation. Again, they suggest to partition the domain of the primary key. At the same time, they present an example in which this measure leads in turn to new problems.

[20] Burns (1990a):135.

[21] Burns (1990b):37.

[22] Burns (1990b):37.

[23] Jajodia/Sandhu (1991c):70.

[24] 'Our approach is to allow the parent record to be deleted, and to leave the child records in place.' Maimone/Allen (1991):56.

[25] Maimone/Allen (1991):58.

- there are three groups of users: $G_1 = \{u_1\}$, $G_2 = \{u_1, u_2\}$ and $G_3 = \{u_1, u_2, u_3\}$
- a database is associated with each group: D_1, D_2, and D_3; D_1 is the open database, ie nothing should be kept secret from u_1, and D_2, and D_3 are distortions of D_1 such that – according to the group members – u_1 can state confidentiality demands for u_2, u_3, and u_2 can state confidentiality demands for u_3.

According to Spalka/Cremers (1999) a successful enforcement of a confidentiality demand is a distortion of the truth value that yields a single distorted model, eg if the tuple α should be kept secret from u_3, then α's truth value in D_3 is opposite to its truth value in D_1.

3.1 Dynamic violation

Let us first have a look at this situation in a general database D and one of its distortions D'. All elements of C, the integrity constraints, are universally quantified clauses, ie a disjunction of literals.

In the dynamic case, the effect of a confidentiality demand stated for a tuple α does not violate any integrity constraint. However, in order to respect the user's powers we must ensure that he cannot execute an authorised transaction, ie one that is within his powers, that is valid in his local database but invalid in the global database.

Given a possible dynamic violation, our idea to enforce confidentiality is to try to ensure that whenever a transaction yields a violated instance of an integrity constraint with respect to D it will also yield a violated instance of an integrity constraint with respect to D'. Each such instance has the form

$$\psi\pi = \eta_1 \vee \ldots \vee \eta_k \vee \varepsilon_1 \vee \ldots \vee \varepsilon_{n-k}$$

such that:

- each η_j is a truthful literal
- each ε_i is a distorted literal
- α or $\neg\alpha$ is among the distorted ε-literals

$\psi\pi$ has the same truth value in D and in D', if k=n, ie all links of $\psi\pi$ are truthful and neither α or $\neg\alpha$ is among them. This trivial case guarantees that this instance of the integrity constraint will always have the same truth value in both the global and local databases, ie a transaction accepted locally will also be accepted globally and if it is rejected by the global database, then it will also be rejected by local database and the user has a local explanation for the failure.

Let $k<n$ and α or $\neg\alpha$ is among the distorted ε-links of $\psi\pi$. The instance $\psi\pi$ is satisfied, ie at least one of its links is true. According to the

observation of powers and knowledge, none of the distorted ε_i is in R_u or K_u. Thus, the effect of every local transaction is limited to the state's truthful, undistorted part, that is, a local transaction can change only the η-links' truth values (simultaneously in both the local and global databases). Therefore, keeping in mind that each ε_i has in D the opposite truth value than in D', if there is at least one ε_i the truth value of which in D' is False, then $\psi\pi$ clearly cannot become false in D while it remains true in D'. Again, integrity is not at threat.

Let us finally turn our attention to the dangerous case. Let $k<n$ and all ε_i be true in D'. The global database's integrity can be threatened if there is a single local transaction (or a sequence thereof) which sets all η_j to False, for then $\psi\pi$ remains true in D' but turns false in D. To prevent this from happening we can, firstly, try to find an η_j we can force to stay true, or, secondly, try to find an instance $\varphi\sigma$ we can force to turn to False in D' whenever $\psi\pi$ turns to False in D. The first case is simple: check if there is an η_j which is true in D' and satisfies also the following conditions:

- η_j is not in K_u: it respects the user's knowledge, ie the user can only learn the truth value of η_j from the database
- η_j is not in R_u: it respects the user's powers, ie the user cannot alter our distortion
- the change of the truth value of η_j does not violate any other integrity constraint

If there is none such literal we must examine the second way. We now need a, not necessarily different, integrity constraint φ and a substitution σ such that:

- $\varphi\sigma$ is ground
- $\psi\pi = \eta_1 \vee \ldots \vee \eta_k \vee \xi_1 \vee \ldots \vee \xi_{n-k}$, $\varphi\sigma$ coincides with $\psi\pi$ in the truthful η-links
- all ξ_i are false in D'
- the confidentiality demand for all ξ_i is satisfiable

If we can find such a φ and σ, we make each ξ_i an alias; if we can find more than one combination, pick one or let the user choose one; if there is none, the confidentiality demand for α is not satisfiable.

3.2 Static violation

In the static case, the effect of a confidentiality demand stated for a tuple α violates a subset W of the integrity constraints C, ie, for all ψ in W there is a finite set of substitutions Π_ψ such that for all π in Π_ψ $\psi\pi$ is ground, α or $\neg\alpha$ is among the links of $\psi\pi$ and $\psi\pi$ is false in D', ie violated.

Given a static violation, the idea to enforce confidentiality is to try to change the truth value of each instance $\psi\pi$ in D to True. We are not allowed to change an ε_i's truth value in D' for its distortion is a deliberate consequence of a previous confidentiality demand. Thus we can only achieve our goal by reversing the truth value of an η_j. However, our choice is limited to those η_j which also satisfy the conditions for truth-reversal in the dynamic case.

Each such η_j is called a candidate for an alias, and that η_j actually selected from among all the candidates is called an alias for α and ψ. If the set of candidates is empty, then the confidentiality demand for α is not satisfiable. Otherwise, we have again decided to let the user pick a candidate he considers most appropriate.

3.3 Remark

This theory for secure databases supporting primary key and foreign key constraints is already implemented in a prototype a copy of which can be freely obtained by request to the authors.

4. CONCLUSION

When dealing with confidentiality and integrity in secure databases most previous works took the view that one can or must be traded against the other. We have shown that integrity is a fundamental property of all databases, open and secure ones, and must never be violated or sacrificed. Therefore, whenever a database acquires additional properties or abilities, these must always be introduced in a manner that respects and preserves integrity – there can be no trade-off. Confidentiality is always connected to a distortion of the open database and there are two elements of the database that can be distorted: its signature, viz its scheme, and its state. A distortion of the scheme is a permanent one and, thus, it is useful, whenever the confidentiality demands have a recurring pattern. This work focuses on confidentiality demands which need not be anticipated in advance. Our method to enforce them has two properties. Firstly, whenever the database determines that a confidentiality demand cannot be brought into accord with integrity it is rejected as unsatisfiable. And, secondly, if recognised by the database as satisfiable, our method computes if and how many additional distortions of the state, which we call aliases, are needed to enforce it in a way that preserves present integrity and prevents future violation of integrity. Since this method has a sound formal background, the statements and results can be verified in a rigid proof. As an example, we have demonstrated its application to a primary key constraint. We have a complete proof for its application and limits to primary key and foreign key constraints, although general constraints in databases with rules still lie ahead.

5. REFERENCES

Bonatti, Piero, Sarit Kraus and V.S. Subrahmanian. (1992) 'Declarative Foundations of Secure Deductive Databases'. Ed Joachim Biskup and Richard Hull. *4th International Conference on Database Theory – ICDT'92*. LNCS, vol 646. Berlin, Heidelberg: Springer-Verlag. pp 391-406. [Also in: *IEEE Transactions on Knowledge and Data Engineering* 7.3 (1995):406-422.]

Burns, Rae K. (1988) 'An Application Perspective on DBMS Security Policies'. Ed Teresa F. Lunt. *Research Directions in Database Security.* 1st RADC Database Security Invitational Workshop 1988. New York et al: Springer-Verlag, 1992. pp 227-233.

-----. (1990a) 'Referential Secrecy'. *1990 IEEE Symposium on Research in Security and Privacy.* IEEE Computer Society Press. pp 133-142.

-----. (1990b) 'Integrity and Secrecy: Fundamental Conflicts in the Database Environment'. Ed Bhavani Thuraisingham. *3rd RADC Database Security Workshop 1990.* Bedford, Massachussets: Mitre, 1991. pp 37-40.

Cremers, Armin B., Ulrike Griefahn and Ralf Hinze. (1994) *Deduktive Datenbanken.* Braunschweig: Vieweg.

Das, Subrata Kumar. (1992) *Deductive Databases and Logic Programming.* Wokingham, England: Addison-Wesley.

Denning, Dorothy E., Teresa F. Lunt, Roger R. Schell, Mark Heckman and William R. Shockley. (1987) 'A Multilevel Relational Data Model'. *1987 IEEE Symposium on Security and Privacy.* IEEE Computer Society Press. pp 220-234.

Gajnak, George E. (1988) 'Some Results from the Entity/Relationship Multilevel Secure DBMS Project'. Ed Teresa F. Lunt. *Research Directions in Database Security.* 1st RADC Database Security Invitational Workshop 1988. New York et al: Springer-Verlag, 1992. pp 173-190.

Garvey, Thomas D., and Teresa F. Lunt. (1991b) 'Cover Stories for Database Security'. Ed Carl E. Landwehr and Sushil Jajodia. *Database Security V.* IFIP WG11.3 Workshop on Database Security 1991. Amsterdam: North-Holland, 1992. pp 363-380.

Haigh, J. Thomas, Richard C. O'Brien and Dan J. Thomsen. (1990) 'The LDV Secure Relational DBMS Model'. Ed Sushil Jajodia and Carl E. Landwehr. *Database Security IV.* IFIP WG11.3 Workshop on Database Security 1990. Amsterdam: North-Holland, 1991. pp 265-279.

-----, -----, Paul D. Stachour and D.L. Toups. (1989) 'The LDV Approach to Database Security'. Ed David L. Spooner and Carl E. Landwehr. *Database Security III.* IFIP WG11.3 Workshop on Database Security 1989. Amsterdam: North-Holland, 1990. pp 323-339.

Jajodia, Sushil, and Ravi S. Sandhu. (1991) 'Enforcing Primary Key Requirements in Multilevel Relations'. Ed Rae K. Burns. *Research Directions in Database Security IV.* 4th RADC Multilevel Database Security Workshop 1991. Bedford, Massachussets: Mitre, 1992. pp 67-73.

Landwehr, Carl E. (1981) 'Formal Models for Computer Security'. *ACM Computing Surveys* 13.3:247-278.

Maimone, Bill, and Richard Allen. (1991) 'Methods for Resolving the Security vs. Integrity Conflict'. Ed Rae K. Burns. *Research Directions in Database Security IV.* 4th RADC Multilevel Database Security Workshop 1991. Bedford, Massachussets: Mitre, 1992. pp 55-59.

Meadows, Catherine, and Sushil Jajodia. (1987) 'Integrity Versus Security In Multi-Level Secure Databases'. Ed Carl E. Landwehr. *Database Security.* IFIP WG11.3 Initial Meeting 1987. Amsterdam: North-Holland, 1988. pp 89-101.

Morgenstern, Matthew. (1987) 'Security and Inference in Multilevel Database and Knowledge-Base Systems'. *1987 ACM SIGMOD Conference / SIGMOD Record* 16.3:357-373.

-----. (1988) 'Controlling Logical Inference in Multilevel Database Systems'. *1988 IEEE Symposium on Security and Privacy.* IEEE Computer Society Press. pp 245-255.

Qian, Xiaolei. (1994) 'Inference Channel–Free Integrity Constraints in Multilevel Relational Databases'. *1994 IEEE Symposium on Research in Security and Privacy.* IEEE Computer Society Press. pp 158-167.

Reiter, Raymond. (1984) 'Towards a Logical Reconstruction of Relational Database Theory'. Ed Michael L. Brodie, John Mylopoulos and Joachim W. Schmidt. *On Conceptual Modeling.* New York: Springer-Verlag. pp 191-238.

Sandhu, Ravi S., and Sushil Jajodia. (1993) 'Referential Integrity in Multilevel Secure Databases'. *16th National Computer Security Conference.* NIST/NCSC. pp 39-52.

Sicherman, George L., Wiebren de Jonge and Reind P. van de Riet. (1983) 'Answering Queries Without Revealing Secrets'. *ACM Transactions on Database Systems* 8.1:41–59.

Spalka, Adrian, and Armin B. Cremers. (1997) 'Structured name-spaces in secure databases'. Ed T. Y. Lin and Shelly Qian. *Database Security XI.* IFIP TC11 WG11.3 Conference on Database Security. London at al: Chapman & Hall, 1998. pp 291-306.

-----, -----. (1999) 'The effect of confidentiality on the structure of databases'. *Database Security XIII.* IFIP TC11 WG11.3 Conference on Database Security.

Stachour, Paul D. (1988) 'LOCK Data Views'. Ed Teresa F. Lunt. Research Directions in Database Security. *1st RADC Database Security Invitational Workshop 1988.* New York et al: Springer-Verlag, 1992. pp 63-80.

-----. (1989) 'SCTC Technical Note: Organizing Secure Applications "by Name"'. Ed Teresa F. Lunt. *Research Directions in Database Security II.* 2nd RADC Database Security Workshop 1989. Menlo Park, CA: SRI.

Thuraisingham, Bhavani M. (1991) 'A Nonmonotonic Typed Multilevel Logic for Multilevel Secure Data/Knowledge Base Management Systems'. *The Computer Security Foundations Workshop IV.* IEEE Computer Society Press. pp 127-138.

-----. (1992) 'A Nonmonotonic Typed Multilevel Logic for Multilevel Secure Data/Knowledge Base Management Systems – II'. *The Computer Security Foundations Workshop V.* IEEE Computer Society Press. pp 135-146.

CHAPTER 19

Extending SQL's Grant Operation to Limit Privileges

Arnon Rosenthal, Edward Sciore
MITRE Corporation and Boston College
arnie@mitre.org, sciore@cs.bc.edu

Key words: Access controls, SQL, limited privilege, Grant/Revoke

Abstract: Privileges in standard SQL are unconditional, forcing the grantor to trust the recipient's discretion completely. We propose an extension to the SQL grant/revoke security model that allows a grantor to impose limitations on how the received privilege may be used. This extension also has a non-traditional implication for view security. Although our examples are from DBMSs, most results apply to arbitrary sets of privileges, in non-database software.

1. INTRODUCTION

Recent database security research has had distressingly little influence on DBMS vendors. The SQL security model has had few extensions in the past 20 years, except for the recent addition of role-based access controls. This paper extends SQL grant/revoke semantics to include a *privilege-limitation mechanism.* Our goal is to present a model which has a small number of new constructs (and thus has a reasonable chance at vendor implementation and adoption), but covers significant unmet security needs.

In standard SQL, a user who has a privilege is able to use it in any circumstance. By attaching limitation predicates to a grant, we refine this "all or nothing" mechanism. For example, a limitation predicate may restrict a command to certain days or hours, to members or non-members of certain groups, to users above a certain rank, to tables above a threshold size, or to requests that are received along a trusted path.

Limitations seem particularly important in large enterprise or multi-enterprise systems, where it may be difficult to impose sanctions for improper use of a privilege. They also can reduce the scope for damage by an intruder who misuses legitimate users' privileges.

Our privilege limitation model is motivated by two principles:

- *The system should have a unified, flexible means of limiting privileges, rather than multiple overlapping mechanisms.*
- *The ability to grant (and to limit grants of others) should respect the natural chains of authority.*

The first principle implies that "revoking a privilege" and "imposing additional limits on an existing grant" are facets of the same concept. For example, imposing a limitation predicate of *false* should be equivalent to revoking the privilege. More generally, modifying the predicate of an existing grant should be equivalent to granting the privilege with the new predicate and revoking the old one. We thus aim to simplify [Bert99], which has separate treatments for SQL-like cascading revoke of entire privileges (without reactivation) and negative authorizations (reactivate-able partial limitations, without cascade).

The second principle guides how grant authority is passed. A user, when granting a privilege, must pass on at least as many limitations as he himself has. Moreover, by modifying the limitations on an existing grant G, a user can propagate those modifications to all grants emanating from G. For example, the creator of a table in a distributed system might authorize remote administrators to grant access to their users, subject to some general limitations; these administrators might further limit access by individual users, as appropriate for each site. If the creator subsequently decides that additional limitations are necessary, he only needs to modify his grants to the remote administrators.

The second principle also implies that a subject x can limit *only* those grants that emanate from a grant he has made. If user y has received grant authority independently of x, then x cannot restrict y's use of that power. To see the need for this principle, imagine that the "Vote" privilege has been granted (with grant option) to the head of each United Nations delegation. Imagine the denial-of-service risk if, as in [Bert99], each could impose limitations on others.

Section 2 describes the principles that underly our approach, and extends SQL grant syntax to allow limitation predicates. Section 3 defines and illustrates the semantics of predicate-limited grants. Section 4 extends the theory to views. Section 5 briefly shows how our model addresses many of the needs perceived in previous work. Section 6 summarizes and presents open research problems.

2. ACCESS CONTROL BASICS

We present our new model gradually. In this section we state the SQL model in terminology that will be useful in the general case. We also show how SQL grants are a special case of limited grants.

A *subject* is a user, group, or role. We treat each subject as atomic; inheritance among subjects (e.g., from a group to its members) is left for future research. A database object is a portion of the database that requires security control, such as a table or procedure. Each database object has a set of operations. For example, table T will have operations such as "insert into T", "select from T", etc.

There are two kinds of *action* associated with an operation: *executing* the operation, and *granting* an authorization for it. A subject issues a *command* to tell the system to perform an action.

Standard SQL has two forms of the grant command. "**grant** θ **to** s", authorizes s to perform execute commands for operation θ. To authorize s to perform both execute and grant commands for θ, one issues the second form,

grant θ ***to** s **with grant option.***

To specify grants with limitations, we extend the syntax to include two (optional) predicates:

grant θ **to** s [**executeif** P_1] [**grantif** P_2]

P_1, called the *execute*-predicate (or *exec_pred*) of the grant, restricts the conditions under which subject s can execute operation θ. P_2, the *grantonward-predicate (or gr_pred)* of the grant, restricts the conditions under which s can grant θ onward to others.

Each operation θ has an *authorization graph*, a rooted labeled digraph that represents the current (non-revoked) grants for θ. We denote it AG_θ, or just AG if θ is implied. The graph has one node for each subject; the root node corresponds to the creator of θ. There is one edge e_G for each unrevoked grant command G (and we refer interchangeably to G or e_G); a grant by s_1 to s_2 corresponds to an edge from node s_1 to s_2. Edge e_G is labeled with G's two predicates.

A *chain* to *s* is an acyclic path $C \equiv \langle G_1, \ldots, G_n \rangle$ in **AG** such that s_1 is the root, each G_i goes from s_i to s_{i+1}, and s_{n+1} is s. By convention, the predicates associated with G_i are denoted gr_pred_i and $exec\_pred_i$.

In the general case, G's predicates can reference G's command state (as discussed in Section 3). In the special case of grants in standard SQL, the exec_pred P_1 is always the constant true (that is, no restriction applied during execution), and the gr_pred P_2 is either *false* (if no grant option) or *true* (if with grant option). We call AG a SQL *authorization* graph if every exec_pred is the constant predicate true and every gr_pred is one of {*true*, *false*}.

The authorization graph AG determines whether a subject s is allowed to perform a command. In particular, AG must have a chain to s that *justifies* performing the command. The general definition of justification appears in Section 3. In the special case of standard SQL, a chain justifies a grant command if all its edges have the grant option; a chain justifies an execute command if all its edges (except possibly the last) have the grant option. More formally:

Definition (for SQL grants): Let $C \equiv <G_1,\ldots,G_n>$ be a chain to s.

- C is *SQL-valid* if $\{gr\_pred_i \mid i = 1, \ldots, n-1\}$ are all *true*. An edge is SQL-valid if it is part of a SQL-valid chain.
- If C is SQL-valid, then C is said to *SQL-justfy* execute commands.
- If C is SQL-valid and gr_pred_n is true, then C is said to *SQL-justify* grant commands.

There are two purposes to these rather elaborate formalizations of a simple concept. First, validity becomes non-trivial when we include general limitation predicates, and we wish to introduce the terminology early. Second, chains (and hence edges) can become invalid what a grant is revoked. In this case, it is the responsibility of the system to automatically revoke all invalid edges.

SQL grants correspond naturally to SQL authorization graphs. That is, if every edge in AG came from a SQL grant, then the graph is an SQL authorization graph. Also, when revoke deletes edges from a SQL authorization graph, the result is still a SQL authorization graph. Section 3.7 will show that our general concepts of validity and justification reduce to the above, on SQL authorization graphs.

3. PREDICATE-LIMITED GRANTS

Section 2 introduced authorization graphs, and defined, for the special case of SQL (unrestricted) grants, how valid chains can justify commands from a subject. This section considers the general case. In particular, justification becomes command-specific – a chain can justify a command only if the command's state satisfies the appropriate limitation predicates. Definitions are given in Sections 3.1 through 3.5. Section 3.6 considers workarounds for an implementation difficulty that does not arise in standard SQL. Section 3.7 shows that we cleanly extend SQL semantics.

3.1Command States

Each command has an associated *state*, which consists of:

- values for environment variables at the time the command was issued;

- the contents of the database at the time the command was issued; and
- values for the arguments of the command.

Example environment variables include $USER (the subject performing the command), $TIME (the time of day when the command was submitted), $LOCATION (from which the command was submitted), $AUTHENTICITY (the certainty that the requestor is authentic), $TRUSTEDPATH (whether the command arrived over a secure connection), and $GLOBALSTATUS (e.g., whether the system is in "emergency mode").

Example argument values are $NEW_TUPLE (for insert and modify commands), $OLD_TUPLE (for modify), and $GRANTEE (for grant commands). Interesting portions of the database state include group and role memberships (is this worker on the night shift?), local status (is a particular patient in emergency mode?), and cardinality (are the tables underlying an aggregate view large enough to preserve anonymity?).

3.2 Limitation Predicates

A *limitation predicate* is a Boolean function without side effects. The inputs to this function are references to a command state – arguments, environmental variables, and database contents. If P is a limitation predicate and C is a command, we write *P(C)* to denote the truth value of P given inputs from the state of C.

We do not propose a particular syntax for predicates. For a DBMS, SQL-like expressions (with embedded environment variables and functions) seem appropriate.

Example. A predicate that evaluates to *true* if the time of the command is during normal working hours or if the subject works the night shift:

($TIME between <8am, 6pm>) or ($USER in NightShift)

Example. A predicate that evaluates to *false* if the grant command is between a particular pair of users: not ($USER = Boris and $GRANTEE = Natasha)

Example. A predicate that restricts a user from inserting high-priced tuples into a table: ($NEW_TUPLE.Price < 100)

3.3 Motivating Examples

Suppose the creator of table *Items* issues the following grant G_1:

grant insert **on** Items **to** joe
executeif ($TIME **between** <8am, 6pm>)

grantif ($USER **in** Manager) **and** (**not** $GRANTEE = mary)

Let θ be the operation "insert on Items". Subject *joe* is allowed to execute θ only between 8am and 6pm. Joe is allowed to grant θ only when he is in the *Manager* role, and the (potential) grantee is not *mary.*

In the above grant G_1, the table creator (who has unlimited authority on its operations) issued the grant, and so Joe's privileges are limited exactly by the specified predicates. Now suppose that Joe issues the following grant G_2 while he is a manager:

grant insert **on** Items **to** amy
executeif $DAY = monday
grantif $TRUSTEDPATH

We first note that Joe was allowed to issue G_2, because he was a manager at the time of the grant, and the grantee is Amy, not Mary. Now suppose that after issuing G_2, Joe is removed from the *Manager* role. Although Joe is no longer able to issue grant commands, grant G_2 will not be invalidated – G_1's predicates are evaluated using the state of G_2, which is taken from *the time the command was issued.*

We next consider what privileges Amy has. Since Joe cannot give Amy fewer restrictions than he has, his restrictions must be added to those of G_2. Thus Amy's effective exec_pred is *($TIME between <8am, 6pm>) and ($DAY=monday),* and her effective gr_pred is *($USER in Manager) and (not $GRANTEE = sue) and ($TRUSTEDPATH).*

3.4 Semantics

As before, and throughout this section, let C =<G_1,...,G_n> denote a chain to subject s. Each G_i has predicates gr_pred_i and $exec\_pred_i$. The definition uses a subtle mutual recursion, and the theorem gives an alternative form.

Definition (general case for grants):

- C is *valid* if n=1 (that is, C consists of a single edge from the root).
- C is *valid* if for each i, the initial subchain <G_1,...G_{i-1}> justifies G_i.
- C *justifies a grant* G from s if C is valid and for each edge G_k in the chain, $gr\_pred_k(G)$ = *true*.

Theorem 1: *C is valid iff for each G_j, for all its predecessors $k<j$, $gr\_pred_k(G_j)$* = true.

Definition: *An edge G is* valid *if it is justified by some chain. An authorization graph is* valid *if all its edges are valid.*

Theorem 2*: In a valid authorization graph, all nodes with outgoing edges have at least one incoming valid chain.*

Definition (general case for execution): C *justifies an execution command* E if C is valid and for each edge G_k in the chain, $exec\_pred_k(G)$ = *true*.

A grant G with an exec_pred of *false* is useless, regardless of the gr_pred. The grant authorization can be passed on to others, but the effective exec_pred along any chain involving G will be false, and thus the operation can never be executed.

3.5 An Example to Illustrate the Subtleties

Privileges are passed along valid chains, each of which effectively carries a pair of predicates, the conjunction of its gr_preds and the conjunction of its exec_preds. Even in a valid graph, some chains can be invalid, and one cannot then use them to justify commands. To illustrate this, consider the following authorization graph:

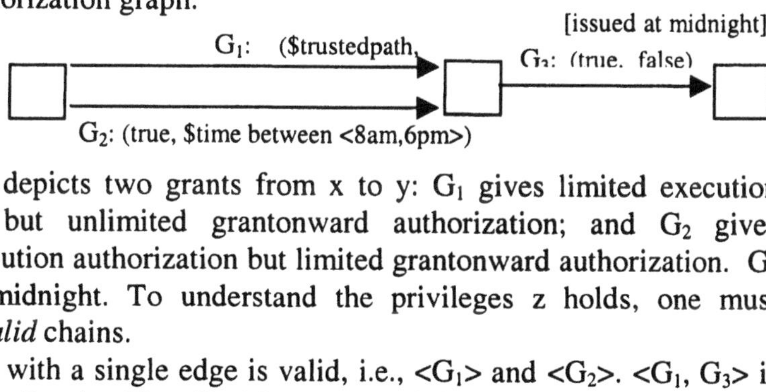

The graph depicts two grants from x to y: G_1 gives limited execution authorization but unlimited grantonward authorization; and G_2 gives unlimited execution authorization but limited grantonward authorization. G_3 is issued at midnight. To understand the privileges z holds, one must consider the *valid* chains.

Each chain with a single edge is valid, i.e., $<G_1>$ and $<G_2>$. $<G_1, G_3>$ is valid because $<G_1>$ justifies G_3 (since gr_pred_1 is the constant *true*). $<G_2, G_3>$ is not valid, because G_3 is not justified by $<G_2>$, because the state of G_3 has $time=midnight. Hence, commands by z can be justified only by $<G_1, G_3>$. An execution command by z can be justified only if it satisfies the exec_preds from $<G_1, G_3>$, i.e., arrived with *$trustedpath=true*. (If G_3 had instead been issued at 10am, then $<G_2, G_3>$ would be valid, and the effective exec_pred for z would be *true*.)

3.6 Maintaining Validity

To evaluate incoming commands, one needs to know which chains are valid. Since grants' states do not change, one can evaluate each relevant predicate just once, at some time after the grant state is created. When w executes a grant command G ≡ (w,x), each newly-created acyclic chain in AG involving G needs to be tested for validity. There are two cases:

- *G is the last edge on the chain;*
- G is in the middle of the chain.

In both cases, there are issues of algorithmic efficiency, which are outside our scope. The first case is somewhat easier, because the command state for G is currently available to be used in checking the chain's gr_preds. In the second case, there is a more basic complication: We cannot expect the entire system state from the last grant on the chain to have been retained (including the database of that time).

For example, consider the authorization graph of Section 3.5, and suppose subject x issues the following grant command (call it G_4):

grant θ **to** y **executeif** true **grantif** ($USER in Accountant)

In order to determine if the new chain C' ≡ <G_4, G_3> is valid, we need to see if G_4 justifies G_3, i.e., to evaluate whether G_3 satisfies the predicate *$USER in Accountant*. To do so, we must have retained enough state of the earlier grant G_3 to know whether y was in *Accountant* at the time G3 was issued.

Consequently, both the semantics and pragmatics need to adjust. Pragmatically, an organizational policy could specify what portion of the system state that will be retained, and writers of Grant predicates would endeavor to use only that portion. The saved portion of the state may be extended over time, as the need for additional information is better understood.

Formally, if an edge predicate in C_{new} references state information that was not saved, then the system must determine how to assign a value to the predicate. We propose that the system treats unknown state information as a no-information SQL Null. If such grants are permitted, then the order in which Grant commands are received affects what information is available to evaluate predicate validity. To keep the system sound (i.e., not allowing grants that users would not want), we require that predicates be monotonic in information state – i.e., do not use "is Null".

3.7 Standard SQL as a Special Case

We now consider the connection between limitation predicates and standard SQL. An SQL grant without grant option gives arbitrary execute privilege and no grant privilege; thus it should be equivalent to

grant θ **to** s **executeif** true **grantif** false

An SQL grant with grant option gives arbitrary execute and grant privilege, and thus should be equivalent to

grant θ **to** s **executeif** true **grantif** true

This correspondence is confirmed in the following theorem:

Theorem 3: Consider a SQL authorization graph AG. Then:

- *A grant or execute command, or an edge, or a graph, is valid iff it is SQL-valid.*
- AG *can be constructed by a sequence of SQL grants.*
- *The validity of a grant or execute command is independent of the command state. It depends only on the valid chains to the issuing subject (i.e., the subject's privileges).*

If we use the conventions that an omitted executeif clause has a default value of *true,* that "with grant option" is an alternate syntax for grantif *true,* and an omitted grantif clause has a default value of *false*, then standard SQL syntax is incorporated seamlessly into ours.

4. LIMITED PERMISSIONS ON VIEWS

Databases have a rich theory for views; in this respect, they are more expressive than operating systems, information retrieval systems, and middleware. Several guidelines drove our extension of "limited privileges" theory to views. We wish again to satisfy the principles of Section 1, notably, to have recognizable chains of authority. We also preserve the usual amenities of view permissions: Grant/revoke from a view must behave as if the view were an ordinary table, and one can grant access to a view but not to the whole underlying table.

We present only an abbreviated treatment, largely through example, due to page limits. Specifically, we examine only the privileges that the creator has, and assume that only grants have limitation predicates (i.e., all exec_preds are *true*). These restrictions, and the dictatorial power of the view creator, will be relaxed in future work.

For each view, we define an authorization graph as if the view were an ordinary table, except that the creator does not get unlimited privileges. Let $V=Q(T_1,\ldots,T_m)$, and suppose for the moment that the exec_pred of each T_i is simply *true.* Then the semantics are: the view creator (and the initial node of the view's authorization graph) is initialized with a grant limitation that is the intersection of these predicates, (If a view creator were not subject to these limitations, a user with limited access to table T could escape the limitations by creating the view "Select * from T".)

We now sketch several extensions for the model of view privileges.

First, consider the view V defined by "Select A_1, A_2 from T". In conventional SQL, a view creator may want to grant the privilege on the operation *select from view V* to users who do not have authority on the base table T. But suppose the creator suffers from a limitation predicate on T, and hence also on V. Who is empowered to make grants that loosen the limitations on the view? Thus far, nobody has this very useful right.

To cure this (and several other ills), in future work we will move away from treating a view as an object to be owned. Instead, it will be seen as derived data, for which certain permissions are justifiable. To start with, any possessor of a right on T can grant that right on V. (We are currently assuming the view definitions to be readable by all interested parties. Under this assumption, any subject with access to T could just define their own view, identical to V, and then grant the privilege.)

Next, consider a view over multiple tables, e.g., "Select A_6, A_7 from T_1 join T_2". Oracle SQL specifies that the creator's privileges on the view are the intersection of the creator's privileges on the input tables. In [Ro00] we apply the same rule to non-creators. It extends easily to handle grants with limitation predicates on just execute – the creator's limitations are the intersection of the limitations on all inputs. For the general case, a more complex graphical treatment is needed to capture that a privilege on a view requires a valid chain (appropriately generalized) on every one of the view's inputs.

5. COMPARISON WITH PREVIOUS WORK

We compare our work with several recent, ambitious approaches. We consider only the part of each work that seems relevant to predicate-limited grants.

[Bert99] is the culmination of a series of papers that offer powerful alternatives to SQL. In [Bert99], two rather independent ways to lessen privileges are proposed. First, there is SQL-like cascading Revoke, without explicit predicates. Second, there are *explicit* negative authorizations, which temporarily inactivate base permissions (node privileges, not grant edges) that satisfy an explicit predicate p. (We can achieve the same effect by ANDing a term *(not p)* to the execution predicate for edges out of the root.) That model includes a large number of constructs, both for vendors to implement and for administrators to learn and use. Administrators must manage the additional privilege of imposing negative authorizations. The negative authorizations can be weak or strong, and there are axioms about overriding and about breaking ties. The model may be too complex to serve as the basis for a practical facility.

We believe that limitation predicates provide a simpler model that still meets the requirements identified in [Bert99]. Our model also improves on [Bert99] in two other areas – scoping of limitations, and views. Their negative authorizations are global, while our limitation predicates apply only along paths in the authorization graph. This scoping greatly reduces the chance of inadvertent or malicious denial of service. For views, [Bert99 section 2.3] adopts a very strong semantics for negative authorization – that absolutely no data visible in the view be accessible. Observing that implementation will be very costly, they then specify that there should be no limitations on views. By settling for less drastic controls, we are able to provide several useful capabilities (as described in Section 3). [Bert98] provides syntax for a special case of limitation predicates, namely those that specify time intervals when the privilege can be exercised.

Another important predecessor to our work is [Sand99], which proposes "prerequisites" (analogous to our limitation predicates) for onward privileges. The model limits only onward privileges, not execution privileges, and administrators must manage grants for the right to revoke each privilege. [Glad97] also has an effective notion of prerequisites, but has no direct support for granting privileges onward.

The Oracle 8i product supports "policy functions", which allow administrator-supplied code to add conjuncts to a query's Where clause. This mechanism is powerful, but difficult to understand. For example, it can be quite difficult to determine: "Based on the current permissions, who can access table T?". There does not appear to be an analogous facility for gr_preds.

Finally, limitation predicates can capture much of the spirit of Originator Control (ORCON) restrictions, such as "You can must get the originator's prior permission before you ship a document outside some group G" [McCo90]. (However, we assume commercial-style discretionary controls on granting and using privileges, not on users' outputs.) We thus assume that a user s passes the information to s2 by Granting s2 the right to read the original document (or a DBMS-controlled replicate located closer to s2). If s has a right to pass information within a group FRIENDS but not outside, the grant to s carries the gr_pred that "grantee ε FRIENDS". We conjecture that other ORAC policies in [McCo90] can be similarly approximated.

6. SUMMARY

This paper represents an initial theory that we believe deserves follow-up. The main contributions of the work are to state principles for a limitation model, and then to provide semantics that satisfy these principles. We also extended limitation semantics to permissions on views. (Previous work in non-database models naturally did not consider this issue.)

Our approach makes several advances over previous proposals.

- *Model Economy:* The model integrates Grant and Execute privileges, consistently. It cleanly extends SQL. An earlier (longer) version of this work showed that it was modular, cleanly separable from reactivation.
- *Easy administration:* The model naturally extends SQL concepts, and accepts all SQL grants. No separate "Limit" privilege need be managed.

- *Limitations respect lines of authority:* Only a grantor or a responsible ancestor has the authority to limit or revoke a user's privilege.
- *Flexibility in limitations:* Designers can give any degree of power to limitation predicates. For a pure security system (unconnected to a DBMS), one could have queries only over security information plus request parameters (e.g., time, trusted path). For a DBMS, one could allow any SQL predicate.
- *Views:* Limitations on underlying tables apply in a natural way to views.

Further work is necessary, of course. The top priority (beyond our resources) would be to implement these features, both as proof of concept and to gather users' reactions. Traditional research questions include extending the theory (to support roles, reactivation and dynamic reevaluation of predicates, a fuller treatment of limitations on views, and policies that modify operations' execution), and efficient implementation.

The pragmatic questions are equally important. Would users see limitations as important, and would they do the administrative work to impose them? How much generality is needed? How does this model compare with security policy managers for enterprises or for digital libraries [Glad97]. Finally, what tools are needed to make it all usable?

7. REFERENCES

[Bert98] E. Bertino, C. Bettini, E. Ferrari, P. Samarati, "An access control model supporting periodicity constraints and temporal reasoning," *ACM Trans. Database Systems*, Vol. 23, No. 3, Sept. 1998, pp. 231 – 285.

[Bert99] E. Bertino, S. Jajodia, P. Samarati, "A Flexible Authorization Mechanism for Relational Data Management Systems," *ACM Trans. Information Systems,* Vol. 17, No. 2, April 1999, pp. 101-140.

[Cast95] S. Castano, M. Fugini, G. Martella, P. Samarati, *Database Security,* ACM Press/Addison Wesley, 1995.

[Glad97] H. Gladney, "Access Control for Large Collections," *ACM Trans. Information Systems,* Vol. 15, No. 2, April 1997, pp. 154-194.

[ISO99] ISO X3H2, *SQL 99 Standard,* section 4.35.

[McCo90] C. McCollum, J. Messing, L. Notargiacomo, "Beyond the Pale of MAC and DAC – Defining new forms of access control," *IEEE Symp. on Security and Privacy,* 1990.

[Ros00] A. Rosenthal, E. Sciore, "View Security as the Basis for Data Warehouse Security", CAiSE Workshop on Design and Management of Data Warehouses, Stockholm, 2000. Also available at http://www.mitre.org/resources/centers/it/staffpages/arnie/

[Sand99] R. Sandhu, V. Bhamidipati, Q. Munawer, "The ARBAC97 Model for Role-Based

CHAPTER 20

LANGUAGE EXTENSIONS FOR PROGRAMMABLE SECURITY

J. Hale, R. Chandia, C. Campbell, M. Papa and S. Shenoi

Abstract Software developers rely on sophisticated programming language protection models and APIs to manifest security policies for Internet applications. These tools do not provide suitable expressiveness for fine-grained, configurable policies. Nor do they ensure the consistency of a given policy implementation. Programmable security provides syntactic and semantic constructs in programming languages for systematically embedding security functionality within applications. Furthermore, it facilitates compile-time and run-time security-checking (analogous to type-checking). This paper introduces a methodology for programmable security by language extension, as well as a prototype model and implementation of JPAC, a programmable access control extension to Java.

Keywords: Cryptographic protocols, simulation, verification, logics, process calculi

1. INTRODUCTION

Internet computing is a catalyst for the development of new programming language protection models and security APIs. Developers rely on protection models to check code integrity and guard memory boundaries at compile-time and run-time [4, 9]. Developers use security APIs to manifest security policies tailored to their applications. Together, protection models and security APIs comprise the state of the art for safeguarding applications running in open environments. However, these tools do not ensure that a security policy articulated with an API is consistent or viable. Moreover, very little is available to programmatically link elements in a protection model with a security API. As a result, security APIs are commonly used in an *ad hoc* fashion yielding unpredictable security policies.

Programmable security provides syntactic and semantic constructs in programming languages for systematically embedding security functionality within applications [12]. Developers use special syntax to express security policies within code in the same way that types are used to express constraints on variable behavior. This approach facilitates compile-time and run-time security-checking (analogous to type-checking) to verify that no potential security policy violations occur within a program.

This paper introduces a methodology for extending programming languages with programmable security services. The methodology is first described, followed by the authorization model adopted for programmable access control. Finally, the design and prototype implementation of our programmable access control solution in Java is presented.

2. PROGRAMMABLE SECURITY

Programmable security links security services to programming language syntax extensions to facilitate the expression and systematic implementation of security policies in applications. Developers use programmable security expressions to specify authorization policies for principals and data elements, authentication protocols for proxies, audit procedures for program modules, and secure communication channels for distributed systems.

The implementation of native programmable security services in new languages offers language architects greater freedom, allowing them to escape the "golden handcuffs" of compatibility. However, extending popular languages has the advantage of immediate relevance to a large audience of developers.

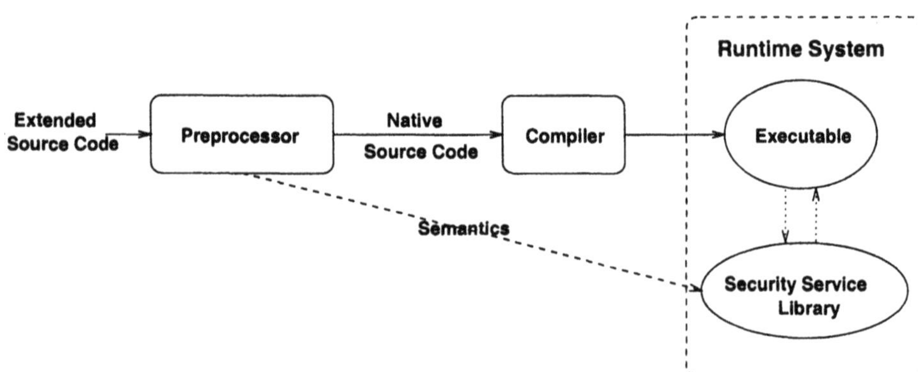

Figure 1. Programmable security methodology.

Figure 1 illustrates an extensional methodology for implementing programmable security. This approach introduces two elements to a programming system; a preprocessor (a similar preprocessing approach has been taken to add genericity to the Java language [3]) and a security service library. The preprocessor employs a parser designed with an augmented grammar to accept expressions in the extended language.

The augmented grammar adds production rules and keywords to the original grammar, binding security services to the programming system. The preprocessor actually plays two roles; (i) checking for security violations within the extended source code and (ii) translating the extended source code into native source code.

The preprocessor relies on the security service library API to derive native source code implementing the specified security functionality. The resulting source code is passed to a native compiler to produce an executable. The security service library can be linked at compile-time or run-time to perform security violation checks during execution.

3. AUTHORIZATION MODEL

Our programmable access control solution relies on a simplified version of the ticket-based authorization model originally described in [12, 13, 14] and refined in [6]. We adopt the ticket-based scheme because it permits policy expression in a variety of authorization models and a straightforward implementation in message passing systems.

Messages requesting access to remote resources are between nodes in an object hierarchy (where any object can also play the role of a subject). Tickets embedded in messages as unforgeable tokens are analogous to capabilities [7, 8, 16, 17], conveying privileges of message originators. Message passing only occurs directly between two adjacent object nodes, as formally specified with the following rule:

$$(1) \quad Adj\ s\ o_1\ o_2 = Parent\ s\ o_1\ o_2\ \vee\ Parent\ s\ o_2\ o_1.$$

$Adj\ s\ o_1\ o_2$ is true whenever objects o_1 and o_2 are adjacent in a hierarchical object structure at a given state s. $Parent\ s\ o_1\ o_2$ is true when, in state s, o_1 is the parent of o_2.

Conceptually, tickets represent *keys* held by subjects that match *locks* held by objects. Keys are checked for matching object locks to authorize access requests.

$Key\ s\ o_1\ t$ is true when o_1 has a key named t in state s. $Lock\ s\ o_1\ o_2\ t$ is true when o_1 has a lock named t on object o_2 in state s. (The hierarchy described below mandates that o_1 and o_2 be *adjacent* for o_1 to hold such a lock.) We can define key/lock matching by an object o_2 as

$$(2) \quad Match\ s\ o_1\ o_2\ o_3 \ = \ \exists\, t.\ Key\ s\ o_1\ t\ \wedge\ Lock\ s\ o_2\ o_3\ t.$$

This predicate defines when a message has permission to access o_3 on behalf of o_1 in o_2. Every message must be authorized for delegation at every inteverning object in the hierarchy. The access request itself is checked only at the destination object.

Another predicate represents the goal of a message. $Access\ s\ o_1\ o_2$, specifies that o_1 can access o_2 from its point of origin in state s. Now we can complete the formalization by creating an inductive definition for access between nodes in a hierarchy with the addition of two rules:

$$(3) \qquad Access\ s\ o_1\ o_1 \ = \ true$$

and

$$(4) \qquad Access\ s\ o_1\ o_2 \ \wedge\ Match\ s\ o_1\ o_2\ o_3 \ \Rightarrow\ Access\ s\ o_1\ o_3.$$

Rule 3 indicates that objects always have access to themselves, and forms a base case for inductive access checking. Rule 4 provides the inductive step, stating that if o_1 can access o_2, and if o_1 holds a key matching a lock in o_2 for o_3, then o_1 can access o_3.

4. PACKAGE-BASED ACCESS CONTROL

This section presents a programmable package-based protection scheme for Java. The system (JPAC) uses syntax extensions to provide developers with discretionary and fine-grained access control for Java applications. Note that JPAC extends, not replaces, the existing Java security architecture. Developers can use JPAC to confine access to program elements based on the package identity of requesting elements.

Figure 2 presents the JPAC syntax extensions used to express package-based protection. Extensions are based on the syntax described in The Java Language Specification documents [2, 21, 22, 23]. The EBNF productions in Figure 2 change the way a compilation unit is named by making `PackageDeclaration` mandatory and adding a `Properties` production to it. Unnamed compilation units are specified by declaring a nameless package.

Three examples of legal compilation units can be found at the bottom of Figure 2. A package `faculty` specifies that its elements can be accessed by a package named `admin`. Associating the keyword `guarded` with the `student` package specifies that its elements can be accessed by any other package using our ticket-based protection scheme. The package `other`, using the keyword `unsecured`, specifies that any package can access its elements, even those that are not compiled under our architecture (useful for interfacing with APIs or other external code).

Synchronization clauses or exceptions are not controlled in our design. Public, private, protected and package-level protection modes are enforced as usual, with package-based protection specifications imparting additional authorization constraints.

```
CompilationUnit:
   PackageDeclaration [ ImportDeclarations ] [ TypeDeclarations ]
PackageDeclaration:
   package [ PackageName ] Properties
Properties:
   protection { [ Property ] }
Property:
   PackageName ; ( PackageName )*
   guarded ;
   unsecured ;
```

```
package faculty
      protection {
   admin; }
class MyClass {
   . . . }
```

```
package student
      protection {
   guarded; }
class MyClass {
   . . . }
```

```
package other
      protection {
   unsecured; }
class MyClass {
   . . . }
```

Figure 2. Extended syntax.

The JPAC semantics are derived from the ticket-based authorization scheme and object hierarchy described earlier. Every JPAC system consists of a root object, and within it a collection of objects mapped to JPAC-protected packages – each associated with its own message handler. Classes and instances are regarded as components of their enclosing packages and use their package's message handler to pass messages conveying access requests/replies across package boundaries.

A unique token is defined for each protected package. A lock/key pair is generated from the token for each of the packages listed in the protection declaration clause. The lock is held in the protected package's access control list, while keys are delivered to the packages for whom access is granted. A special token representing "everyone" is defined to build a key for distribution to all objects in the JPAC system. Packages with guarded protection status hold the "everyone" lock, enabling access by all JPAC objects, but not by external Java code.

JPAC program elements are organized into an object hierarchy. A root object resides at the top of the hierarchy, below it are objects modeling packages, classes and instances. Access requests are carried by messages that flow from the message handler of the package representing the request source to the message handler of the destination package.

Our prototype implements package protection with filter operations performed by message handlers. Messages contain fields identifying the source, the destination and the keys of their originator. Each time a

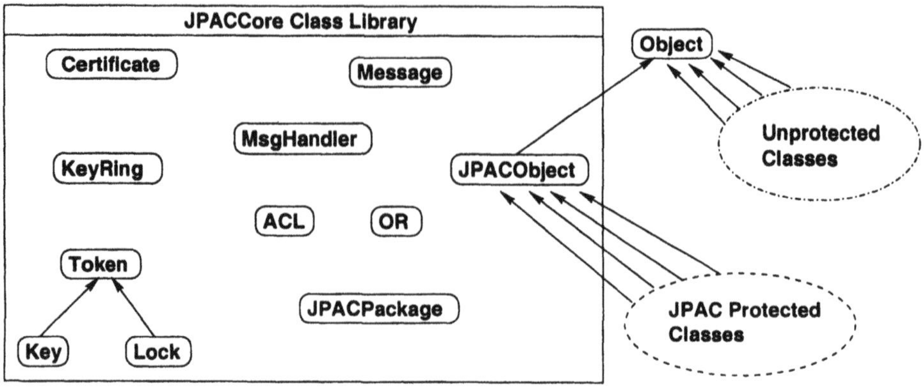

Figure 3. JPAC class hierarchy.

message is received by a message handler it verifies keys contained in the message against locks held in a package access control list.

5. JPAC IMPLEMENTATION

JPAC integrates a set of classes to model a message passing hierarchy for program elements, a preprocessor for extended source code translation, and a run-time ticket management software architecture. The class hierarchy comprising the security service library is shown in Figure 3.

5.1. OBJECT HIERARCHY

The JPAC implementation adds a `MessageHandler` class and a class for each package to dispatch access control in an object hierarchy. Instances of `MessageHandler` are associated with each of the newly created package classes. Package classes hold package-specific data, guiding `MessageHandler` initialization. All package classes inherit their behavior from the `JPACPackage` abstract class.

Figure 4 shows the source code for a JPAC class `Learn`, including a protection clause restricting access to the `faculty` package. Resulting package classes are named as "Package_X", where "X" is a flattened version of the package name. This simple naming convention for package classes helps avoid name clashes in JPAC.

5.2. PREPROCESSING

The preprocessor performs various transformations on program elements in extended source code to authenticate calling subjects, effect secure method dispatch and respect all forms of variable access. Variable and method access is validated with a certificate placed in an extra

Learn.jpac:

```
package student protection {
faculty;
}

public class Learn extends tools.BBSClient {
    public int addMsg(String msg) {
        super.addMsg(msg);
        return noOfMsgs++;
    }
    protected int version = 1.0;
    // the method public int getNoOfMsgs() and the field
    // public int noOfMsgs are inherited from class tools.BBSClient
}
```

Figure 4. Package-based Java protection code.

parameter generated by the preprocessor. Finally, the preprocessor must successfully integrate Java interfaces and unsecured packages with JPAC systems.

5.2.1 Methods. JPAC method calls are transformed to include an authenticating certificate placed in the extra parameter generated by the preprocessor. The method `checkOut()` in the `MessageHandler` of the current package class checks if a message can reach the destination, and returns a certificate for the callee method.

Extending Java's protection model to permit discretionary access control provides a unique set of challenges to the preprocessor. For example, protected classes may invoke unsafe methods in inherited classes. Protected classes in JPAC inherit from the `JPACObject` class, which provides safe replacements for methods in `java.lang.Object`. If a method from Object is used, a `JPACAccesDeniedException` exception is thrown.

Inheritance and dynamic linking in Java also produce an interesting problem. Any call destined for a class in some package can arrive, due to inheritance, to another class in a different package. If this is allowed, legitimate calls could be denied just because inheritance was used. The JPAC solution is to produce proxy methods in the inheriting class that forward calls to the parent class.

Another complication results from the fact that all constructors call their parent's default constructor. When a call to the parent's constructor is missing in a JPAC constructor, one is placed with a fresh certificate in the first statement of the constructor body.

5.2.2 Variables. Direct variable reads and writes are emulated with accessor methods, which authorize access by validating certificates in the same way as JPAC methods. These accessor methods inherit protection levels from their variables. Furthermore, if a variable is static then the accessor method is made static as well. Variables in the JPAC code are then set to private-level protection in the transformed Java code, preventing unauthorized access.

JPAC accessor method names are chosen to reflect not only the name of the variable, but also the class (or interface) that contains it. When variable accesses are found in JPAC code, the preprocessor determines the type where the variable is stored and generates the appropriate call as needed.

5.2.3 Interfaces and Unprotected Packages. JPAC interfaces are translated similar to classes, except that interface variables are implicitly static, public and final, making them impossible to "privatize." JPAC moves interface variables into specially constructed classes making it possible to change their access level to private and to add accessor methods. Wherever a JPAC interface variable is referenced, a call to the appropriate accessor method is substituted. Naming of interface variables and accessor methods is performed in the same way as for class variables.

Classes and interfaces in unsecured packages are considered unprotected by the JPAC system extensions. Unsecured classes and interfaces are useful in that they can directly subclass `Object` (the core Java system class) and other unprotected classes. Classes and instances in unsecured packages do not adopt the additional certificate parameter for methods or accessor methods for variables. The only modifications are the transformation of calls to methods and variables in classes belonging to protected packages and the addition of a package class.

5.3. TICKET MANAGEMENT

The ticket management software architecture in Figure 5 serves as an execution model for the ticket-based access control scheme described earlier. The architecture supports message passing in a hierarchy of handlers to validate inter-package access.

5.3.1 Keys, Locks and Rings. Key and lock objects provide a basis for constraining access, while messages encapsulate authorization requests. Tokens, which model keys and locks, are characterized by an abstract class (`Token`) containing a unique identifier and an abstract method to match keys and locks. A simple protocol ensures that a lock and its matching key are created simultaneously to guarantee their authenticity.

The `match()` method checks keys and locks by computing an encrypted key value and comparing it to the value of the lock.

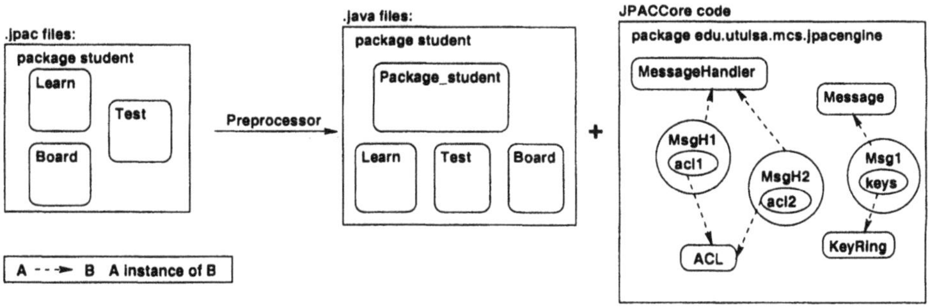

Figure 5. Software architecture.

Access control lists maintained within each package class store locks and keys. The access control list class (**ACL**) provides methods to add and remove keys from a key ring. Instances of the **KeyRing** class are passed between message handlers to facilitate inter-package access by presenting keys to match with locks in destination package access control lists.

To access a variable or method in another package, the key ring is passed as a parameter to the **match()** method of the destination **ACL**. The **match()** method passes each lock to a method of the key ring which checks every key for a match. If a key fits, the key ring returns a copy of the key to the **ACL** for verification, and access is granted. When a foreign package attempts to gain access to a local package, the local package receives a copy of the foreign key registry.

5.3.2 Message Handlers. The centerpiece of the software architecture is the message handler, which effects message passing between objects. Messages are used only for authorization and consist of a key ring, a source and destination identifier, and a certificate. Key rings that accompany messages embody the rights of the message originator. Messages are passed between objects via resident message handlers, authorized at each stop, until they reach their final destination.

Static methods in the **MessageHandler** model behavior for the root JPAC domain. A static code block creates a new message handler for each package class. The **MessageHandler** constructor obtains a reference to program units above it in the hierarchy. If such a reference is to a unit that has not yet been instantiated, that unit's static code will execute, creating its parent object. The result of this domino effect is that when any package is first accessed, message handlers for it and every other package above it in the hierarchy are initialized.

6. COMPARISONS WITH OTHER WORK

Object-oriented programming languages employ protection schemes based on classes, variables and methods. Java 1.0 provides packages to group program units (classes and interfaces), creating access boundaries [2, 4]. Java 1.2 lets developers define protection domains to specify sets of classes sharing identical permissions [10, 11]. The added functionality is given in an API. Wallach *et al.* propose extensions to the Java security model that employ capabilities and namespace management techniques [26]. Java capabilities are implemented based on the fact that references to objects cannot be fabricated due to Java's type safety features. The disadvantage of these approaches is that no significant compile-time security checking can be performed.

Early work in [5] describes a compile-time mechanism to certify that programs do not violate information flow policies, while [1] provides a flow logic to verify that programs satisfy confinement properties. Static analysis of security properties has re-emerged as a promising line of research because it eliminates much of the need for costly runtime checks. It also prevents information leakage that can occur at runtime.

In [25], Volpano *et al.* recast the information flow analysis model in [5] within a type system to establish its soundness. This work led to a sound type system for information flow in a multi-threaded language [20]. JPAC differs in that it promotes a foundational authorization model as a common substrate for various access control schemes to support the static analysis of secure program interoperability.

Van Doorn *et al.*, extend Modula-3 network objects with security features in [24]. Secure network objects (SNOs) bind programming languages into service for integrating security into objects and methods. SNOs promote subtyping for specifying security properties of objects.

Myers and Liskov describe a decentralized information flow control model in [19]. Security label annotations can be inferred and type-checked by a special compiler to verify program information flow properties. Myers implemented these ideas in JFlow, a variant of Java that integrates statically checked information flow annotations with advanced programming language features such as objects, subclassing and exceptions [18].

The SLam calculus is a typed λ-calculus that tracks relevant security information of programming elements [15]. A compiler that executes static checks enforces the type system rules to guarantee program security. Types in SLam are monomorphic and static, but the system has been shown to be extensible to concurrent and imperative programming.

7. CONCLUSIONS

Programmable security allows developers to express verifiable protection policies with special syntax. Preprocessors can be used to extend existing programming languages with syntactic constructs tied to security service libraries, yielding a programmable solution that is interoperable with systems developed in the original language. Our programmable access control prototype, JPAC, extends the Java programming language with syntax for expressing package-level discretionary policies. JPAC classes and interfaces can be seamlessly integrated within native Java applications, allowing developers to customize protection policies for selected software components. In addition, the semantic foundation of the JPAC architecture permits the design and implementation of more fine-grained authorization models for class-based and instance-based protection.

References

[1] Andrews, G. and Reitman, R. (1980) An axiomatic approach to information flow in programs. *ACM Transactions on Programming Languages and Systems*, **2(1)**, 56–76.

[2] Arnold, K. and Gosling, J. (1998) *The Java Programming Language, 2nd Edition.* Addison-Wesley, Reading, Massachusetts.

[3] Bracha, G., Odersky, M., Stoutamire, D. and Wadler, P. (1998) Making the future safe for the past: Adding genericity to the Java programming language *Object Oriented Programming: Systems, Languages and Applications (OOPSLA)* ACM SIGPLAN Notices **33(10)**, 183–200.

[4] Dean, D., Felten, E. and Wallach, D. (1996) Java security: From HotJava to Netscape and beyond. *Proceedings of the IEEE Symposium on Research in Security and Privacy*, 190–200.

[5] Denning, D. and Denning, P. (1977) Certification of programs for secure information flow. *Communications of the ACM*, **20(7)**, 504–513.

[6] Dionysiou, I. (2000) *A Formal Semantics for Programmable Access Control*, Masters Thesis, Washington State University.

[7] Fabry, R. (1974) Capability-based addressing. *Communications of the ACM*, **17(7)**, 403–412.

[8] Gilgor, V., Huskamp, J., Welke, S., Linn, C., and Mayfield, W. (1987) Traditional capability-based systems: An analysis of their ability to meet the trusted computer security evaluation criteria, Institute for Defense Analyses, IDA Paper P-1935.

[9] Gong, L. (1998) Secure Java class loading. *IEEE Internet Computing*, **2(6)**, 56–61.

[10] Gong, L., Mueller, M., Prafullchandra, H. and and Schemers, R. (1997) Going beyond the sandbox: An overview of the new security architecture in the Java Development Kit 1.2. *Proceedings of the USENIX Symposium on Internet Technologies and Systems*, 103–112.

[11] Gong, L. and Schemers, R. (1998) Implementing protection domains in the Java Development Kit 1.2. *Proceedings of the Internet Society Symposium on Network and Distributed System Security*, 125–134.

[12] Hale, J., Papa, M. and Shenoi, S. (1999) Programmable security for object-oriented systems, in *Database Security, XII: Status and Prospects* (ed. S. Jajodia), Kluwer, Dordrecht, The Netherlands, 109–126.

[13] Hale, J., Threet, J. and Shenoi, S. (1998) Capability-based primitives for access control in object-oriented systems, in *Database Security, XI: Status and Prospects* (eds. T.Y. Lin and X. Qian), Chapman and Hall, London, 134–150.

[14] Hale, J., Threet, J. and Shenoi, S. (1997) A framework for high assurance security of distributed objects, in *Database Security, X: Status and Prospects* (eds. P. Samarati and R. Sandhu), Chapman and Hall, London, 101–119.

[15] Heintze, N. and Riecke, J. (1998) The SLam calculus: Programming with security and integrity. *Proceedings of the Twenty-Fifth ACM SIGPLAN-SIGACT on Principles of Programming Languages*, 365–377.

[16] Karger, P. (1984) An augmented capability architecture to support lattice security. *Proceedings of the IEEE Symposium on Research in Security and Privacy*, 2–12.

[17] Karger, P. (1988) Implementing commercial data integrity with secure capabilities. *Proceedings of the IEEE Symposium on Research in Security and Privacy*, 130–139.

[18] Myers, A. (1999) JFlow: Practical mostly-static information flow control. *Proceedings of the Twenty-Sixth ACM SIGPLAN-SIGACT on Principles of Programming Languages*, 229–241.

[19] Myers, A. and Liskov, B. (1997) A decentralized model for information flow control. *Proceedings of the Sixteenth ACM Symposium on Operating System Principles*, 129–142.

[20] Smith, G. and Volpano, D. (1998) Secure information flow in a multi-threaded imperative language. *Proceedings of the Twenty-Fifth ACM SIGPLAN-SIGACT on Principles of Programming Languages*, 355–364.

[21] Sun Microsystems. (1999) Clarifications and Amendments to The Java Language Specification. http://www.java.sun.com/docs/books/jls/clarify.html.

[22] Sun Microsystems. (1997) Inner Classes Specification. http://java.sun.com/products/jdk/1.1/docs/guide/innerclasses/spec/innerclasses.doc.html.

[23] Sun Microsystems. (1999) Clarifications and Amendments to the Inner Classes Specification. http://www.java.sun.com/docs/books/jls/nested-class-clarify.html.

[24] Van Doorn, L., Abadi, M., Burrows, M. and Wobber, E. (1996) Secure network objects. *Proceedings of the IEEE Symposium on Research in Security and Privacy*, 211–221.

[25] Volpano, D., Smith, G. and Irvine, C. (1996) A sound type system for secure flow analysis. *Journal of Computer Security*, **4(3)**, 167–187.

[26] Wallach, D., Balfanz, D., Dean, D. and Felten, E. (1997) Extensible security architectures for Java. *Proceedings of the 16th Symposium on Operating Systems Principles*, 116–128.

CHAPTER 21
PROTECTING PRIVACY FROM CONTINUOUS HIGH-RESOLUTION SATELLITE SURVEILLANCE

Soon Ae Chun and Vijayalakshmi Atluri

MSIS Department and CIMIC

Rutgers University, Newark, NJ 07102

{soon,atluri}@cimic.rutgers.edu

Abstract Privacy refers to controlling the dissemination and use of personal data, including information that is knowingly disclosed, as well as data that are unintentionally revealed as a byproduct of the use of information technologies. This paper argues that the high resolution geospatial images of our earth's surface, produced from the earth observing satellites, can make a person visually *exposed,* resulting in a technological invasion of personal privacy. We propose a suitable *authorization model for geospatial data* (GSAM) where controlled access can be specified based on the region covered by an image with privilege modes that include `view`, `zoom-in`, `overlay` and `identify`.

1. INTRODUCTION

In the new millennium, 31 satellites, funded by both governments and private corporations, will be capable of providing land cover data at resolutions of 1 to 30 meters in orbit. As low-cost, highly responsive commercial satellite systems become operational, high resolution imagery is expected to become a regular input to consumer products and information services. Remote sensing data sales and services are predicted to grow into a $2 billion dollar market by the beginning of the 21st century [1].

There are numerous benefits to society in the constructive use of low cost satellite imagery. Examples include environmental monitoring, map making, disaster relief, infrastructure planning, national security, pinpointing of prospective sites to aid miners and drillers in planning access to natural resources, and detecting distressed crops early before such stress is visible to the human eye. Up-to-date satellite images can assist businesses in planning the placement of consumer outlets and manufacturing facilities, and help demographic analysts locate their target markets. Images can be used to aid police and fire crews to respond more quickly to distress calls, and to direct vehicle flows depending on observed traffic situations.

Motivation: While high resolution low cost satellite imagery enjoys many benefits, there are significant threats to privacy due to the commercial availability of high-resolution imagery in near real-time fashion. Public entities, such as local governments or public utility companies, collect, use and disseminate large amounts of personal information. Combination of this publicly available personal data pool with high resolution image data coupled with the integration and analysis capabilities of modern GIS systems providing geographic keys such as longitude and latitude, can result in a technological invasion of personal privacy. A person can not only be identified by name or address, but can be *visually exposed.* Therefore, in the near future, it may be technically feasible for anyone to observe, record and measure the outdoor activities of anyone, at any place in the world (from backyard pools to nuclear plants), almost at any time. For example, one can clearly identify the objects in the high-resolution image shown in figure 1. Many scenarios can be envisioned that may threaten the privacy of individuals or organizations; some are listed below.

Figure 1. A high resoultion image

1. Observation of military operations or movements of agents of foreign countries can be achieved by the click of a mouse [7].

2. Unauthorized surveillance of a person's outdoor activities by a stalker or a burglar may help planning a break-in into a home. Tracking of residents entering and leaving the house through observing high resolution images over a period of time can simply be done on his computer.

3. Tracking of the shipping volumes and patterns of a company by observing the number of trucks being loaded and unloaded can be valuable for a competing business enterprise.

These are some scenarios that depict the need for access control for high resolution geospatial image data. Although there are no policies or laws in place yet, they appear to be inevitable [7]. Aside from protecting privacy of individuals from near real-time high-resolution satellite surveillance, the need for controlled access to images arises because of different reasons:

1. Concept based filtering: Filtering of images is needed, for example, to prevent children from accessing objectionable images available on the web. While traditionally access control is provided at the server, filtering requires access control at the client.

2. Controlled access to images: Prevention of unauthorized access may be needed for providing controlled distribution of images to subscribers.

3. Content based access control: Prevention of access may be needed for certain images based on their content, for example, to prevent the public from accessing images of all vehicles with a color distribution used by the military.

Related Work: While there exists no work on providing access control for geospatial images, recently, a number efforts have been made to screen objectionable images using shape detection, object recognition, people recognition, face recognition, and content-based image retrieval. They include (1) filtering of images of naked people using a skin filter and a human figure grouper [3, 4], and (2) using a content-based feature vector indexing where an image is matched against a small number of feature vectors obtained from a training database [5, 6]. However, these approaches filter all images that match a set of criteria, but do not provide controlled access that facilitates access to images for legitimate users.

Our Contribution: A suitable access control for protecting privacy due to unauthorized high-resolution surveillance should not only be based on the spatial extent of images but also be based on their resolution. While a low resolution image may be revealed to the user regardless of its location coordinates, a high resolution image may not be accessed, except in the region where the user has access permission. For example, a factory owner may access every detail pertaining to his own operations, but should be prohibited from accessing the images that reveal the details of his competitor's operations. To the best of our knowledge, there does not exist any authorization model suitable for geospatial images. In this paper, we propose an authorization model that can provide access control for geospatial images based on their spatial extent and resolution, called *Geo-Spatial Authorization Model* (GSAM). Our access control model will use publicly available user information, such as property ownership and voter registration records to determine the spatial extent that the user is allowed to access, which in turn is used to determine the appropriate image(s), or a portion of it, from the image database. To accomplish this, GSAM supports, in addition to the conventional privilege modes such as `read`, `insert`, `delete` and `modify`, privilege modes such as `view`, `zoom-in`, `overlay` and `identify` that can be defined based on the allowed resolution level for a given user.

We provide access control in two ways. (1) We *control the depth* a user can traverse, thereby controlling the resolution of the images (s)he can access. For example, anyone can access a low resolution image such as the New Jersey state map, but access to a 1 meter resolution image of an individual's house is prohibited as it may infringe on the privacy of that individual. (2) We *control the extent* a user can view. That is, a user is given access to high resolution images (say 1 meter), only for certain regions (typically the property (s)he owns, public parks, etc.) but not to all regions.

2. BACKGROUND ON GEOSPATIAL IMAGES

Geospatial images can either be *digital raster images* that store images as a number of pixels, or *digital vector data* that store images as points, lines and polygons. Typically, satellite images, digital orthophoto quads and scanned maps are raster images, while maps of vector type (e.g. a Shape file), digital line graphs, or census TIGER data are vector images. Other non-image geospatial data sets are data with locational information, such as census data, voter registration, land ownership data, and land use data.

Since the main focus of this paper concerns protecting privacy from high-resolution satellite surveillance, we provide more details on satellite imagery. Satellite images are a product of Remote Sensing. Remote sensing is a technology for sampling radiation and force fields to acquire and interpret geospatial data. Geospatial data are used to develop information about features, objects, and classes on Earth's land surface, oceans, and atmosphere. Remote sensing of the Earth traditionally has used reflected energy in the visible and infrared regions and emitted energy in the thermal infrared and microwave regions. It gathers radiation that can be analyzed numerically or used to generate images whose variations represent different intensities of photons associated with a range of wavelengths that are received at the sensor. Satellite images are pictorial representation of target objects and features in different spectral regions. Each sensor (commonly with bandpass filters) is tuned to accept and process the wave frequencies (wavelengths) that characterize each region. Each region normally shows significant differences in the distribution (patterns) of color or gray tones. A chief use of satellite image data has been in classifying different features in a scene into meaningful categories or classes. The image then becomes a thematic map (the theme is selectable, e.g., land use; geology; vegetation types; rainfall). Satellite data have the following characteristics:

1. The satellite's orbital information is changing; hence it is hard to obtain images whose spatial coverages are exactly the same.

2. There are variabilities of images coming from different satellites and sensors, even if they observe the same region. Typically different sensors capture different characteristics of earth surface, e.g. land coverage and weather.

3. Different sensors provide images of different resolution levels, from low to high. For example, the Advanced Very High Resolution Radiometer (AVHRR) is a broad-band, four or five channel (depending on the model) scanner, sensing the visible (red, green, blue), near-infrared, and thermal infrared portions of the electro-magnetic spectrum. It produces 1km resolution images. Landsat Thematic Mapper (TM) provides multispectral imagery at 25m ground resolution. Radar sensors can transmit 5 to 10 meter resolution images. Sensors from the IKONOS satellite launched by Space Imaging/EOSAT promises to provide 1m Panchromatic and 4m Multispectral (blue, green, red, near-IR) data.

4. For any remotely sensed image, there is a trade-off between spatial resolution, area of extent, and data volume. If the data volume is to be held constant, a high-resolution image will cover a small area, while a low-resolution image will cover a large area. The systems intended for the identification of land cover and land use have focused on moderate resolutions between 5 and 30 meters and swaths of 100 to 200 kilometers, while the high resolution satellites are designed with 1 to 3 meters resolution and 4 to 40 kilometer swaths.

5. Each satellite image undergoes the process of georectification which involves two steps: georegistration and geocorrection. Geocorrection of the image is needed since the distances and directions in satellite images do not correspond to true distances and directions on the ground due to the variability of satellite position. Georegistration registers each image with a known coordinate system (e.g. longitude, latitude), reference units (e.g. degrees) and coordinates of left, right, top and bottom edges of the image.

3. AUTHORIZATION MODEL FOR GEOSPATIAL DATA (GSAM)

In this section, we formally present GSAM, an authorization model suitable for providing controlled access to geospatial data. Let $S = \{s_1, s_2 \ldots\}$ denote a set of subjects, $O = \{o_1, o_2 \ldots\}$ a set of objects, and M={*view, zoom-in* ... } a finite set of privilege modes. In the following, we describe in detail the image objects and privilege modes, and present the formalism for authorization specification.

3.1. IMAGE OBJECTS

Image objects can either be raster or vector images. Vector objects describe geographic map features such as roads, parcels, soil units, or forest stands. It can contain several feature classes, such as arc, node, polygon, label point, annotation, tic, and coverage extent. Each raster image object O_i is represented as a tuple, $< id, l, g, h, w, r, t >$, where *id* is a unique identifier and *l, g, h,* and *w* are *latitude, longitude, height,* and *width*, respectively, that represent the spatial extent of the image. *r* is for *resolution* of O_i, while *t* represents the *download timestamp*. Each vector object, O_v, is represented as a tuple, $< id, l, g, h, w, t, k >$, where *id* is a unique identifier and *l, g, h,* and *w* are *latitude, longitude, height,* and *width*, respectively, that represent the spatial extent of the vector file. The symbol *t* denotes the *last update timestamp*. The symbol *k* denotes a *link* that links tabular data of geographic features contained in the vector object, O_v.

There is a set of access functions associated with each object. Given an image object, O_i, the function *rectangle*(*id*) would retrieve the rectangular region (l, g, h, w) of the object. Similarly *resolution*(*id*) would return *r*.

3.2. PRIVILEGE MODES

In our model, we support two types of privilege modes – *viewing* and *maintenance*. The viewing modes include `view`, `zoom-in`, `overlay`, and `identify`, and the maintenance modes are `insert`, `delete` and `update`. The `view` privilege allows a user to see an image object covering a certain geographic area within a permitted resolution level.

The `zoom-in` privilege allows a user to view an image covering a certain geographic area at a higher resolution. Unlike conventional privilege modes that allow or deny access, this privilege specifies the level of zoom-in allowed, and is therefore expressed with an associated value, called `zoom level` (for example, `zoom-in:10`). The access control algorithm interprets this value and determines the level of resolution of the image that is allowed to be viewed by the user. Note that given an image, zooming-in can also be achieved using zoom-in algorithms, but the quality of the image decreases so that the result becomes useless, if zooming is done beyond a certain level. Thus the level of zoom-in a user is allowed should be determined based on the level (s)he can attain after applying the `zoom-in` algorithm. That is, if a user is allowed a zoom-in level of l_z, the access control algorithm must make sure that the user is given an image with a resolution of at most r that can not be zoomed-in to a resolution higher than l_z without losing its content. The functionality of providing the desired level of zoom-in is achieved by storing multiple images with different levels of resolution. Thus, if a user is allowed to access a region at a certain level of resolution, zooming-in is accomplished by retrieving a higher resolution image.

The `overlay` privilege allows users to generate composite images, where a composite image is constructed by *overlaying* one image on top of another. Although each individual image in isolation can be viewed by a user, sometimes an overlayed image may reveal more information than the user is allowed to access. Overlaying the street map on a high resolution image may help pin-pointing a person's private property and viewing it in realtime.

The `identify` privilege allows the user to view the tabular data linked to an image. The data linked to the image, for example the ownership information, when shown with a high resolution image may provide visual exposure of a person's private property.

While the `insert` privilege allows a user to insert an image object into the database, the `delete` privilege allows her to remove images. The `update` privilege allows a user to replace one image with another as well as modify the attributes of the image, such as latitude, longitude, resolution, and link. In addition, it allows the user to update the tabular data linked to the image.

3.3. AUTHORIZATION

An authorization in GSAM is specified as follows:

Definition 1 An authorization a is a triple $\langle sub, obj, pr\rangle$, where
sub is a subject $s \in S$,
obj is (i) an object *id* of an object $o \in O$,
(ii) a region represented as a rectangle with (latitude, longitude, height, width), or
(iii) a set of object *id*s, and
pr is (i) a single privilege mode $m \in M$ or
(ii) a set of privilege modes $\{m_1, m_2, \ldots\} \subseteq M$.

An object in our authorization specification can be a single image, a set of images, or a region. Although the region could be any polygon, for the sake of simplicity, in this paper, we limit it to represent only rectangles. The privilege *pr* in an authorization triple may be composite, that is, may contain more than one privilege mode, which is especially useful when used with `overlay`. That is the case because, a subject may be allowed to overlay an image over another low resolution image, but not over a high resolution image. In order to specify such access control policies, we need a combination of both `zoom-in` and `overlay`.

In our model, as can be seen from the above definition, authorizations will allow one to specify that a subject is allowed to view a specific image or region with a specific resolution, or is allowed to overlay a set of images with a specific resolution. Following are some examples of authorizations.

$a_1 = \langle John, (50, 60, 10, 10), (zoom-in : 8)\rangle$, $a_2 = \langle Mary, 123, view\rangle$

$a_3 = \langle Ann, \{123, 456\}, overlay\rangle$, $a_4 = \langle Tom, \{123, 456\}, (overlay, *, 8)\rangle$

Above authorizations can be interpreted as follows: a_1 specifies that John is allowed to access a region centered at point (50,60) with width and height of 10, with a zoom-in level of 8. a_2 specifies that Mary can view the object with the object id 123. a_3 specifies that Ann is allowed to overlay objects 123 and 456. Finally, a_4 specifies that Tom is allowed to overlay images 123 and 456 where the highest resolution level of object 456 is 8.

We use $a(sub), a(obj)$ and $a(pr)$ to denote the subject, object and privilege of a, respectively. Moreover, to denote the attributes of each component in a, we use the notation $component_{attribute}$. For example, $a(pr_{zoomin})$ represents the zoom-in level specified in the privilege mode of a. We denote the set of all authorizations as *geo-spatial authorization base*, $GSAB$.

4. ACCESS CONTROL

When a subject requests to access images covering a specific geographic region at a specific resolution level, the access control mechanism must evaluate whether such a request can be granted. We define the Access Request by a user, ur, as follows:

Definition 2 [Access Request] An *access request* is a triple $ur = \langle s, o, pr\rangle$, where s is the subject, pr is the privilege mode, and o is the object which can be either of the following two: (i) a tuple (l, g, h, w, r) where (l, g, h, w) represents the requested rectangle that consists of latitude, longitude, height and width, and r represents the level of resolution, or (ii) a set of object *ids*.

According to the above definition, a user may request to access an object by specifying its object id, or may request to access a rectangular region by specifying its latitude, longitude, height and width. We use

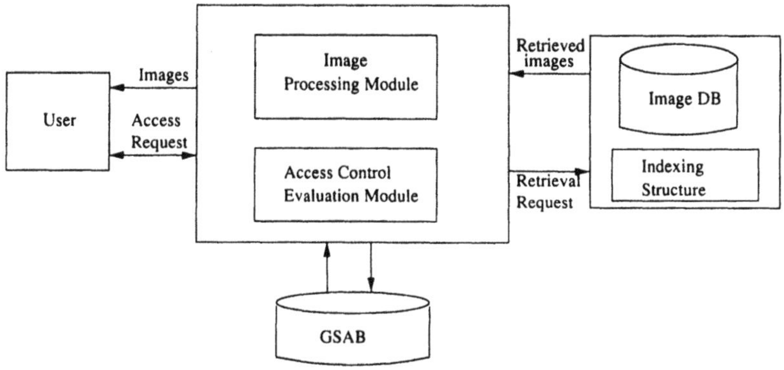

Figure 2. The System Architecture

$ur(s), ur(o)$ and $ur(pr)$ to denote the subject, object and privilege mode specified in ur, respectively.

When a subject requests to access images covering a specific geographic region at a certain resolution level, the access control module (refer to figure 2) verifies whether there exists an authorization such that the object region specified in the authorization *overlaps* with (or contains) the requested object area. As a first step, it determines all the authorizations relevant to the access request. Access is denied if no relevant authorization exists. Then the authorization evaluation module determines either a set of object ids or a rectangular region that is allowed to be viewed by the subject and sends a request to the image database. Since the region allowed to be viewed by the subject may not match exactly with the image(s) returned, the images returned from the image database need to be edited, namely assembled and/or cropped. This function is performed by the image processing module. Given an authorization base $GSAB$, the following algorithm describes how an access request ur with view, zoom-in and overlay modes can be evaluated.

```
Algorithm 1 [Authorization Evaluation]
input: ur
output: set of images
begin
1.Find the set of authorizations A(ur) in GSAB such that
      foreach a ∈ A(ur)
         (a(s) = ur(s)) ∧ (a(pr) = ur(pr))
2.ifA(ur) = ∅
then return (''Access denied'')
else {
        while A(ur) ≠ ∅ {
            foreach a ∈ A(ur)
            case ur(pr) ='view':  {
               if ((a(o) is id) ∧ (ur(o) is id))
               then{if (a(o) = ur(o))
                    then RETRIEVE-IMAGE-WITH-ID FROM ImageDB
                          WHERE imageid = a(o) }
               if ((a(o) is id) ∧ (ur(o) is not id))
               then{if (overlap(retangle(a(o)), rectangle(ur(o))) ≠ ∅)
```

```
                then RETRIEVE-IMAGE-WITH-ID FROM ImageDB
                    WHERE imageid = a(o) }
            if ((a(o) is not id) ∧ (ur(o) is not id))
            then {
                area = overlap(rectangle(a(o)), rectangle(ur(o)))
                RETRIEVE-IMAGES-WITH-AREA FROM ImageDB
                WHERE overlap(area(image), area) ≠ ∅ ∧
                    resolution(image) ≥ resolution(a(o))
                PROCESS-IMAGES (area, images) }
            A(ur) = A(ur) − a }
        case ur(pr) ='zoom-in': {
            resolution(ur(o)) = ur(pr_zoom-in)
            if ((a(o) is id) ∧ (ur(o) is id))
            then{if (a(o) = ur(o))
                then  RETRIEVE-IMAGE-WITH-ID FROM ImageDB
                      WHERE imageid = a(o) }
            if ((a(o) is id) ∧ (ur(o) is not id))
            then {if ((resolution(a(o)) ≤ resolution(ur(o)))∧
                      overlap(rectangle(a(o)), rectangle(ur(o))) ≠ ∅)
                  then RETRIEVE-IMAGE-WITH-ID FROM ImageDB
                      WHERE imageid = a(o) }
            if ((a(o) is not id) ∧ (ur(o) is not id))
            then { if (resolution(a(o)) ≤ resolution(ur(o)))
                  then {area = overlap(rectangle(a(o)), rectangle(ur(o)))
                      RETRIEVE-IMAGES-WITH-AREA FROM ImageDB
                      WHERE (overlap(rectangle(image), area) ≠ ∅)∧
                         (resolution(image) = resolution(ur(o))) }
                      PROCESS-IMAGES (area, images) }
                  A(ur) = A(ur) − a }
        case ur(pr) ='overlay': {
            if (((a(o_i) is id) ∧ (ur(o_i) is id)) ∧ ((a(o_j) is id) ∧ (ur(o_j) is id)))
            then{ RETRIEVE-IMAGE-WITH-ID FROM ImageDB
                      WHERE imageid = a(o_i) ∪ imageid = a(o_j) }
            if ((a(o_i) is id) ∧ (a(o_j) is id)) ∧ ((ur(o_i) is not id) ∧
                (ur(o_j) is not id)))
            then  {
                if (overlap(rectangle(a(o_i)), rectangle(ur(o_i))) ≠ ∅)
                then { RETRIEVE-IMAGE-WITH-ID FROM ImageDB
                      WHERE imageid = a(o_i) ∧ resolution(image) ≥ resolution(a(o_i)) }
                if (overlap(rectangle(a(o_j), rectangle(ur(o_j))) ≠ ∅)
                then { RETRIEVE-IMAGE-WITH-ID FROM ImageDB
                      WHERE imageid = a(o_j) ∧ resolution(image) ≥ resolution(a(o_j)) }
                area = overlap(rectangle(ur(o_i)), rectangle(ur(o_j)))
                PROCESS-IMAGES(area, images) }
            if ((a(o_i) is not id) ∧ (a(o_j) is not id))
                ∧ ((ur(o_j) is not id) ∧ (ur(o_j) is not id)))
            then { R_i = overlap(rectangle(ur(o_i)), rectangle(a(o_i)))
                  R_j = overlap(rectangle(ur(o_j)), rectangle(a(o_j)))
                  if (overlap(R_i, R_j) ≠ ∅)
                  then {
                      RETRIEVE-IMAGES-WITH-AREA from IMAGEDB
                      WHERE overlap(rectangle(image), R_i) ≠ ∅∧
                          resolution(image) ≥ resolution(a(o_i))
                          resolution(image) ≤ resolution(ur(o_i))
                      RETRIEVE-IMAGES-WITH-AREA from IMAGEDB
                      WHERE overlap(rectangle(image), R_j) ≠ ∅∧
                          resolution(image) ≥ resolution(a(o_j))
                          resolution(image) ≤ resolution(ur(o_j))
                      PROCESS-IMAGES (overlap(R_i, R_j), images) }}
            A(ur) = A(ur) − a } } }
end
```

Procedure PROCESS-IMAGES

```
input:  area, retrieved-images
output:  images covering only area
begin
      foreach image i ∈ images
         chop (area, i)
      for each imageset I ∈ same resolution level {
         images = assemble-area (area, I)
```

```
        return(images) }
end
```

This algorithm considers three cases for evaluating each privilege mode. In the first case, both the access request and authorization are specified with image ids. In this case, evaluation of an access request is done by testing whether the ids are the same. In the second case, the access request is specified as a rectangular region, but the authorization is specified with an image id. In this case, evaluation involves determining the overlapping region of the image specified in the authorization with the requested region. If the overlapping region is empty, access is denied. Otherwise, appropriate request is sent to the image database to retrieve the image. The case where authorization is specified with a region and the access request is specified as an id can be dealt with in a similar manner. Therefore, this is not included in the algorithm. In the third case, both the access request and the authorization are specified as rectangular regions. In this case, the overlapped region must be determined first. The area is then used to retrieve the relevant images.

Further processing is done by the procedure PROCESS-IMAGES if the area covered by the retrieved images does not coincide with the region authorized to be viewed by the subject. In this case the image is cropped. If more than one image are retrieved, they are first assembled together before cropping.

5. CONCLUSIONS AND FUTURE RESEARCH

In this paper, we have argued that near-continuous surveillance through high resolution satellite images when combined with geographic information could be a threat to privacy. In order to address this issue, we presented a suitable access control model, called Geospatial Authorization Model (GSAM). GSAM supports privilege modes including `view`, `zoom-in`, `overlay` and `identify` that are essential for providing constrained access to geospatial data based on the region covered by an image. Our future research spans a number of directions. We plan to extend the authorization specification GSAM with temporal attributes. Unlike conventional authorizations that can be implemented as lists, authorizations in GSAM involve spatial attributes. In such a case, managing the authorization base and searching for authorizations based on the spatial extent is not trivial. Therefore, we intend to investigate techniques to maintain the authorization base. We plan to devise methodologies to verify the consistency of the authorization specification, analyze conflicts occurring due to simultaneous presence of contains, overlap and other operations, and strategies to resolve these conflicts. We have demonstrated in [2] how access control can be efficiently enforced using a spatial indexing structure called MX-RS quadtree. In future research we will build an indexing structure suitable for image access control in more general cases, where images at the same resolution level do not have fixed spatial extents. In addition, we intend to consider including the temporal aspects into the indexing structure. We also plan to investigate methods for providing refined access control where different geospatial information sets, such as health data and income data are integrated with image and map data.

Acknowledgments

The concept of access control for high resolution satellite imagery was conceived through discussions with Geoff Henebry. We acknowledge Francisco Artigas for the information on geo-spatial images, their analysis and processing. We thank James Geller for commenting on an earlier draft of this paper. The work was partially supported by the National Science Foundation under grant IRI-9624222 and the Meadowlands Environmental Research Institute as a grant from the Hackenack Meadowlands Development Commission.

References

[1] Jonathan Ball. Satellite remote sensing. *TCS Remote Sensing and GIS web page.*

[2] Soon Ae Chun and Vijayalakshmi Atluri. Protecting privacy from continuous high-resolution satellite surveillance. Technical report, CIMIC, Rutgers University, November 1999.

[3] M. Fleck, D. Forsyth, and C. Bregler. Finding naked people. In *Proceedings of 4th European Conference on Computer Vision*, pages 593–602, 1996.

[4] D. et al Forsyth. Finding pictures of objects in large collections of images. In *Proceedings of International Workshop on Object Recognition*, pages 69 – 142, 1996.

[5] James Ze Wang, Jia Li, Gio Wiederhold, and Oscar Firschein. System for Classifying Objectionable Websites. In *Proceedings of the 5th International Workshop on Interactive Distributed Multimedia Systems and Telcommunication Services (IDMS '98)*, volume LNCS 1483, pages 113–124. Springer Verlag, September 1998.

[6] James Ze Wang, Gio Wiederhold, and Oscar Firschein. System for Screening Objectionable Images Using Daubechies' Wavelets and Color Histograms. In *Proceedings of the 4th European Workshop on Interactive Distributed Multimedia Systems and Telcommunication Services (IDMS '97)*, volume LNCS 1309. Springer Verlag, September 1997.

[7] Robert Wright. Private Eyes. *The New York Times Magazine*, September 1999.

CHAPTER 22

Database Security Integration Using Role-Based Access Control

Sylvia Osborn
Department of Computer Science, The University of Western Ontario
London, Ontario, Canada, N6A-5B7
sylvia@csd.uwo.ca

Abstract: Role-based access control provides very flexible mechanisms for managing access control in complex systems. The role graph model of Nyanchama and Osborn is one example of how role administration can be implemented. In previous research, we have shown how the access control information of existing systems can be mapped to a role graph. In this paper, we extend this research by showing how, when two systems are being integrated, their role graphs can also be integrated.

Keywords: role-based access control, database integration, security integration

1. INTRODUCTION

Database interoperability and federated databases have been the subject of much research [13]. The architecture of federated databases requires each participating database system to provide an export schema for the data it is willing to share. Most research in this area has focused on the subsequent integration of the database schemas into a federated schema. Much less work has been done on integrating the access control information in a meaningful way.

Recently, there has been a great deal of activity concerning role-based access control (RBAC), for general system security as well as database security. Database security, like systems security, falls into two broad categories: discretionary access control (DAC), typically found in commercial relational database packages, and mandatory access control (MAC) typified by a security lattice and mandatory labelling of subjects and objects [2]. Many systems today require access control, which has properties somewhere between these two extremes. RBAC has been shown to be capable of modelling this broad spectrum of security requirements. To date, no one has examined interoperability of RBAC systems.

Research has been done on interoperability of security systems; some of this work is cited here. Bonatti et al. has looked at merging two MAC lattices [1]. [7,4] and [15] have examined the specification of authorisation at both the local level and the federated level. Tari's DOK system is based on constraint checking, and focuses on providing a secure architecture [14]. Jonscher and Dittrich's Argos system has roles, but the focus of the security mechanism is to interpret individual queries in a consistent manner [6].

In this paper, we provide a first step in the integration of systems whose access control is represented by role graphs [8]. Once two systems' role graphs have been integrated, further design of the access control for the federation can proceed by using RBAC administration algorithms to enhance the initial federated role graph. The role graph model is introduced in the next section. Section 3 contains a discussion of the integration of two role graphs. Section 4 presents the algorithm. Two examples, one discretionary and one mandatory, are presented in Section 5, followed by conclusions.

2. ROLE-BASED ACCESS CONTROL

Role-based access control facilitates the management of permissions in systems with large numbers of users, objects and permissions [12]. Roles correspond to job functions, and have names which reflect this.

2.1 The Role Graph Model

The role model of Nyanchama and Osborn [9] emphasises three important entities in modelling access control in a complex system: users, roles, and privileges. A privilege consists of an object and an access mode on the object. Access modes could be as simple as read or write in traditional security models, or very complex methods on objects. *Roles* are sets of privileges. We use the term *group* to refer to sets of users. In our reference model, we emphasise three planes: the user/group plane, the role plane and the privileges plane.

As well as the three basic entities, there are relationships among the entities which provide a rich way of modelling who is allowed to do what to what. Implications can exist among privileges within the privileges plane: for example, an update privilege might imply a read privilege. Users can be assigned to groups, such as ``the Physics Department'' or ``Project Alpha'', and the groups can be related to each other in the user/group plane. Role-role relationships can exist: the set of privileges assigned to the secretary role might be a subset of those assigned to the manager role. As well as these relationships, there are assignments of users/groups to roles, and assignments of privileges to roles. Following through from a user to the roles the user is assigned to, and the privileges assigned to these roles, one can then determine the details of access control. At the same time, by being able to create groups and roles that correspond to the application area, the flexibility of management of access control is greatly enhanced.

In our role graph model [9], we model the role-role relationships by an acyclic directed graph we call the *role graph*. In this graph, the nodes represent roles and the edges represent the *is-junior* relationship. A role is represented by a pair (rname, rpset), giving the role name and privilege set respectively. Role r_1 *is-junior* to role r_2 iff $r_1.rpset \subset r_2.rpset$. We also say that r_2 *is senior to* r_1. By specifying that role r_1 is-junior to r_2, one makes available all the privileges of r_1 to any user or group authorised to role r_2. We require that two roles have distinct privilege sets, i.e. that the graph be acyclic, so that each role offers a unique set of privileges. We distinguish between the *direct* privileges of a role, which are privileges not found in any of the role's juniors, and *effective* privileges, which are all the privileges contained in a role either as direct privileges or ``inherited" from one of the junior roles. The model does not deal with negative privileges. We also include in each role graph two distinguished roles: MaxRole and MinRole. MaxRole contains all the privileges in the system. MinRole.rpset may be empty. It is not necessary for every role to have users or groups assigned to it.

Role graphs have the following *Role Graph Properties*: (1) There is a single MaxRole. (2) There is a single MinRole. (3) The Role Graph is acyclic. (4) There is a path from MinRole to every role r_i . (5) There is a path from every role r_i to MaxRole. (6) For any two roles r_i and r_j, if $r_i.rpset \subset r_j.rpset$, then there must be a path from r_i to r_j. By convention, we draw the role graphs with MaxRole at the top, MinRole at the bottom, all edges going up the page, and without redundant edges.

We have, in our previous research, introduced algorithms for inserting and deleting roles, edges, and privileges [8,9]. With these algorithms, role management is a dynamic process, since roles can be altered quite easily, and the structure of the role graph (i.e. the interactions between the roles) can be changed quite frequently if required. All the algorithms run in time polynomial in the size of the role graph and the size of the privilege sets [9]. In [10] we describe how to map a role graph onto the system tables for a relational database system so that the same permissions described by the role graph can be maintained by the resulting relational database. We also show

how to take the permission tables from a relational database and form an equivalent role graph. Going in this direction gives roles with system-defined names, which can subsequently be given more meaningful names using the role graph tools. We have also shown how to map Unix permissions onto roles [5]. Oracle currently allows roles to be used to help specify access control [3], although their mechanisms are not as rich as our role-graph algorithms. It has even been shown that mandatory access control can be modelled by roles [11]. So, it is reasonable to assume that if two database systems or two other complex systems are to be integrated, their access control portion can be represented by a role graph.

2.2 Some Algorithms

In [9], algorithms are given for a number of role graph operations. Of interest in this paper are the two role insertion algorithms. The first, which we will call Insert1, takes a role graph, a role name, a set of what are to be the direct privileges, the proposed immediate senior and junior roles. The algorithm creates edges from these proposed juniors to the new role, edges from the new role to the proposed seniors, computes the effective privileges of the new role from the proposed direct privileges and the juniors' effective privileges, and then reestablishes the role graph properties. The algorithm aborts if a cycle would be created (which would create redundant roles), leaving the graph unchanged.

The second role insertion algorithm, which we will call Insert2, takes a role graph, a role name, a set of what are to be the effective privileges, and inserts the role into the graph. It generates all edges to juniors and seniors, as determined by comparing effective privileges, and reestablishes the role graph properties. The algorithm aborts if the new role duplicates an existing role.

Both of these algorithms are polynomial in the size of the role graph and the number of privileges in the privilege sets [9].

3. INTEGRATING ACCESS CONTROL

Suppose we have two database systems each of whose access control is described by a role graph. According to our reference model, we have three different kinds of information: the users, the roles, and the privileges. Both users and roles are represented by names. For the users, we assume that either user names are universal or that a one-to-one mapping can be constructed by the security administrator in a deterministic way. We ignore user groups here, and just concentrate on individual user-role assignments.

The role names involve the use of natural language with all its ambiguities. For this reason, we propose that if two systems have matching role names, they will be presented to a human being, whom we shall call the security administrator or SA, to verify that they are intended to be the same. As well, as described below, we will present roles which seem to have similar privileges but different names to the SA to verify whether they should be considered to be the same role, in which case they can be merged. This decision will always be made by the SA.

Privileges are composed of an object name and an operator name. In integrating two systems, there may be underlying data objects which should be regarded as ``the same". We assume that database integration techniques have been used to decide which objects from systems 1 and 2 should be regarded as the same. We make a similar assumption concerning operator names. If the operations are applications or packages, we assume that database integration techniques can be used to decide, for example, the ``hire" application in one system is the same as the ``create-new-employee" application in the other. In the worst case, every program and application can be broken down into a set of reads and writes on individual database objects. So if the integration of the database objects has been done, and the code for the applications analysed, complex operations can be compared to see if they represent the same privilege.

For the sake of the following discussion, if systems 1 and 2 are to be integrated, then for any two database objects or operations deemed to be the same, the object name or operation name in system 2 has been mapped onto that of system 1. The following notation will be used: system 1, $S_1(U_1, R_1, P_1)$ and system 2, $S_2(U_2, R_2, P_2)$ consist of three sets: users (U_1 and U_2), roles (R_1 and R_2), and privileges (P_1 and P_2). As well as these, there are two role graphs: $RG_1(R_1, \rightarrow_1)$ and $RG_2(R_2, \rightarrow_2)$. In turn, each P_i consists of object-operation pairs. There are 8 cases to consider:

1. U_1 and U_2 are disjoint; R_1 and R_2 are disjoint; P_1 and P_2 are disjoint
2. U_1 and U_2 are disjoint; R_1 and R_2 are disjoint; P_1 and P_2 not disjoint
3. U_1 and U_2 are disjoint; R_1 and R_2 not disjoint; P_1 and P_2 are disjoint
4. U_1 and U_2 are disjoint; R_1 and R_2 not disjoint; P_1 and P_2 not disjoint
5. U_1 and U_2 not disjoint; R_1 and R_2 are disjoint; P_1 and P_2 are disjoint
6. U_1 and U_2 not disjoint; R_1 and R_2 are disjoint; P_1 and P_2 not disjoint
7. U_1 and U_2 not disjoint; R_1 and R_2 not disjoint; P_1 and P_2 are disjoint
8. U_1 and U_2 not disjoint; R_1 and R_2 not disjoint; P_1 and P_2 not disjoint

We will first discuss isolated cases, and then the whole process.

Consider first cases 1 and 5. Since both the role sets and the privilege sets are disjoint, the role graphs can be combined as shown in Figure 1.

Once the new role graph is created, users in U_1 remain assigned to all the roles they were assigned to in S_1, and similarly, users in U_2 can remain assigned to all the roles they were assigned to in S_2. This user assignment is the same whether or not U_1 and U_2 are disjoint. After the two role graphs are merged, the role graph algorithms can be used to fine-tune the result. For example, MaxRole and MinRole from the original graphs can be deleted if they have no users assigned to them.

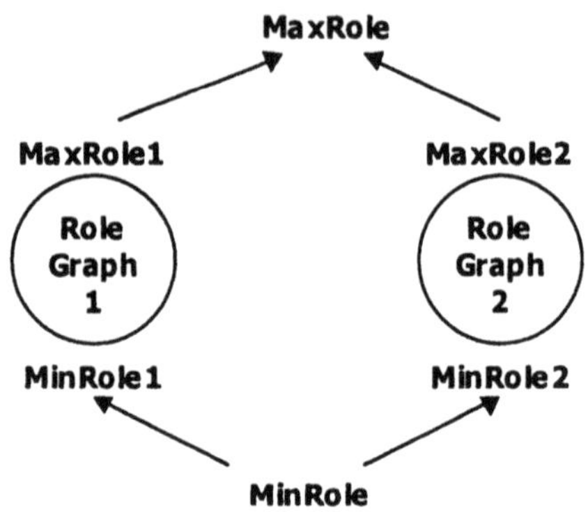

Figure 1. Disjoint Roles and Privilege Sets

Now consider cases 2 and 6. In both cases the privilege sets are not disjoint (they have non-empty intersection). First, consider the result graph to be RG_1. For each role r_i in R_2, insert r_i with its rname and effective privileges into RG_1 using Insert2. Insert2 may report that a duplicate role exists. Since duplicates are not allowed in our role graphs, this insertion will be rejected. I.e., the two roles have equal effective privilege sets, and we can treat this as merging the two roles. Role r_i should be mapped to the role that it is found to be equivalent to. The system must keep track of these mappings. After the role graph merging is complete, the usual role graph algorithms can be used to rename roles, etc.

Once the role graphs have been merged, the user assignments have to be looked at. If U_1 and U_2 are disjoint, then the users from U_1 are assigned to the roles they were assigned to in RG_1, and the users from U_2 are assigned to the roles they were assigned to in RG_2 or whatever they got mapped into. If U_1 and U_2 are not disjoint, then we begin by assigning the users from U_1 to their original roles. For each user in U_2, a situation can arise as shown in Figure 2. Suppose a user A in U_1 was assigned to role r3 in S_1 and to r8 in S_2. Further suppose that roles r2 and r9 are merged. According to S_2, this user should not be assigned to the privileges in r9. However, according to S_1, this user was given these privileges. The merging makes it appear from S_2's point of view that user A would receive new privileges (even though the integration has equated whatever privileges make up r2 and r9). In any case, the SA should be notified so that a decision can be made regarding this user's role assignments in the integrated system.

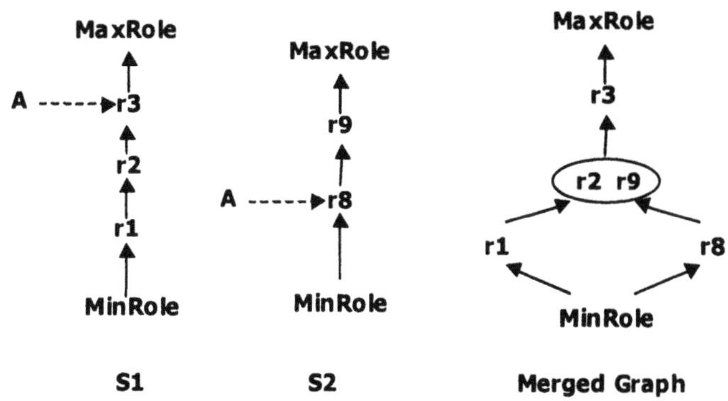

Figure 2. Merging two roles

Now consider cases 3 and 7: some duplicate role names, but no duplicate privileges. In particular, consider one role name which corresponds to a role in both graphs, but whose privilege sets are disjoint. This situation has to be handled by the SA. There are two possibilities: (1) one of the (duplicate) role names should be changed. If this is done, we are back to cases 1 and 5. (2) the SA may want to keep this common role. An example of this is an accounting role in two systems, say payroll and purchasing, which have no duplicate objects and therefore no duplicate privileges. Let the two duplicate roles be denoted by *s* from S_1 and *r* from S_2 and let the common name be *n*. To keep a role with name *n*, insert a new role with *n* as its name, *s* and *r* as its immediate juniors. The new role has no direct privileges. The immediate seniors of the new role will be established by the algorithm. Roles *s* and *r* need to be renamed (to some *s*' and *r*'). The new role, then, has the union of the privileges of the roles, which had the same name in the two original systems. The new role needs to be flagged for user assignment - users assigned to the original *r* and *s* may or may not be assigned to the new role instead of to *s* or *r* - this decision should be made by the SA.

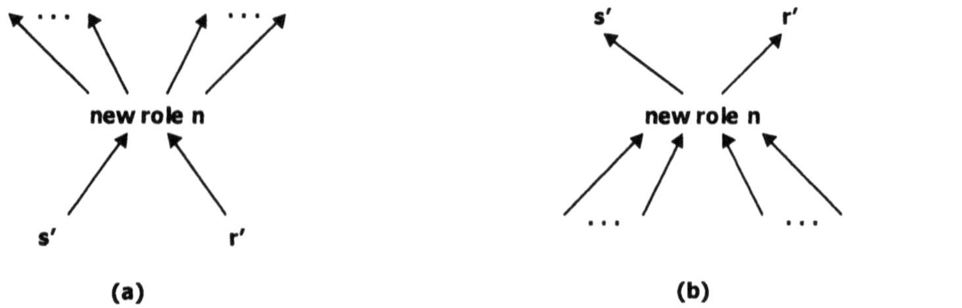

Figure 3. Common names with (a) disjoint privileges, (b) common privileges

Finally, cases 4 and 8: (some) duplicate role names, and (some) duplicate privilege names. Two roles with distinct names and duplicate privileges were handled by cases 2 and 6. Two roles with duplicate names and completely disjoint privileges were handled by cases 3 and 7. Completely duplicate privilege sets with duplicate role names can just be merged. The interesting case is if we have duplicate role names and some overlap of the privileges. Suppose we have two such roles, *s* from S_1, and *r* from S_2. What we suggest here is to create a new role with the common name *n*, which contains all the privileges of the intersection of the privileges of *s* and *r*, rename *s* and *r* (to some *s*' and *r*'), insert the new role with *s*' and *r*' as its immediate seniors. This situation is shown in Figure 3. Each such role should be assigned to all users who were assigned to *s* in S_1 and those assigned to *r* in S_2. The new role will be implicitly assigned to all such users if the users assigned to *s* (*r*) in the original role graph are assigned to *s*' (*r*') in the merged graph.

The overall algorithm proceeds, then, by taking one of the input role graphs and inserting the roles from the second graph one at a time into it, taking the above cases into account.

4. THE ALGORITHM

In the algorithm, we merge all the cases above by starting with one of the role graphs, and inserting the roles from the second graph into it. One problem that arises is that in the cases shown in Figure 3(a) and (b), when the new role is inserted, not all of the seniors or juniors of the original role from RG_2 may have been inserted yet. This is handled by noting that the graph itself has redundant information - the effective privileges can be deduced from the edges, and vice versa. For Insert1, the privileges given with the new role are what are believed to be the direct privileges, but if they are found to be redundant (present in an immediate junior), the role insertion algorithm will clean this up. So, if, when we use Insert1, we give it the effective privileges as what we think will be the direct privileges, when all the roles have been inserted, and the graph edges and paths cleaned up, the required juniors or seniors will be connected as expected. The algorithm is given next.

The output of the algorithm is a merged role graph that retains all of the information contained in the original two role graphs. Specifically all of the original roles are present, possibly with new names given by the mapping m, and each of these roles retains its original effective privilege set. Furthermore, any roles originally junior or senior to any role are still in this relationship in the new graph.

```
Algorithm GraphMerge
Inputs S1(U1, R1, P1), S2(U2, R2, P2),//the two systems,
RG1(R1,→1), RG2(R2,→2),//the two role graphs,
URA1, URA2 // the user-role assignments.
Output: NewRG(R,→) // a single role graph
  m(R1), m(R2) // mappings of original roles onto R.
Method:
  NewRG = RG1;
  for each role r in R2
       if name(r) any role name in NewRG (cases 1 and 5)
      then Insert2(NewRG, name(r), effective(r));
              if duplicates, then m(r) = name(duplicate);
              //(cases 2 and 6)
       else (role name equals to a role s in NewRG)
              if effective(r) effective(s) //(cases 3 and 7)
           ask SA if r should be renamed;
           if yes then m(r) = newname;
              Insert2(NewRG, m(r), effective(r))
           else n = name(r);
              m(r) = r';
          m(s) = s";
              Insert2(NewRG, name(r'), effective(r));
              Insert1(NewRG,n,effective(r)∪effective(s),ϕ,
                   {s"∪r'});
         else //(cases 4 and 8)
           if effective(r) = effective(s)
              then m(r) = s //merge the two roles)
              else n = name(r);
                m(r) = r';
                m(s) = s";
                Insert2(NewRG, name(r'), effective(r));
                Insert1(NewRG,n,effective(r)∩effective(s),
                     {s"∪ r'}, ϕ);
 for each u in U1 //(now look at user-role assignment)
       for each role r that u is assigned to in URA1
        assign u to m(r);
  for each u in U2
       for each role r that u is assigned to in URA2
         if u is assigned to role s in NewRG senior to
            m(r) or junior to m(r)
         then notify the SA for intervention
         else assign u to m(r);
  for each new role created by the algorithm
         notify the SA to specify user assignments;
```

Figure 4. Role Graph Integration Algorithm

5. AN EXAMPLE

We will illustrate the process by presenting an example showing two traditional relational databases using standard (discretionary) access control. System 1 is an Oracle database with relations Staff and Accounts. It has an Admin role with rights: read Staff, update Accounts and read Accounts. A Clerk role has rights: read Accounts and insert Accounts. User U1 has been granted the right to update Staff, and to perform role Admin. User U2 has been granted role Admin and users U3 and U4 have been granted role Clerk.

System 2 is a relational database whose access control has been specified in a traditional relational database way, without roles. The method given in [10] has been used to derive a role graph from the permission tables. As a result, the roles have generic names.

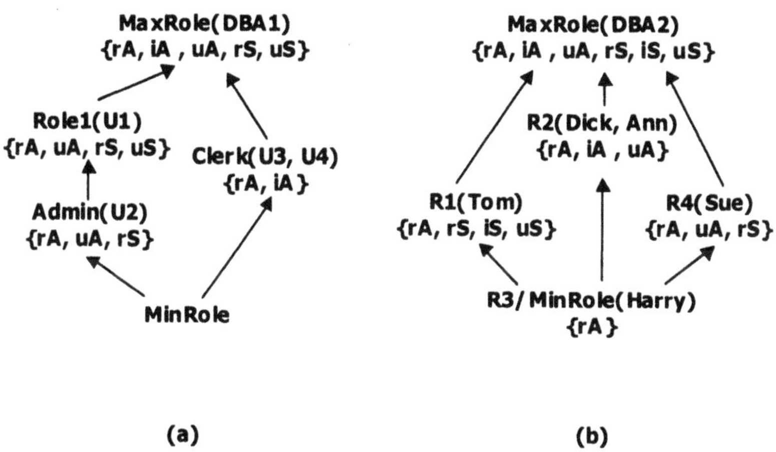

Figure 5(a,b). Input role graphs

The two role graphs are shown in Figure 5(a) and (b). We have shown the users in brackets beside the role names, and the effective privileges (using rA for read Accounts, iS for insert to Staff, etc.) below the role names. Both systems have a database administrator assigned to MaxRole.

When MaxRole from RG_2 is inserted into NewRG, the SA will be asked if one of them should be renamed. If the answer is yes, the role graph shown in Figure 6 results. If the answer is no, the MaxRole from RG_2 is inserted, and then the altorithm will try to insert a role with the union of the privileges of the rwo MaxRoles. This equals the privileges of MaxRole2, so this second insert aborts. The only difference is the ultimate role names (which can be changed later). Note that the Admin role from RG_1 and role R4 from RG_2 are merged.

Figure 6 shows the default user assignments. If U1 happens to be Sue from System2, the SA will be notified and can decide whether or not she should be assigned to Role1 or to R4/Admin in the integrated system.

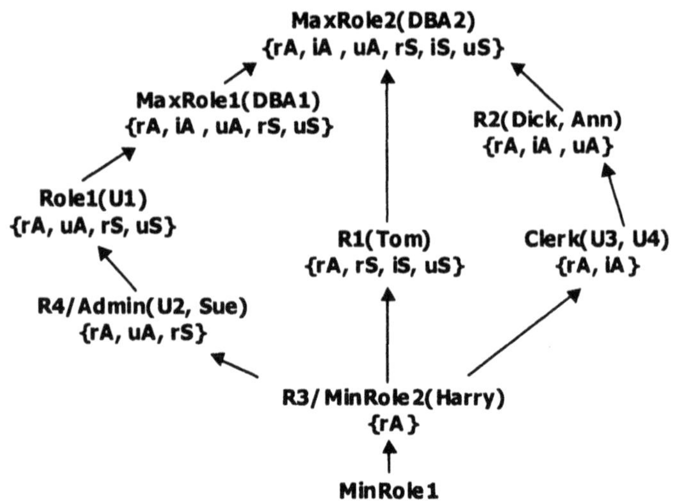

Figure 6. Merged role graph

6. SUMMARY

We have shown how, using our role graph algorithms, we can devise an algorithm for merging two role graphs. This algorithm is particularly useful in integrating the security systems of two databases, which are to be integrated. Because of the wide applicability of role-based access control, this technique can be used in a wide variety of integration activities.

References

[1] P.A. Bonatti, M.L. Sapino, and V.S Subrahmanian. Merging heterogeneous security orderings. In Martella Bertino, Kurth and Montolivo, editors, *Computer Security - ESORICS96, LNCS1146*, pages 183-197. Springer-Verlag, 1996.

[2] S. Castano, M. Fugini, G. Martella, and P. Samarati. *Database Security*. Addison-Wesley, 1994.

[3] Oracle Corporation. *Oracle Version 7, Chapters 6 & 7.* http://www.oracle.com/security/html/chap_6.html, 1995.

[4] S. di Virmercati and P. Samarati. An authorization model for federated systems. In Martella Bertino, Kurth and Montolivo, editors, *ESORICS96, LNCS 1146*, pages 99-117. Springer-Verlag, 1996.

[5] L. Hua and S. Osborn. Modeling unix access control with a role graph. In *Proc. International Conference on Computers and Information*, June 1998.

[6] D. Jonscher and K.R. Dittrich. Argos - a configurable access control system for interoperable environments. In *Database Security IX, Status and Prospects*.

[7] D. Jonscher and K.R. Dittrich. An approach for building secure database federations. In *Proceedings of 20th VLDB Conference*, pages 24-35, 1994.

[8] M. Nyanchama and S. L. Osborn. Access rights administration in role-based security systems. In J. Biskup, M. Morgenstern, and C. E. Landwehr, editors, *Database Security, VIII, Status and Prospects WG11.3 Working Conference on Database Security*, pages 37-56. North-Holland, 1994.

[9]M. Nyanchama and S. L. Osborn. The role graph model and conflict of interest. *ACM TISSEC*, 2(1):3-33, 1999.

[10] S.L. Osborn, L.K. Reid, and G.J. Wesson. On the interaction between role based access control and relational databases. In *Database Security X, Status and Prospects*.

[11] R. Sandhu. Role hierarchies and constraints for lattice-based access controls. In *Computer Security - ESORICS 96, LNCS1146*, pages 65-79. Springer Verlag, 1996.

[12] R. Sandhu, E.J. Coyne, H.L. Feinstein, and C.E. Youman. Role-based access control models. *IEEE Computer*, 29:38-47, Feb. 1996.

[13] A.P. Sheth and J.A. Larson. Federated database systems for managing distributed, heterogeneous, and autonomous databases. *ACM Computing Surveys*, 22(3):183-236, Sept. 1990.

[14] Z. Tari. Designing security agents for the dok federated system. In Lin and Qian, editors, *Database Security XI*, pages 35-59. Chapman & Hall, 1997.

[15] M. Templeton, E. Lund, and P. Ward. Pragmatics of access control in mermaid. *IEEE-CS TC Data Engineering*, pages 33-38, Sept. 1987.

CHAPTER 23

USER ROLE-BASED SECURITY MODEL FOR A DISTRIBUTED ENVIRONMENT *

S. Demurjian, T.C. Ting, J. Balthazar, H. Ren, and C. Phillips
Computer Science & Engineering Department, The University of Connecticut
steve@engr.uconn.edu, ting@engr.uconn.edu

P. Barr
The Mitre Corporation, Eatontown, New Jersey
poobarr@mitre.org

Abstract A distributed resource environment (DRE) allows distributed components (i.e., servers, legacy systems, databases, COTs, printers, scanners, etc.) to be treated akin to OS resources, where each component (resource) can publish services (an API), that are then available for use by clients and resources alike. DREs have lagged in support of security. To address this deficiency, this paper concentrates on proposing a technique for seamlessly integrating a role-based security model, authorization, authentication, and enforcement into a DRE, including our prototyping with the JINI DRE.

Keywords: Security, roles, distributed computing, authorization, authentication.

1. INTRODUCTION AND MOTIVATION

The emergence of distributed computing technology such as DCE [10], CORBA [7], and DCOM [5], has enabled the parallel and distributed processing of large, computation-intensive applications. The incorporation of security has often been dependent on programmatic effort. For example, while CORBA has confidentiality, integrity, accountability, and availability services, there is no cohesive CORBA service that ties to-

*This work partially supported by the Mitre Corporation and a AFOSR grant.

gether them with authorization and authentication. However, there has been significant progress in distributed authentication in Kerberos [6] and Cheron [3], security metric analysis and design [9], Internet security via firewalls [8], role-based access control on Web-based intranets [12], and security for mobile agents [14, 15].

Our specific interest is in distributed applications that plug-and-play, allowing us to plug in (and subtract) new "components" or *resources* where all of the resources (e.g., legacy, COTS, databases, servers, etc.) have services that are published (via APIs) for use by distributed application components. The resources, their services, and the clients, interacting across the network, comprise a *distributed resource environment (DRE)*. Our goal in this paper is to leverage the infrastructure of a DRE to support and realize role-based security. In such a setting, we propose specialized security resources that interact with non-security resources and clients, to authorize, authenticate, and enforce security for a distributed application in a dynamic fashion. To demonstrate the feasibility of our approach, we exploit Sun's DRE JINI [1]. JINI promotes the construction and deployment of robust and scalable distributed applications. In JINI, a distributed application is conceptualized as a set of services (of all resources) being made available for discovery and use by clients. Resources in JINI discover and then join the Lookup Service, registering their services for network availability. However, JINI lacks the ability to restrict what a client can and cannot do, i.e., the services of a resource are available to any and all clients without restriction.

Our main purpose of this paper is to examine the incorporation of a role-based approach to security within a DRE, in general, and JINI, in particular, which supports the selective access of clients to resources. We propose security specific resources for authorization of clients based on role, authentication of clients, and enforcement to insure that a client only uses authorized services. We provide role-based access to services based on our previous object-oriented efforts [2], without programmatic changes to a resource, allowing the resource to dynamically discover security privileges from security resources. In the remainder of this paper, Section 2 provides brief background on JINI, Section 3 proposes a role-based security model for a DRE, Section 4 synopsizes our prototyping with JINI, and Section 5 contains our conclusions.

2. JINI

JINI allows stakeholders to construct a distributed application by federating groups of users (clients) and the resources that they require [1]. In JINI, the resources register services which represent the methods (similar to an API) that are provided for use by clients (and other resources). A Lookup Service is provided, and operates as a clearinghouse for resources to register services and clients to find services. The Lookup Service arbitrates all interactions by resources (e.g., discovering Lookup Services, registering services, renewing leases, etc.) and by clients (e.g., discovering Lookup Services, searching for services, service invocation, etc.). After discovery has occurred, the resources register their services on a class-by-class basis with the Lookup Service. The class is registered as a service object which contains the public methods available to clients coupled with a set of optional descriptive service attributes. The service object is registered as a proxy, which contains all of the information that is needed to invoke the service. One limitation of this process is that once registered, a resource's services are available to all clients. The registration of services occurs via a leasing mechanism. With leasing, the services of a resource can be registered with the Lookup Service for a fixed time period or forever (no expiration). The lease must be renewed by the resource prior to its expiration, or the service will become unavailable. From a security perspective, the lease that is given by a resource to its services is not client specific. Once leased, a service is available to all, even if the service was intended for a targeted client or group of clients. Our work seeks to overcome this limitation.

3. A DRE ROLE-BASED SECURITY MODEL

In a DRE, all of the different resources are treated in a consistent fashion, allowing all of the clients and resources to be seamlessly integrated. Clients consult the Lookup Service to locate and subsequently execute the services of the found resource that are necessary to carry out their respective tasks. However, DREs are lacking in their support of security. When a resource registers its services with the Lookup Service, there is no way for the resource to dictate which service can be utilized by which client. If the resource wants to control access to its services, it must do so programmatically, putting in client-specific code within the implementation of the service. We are extending the security capabilities of a DRE to allow resources to selectively and dynamically control who can access its services (and invoke their methods), based on the role of the client. Our solution exploits the DRE, by defining dedicated resources to authorize, authenticate, and enforce role-based security for the distributed application. The remainder of this section is organized to propose and discuss: a software architecture for role-based security in a DRE (Section 3.1), the security resources and services for such an architecture (Section 3.2), and the usage of the solution by clients and resources (Sections 3.3 and 3.4).

3.1. A SOFTWARE ARCHITECTURE

A software architecture for supporting role-based security in a DRE is presented in Figure 1.1, and contains: a set of clients that seek to utilize a set of resources, one or more Lookup Services that allow clients to find resources (and their services), and three security-specific resources.

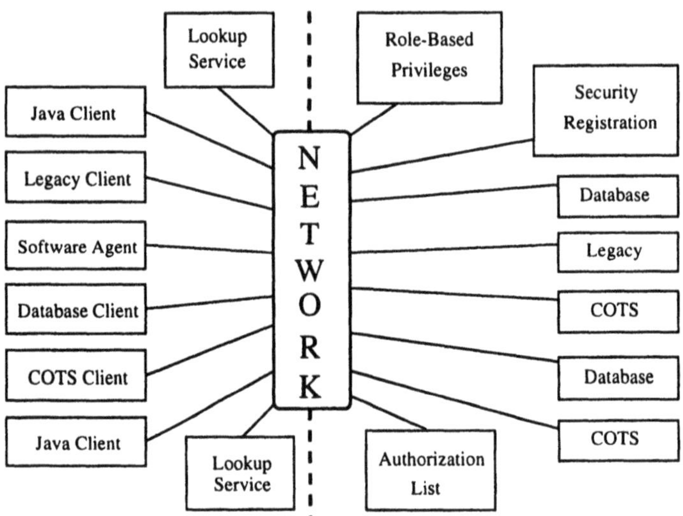

Figure 1.1. General Architecture of Clients and Resources.

The *Role-Based Privileges* resource tracks the services of each resource, and for every service, the methods that are defined. Each user role may be granted access at varying levels of granularity, allowing a role to be assigned to a resource (able to use all services and their methods), to a service (able to use all of its methods), or to individual methods (restricted to specific methods of a service). The *Authorization-List* resource maintains a list of all users, and for each user, tracks the roles that they have been authorized to play. Finally, the *Security Registration* resource tracks the current active users uniquely identified by a triad of <name, IP address, user role>. The architecture supports:

1 Role-based authorization to grant and revoke resources, their services, and their methods for use by clients. This is accomplished using the Role-Based Privileges and Authorization-List resources.

A special security client (see Section 3.3) can be utilized by the security officer to manage this security data.

2 Client authentication for the verification of the identity and role of client. This is supported by the Security Registration resource, which tracks all active clients (name, IP address, role), and is used by resources whenever a client attempts to access a service.

3 Customized resource behavior so that the client and its role dynamically determines if a particular service of a resource can be used. A resource utilizes all three security specific resources to control access to its services by clients.

The term client is used in a general sense; resources can function as clients to access other resources as needed to carry out their functions.

3.2. SECURITY RESOURCES/SERVICES

This section examines the Role-Based Privileges, Authorization List, and Security Registration resources (see Figure 1.1) via a role-based approach to discretionary access control [2, 4, 11, 13]. In a DRE, the computational and abstraction model is to define, for each resource, a set of one or more services, and for each of the services, to define a set of one or more methods. However, there is no a priori way to selectively control which client can utilize which resources (and its services and their methods). We leverage our past work [2] on selectively allowing the methods defined on object-oriented classes to be assigned on a role-by-role basis as a basis to selectively control which clients can access which services and methods of which resources. The role-based security model presented herein will focus on the ability to grant and revoke privileges on resources, services, and/or methods to clients playing roles.

3.2.1 Role-Based Privileges Resource. This resource is utilized by the security officer to realize the defined security policy for a distributed application to: define user roles; grant access of user roles to resources, services, and/or methods; and, when appropriate, revoke access. The Role-Based Privileges resource is utilized by the resources (e.g., legacy, COTS, database, Java server, etc.) that comprise the distributed application to dynamically determine if a client has the required permission to execute a particular service. To facilitate the discussion, consider the definitions:

Definition 1: A *Resource* is a system (e.g., a legacy, COTS, database, Web server, etc.) that provides functions for the distributed application via a collection of n services, $S_1, S_2, ..., S_n$.

Definition 2: A *Service*, $S_i, i = 1..n$, is composed of p_i methods M_{i1}, M_{i2}, ..., M_{ip_i} where each method M_{ij}, $j = 1..p_i$ is similar to an object-oriented method, and each method represents a subset of the functionality provided by the service.

Definition 3: A *Method* M_{ij}, $j = 1..p_i$ of a service S_i is defined by a signature (method name, parameter names/type, and return type).

Definitions 4, 5, and 6: Each resource has a unique *resource identifier* that allows the DRE to differentiate between replicated resources. Each service has a unique *service identifier* to distinguish the services within a particular resource. Each method has a unique *method signature* that permits overloading of method names while allowing the methods of the same service to be distinguished.

Each triple of <resource identifier, service identifier, method signature> uniquely identifies the method across the distributed application.

Given these definitions, we can now define the concept of user role. In our past work [2], we proposed a user-role definition hierarchy to characterize the different kinds of individuals (and groups) who all require different levels of access to an application. For the purposes of this discussion, we focus on the leaf nodes of the hierarchy.

Definition 7: A *user role, UR*, is a uniquely named entity that represents a specific set of responsibilities against an application. Privileges are granted and revoked as follows:

- UR can be granted access to resource R, denoting that UR can utilize all of R's services, $S_1, S_2, ..., S_n$, and, for all $S_i, i = 1..n$, all of the p_i methods $M_{i1}, M_{i2}, ..., M_{ip_i}$.
- UR can be granted access to a subset of the services of resource R, denoting that UR can utilize all of the methods defined by that subset.
- UR can be granted specific access to a method via the triple of <resource identifier, service identifier, method signature>.

Once granted, access to resources, services, and/or methods can be selectively or entirely revoked by a security officer. The granularity of user roles may be fine or coarse at the discretion of a security officer. Given these definitions, the Role-Based Privileges resource maintains: a *resource list*, indexed by <resource identifier> and for each resource, a list of all user roles granted access; a *service list*, indexed by <resource identifier, service identifier>, and for each service, a list of all user roles granted access; a *method list*, indexed by <resource identifier, service

identifier, method signature>, and for each method, a list of all user roles granted access; and a *user-role list*, indexed by <role name, role identifier>, and for each user role, a list of all resources, services, and/or methods, to which that user roles has been granted access. The information of the Role-Based Privileges resource can be manipulated by the different clients that are part of the distributed application:

- Each resource must register with the Role-Based Privileges resource, so that the master resource list, service list, and method list, can be dynamically modified. Resources must be allowed to register and un-register services/methods. The Register service in Figure 1.2, supports these actions.
- Each resource, when consulted by a client (e.g., GUI, software agent, another resource, etc.), asks the Security Registration resource if the client has registered, (see Section 3.2.3) and if so, asks the Role-Based Privileges resource if the client has been granted access to a service/method pair based on the role of the client. The Query Privileges service in Figure 1.2 supports these actions.
- There is a Security Client (see Section 3.3), utilized by the security officer to define and remove user roles and to grant and revoke privileges (resources, services, and/or methods). The Grant-Revoke-Find service in Figure 1.2 supports these actions.

To simplify the presentation, we have omitted return types. For example, the majority of the methods will return a success/failure flag, the Check_Privileges will return a yes/no, and the Finds will return result sets. Note that the services in Figure 1.2 represents a general characterization of the services for all three security specific resources.

3.2.2 Authorization-List Resource. This resource maintains profiles on the clients (e.g., users, tools, software agents, etc.) that are actively utilizing services within the distributed application. The identification of users is more problematic in a distributed setting, since a user may not be an actual person, but may be a legacy, COTS, database, agent, etc. This leads to the definition:

Definition 8: A client profile, CP, characterizes all of the pertinent information needed by a resource to dynamically verify whether a client can access the desired triple of <resource identifier, service identifier, method signature>.

The Authorization-List resource maintains the client profiles using two services (see Figure 1.2). The Client Profile service is utilized by the

Role-Based Privileges Services

Register Service

```
Register_Resource (R_Id);
Register_Service (R_Id,S_Id);
Register_Method (R_Id, S_Id, M_Id);
UnRegister_Resource (R_Id);
UnRegister_Service (R_Id, S_Id);
Unregister_Method (R_Id, S_Id, M_Id)
```

Query Privileges Service

```
Check_Privileges (UR_Id, R_Id, S_Id, M_Id)
```

Grant-Revoke Service

```
Grant_Resource (UR_Id, R_Id);
Grant_Service (UR_Id, R_Id, S_Id);
Grant_Method (UR_Id, R_Id, S_Id, M_Id);
Revoke_Resource (UR, R_Id);
Revoke_Service (UR, R_Id, S_Id);
Revoke_Method (UR, R_Id, S_Id, M_Id);
Find_AllUR_Resource (UR, R_Id);
Find_AllUR_Service (UR, R_Id, S_Id);
Find_AllUR_Method (UR, R_Id, S_Id, M_Id);
Find_UR_Privileges (UR)
```

User Role Service

```
Create_New_Role (UR_Name, UR_Disc, UR_Id);
Delete_Role (UR_Id);
Find_UR_Name (UR_Name);
Find_UR_Id (UR_Id);
```

Authorization-List Services

Client Profile Service

```
Create_New_Client (C_Id);
Delete_Client (C_Id);
Find_Client (C_Id);
Find_All_Clients ();
```

Authorize Role Service

```
Grant_UR_Client (UR_Id, C_Id);
Revoke_UR_Client (UR, C_Id);
Find_AllUR_Client (C_Id);
Find_All_Clients_UR (UR);
Verify_UR_Client (UR, C_Id);
```

Security Registration Services

Register Client Service

```
Register_Client (C_Id, IP_Addr, UR);
UnRegister_Client (C_Id, IP_Addr, UR);
IsClient_Registered (C_Id);
Find_Client (C_Id, IP_Addr);
Find_All_Active_Clients ();
```

Figure 1.2. The Services and Methods for Security Resources.

security officer, via a Security Client (see Section 3.3), to create and manage the profiles for clients. The Authorize Role service is also utilized to verify whether a client has registered with a role (see Section 3.4).

3.2.3 Security Registration Resource. This resource is utilized by clients for identity registration (client id, IP address, and user role) and by the Security Client (see Section 3.3). The Register Client service (see Figure 1.2), allows a client to have access to resources and their services. Every non-security resource utilizes the Security Registration resource to dynamically determine if the client trying to invoke the service has registered via the IsClient_Registered method. If the client has not registered, the resource will deny service.

3.3. SECURITY CLIENT PROCESSING

To further explain the security processing in the DRE, Figure 1.3 contains a depiction of a Security Client and a General Resource (e.g., legacy, COTS, database, etc.). For the Security Client, Figure 1.3 contains the services from the three security resources that can be used to establish the security policy by creating/finding clients, authorizing roles to clients, and granting, revoking, and finding the privileges that a role has against a resource, service, and/or method. For the General Resource, there is the requirement to register itself, its services, and their methods with the Role-Based Privileges resource (see Figure 1.3). Registration allows entries to be created on the resource, service, and method lists that can then be accessed via the Security Client. Note that the Security Client and General Resource must discover the services in Figure 1.3, prior to their invocation, as represented by the dashed arrows.

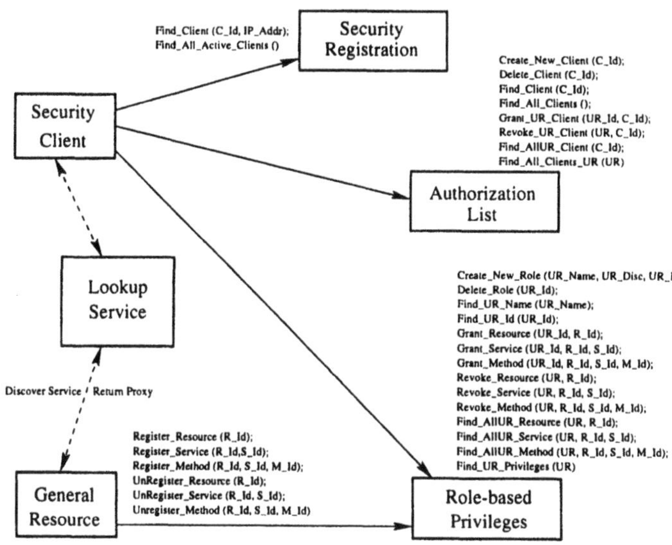

Figure 1.3. Security Client and Database Resource Interactions.

3.4. CLIENT PROCESSING

Finally, to fully illustrate the process, we present an example in Figure 1.4, with flow via the numbered service invocations and returned results. To reduce the confusion in the figure, we have omitted all of the discoveries and proxy returns that would be required for the actions labeled 1, 2, 5, 6, and 8. The actions that occur can be illustrated with the method call represented by the arrow labeled 1. Register_Client. Prior to this method call, the GUI Client would ask the Lookup Service for a resource that provides the Register Client Service (part of the Security Registration resource as shown in Figure 1.2). The Lookup Service would return a proxy to the Register Client Service, and the GUI would use this proxy to execute the Register_Client method.

With the discovery/proxy process described, the example begins by the client making itself known by registering with the Security Registration resource. The arrows labeled 1, 2, 3, and 4 facilitate the registration process, by requiring the client to register itself with the

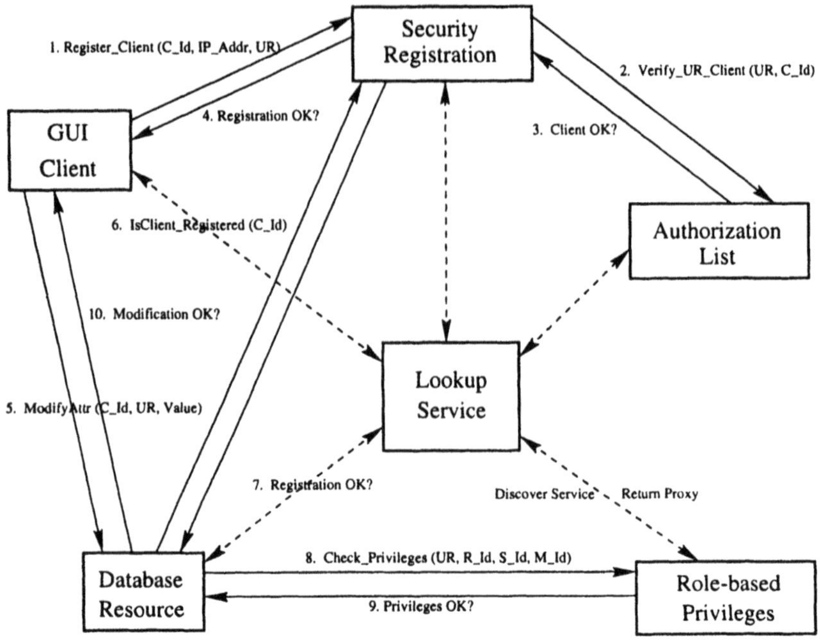

Figure 1.4. Client Interactions and Service Invocations.

Security Registration resource (arrow 1), which in turn interacts with the Authorization-List resource to determine if the client has been authorized to play the desired role (arrow 2). Arrows 3 and 4 complete the process and will return either success or failure. For this discussion, we assume that success is returned. Note that clients that have not registered will still be able to discover resources and services via the Lookup Service. But, they will be prohibited from executing those services if they have not registered. After the Client has successfully registered, it can then discover services via the Lookup Service. Suppose that the Client has discovered the ModifyAttr method that is part of the Update Database Service for the Database Resource (arrow 5 in Figure 1.4). When the Database Resource receives the ModifyAttr invocation request, the first step in its processing is to verify if the client has registered by interacting with the Security Registration resource (arrows 6 and 7). If so, then the Database Resource must then check to see if the client playing the particular role has the required privileges to access the ModifyAttr method, which is accomplished via arrows 8 and 9 by consulting the Role-Based Privileges resource. If the Database Resource receives a response to indicate that the GUI Client has the privileges to access the method, it will then execute the ModifyAttr method and return a status to the Client (arrow 10).

4. PROTOTYPING WITH JINI

This section reviews our prototyping efforts with JINI to support our security model as presented in Section 3. We have implemented the prototype on Windows NT 4.0, LINUX, and UNIX computing platforms, using Java 1.3, MS Access and ORACLE for database management, and JINI 1.3. To support the prototyping effort, we employ a university application where students can query course information and enroll in classes, and faculty can query and modify the class schedule. Our prototype has fully designed and implemented the security resources: Security Registration, Role-Based Privileges, and Authorization-List. These resources, along with two Security Client GUIs, one for policy making and one for policy enforcement (authorizations), make up a reusable Security Client (see Section 3.3) and its security services (Figure 1.2). A security officer can now define, manage, and modify the security privileges dynamically in support of university security policy. Note that additional details on our prototyping can be found at our web site for this project [16].

5. CONCLUSIONS AND FUTURE WORK

In this paper, we proposed and explained an approach that can authorize, authenticate, and enforce a role-based security solution that operates within a DRE. As presented in Section 3, our architecture (see Section 3.1) defined the basis of a role-based security model for a DRE, specified Security Registration, Authorization-List, and Role-Based Privileges resources and their services (see Section 3.2), and detailed the processing of both clients and resources (see Sections 3.3 and 3.4). We prototyped our model from Section 3 using JINI as described in Section 4, and including the clients, resources, security resources, and a Security Client on heterogeneous hardware/OS platforms. The work presented herein represents the first step in an ongoing effort with one doctoral and two masters students. There are a number of issues under investigation: negative privileges to specifically define which resources, services, and/or methods are not available to a client based on role; incorporation of timing and timestamp to allow privileges to expire for a client based on role, which is related to the JINI leasing mechanism; definition and utilization of predicates to allow methods to be invoked by clients only if parameter values are within authorized ranges; and, investigation of the incorporation of our role-based security model and concepts for a DRE into an agent-based environment. Overall, we are concentrating our efforts to define security solutions for distributed applications operating within a DRE.

References

[1] K. Arnold, et al., *The JINI Specification*, Addison-Wesley, 1999.

[2] S. Demurjian and T.C. Ting, "Towards a Definitive Paradigm for Security in Object- Oriented Systems and Applications", *Journal of Computer Security*, Vol. 5, No. 4, 1997.

[3] A. Fox and S. Gribble, "Security on the Move: Indirect Authentication Using Kerberos", *ACM MOBICON 96*, Rye, NY, 1996.

[4] F. H. Lochovsky and C. C. Woo, "Role-Based Security in Data Base Management Systems", in *Database Security: Status and Prospects*, C. Landwehr (ed.), North-Holland, 1988.

[5] Microsoft Corporation, *The Component Object Model (Technical Overview)*, Microsoft Press, Redmond, WA, 1995.

[6] C. Nueman and T. Ts'o, "An Authorization Service for Computer Networks", *Comm. of the ACM*, Vol. 32, No. 9, Sept. 94.

[7] Object Management Group, *The Common Object Request Broker: Architecture and Specification, Rev. 2.0*, MA, July 1995.

[8] Oppliger, R. "Internet Security: Firewalls and Beyond", *Comm. of the ACM*, Vol. 40, No. 5, May 1997.

[9] M. Reiter and S. Stubblebine, "Authentication Metric Analysis and Design", *ACM Trans. On Information and System Security*, Vol. 2, No. 2, May 1999.

[10] W. Rosenberry, D. Kenney, and G. Fischer, *Understanding DCE*, O'Reilly & Associates, 1992.

[11] R. Sandhu, et al., "Role-Based Access Control Models", *IEEE Computer*, Vol. 29, No. 2, Feb. 1996.

[12] R. Sandhu and J. Park, "Decentralized User-Role Assignment for Web-based Intranets", *Proc. of the 3rd ACM Wksp. on Role-Based Access Control*, Fairfax, VA, Oct. 1998.

[13] D. Spooner, "The Impact of Inheritance on Security in Object-Oriented Database Systems", in *Database Security, II: Status and Prospects*, C. Landwehr (ed.), North-Holland, 1989.

[14] V. Swarup, "Trust Appraisal and Secure Routing of Mobile Agents", *Proc. of 1997 Workshop on Foundations for Secure Mobile Code (DARPA)*, March 1997.

[15] Walsh, T., Paciorek, N., and Wong, D. "Security and Reliability in Concordia", *Proc. of the 31st Hawaii Intl. Conf. on System Sciences (HICSS'98)*, 1998.

[16] http://www.engr.uconn.edu/ steve/urbsdreproj.html

CHAPTER 24

WorkFlow Analyzed for Security and Privacy in using Databases

Wouter Teepe, Reind van de Riet and Martin Olivier
[1]*Department of Artificial Intelligence, State University of Groningen, Groningen, The Netherlands, email: wouter@teepe.com* [2]*Department of Mathematics and Computer Science, Vrije Universiteit, Amsterdam, The Netherlands, email: vdriet@cs.vu.nl*
[3]*Department of Mathematics and Computer Science, Rand University, Johannesburg, South Africa, email: molivier@rkw.rau.ac.za*

Key words: Security & Privacy and Database systems, Workflow, Cyberspace, Object-Oriented Databases

Abstract: When companies interchange information about individuals, privacy is at stake. On the basis of the purpose of the information interchange, rules can be designed for an agent (Alter-ego) to determine whether the requested information can be provided. This purpose can be derived from a WorkFlow specification according to which employees (agents) of one company are executing their tasks. Direct information flow as well as information which might flow through private and covert channels is considered.

1. INTRODUCTION

In a study, being conducted for many years, we have introduced the notion of Alter-ego, which is an object/agent, representing people in Cyberspace and acting on behalf of these people (see [vdRB96b]). We are in particular interested in the problem of protecting someone's privacy.

In choosing a company for certain services, like an insurance, an individual will not only look at conditions such as financial costs and benefits, but also at less tangible conditions such as privacy rules held in that company. After inspection of these rules a client can decide to accept an offer.

In the near future we expect that the privacy conditions are treated even more seriously, in that the client demands that an agent is placed in that company which checks the behaviour of the employees in that company. This agent may inspect WorkFlows according to which these employees are working. Actually, the situation can be even more complicated by considering the cooperation of this company (A) with another company (B), who is interested in information about the individual. The agent may then decide whether to give that information or not. Also in this case the agent may inspect the WorkFlow according to which employees in company B are working; in order to determine whether it is of the interest of the individual or contrary to his/hers privacy concerns.

The main point of this paper is therefore to analyze a WorkFlow specification to find out properties relevant for privacy protection. A simple example will make clear what kind of properties we mean. Suppose the company is an insurance company and the individual wants to be sure that decisions within this company about policies and about claims are made without taking into account specific properties of the individual, such as the colour of the skin or marital and social status. Using the tools described in this paper that individual can carry out this analysis.

It is assumed that two companies A and B have organized the work of all their employees in the form of a WorkFlow (abbreviated in the following as WF). Although WF systems have been in existence for a number of years, the trend towards greater interconnection will greatly impact such systems. On the one hand, interaction will involve more and more non-human participants. On the other hand the participants in WF processes will become more and more unrelated. The key to secure implementation of future generation WF systems is proper authentication and authorization of participants in a WF process. It is our contention that Alter-egos (see the next section) are particularly suitable for authentication, while roles are particularly suitable for authorization. We have presented these ideas in [GRBO97].

These WFs are open for inspection. From them one can determine whether employees have the proper information to perform their tasks, but also whether they may have too much information about an individual, or even when they can conspire/cooperate with other employees and then are able to derive private information about the individual, using special channels. For the agent or Alter-ego in company A it is possible to analyze these WFs. The outcome can be used in two different ways:

1. To determine whether a company is trustworthy with respect to keeping privacy rules the employees have (just) enough information about the individual, and

2. to decide whether to respond to a query which is sent to company A by one of B's employees taking into account the information this employee already has about the individual as derived from the WF; this is depicted in figure 1.

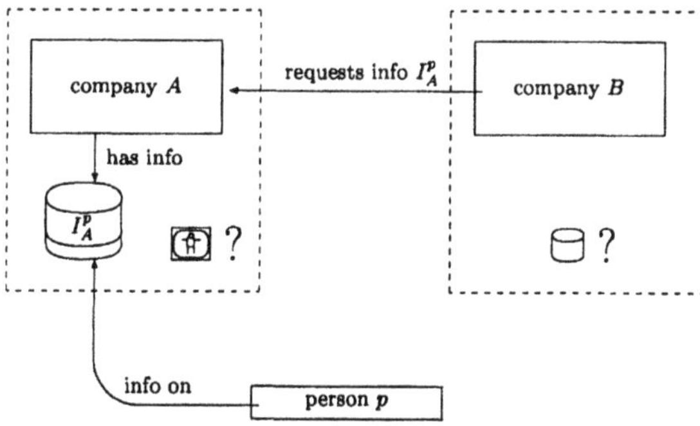

Figure 1: A Company keeping information about person P_i, B asks it.

In the next section we will sketch a bit of the framework in which we are doing our research, i.c. the notion of Alter-ego and introduce the COLOR-X system which we use to specify WF diagrams. In the following section we then shall see how the COLOR-X diagrams can be represented as a Prolog database, so that analysis programs can be written in Prolog. The purpose is to analyze beforehand what each agent in B knows about P; that is to say: what s/he has to know in order to do the task specified, and what s/he may know when using information sent by cooperating/conspiring colleagues, flowing through a private and covert channels.

In the next section we will see how the privacy rules may use the knowledge provided in the analysis of the WF diagram. Finally, we will give some conclusions and hints for future work.

2. BACKGROUND

2.1 Alter-egos

For our research in Security & Privacy in Cyberspace, we assume that individuals, either in an office environment, or in their homes, will be represented in Cyberspace by objects, called Alter-egos, in the sense of Object-Oriented Technology. The identifier of this object may be considered a combination of Social Security Number and e-mail address. The contents of these objects represent the properties of the persons for which they are Alter-ego; their behaviour can be seen as the behaviour of agents acting on behalf of these persons. They were introduced in [GRBO97], where it was shown how these Alter-egos can be structured and how Security and Privacy (S&P) aspects can be dealt with questions around responsibility and obligations of Alter-egos have been discussed in [vdRB96b, vdRB96a].

2.2 The WorkFlow system COLOR-X

In this section we briefly describe the COLOR-X system in which it is possible to specify a WF diagram. In Workflow management (WFM) applications there are tasks to be completed by some organization, but the organization procedures require that this task will be carried out in steps where each step is executed by a different individual and no step can be performed before the steps it depends on are completed [GHS95]. We will show how S&P rules can be derived from COLOR-X diagrams.

WFM tools are currently being used to specify how people and information systems are cooperating within one organization. There are at least three reasons why WFM techniques are also useful in Cyberspace. First, organizations tend to become multi-national and communication takes place in a global manner. Secondly, more and more commerce is being done electronically. This implies that procedures have to be designed to specify the behaviour of the participants. These procedures may be somewhat different from ordinary WFM designs, where the emphasis is on carrying out certain tasks by the users, while in commerce procedures are based on negotiating, promises, commitments and deliveries of goods and money. However, as we will see, these notions are also present in the WFM tool we will use. Thirdly, people will be participants in all kinds of formalized procedures, such as tax paying or home banking.

2.3 Workflow and Security

This being said, how can we derive security and privacy rules from the Workflow diagrams (WFDs)? Specifying tasks and actions of people working in an organization naturally also involves the specification of their responsibilities [vdRB96b, vdRB96a, GRBO97]. This is what WFDs usually do. Responsibility implies access to databases to perform certain actions on data of individuals.

A Workflow Authorization Model is proposed in [AH96]. Authorization Templates are associated with each Workflow task and used to grant rights to subjects only when they require the rights to perform tasks. A Petri net implementation model is also given.

3. THE INSURANCE-CLAIM APPLICATION

The following example is about the treatment of a claim within an Insurance Company IC, concerning a trip booked with a Travel Agent TA. First we describe the processes in natural language, using numbers identifying the actions for easy identification with the boxes used in the COLOR-X diagram, following next.

There is an Insurance Company, IC, Furthermore there are persons, which can be employees of the IC. An employee can be an approver, a travel agent, an expert or a cashier. Also a person can be a submitter of a claim. The static (incomplete) structure op the submitter is depicted in figure 2.

```
type person is_a thing        type submitter is_a person
  has_a name
  has_a address
```

Figure 2: The static structure of submitter.

Next follows the text of the Claim example. The numbers refer to the numbered boxes in the diagram.

1. A submitter SU sends in a triple of data (the trip TR, the incident IN, the amount AM1) to the approver AP of the insurance company IC.
2. AP receives the message from SU and creates an object called claim, CL, from the triple sent and asks the travel agent TA to verify the claim (possibly) within one week.
3. TA tries to verify CL within one week and return the answer to AP
4. Upon not receiving an answer from TA, AP assumes the claim is not OK and informs the submitter SU accordingly. (in a more realistic setting AP would send a reminder to TA). Upon receiving an answer from TA, which is "not OK", AP informs SU that the claim is not OK.
5. When TA's answer is positive and the amount is smaller than $100, AP asks the cashier CA to transfer the money to SU's Bank and informs SU.
6. Upon receiving an answer from TA, which is "OK", and the amount not being smaller than $100, AP asks an expert EX to look at the claim and AP informs SU appropriately.
7. EX treats CL and reports the decision to AP, which, in case the claim is found "not OK", handles as above in 4;
8. when "OK", AP determines the amount AM2 to be paid to SU and asks the cashier CA to transfer the money to SU's Bank;
9. CA pays the amount AM2 to SU's Bank.

We now give some clarification of the COLOR-X specification in figure 3.

- each box of actions has a mode: PERMIT, NEC or MUST. MUST means an obligation based on some negotiating in the past: as we are not sure

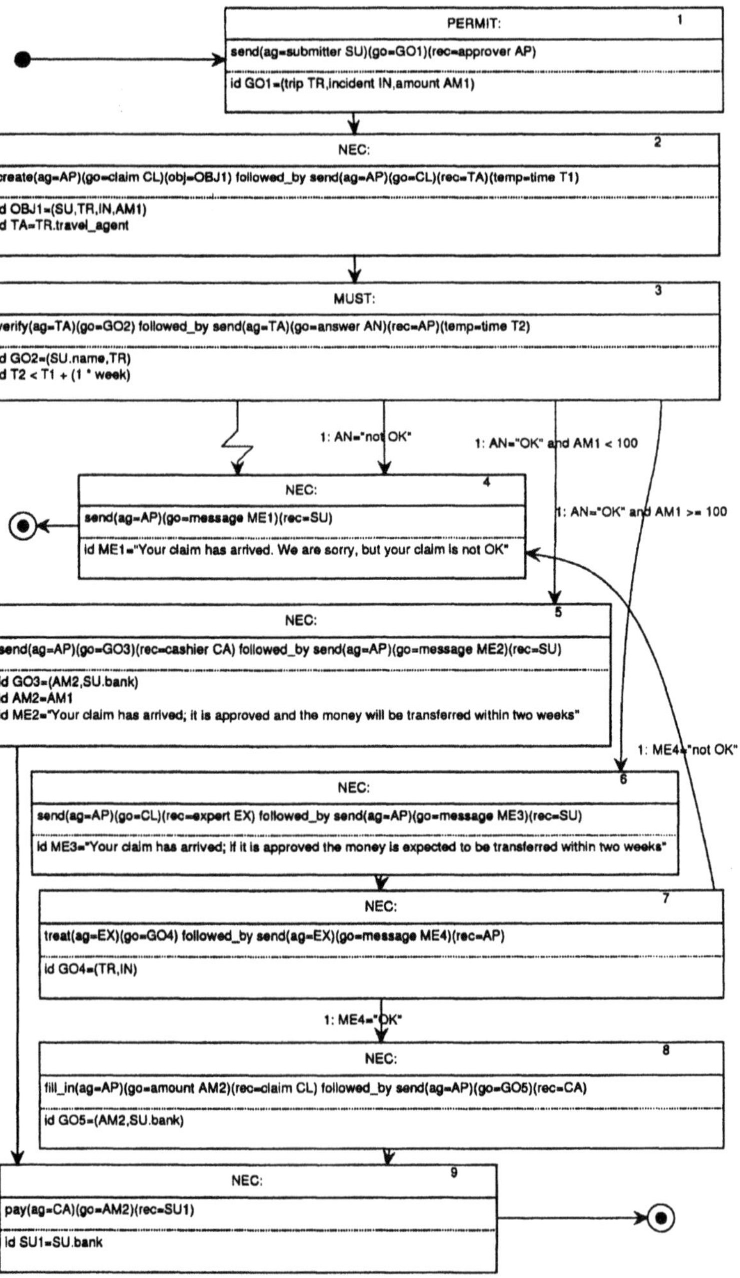

Figure 3: The claim example

– that the action is actually carried out within the prescribed time it is necessary to define a counter measure indicated by the lightning arrow. The mode NEC means we can be sure the action is necessarily carried

out by the system. PERMIT means there are no pre-conditions: the actions in the box can be executed;
- the actions are described in a formal language involving the participants and their roles.

It is important to notice that in sending a message from an agent A to a receiver R only the object identifiers are readable by R, not the contents. Only when the Workflow specifies that R has to do something with the contents of the object, it is allowed to read this.

4. THE REPRESENTATION OF COLOR-X DIAGRAMS IN PROLOG

Before stating for what purpose the WorkFlow WF is going to be analyzed we give three examples:

1. Suppose an agent like the travel agent TA asks information to company A, say the marital status of the submitter SU. The submitter's agent in A could refuse to respond because the analysis of WF shows that TA knows the trip TR and SU's name. The agent may reason as follows: TA knows TR, which was a trip for married people, if TA also knows that SU is single, TA may sue SU for bringing with him/her a partner to which s/he was not married.
2. Now the travel agent asks for the submitter's age. Although it is not certain that TA knows the incident IN, it is possible that the approver AP sends this information to TA using the message in which a reference to the claim is written. In this case some kind of "private" channel is used between AP and TA. When TA combines the contents of IN with the knowledge of the age of SU, TR finds out that the incident concerned illegally driving a car because SU was too young.
3. The cashier CA seems to know only the amount to be paid and the submitter's bank and it seems that no privacy problem can occur, however, suppose the amount is very high, so that CA may want to know SU's name. By conspiring with the approver AP and the travel agent TA, using a private channel, CA can get SU's name indeed.

The three examples show that the analysis has to reveal what each employee knows about the individual, here the submitter SU. It also reveals that we need to know what each employee might know about the individual, by cooperating/conspiring with other employees, using private channels. So lists have to be made for each employee in an action what s/he knows according to the WF and what s/he may know additionally when another agent sends him/her a message with more information than the information prescribed in the WF.

4.1 About the verbs being used

We have to say something about the verbs describing the actions. Evidently, "send(ag=S, go=M, rec=R, ...)" means: S sends a message M to R. M may a tuple, as in "(trip TR, incident IN, amount AM1)" or an object identifier, as in: "go=CL", or an unspecified thing as in "go=answer". There are also verbs denoting some specific action as: "verify", "treat", or "pay". For these actions it is necessary that the contents of their parameter "goal" is known on the basis of "need to know". The "create" and "fill_in" actions are also special as they bring new objects into being. For these actions detailed knowledge about their parameter "goal" is not needed. The computer can carry out these actions without the agent knowing these details.

COLOR-X is a system which has been designed with Linguistics in mind, in fact it is based on the linguistic theory Functional Grammar [Dik89,Bur96], while the proper working of the COLOR-X system requires a connection with a Lexicon, such as WordNet [Fel98], in which the meaning of words and concepts is stored. In our case we would like the Lexicon making the distinction between these different kinds of verbs: "send" is a communicative verb, while "treat" and "verify" are verbs connected with the notion of performing. To "create" and "fill_in" are verbs connected to "making something new".

4.2 About the identifiers being used

In the WF many identifiers are being used. They may denote objects, such as SU, the submitter, or CL a new object created to handle the claim. They also may denote attributes, usually with information about the submitter, in which case privacy may be a concern, or about the claim. Some identifiers are made within the WF, such as AN, denoting an answer used within a message, or TA being a shorthand for "TR.travel_agent". It is not the case that only the identifiers belonging to information about the submitter are important for privacy. Identifiers whose values are created in the WF can also reveal important information about the submitter, like the amount of money AM2, which says something about the trip and accident of the submitter.

4.3 About the representation of the WorkFlow in Prolog

The representation of the WF is adapted to the above analysis; facts and functors are used for: nodes, processes, actions, roles, identifiers, constraints, comparisons, expressions, edges, types and attributes. As WFs can be run through in different ways, these have to be administered in the form of flows. For our example there are five flows possible, given in figure 4. In general there may be an infinite number of flows, so in order for the analysis program not to loop, it is also necessary to find cycles in the WF. The numbers in this figure are the index numbers of the nodes in the claim CEM, the arrows are transitions. If there are multiple possibilities for following a transition then this is indicated above the arrow. If there is only one possibility then this is notated as a single →. Transitions that occur when a "MUST" condition is violated, are notated as ↯.

#1 0 → 1 → 2 → 3 ↯ 4 → -1

#2 0 → 1 → 2 → 3 →(AN="not OK")→ 4 → -1

#3 0 → 1 → 2 → 3 →(AN="OK" and AM1<100)→ 5 → 10 → -1

#4 0 → 1 → 2 → 3 →(AN="OK" and AM1>=100)→ 6 → 7 →(ME4="not OK")→ 4 → -1

#5 0 → 1 → 2 → 3 →(AN="OK" and AM1>=100)→ 6 → 7 →(ME4="OK")→ 8 →9 → -1

Figure 4: Flows of the claim CEM.

In table 1 we see a list of the identifiers for the claim example. The second column indicates the identifiers which have to be known by the agent in order to do its work. Evidently, in order to be able to carry out the "pay" action, CA must have access to the contents of "AM2" and "SU.bank". The approver AP in node 8, however, who sends the tuple "(AM2, SU.bank)" object to CA does not need to know the contents of this tuple, it is just sufficient to know its object identifier. He can send this identifier to CA as if it is put in a closed envelope. A special case is formed by identifiers like "AM2", being sent by EX, as part of the message ME4. From the WF we cannot see what is the contents of this identifier. In fact it is the outcome of the "treat" action. Or it comes from the assignment "AM2=AM1". The question is whether this identifier is also interesting from the standpoint of SU's privacy. It seems that it is harmless when it is used by the cashier CA. This is only seemingly the case: from the height of the amount the kind of claim and incident could be deduced.

The third column reveals that CA could know also "SU.name", when namely the approver AP would help him. Indeed AP could know "SU.name" and send it unnoticed, using the message with the above tuple, to CA. On its turn, AP needs TA to know "SU.name". This is called a private channel, the existence of such channels is important as the second and third examples have shown, presented in the beginning of this section. For communicative actions, indicated by such verbs as: send, create and fill_in, only tokens are used to indicate identifiers of pieces of information, such as an object identifier or a pointer, and there is no threat for violating privacy rules. Only when also a right to read or to write is needed, this threat exists, as the contents of objects and messages is at stake. This is the case with actions such as "treat, verify and pay".

node & agent	verb	role	identifiers	identifiers accessed using a private channel
1 SU	send	goal	GO1, TR, IN, AM1	
		rec	AP	
2 AP	create	goal	CL	
		obj	OBJ1, SU, TR, IN, AM1	
	send	goal	CL	
		rec	TA, TR,travel_agent	
3 TA	verify	goal	GO2, SU.name, TR	TR, IN, AM1 (from AP)
	send	goal	AN	
		rec	AP	
4 AP	send	goal	ME1	SU.name (from TA)
		rec	SU	
5 AP	send	goal	GO3, AM1, SU.bank	SU.name (from TA)
		rec	CA	
	send	goal	ME2	
		rec	SU	
6 AP	send	goal	CL	SU.mame (from TA)
		rec	EX	
	send	goal	ME3	
		rec	SU	
7 EX	treat	goal	GO4, TR, IN	SU.name, AM1 (from AP, TA)
	send	goal	ME4	
		rec	AP	
8 AP	fill_in	goal	AM2	
		rec	CL	
	send	goal	GO5, AM2, SU.bank	
		rec	CA	
9 CA	pay	goal	AM2	SU, SU.name, TR (from AP, TA)
		rec	SU.bank	

Table 1: Access of agents to the identifiers in hte claim CEM

5. THE WORKFLOW ANALYZED

The Workflow can be analyzed for several reasons. They may have to do with rather general properties such as: every agent who needs certain information is provided with that information. This is a property concerning the quality of the WF. Our analysis program provides this type of analysis. For our interest in S&P we may see different aspects to be analyzed:

- Are the employees of a company provided with the information needed for their work (need-to-know) and don't have more information at their disposal, which may be contrary to privacy rules/laws.
- The Alter-ego in company A, when deciding to answer a query Q coming from an employee E of company B, can use the knowledge coming out of the analysis in this way: Is the knowledge of E together with the answer to Q enough to entail information about the individual that the individual does not want E to know.

The first aspect is important when analyzing whether the insurance company is making fair decisions, that is decisions which don't take the specific individual into account (such as the information that the submitter SU is a nephew of the approver AP) WF is analyzed whether a decision maker in WF is not using personal information, such as name or address, which he does not need. For our WF this analysis reveals that TA could make use of some personal information, namely SU's name. It can do that not directly, as its only information is the claim object CL, to which it does not have reading access, but because it has reading access to GO2 and because according to the constraint in node 3: "id GO2=(SU.name, TR)", "SU.name" is part of GO2, indeed TA can see SU's name.

The second aspect is demonstrated by the existence of private channels. We have seen in the second and third example how a private channel can be used to jeopardize privacy rules involving conspiring employees. It may be necessary that the management of the insurance company is notified that this type of possible conspiracy exists. In fact it may be the task of an auditor to signal these possible privacy breaches.

The analysis is based on table1 which gives for each agent in an action defined in a node two lists:

1. the identifiers it needs to know in order to do the work specified,
2. the identifiers it might know by conspiring with other employees (using messages for which they are not meant, so creating private channels).

From this table the Alter-ego for our individual can easily determine whether a certain query can be answered or not. Take the query in the first example in the beginning of this section asked by the travel agent TA about the individual's marital status. The table reveals that TA (needs to) know(s) the trip TR, so the individual may want his Alter-ego to refuse the correct answer. In the second example, TA is interested in the individual's age, and if the individual does not trust the TA he can refuse to answer the query.

5.1 Real covert channels

The use of private channels such as we introduced them in the preceding sections, can in principle be detected by the WorkFlow engine, i.e. the underlying machine which governs the carrying out of the WF. The messages sent by all agents involved can be inspected, so that it can be seen that agents are sending each other more pieces of information than is asked for. In the study we describe here another form of using real covert channels has been dealt with also. In this kind of covert channel an agent puts information in some piece of information s/he has produced him/herself, such as changing the amount AM2 from 2000 to 2000.22, where "22" is some predefined code. Or when the information is a character string using lower and uppercase letters in some predefined way. In another report [Tee99] this kind of covert channels is fully analyzed.

6. CONCLUSIONS

We have shown how tools can be built by means of which WF diagrams can be analyzed on privacy aspects. These tools can also be used to analyze other aspects such as quality of the WF specification. Future work has to be carried out around detection of other types of channels. Also the integration of these tools in the Security part of ERP systems is an interesting area.

7. REFERENCES

[AH96] V. Atluri and W-K. Huang. *An extended petri net model for supporting workflows in a multilevel secure environment*. In Proceedings of the 10th IFIP WG 11.3 Working conference on Database Security, pages 199-216, July 1996.

[Bur96] J.F.M. Burg. *Linguistic Instruments in Requirements Engineering*. PhD thesis, Department of Mathematics and Computer Science, Vrije Universiteit Amsterdam, 1996.

[Dik89] S.C. Dik. *The Structure of the Clause*, volume 1 of The Theory of Functional Grammar. Floris Publications, Dordrecht, 1989.

[Fel98] C. Fellbaum, editor. *WordNet: An Electronic Lexical Database*. MIT Press, Cambridge, MA, 1998.

[GHS95] D. Georgakopoulos, M. Hornick, and A. Sheth. *An overview of workflow management: from process modelling to workflow automation infrastructure*. Distributed and Parallel Databases, 3(2):119-154, 1995.

[GRBO97] E. Gudes, R.P. van de Riet, J.F.M. Burg, and M.S. Olivier. *Alter-egos and roles - supporting workflow security in cyberspace*. In Proceedings of the IFIP WG 11.3 Database Security Conference (DBSec'97), Lake Tahoe, USA, 1997

[Tee99] Wouter Teepe. *Privacy-gerichte workflow analyse*. Master's thesis, Rijksuniversiteit Groningen, 1999.

[vdRB96a] R.P. van de Riet and J.F.M. Burg. *Linguistic tools for modelling alter egos in cyberspace: Who is responsible?* Journal of Universal Computer Science, 2(9):623-636, 1996.

[vdRB96b] R.P. van de Riet and J.F.M. Burg. *Modelling alter egos in cyberspace: Who is responsible?* In Proceedings of the World Conference of the Web Society (WebNet'96). AACE, 1996.

CHAPTER 25

Identifying Security Holes in OLAP Applications

JÜRGEN STEGER, HOLGER GÜNZEL, ANDREAS BAUER
Department of Database System
University of Erlangen-Nuremberg
Martensstr. 3
D-91058 Erlangen
Germany

Key words: Data Warehouse, OLAP, Multidimensional Data Model, Inference

Abstract: A data warehouse system is a necessity for fundamental decisions in every enterprise. The integration of data from several internal or external sources and the functionality of modern decision support systems like OLAP tools not only provide broad access to data but also raise security problems. Security concerns are more or less the same as those of other database systems but enriched especially with access and inference control in the multidimensional model. This paper presents an integrated approach for inference and access control not on the physical but on the conceptual level. The question is not only the restriction of relations, but rather the identification and evaluation of the inference problem of hierarchies and dimensions. The possibility to restrict or perturbate data in general, is not an adequate solution. We present some specific problems of a market research company and a solution with an indicator to discover possible attacks and so be able to restrict the access by mechanisms like aggregation, restriction or perturbation.

INTRODUCTION

Whenever managers of large enterprises prepare to make the right decisions, they require detailed information on specific topics. In a dynamic market environment it is crucial to have online information about one's own general business figures as well as detailed information on other companies. Some of the required data come from independent services like market research companies. They provide an additional basis for efficiently making decisions.

One of these third party data providers is the retail research department of GfK AG in Nuremberg. They collect the turnover of goods in different shops on a regular time base and sell this cleansed and aggregated data to companies in the form of trend analysis, market concentration and price class analyses. The market research companies themselves collect and store the provided data in a data warehouse [1]. Typically, users navigate through the data guided by a multidimensional data model which fits best for this application context. Codd introduced the term "Online Analytical Processing" (OLAP, [2]) for the interactive exploration of multidimensional data.

The goal of data warehousing and OLAP is to provide integrated access to data which resided in heterogeneous sources. Each user is able to analyze data and create reports himself. But on the other side the user is now able to receive data he is normally not allowed to. New access control mechanism are required, because the variety of data cause security problems. Access control depends on authorization of a specific user, i.e. not each user should be allowed to see the same data. Commercial products already restrict access to specific classification hierarchy nodes or provide only aggregated data or only parts of a cube.

Beside these static problems, topics like inference come into consideration. The schema and analysis is user-based and therefore inference oriented. Inference stands for inferring new information from already known data. Hence, a solution for an access control must include inference aspects as well. An integrated approach for access and inference control is required on a conceptual level. However, the main problem is not knowing which query or answer is problematic with the available data. This question primarily depends on the data provider. We summarize our work in three steps: Search the data security holes on a conceptual level, illustrated with the scenario of the GfK, give general indicators to address these problems and fix it with restriction or perturbation. The indicators can be precalculated and be integrated into an aggregation mechanism.

The remainder of this paper is organized as follows. In the next section, the structure of the multidimensional data model in general as well as specialities of the retail research at GfK is explained. In section 3, some aspects of inference and access problems are presented. Our indicator solution for these problems is proposed in section 4. The paper concludes with a summary and an outlook on future work.

1. MULTIDIMENSIONAL DATA MODEL

A data warehouse is a database integrating several data sources for analyses aspects. Data is often modelled on a conceptual level with a multidimensional model. We distinguish between a classification schema with the structure of a dimensions and the multidimensional schema which combines several dimensions and measures for a data cube.

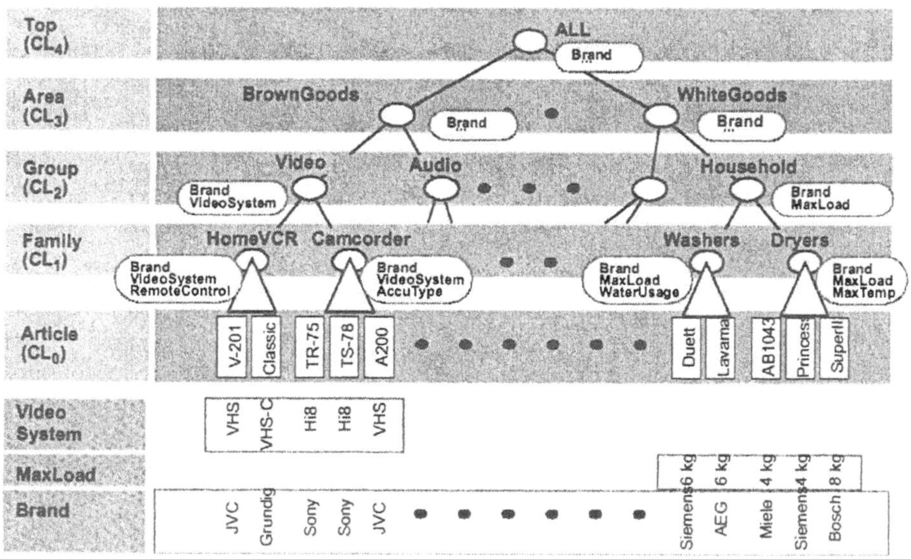

Figure 1: Classification schema and hierarchy of a product dimension

1.1 Classification Schemes and Classification Hierarchies

A classification schema defines the structure of the classification hierarchy. A classification schema *CS* is a partially ordered set of classification levels $(CL \cup \{Top\};\rightarrow)$ where $CL = \{CL_0,...,CL_n\}$. Top is a generic element which is maximal with respect to "$\rightarrow$", i.e. $CL_i \rightarrow Top$ for each $CL_i \in CL$. Figure 1 shows an example of a classification schema of the product dimension. The partial order "$\rightarrow$" allows to place the classification levels in a directed acyclic graph (DAG). Top is generic in the sense that it is not modelled explicitly. CL_0 is the basic level of the DAG and called dimensional element.

Furthermore, each classification level SL_i of a classification schema *CS* has a finite domain $dom(SL_i)$. The instances of a classification level are classification nodes *CN* like HomeVCR for the classification level Family.

The classification nodes establish a tree structure. We assume the domains to be mutually disjoint and dom(Top) is {"ALL"}.

Moreover, the dimensions contain features like video system or brand. This information primarily depends on the instances of the dimensional elements, but can build up an inheritance hierarchy like in figure 1 and also depends on the classification nodes. Commonly, the features build another alternative classification hierarchy.

1.2 Multidimensional Data Structures

After having defined the dimensional data structure, this section deals with the formal definition of the multidimensional schema. A logical data model should clearly separate intension and extension of a data cube ([3]). Otherwise, logical schema design is not independent from the actual instances.

OLAP data cubes in general contain numerical measures, like sales or price. There are different types of measures with regard to their summarizability.

In fact, a multidimensional schema is a collection of possibly aggregated cube cells with a homogeneous structure. Homogeneous means, that all cube cells have the same granularity, i.e. aggregation level, and they contain the same measures. The multidimensional schema C is a structure C[G, M] where $G = (G_1,...,G_n)$ is the granularity consisting of a set of classification nodes, i.e. $G \subseteq CN_{G1} \cup ... \cup CN_{Gd}$ such that for each G_i, $G_j \in G$: $G_i \neg\rightarrow G_j$ and $M = (m_1,...,m_m)$ is a set of measures.

2. INFERENCE PROBLEMATIC

On the one hand, the multidimensional model supports the user in making decisions with its structure and operations based on the classification hierarchy. On the other hand, the user should not be allowed to ask all questions he wants to. In commercial systems, it is possible to deny the access for specific classification nodes or classification levels which can be done along with aggregation. But, a static access control on conceptual level is not enough, because the user is still able to bypass these reglementations through tricky queries. Therefore problems between the user's analysis focus and the data provider's limitations and dynamic aspects of querying in the multidimensional model have to be discussed.

2.1 One-Query-Inference

In this chapter the question is discussed which data can be inferred by one query, i.e. which single query leads to inference problems. The user himself has to search for the explicit data. The gist of a disclosure is to get sensitive data of an individual. In the multidimensional model, we call this a multidimensional related disclosure, because many dimensions are involved in one query. Besides, we distinguish between a refinement and a weighting disclosure.

Refinement

The refinement disclosure is an exact disclosure, i.e. a query specifies a query set. A query consists of measures and a combination of classification nodes from different dimensions. This is used to calculate a value with an aggregate function e.g. SUM over classification nodes. The result of a query is composed of the tuples of the query set.

Two examples of the refinement disclosure will be discussed. The first is called department store problem, the second query-set-smallness. The department store problem relates to a specific case of the market research company GfK. In this case a query set is specified by a query which results in a sum over the sales of a product in only two shops within a period. If this result is known by one of these two shops it can subtract its sales from the result of the query. The difference are the sales of the other shop. In this situation it is possible for one shop to determine the sales of its competitor. Let us explain it with the competitors A and B which are the only department stores in an specific area. The query 'Give me the sales of the department stores in Nuremberg of the TR-75 on the 15.04.1999' asked by A is a sensitive one, because the department store A can calculate the exact result with the subtraction of its own sales in this area and time.

The query-set-smallness can be seen as a generalization of the department store problem. It refers to each query that can be asked to the system and whose query set contains a low number of tuples. For example the query 'Give me the number of all sold TR-75 at the Media market in Nuremberg on the 15.04.1999' is a sensitive query. Its query set contains only one tuple and is therefore identifying.

Weighting

The weighting disclosure can be an exact or an approximative disclosure. Likewise a query set is used to calculate a value. But the feature of this approach is the domination of one or some tuples. They take a special position within the aggregation of the query set.

Related to our case study we found three types: the trade brand, the exclusive model and the weighting disclosure itself. Trade brands are brands whose producer and vendor is identical. Thus a trade brand is only distributed via channels of its own company. An example of a trade brand is Universum because the products of Universum are only sold by the vendor Quelle itself. A problem arises if e.g. the sales of a Universum VR in Nuremberg is known, then it is also known that the video recorder is sold by Quelle in Nuremberg. We call these problems trade brand disclosure.

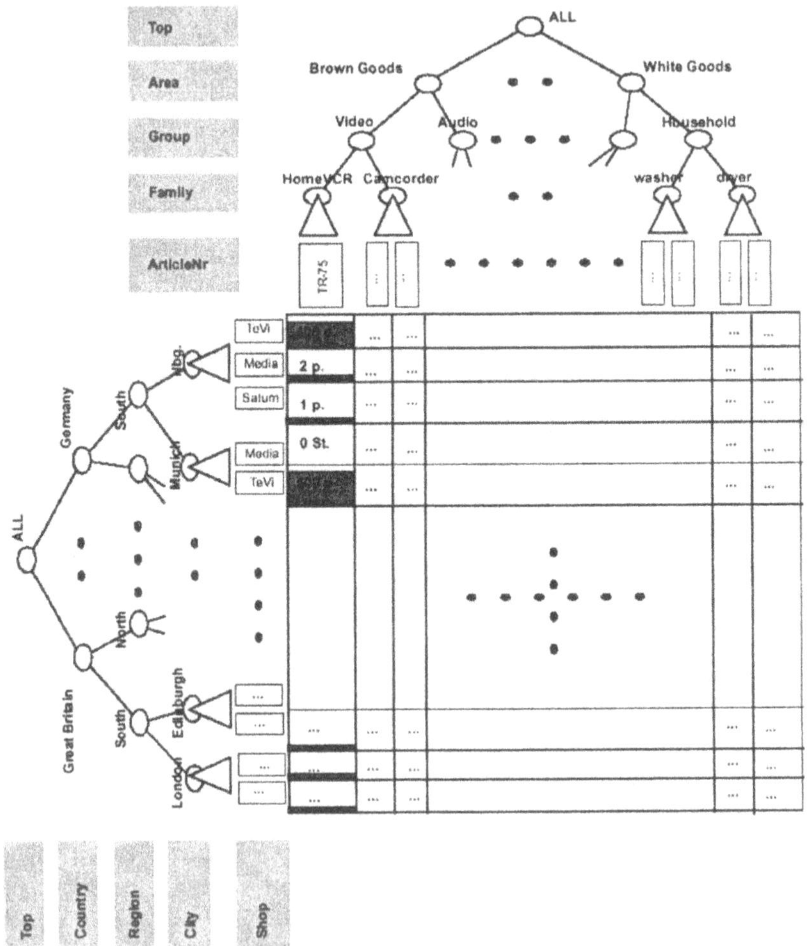

Figure 2: The weighting disclosure

Another issue is the exclusive model disclosure. Exclusive models are products a manufacturer makes only available for one vendor. In contrast to the trade brands the vendor can not be recognized by the vendor name but by the name of the product. An example of an exclusive model is a jubilee model, e.g. Sony delivers to Dixxon a special model with a designation only used for Dixxon. The inference of the exclusive models is similar to the trade brands. For both it is common that a query asking for sales of a trade brand or an exclusive model leads to a disclosure provided by a 100% domination of the tuples of the query set. A 100% domination is if all tuples of the query set contribute to the sensitive result that must not be known.

Sometimes, the domination is not a 100% domination but a k% domination. Logically a k% domination is the aggregation of some values of a combination of classification nodes divided by the aggregation over the same classification nodes of the whole query set. A more general type of disclosure is required as the trade brand or exclusive model disclosure. We call it weighting disclosure.

An example of the weighting disclosure is shown in figure 2. There is the product and shop dimension. Each dimension has its own classification hierarchies. The crosstable shows the number of sales. The query 'Give me the number of all sold TR-75 recorders in Nuremberg' or 'Give me the number of all sold TR-75 in South-Germany' results in a weighting disclosure. Because the first query consists of a three tuple query set (TeVi-, Media-, and Saturn), the TeVi result takes place a 400/403 = 99.3% domination. The second query leads to a 99.6% domination because of the domination of the two TeVi tuples within the query set. The weighting disclosure obviously does not lead to an exact disclosure, but it gives an impression of the sold products of a vendor if you know that domination.

Reducing the Result Set

Another trick to improve the result of a forbidden query is the parallel classification disclosure. It appears if two or more classification nodes of different parallel classifications are used to identify one dimensional element of one dimension without using the name of the dimensional element itself. In general the dimension element of a dimension is an unimportant information. Everybody knows that an electronic product like TR-75 exists. In all multidimensional data models the dimensional elements of all dimensions are well known. But, if there is a parallel classification of a dimension you can combine the classification nodes of different classification hierarchies. With this element it is not apparent for the system that you are on the forbidden level of the classification hierarchy.

In the example in figure 3, the product dimension has two parallel classifications: the hierarchy of the classification nodes and the feature classification. The product classification has a dimensional element which identifies exactly one result in the product dimension (extensional description [4]). The feature classification is not a dimensional classification, but an intensional description. Normally, it classifies not exactly one result, but you reduce the quantity of results. Both together are useful to determine one result in the product dimension, without using the name of the dimensional element. Universum color TV can be determined by an article number or as shown in figure 3 by using two intensional descriptions. The classification node CTV of the product classification and a special feature combination (68cm, stereo, 16:9, 100 Hertz, child prooflock) exists only for a Universum color TV which is equal to a specific product.

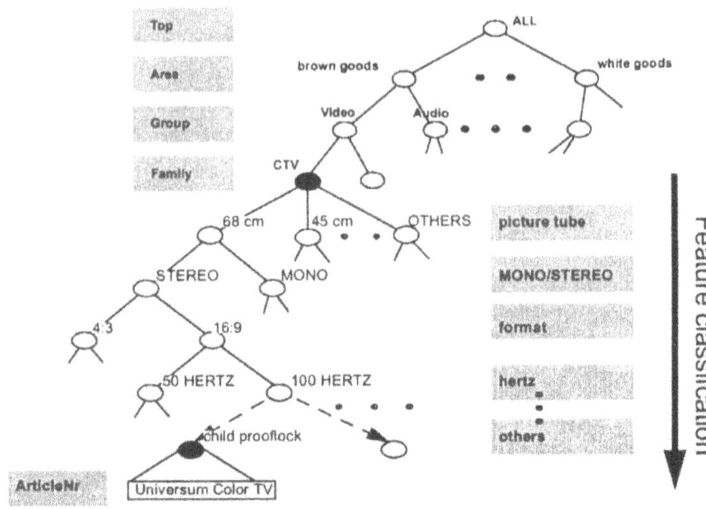

Figure 3: The parallel hierarchies of the product dimension

2.2 Multiple-Query-Inference

The one-query-inference isn't always successful because some static restrictions are able to suppress them. A more efficient and powerful way of getting sensitive data from a data warehouse is to go through a series of queries whose results are combined in a knowledge base (audit based approach). This memory is filled up until the search for sensitive data can be fulfilled. We distinguish two approaches: the intuitive and the theoretical approach.

Intuitive Approach

The intuitive approach is a combination of the parallel-classification- and the multidimensional-related disclosure. Intuitive means that the user is in the position to infer sensitive data without knowledge of mathematical retrieval methods. The user only relies on his knowledge of the market and combines it with the information of the reports to receive sensitive data. If the result isn't detailed enough, he uses the OLAP operations of the data warehouse to refine it stepwise. For example it is possible to get the sales of the trade brand Universum TV in Nuremberg by doing a drill down on the shop dimension to the classification node Nuremberg and on the product dimension to the classification node Color TV and then drill down the feature hierarchy. As the user is aware of the trade brand Universum TV and its characterizing features, he knows that he inferred the sales of the Universum TV of the Quelle shop in Nuremberg. The usage of OLAP operations in this approach bases on the knowledge of the user. They are only tools to infer sensitive data. This kind is used very often in the commercial area, because every manager has background knowledge about the competitors.

Theoretical Approach

A more complex, but efficient way is the theoretical approach. Some years ago, the area of scientific and statistical databases collected various methods of inference techniques and restriction of access. To give a short introduction, some ideas of revealing data are presented in the following.

A very efficient way of revealing particulars of an individual is shown by Denning at al [5]. They use a special characteristic formula called 'tracker' that is composed of the splitting of an forbidden, sensitive statistical query into smaller parts. Once found, a tracker is able to deduce the result of the sensitive query by involving the tracker and the response of a few answerable queries.

Rowe [6] does not try to gain sensitive information of an individual but statistics on a database which may also be sensitive. His approach 'diophantine inference' uses a special kind of diophantine equations that has to be solved to track down sensitive statistics. Palley and Simonoff [7] suggest an algorithm to yield a statistical disclosure of a confidential attribute. A synthetic database is created from the original statistical database. Then regression analysis is applied to it to estimate the hidden attribute. Delugach and Hinke [8] introduced an approach to automatically retrieve sensitive knowledge from a database based on 'Conceptual Graphs'.

All approaches have in common that the original usage was with unstructured data and not focussed on access ideas. The data warehouse environment and the multidimensional model contain the initial point for a new and broad data specific search.

3. INDICATORS FOR VISUALIZATION OF THE SECURITY HOLES

An overview of possible restrictions in statistical and scientific database area is given in [5]. Their methods mainly base on restriction of data and perturbation. A general solution is hard to present, because a generic perturbation contradicts the OLAP ideas and conflicts with economical operations like the distribution analysis, which requires data on a specific detail level. Otherwise a restriction of specific classification nodes, schemes or parts of the cube could be bypassed through other queries.

The main problem is not the restriction or the perturbation but to find a solution showing sensitive areas on the fly. We propose an indicator-based recognition on the conceptual level which can be often precalculated and used for an access control at runtime. Of course, only a small part of data is critical, i.e. not every query contains risks. But, queries on a detailed classification schema level should be handled with care.

An indicator is an inequation finding out that a query is sensitive and can compromise the system. If the inequation is true, it means that a disclosure is obtained; if it is false then the disclosure is not reached. These indicators can be precalculated in conjunction with an aggregation mechanism.

3.1 Indicator for Parallel Classification and Smallness

First we devote on the parallel classification and the smallness disclosure. Both use the same indicator, the smallness indicator:

$$K \leq |K_G| \leq N - K$$

N is the cardinality of the database and k is a threshold value. k depends on the user conditions and the limitations of the data provider. In case of the parallel classification disclosure $|R_G|$ is the cardinality of the used tuples of the dimension G. It recognizes whether a query reaches the classification level of the dimensional element of dimension G. A query is suppressed, if in all dimensions the level of the dimensional elements is reached. Otherwise $|R_G|$ is the cardinality of the query set R_G of the query characterized through its characteristic formula G. But, just as dangerous to find only a some tupels, too much tupels should be suppressed as well, because of the chance of building the compliment.

3.2 Department Store Indicator

The department store disclosure can't be avoided by the smallness indicator. We need a new indicator not to be dodged by a query. The department store indicator is only useful if the competitor, itself a member of the department stores, asks a department store query. Otherwise it should be true if a none member asks it. Of course, problems are still remaining, if other people do the search for these data.

$$\frac{SUM(\langle product, \{x\}\rangle \cap \langle shop, \{a\} \cap \{C\}\rangle, sales)}{SUM(\langle product, \{x\}\rangle \cap \langle shop, \{C\} \cap \{z\}\rangle, sales)} \geq s$$

This notation denotes a query for the sum of sales for a specific product

$$with\ \ s = 1 - \frac{SUM(\langle product, \{x\}\rangle \cap \langle shop, \{b\} \cap \{C\}\rangle, sales)}{SUM(\langle product, \{x\}\rangle \cap \langle shop, \{C\} \cap \{z\}\rangle, sales)}$$

and classification node in the shop dimension. A is a shop, and b its competitor, x is a product e.g. TR-75, z is a shoptype e.g. department store and C is a node of the classification hierarchy at which classification level the query is dangerous or not, e.g. C = 'Nuremberg'. The query in the denominator is the users query. With the instantiation of the variables the users query leads to the indicator s. So the system has to compute the query above - if the quotient is larger or equal than s, determined through the formula s, the query has to be suppressed.

3.3 Trade Brand or Exclusive Model Indicator

Trade brands imply a disclosure through the connection between the producer's and the vendor's and exclusive models between the product's and the vendor's name. The indicator below reveals a trade brand or an exclusive model disclosure.

x is a trade brand or an exclusive model, for C see above and a is the vendor of the trade brand or exclusive model. The query in the denominator is the users query. The query in the numerator has to be computed by the system and divided by the user's query. If the result is 1 the indicator signals that the user's query is a sensitive one.

3.4 Weighting Indicator

As mentioned in chapter 3 there exists a more general disclosure including the trade brand and exclusive model disclosure. The indicator for the weighting problem is described as follows:

$$\frac{SUM(\langle product, \{x\}\rangle \cap \langle shop, \{a\} \cap \{C\}\rangle, sales)}{SUM(\langle product, \{x\}\rangle \cap \langle shop, \{C\}\rangle, sales)} \geq s, s \in [0,1]$$

The difference to the trade brand or exclusive model indicator is that the quotient need not be 1 but over a certain threshold s to indicate a disclosure. The shop variable a need not be a shop of a trade brand or exclusive model but a user determined shop. Again, the query in the denominator is the users query.

4. SUMMARY

To find security holes is a fairly complex project, because both the user and the structure of the data model offer possibilities to achieve sensible data. In this paper, we presented some inference aspects in a market research company, to protect their data in a qualified way. Our indicator solution offers both, to the user a non static limitation and to the data provider the security not to disclose a secret. The next steps in our research will be practical tests with our indicator solution and the examination of data mining methods in this scenario.

REFERENCES

[1] Inmon, W.H.: Building the Data Warehouse, 2. edition. New York, Chichester, Brisbane, Toronto, Singapur: John Wiley & Sons, Inc., 1996

[2] Codd, E.F.; Codd, S.B.; Salley, C.T.: Providing OLAP (On-Line Analytical Processing) to User Analysts: An IT Mandate, White Paper, Arbor Software Cooporation, 1993

[3] Sapia, C.; Blaschka, M.; Höfling, G.; Dinter, B.: Finding Your Way through Multidimensional Data Models, in: 9th International Workshop on Database and Expert Systems Applications (DEXA'98 Workshop, Vienna, Austria, Aug. 24-28), 1998

[4] Lehner, W.; Albrecht, J.; Wedekind, H.: Multidimensional Normal Forms, in: 10th International Conference on Scientific and Statistical Data Management (SSDBM'98, Capri, Italy, July1-3), 1998

[5] Denning, D.E., Denning, P.J., Schwartz, M.D.: The Tracker: A Threat to Statisical Database Security, ACM Transactions on Database Systems, 4(1), March 1979, p. 76-96

[6] Rowe, N.C.: Diophantine Inference on a Statitical Database, Infromation Processing Letters, 18, 1984, p. 25-31

[7] Palley, M.A., Simonoff, J.S.: The Use of Regression Methodology for the Compromise of Confidential Infromation in Statistical Databases, ACM Transactions on Database Systems, 12(4), December 1987, p. 593-608

[8] Delugach, H.S., Hinke, T.H.: Using Conceptual Graphs To Represent Database Inference Secruity Analysis, Journal Computing und Information Technology, 2(4), 1994, p. 291-307

CHAPTER 26

ALGORITHMS AND EXPERIENCE IN INCREASING THE INTELLIGIBILITY AND HYGIENE OF ACCESS CONTROL IN LARGE ORGANIZATIONS

Marc Donner - Morgan Stanley
David Nochlin - Morgan Stanley
Dennis Shasha - New York University
Wendy Walasek - Morgan Stanley

Abstract: Security managers in large organizations must manage the access of tens of thousands of employees on diverse data. Databases store the access control information but the security officers use essentially manual techniques to determine who has too much access and why. We call this task the Audit Problem. The security research community has offered promising frameworks such as role-based access control, but these still leave open the problems of designing the roles and determining group memberships and of demonstrating that there are substantial benefits to be reaped from making a change.

In this paper, we propose a data-mining approach that includes an algorithm that starts with a set of atomic permissions of the form (user, asset, privilege) and derives a smaller but equivalent set (user group, asset group, privilege group). The asset and privilege groups so identified constitute promising roles. The users so identified constitute useful groups.

In this paper we report on actual experience with actual corporate access control data. We built a production role-based access control authorization service, storing the tables in a relational database and transmitting queries as XML 'documents' over MQ message queues.

Our experiments show that the proposed algorithm can reduce the number of permission assertions by a factor of between 10 and 100. With such a reduction, the Audit Problem is brought from the absurd to the plausible.

1. THE PROBLEM

1.1 The players

In any complex environment, there are three sets of players in the access control arena. On the one hand there are the business managers who are constrained by fiduciary responsibility and by specific regulations to establish an appropriate control regime for information. On the other hand there are the software implementers and support staff for whom success is measured by the rapid deployment of powerful software and by its stable operation. Between the two is a collection of auditors, both internal and external, whose role is to ensure that the implementations are at least approximately compliant with the regulations.

These relationships are illustrated in this figure:

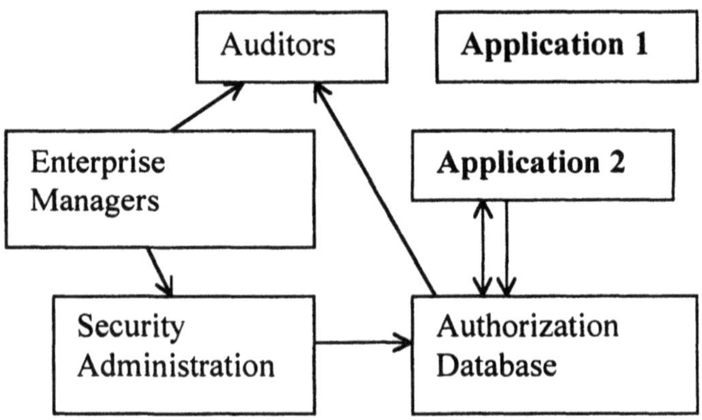

Figure 1.

1.1.1 Enterprise Managers [Policy]

To senior enterprise managers the imperatives of security are risk management and regulatory compliance. How, at minimal cost, can they maintain an acceptable risk profile and comply with the various laws, rules, and regulations governing the enterprise? Enterprise managers know that complexity breeds failure, and so they want clear simple statements of principle. An ideal policy is a one or two page statement in English that unambiguously lays out the goals and objectives and establishes clear guidance to employees seeking decisions.

1.1.2 Software Developers and Integrators [Application 1 and Application 2]

Developers and integrators are typically faced with demands for rapid delivery of software and systems that provide the maximum in functionality and performance at the lowest cost. Most software is produced or procured for a specialized purpose and serves a subset of the organization that is, by nature of being smaller, naturally more coherent. This reduces the perceived need by both the enterprise line staff and the developers for stringent security machinery.

1.1.3 Security Administrators [Security Administration]

Low in the organizational food chain and often neglected in planning access control systems, the security administrators are the keys to the day-to-day interpretation of the security policies and their effective reduction to practice. They have to understand the policies, they need tools that they can use effectively, and their needs must be reflected in the overall access control architecture if it is to be effective. To illustrate this point, imagine a house with excellent locks on every window and door, but installed so inconveniently that to lock or unlock them requires that the homeowner carry a ladder and a box of tools to each window and door. How likely is it that the doors and windows will be locked or unlocked at the appropriate times?

1.1.4 Auditors

Senior managers and a wide variety of external parties, from customers to industry regulators, look to the auditors to reconcile the ideally clear and simple statements of policy and the necessarily complex and messy implementations that emerge from day-to-day activities. Auditors, in turn, look for powerful analytical tools to help them reduce the complexity of the world they discover so that they may answer the questions that are put to them.

1.1.5 Related Work

To quote from a report on this problem at NIST [1], "one of the most challenging problems in managing large networked systems is the complexity of security administration. Today, security administration is costly and prone to error because administrators usually specify access control lists for each user on the system individually. The principle of role based access control (RBAC) is that security should be mapped to an organization's structure. With Role-based Access Control, security is managed at a level that corresponds closely to the organization's structure. Each user is assigned one or more roles, and each role is assigned one or more privileges that are permitted to users in that role."

The notion of authorization hierarchies using roles is certainly present in the SQL databases [2].

In SQL, the owner of a resource can give certain operational rights (e.g. insert, delete, and update) to certain users or groups of users (called roles) on certain objects where an object can be a column, table, or entire database, or even can be defined as a query. The syntax is:

```
GRANT privileges
ON objects
TO roles
```

Non-SQL approaches to the problem include the product from Computer Associates called TopSecret. That system allows positive and negative authorizations, permitting grouping of users into collections, wild cards in object names, and a hierarchy of privileges NONE > ALL > WRITE > READ where > means "takes precedence over". Assets and permissions are grouped into profiles that are distributed to users. Finally, there is a notion of single and variable length wild card characters, so that for example AB*C matches ABXYTC.

Jajoida et alia [3] have proposed a framework for positive and negative access control policies. The framework consists of languages and techniques for making positive and negative access control policies consistent.

The novelty of our work derives mainly from the fact that we must actually solve this problem on large data. In a large bank that originates significant electronic funds transfers people who have excessive permissions could cause significant financial harm. Existing approaches within our organization to reducing such risks are manual and consist of interviewing people and managers about their needs. Our approach here is to aid that work by increasing the intelligibility of the permissions people have.

Why could we define no previous experimental study of access control or algorithms to increase the intelligibility of security? Here's what Prof. Jajodia observed in a personal communication: "There is no study because the general feeling is that groups and roles are helpful. Everybody accepts that." In a way, this paper is meant to show how much help such a technique can provide.

2. A DATA MODEL

2.1 Glossary

Term	Definition
Asset	An ***asset*** is an enterprise thing like an account or a technical thing like an application program or system file.
Asset group	An asset ***group*** is a potentially arbitrary administrative grouping of ***assets***. The groupings are established for enterprise purposes, for instance a set of accounts can be grouped together because they are owned by the same party or are controlled by the same portfolio manager. An asset ***group*** is an ***asset***, so these definitions support potentially arbitrary grouping and clustering.
Person/User [People]	A ***person*** or ***user*** here is a bona fide individual. Each system assigns each person with which it has a relationship a unique ID called the ***userid***. Notice that the establishment of confidence that a particular person should be entitled to act as a particular userid is the responsibility of the ***authentication system***, an external component that provides that service uniformly to all systems within the organization.
User group	A ***user group*** is a potentially arbitrary grouping of ***people***. The groupings are established for

	enterprise purposes, for instance the set of ***people*** authorized to order trades in an account might be such a group.
Privilege	A ***privilege*** is the right to perform some action. In object oriented programming terminology, a ***privilege*** is the right to invoke a specific method. A method might enable you to read data from a specific file or set of files.
Privilege group	A ***privilege group*** is a named collection of ***privileges***.

2.2 The Central Data Structure

Historically, access control databases have provided the capability to assign specific individuals specific rights to specific assets. Some have provided the ability to aggregate one or another of these atomic entities, but in general little aggregation has been available. This has resulted in administrative and analytic headaches as the number of assertions in the access control databases have grown. At Morgan Stanley Dean Witter in

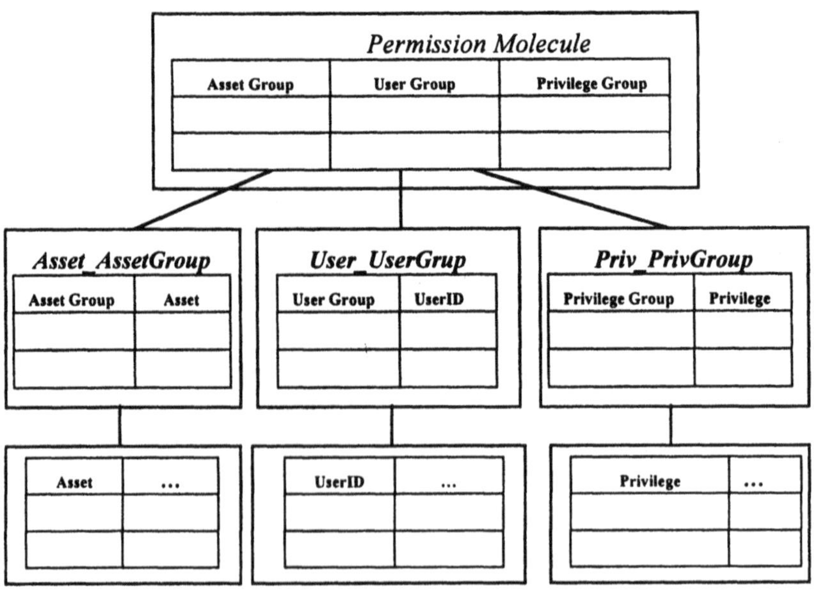

Figure 2 [User_UserGroup and (p,r) is in Priv_PrivGroup]

the Institutional Securities business we use a product named "Top Secret," now from Computer Associates, which permits the grouping of asset-privilege combinations. The operational database for our Top Secret environment has nearly 500,000 assertions. The number is so large that we cannot practically analyze it.

It was our hypothesis when we undertook this work that by providing aggregation for each of the three entities, users, assets, and privileges, we could reduce the number of assertions in the central fact table. As you will see in the result section below, that is exactly what we found.

3. ALGORITHMS AND PROOFS

The data model introduced in section 2 is a framework for grouping assets into asset groups, users into user groups, and privileges into privilege groups. The algorithm of this section transforms a set of atomic relationships into the most economical possible set of groupings.

3.1 Reduction Algorithm for Inferring Molecular Rules:

Input: A set of rules at the atomic level (asset, user, and privilege). This is called **PermissionsAtom**.

Output: A set of rules at the molecular level (asset group, user group, and privilege group). This is called **PermissionsMolecule**.

A description of the groupings

- From asset to asset group (**Asset_AssetGroup**),
- From user to user group (**User_UserGroup**), and
- From privilege to privilege group (**Priv_PrivGroup**).

Correctness Conditions:

If (a, u, p) is in PermissionsAtom, then there exists a row (c, g, r) in PermissionsMolecule such that (a,c) is in Asset_AssetGroup, (u,g) is in User_UserGroup, and (p,r) is in Priv_PrivGroup.

3.1.1

If (c,g,r) is in PermissionsMolecule then for all a, u, p such that (a,c) is in Asset_AssetGroup, (u,g) is in User_UserGroup, and (p,r) is in Priv_PrivGroup, (a, u, p) is in PermissionsAtom.

3.2 Atom to Molecule Reduction Algorithm:

We explain this algorithm along with the following running example. We start with the following atomic table.

Table 1. [Atom to Molecule Reduction Algorithm]

Asset	User	Privilege
a1	u2	p1
a1	u3	p2
a2	u1	p2'
a2	u1	p1

Note: We now present the reduction steps in a particular order. As we show later, the order of reduction matters, so this ordering is only one among several (six, to be precise). But all reductions use the same basic construction.

3.2.1 Asset Reduction Step

For each distinct user-privilege pair (u, p), find the set of assets:

S(u,p) = { PermissionsAtom.asset |
PermissionsAtom.User = u and
PermissionsAtom.Privilege = p
}

For each such set, create a new name, e.g. assetgroup_u_p. Then create a new table, denoted tab1, consisting of these asset groups and their unique user-privilege pairs. Formally, tab1 has three columns (asset group, user, and privilege), where user-privilege together form a key.

In set theoretic notation:

tab1(asset group, user, priv) =
{ (S(u, p), u, p) |
u belongs to PermissionsAtom.user and
p belongs to PermissionsAtom.priv
}

In words: create triples consisting of each possible user u, privilege p, and the associated set of assets, which will be grouped into a new asset group name. In addition create an association between each created set of assets and an asset group name.

In our running example, this would give the following (here, we keep the original sets instead of replacing them by asset group names):

Table 2.

tab1

Asset Group	User	Privilege
{a1, a2}	u1	p1
{a1}	u2	p1
{a1}	u3	p2
{a2}	u1	p2

Asset	Asset Group
a1	c1
a2	c1
a1	c2
a2	c4

Thus, c2 is the name for {a1} whereas c1 is the name for {a1, a2}. So, replacing the sets by their names, we would get another form for tab1:

Table 3.

tab1

Asset Group	User	Privilege
c1	u1	p1
c2	u2	p1
c2	u3	p2
c3	u1	p2

3.2.2 Privilege Reduction Step

The next step consists of grouping the privileges into privilege groups. The strategy is to perform groupings based on user and asset group to create sets of privileges.

tab2(asset group, user, privilege group) =
{ (c, u, { tab1.priv |
tab1.user = u and

```
                tab1.asset_group = c
            }
    ) |
        u belongs to tab1.user and
        c belongs to tab1.asset_group
    }
```

Again, the constraint is that no two rows in tab2 may have the same asset group and user combination of values.

In our running example, this does not diminish the number of rows:

Table 4.
tab2

Asset Group	User	Privilege Group
{a1, a2}	u1	{p1}
{a1}	u2	{p1}
{a1}	u3	{p2}
{a2}	u1	{p2}

3.2.3 User Reduction Step

The next step consists of grouping users into groups. This is the final step and creates the molecular level of grouping that we seek.

```
        PermissionsMolecule(
                asset group,
                user group,
                privilege group) =
                  { ( c,   { tab2.user |

        tab2.privilege_group = r and
        tab2.asset_group = c
          }, r ) |
        r belongs to tab2.privilege_group and
        c belongs to tab2.asset_group
    }
```

In our running example, this does not diminish the number of rows either:

Table 5. [***PermissionsMolecule***]

Asset group	User group	Privilege Group
{a1, a2}	{u1}	{p1}
{a1}	{u2}	{p1}
{a1}	{u3}	{p2}
{a2}	{u1}	{p2}

3.3 Observations:

3.3.1

The general step of reducing based on C given a table T(G1, G2, C) is to form the set

```
T'      ={ ( g1, g2, { T.C |
            T.G1 = g1 and
            T.G2 = g2
           }
     ) |
     g1 belongs to T.G1 and
     g2 belongs to T.G2
  }
```

with the constraint that no two rows in T' have the same g1 and g2 values, in combination. (So, many rows may have g1 in the G1 column and many may have g2 in the G2 column, but only one row will have g1 and g2.)

3.3.2

The transformation satisfies the correctness conditions. We will show this through the use of generalized tables in which there are sets as field values.

3.3.3 Definitions:

The **atomic permission table** has a single user, a single asset, and a single privilege in each row.

A **partly molecular table** has a set of users, a set of assets, and a set of privileges in each row. Any of these sets can be singleton, so even the atomic permission table can be modeled as a partly molecular table in which every field in every row is singleton. A partly molecular table is isomorphic to the intermediate tables in our construction. Each such table has atoms in each field, but some of those atoms represent sets, (e.g. an asset group represents a set of assets). Partly molecular tables are non-first-normal form representations of those sets.

Table 6.

Example:

The partly molecular table for the result of the first reduction is:

Asset	User	Privilege
{a1, a2}	{u1}	{p1}
{a1}	{u2}	{p1}
{a1}	{u3}	{p2}
{a2}	{u1}	{p2}

The **row expansion** of row r in a partly molecular table is the cross product of its sets.

The **expansion** of a partly molecular table is the union of its row expansions.

A **row one-column expansion** of row r on column C is a set of rows of size ||r.C||, each row having one value of r.C and the values contained r for the remaining columns.

The **one-column expansion** of a partly molecular table is the union of its row one-column expansions.

Table 7.

Example:

If we have a table:

Asset	User	Privilege
{a1, a2}	{u1, u3, u4}	{p1,p2}
{a1, a3, a4}	{u2, u4}	{p1}

Then the one-column expansion based on column User would give:

Asset	User	Privilege
{a1, a2}	{u1}	{p1,p2}

{a1, a2}	{u3}	{p1,p2}
{a1, a2}	{u4}	{p1,p2}
{a1, a3, a4}	{u2}	{p1}
{a1, a3, a4}	{u4}	{p1}

Table 8.

The **expansion** (to singleton sets) would give:

Asset	User	Privilege
{a1}	{u1}	{p1}
{a1}	{u1}	{p2}
{a2}	{u1}	{p1}
{a2}	{u1}	{p2}
{a1}	{u3}	{p1}
{a1}	{u3}	{p2}
{a2}	{u3}	{p1}
{a2}	{u3}	{p2}
{a1}	{u4}	{p1}
{a1}	{u4}	{p2}
{a2}	{u4}	{p1}
{a2}	{u4}	{p2}
{a1}	{u2}	{p1}
{a3}	{u2}	{p1}
{a4}	{u2}	{p1}
{a1}	{u4}	{p1}
{a3}	{u4}	{p1}
{a4}	{u4}	{p1}

Observation:

Any ordering of one-column expansions that includes all columns will yield the same set of rows as an expansion.

The operation **unsetting** removes the curly brackets when all sets are singleton. In the example, unsetting yields the following table:

Table 9.

Asset	User	Privilege
a1	u1	p1
a1	u1	p2
a2	u1	p1
a2	u1	p2
a1	u3	p1
a1	u3	p2
a2	u3	p1
a2	u3	p2
a1	u4	p1
a1	u4	p2
a2	u4	p1
a2	u4	p2
a1	u2	p1
a3	u2	p1
a4	u2	p1
a1	u4	p1
a3	u4	p1
a4	u4	p1

The operation **setting** is the inverse of **unsetting**.

Suppose that Ta is an atomic table and P is a partly molecular table. We say that P **conserves** Ta if Ta = the unsetting of the expansion of P. That is, up to reordering Ta is the same as the unsetting of the expansion of P.

Lemma: If P1 is a partly molecular table that conserves Ta and P2 is a reduction of P1, then P2 also conserves Ta.

Proof: Our strategy is to show that reduction is the inverse of expansion. (We assume three columns, though the same argument will apply to any number of columns greater than one.)

When doing a reduction from P1 to P2, we partition P1 by its grouping columns, e.g. user and asset, and compute the set in its grouped column, e.g. privilege, corresponding to each partition. Call the grouping columns G1 and G2 and the grouped column C. Without loss of generality, assume that G1 and G2 are the first two columns. In P2, no two rows have the same G1 and G2 values. Further, no two sets of rows have the same G1 and G2 values in P1 so we can treat the reduction that produces a single row of P2 independently from the reduction for any other row of P2.

Consider the row having values g1 in G1 and g2 in G2 and the corresponding rows in P1 having g1 and g2 as members. Let set c of items from column C be all the items from column C in rows having (g1, g2) as the entries in G1 and G2, respectively.

So, the row (g1, g2, c) in P2 is the reduction of the set of rows in P1 having g1 and g2 as their first two field values. A row one-column expansion of (g1, g2, c) based on C results in ||c|| rows all having g1 and g2 as their first two field values and having a different element in c in the third field of each row.

A one-column expansion based on C is the inverse of reduction based on C. This implies that P1 is the expansion of P2 based on C. Hence, the expansion of P2 has the same set of rows as the expansion of P1.

Therefore P2 conserves Ta because P1 conserves Ta.

Theorem: The molecular Permissions Table that results from the Reduction Algorithm conserves the atomic Permissions Table.

Proof: By induction on the column reductions and from the lemma.

Recursion on this procedure does not help.

It never helps, i.e. reduces the size of the permissions molecule, to do further grouping beyond the above construction. We explain why by concrete example, but the reader will be able to generalize the example.

Suppose that it were useful to group, say, privilege groups into bigger privilege groups. Then there would have to be two rows in PermissionsMolecule with values (g, c, r) and (g, c, r') where privilege groups r and r' are distinct but group g and asset group c are the same.

When privilege groups are created, they are created based on a partition of user-asset group pairs. Users from such pairs later are put into groups. Therefore, no two privilege groups can be associated with the same user and asset group or the same user group and asset group.

3.3.4 Choosing different orderings of reduction may help.

Recall our running example:

Asset	User	Privilege
a1	u1	p1
a1	u2	p1
a1	u3	p2

a2	u1	p2
a2	u1	p1

If we reduce asset first, we get the following groupings after the first step:

Asset group	User	Privilege
{a1, a2}	u1	p1
{a1}	u2	p1
{a1}	u3	p2
{a2}	u1	p2

None of the other reductions shrinks this set any further.
However, if we reduce user first, we get:

User group	Asset	Privilege
{u1, u2}	a1	p1
{u3}	a1	p2
{u1}	a2	p2
{u1}	a2	p1

Now, if we reduce privilege next, we get:

User Group	Asset	Privilege Group
{u1, u2}	a1	{p1}
{u3}	a1	{p2}
{u1}	a2	{p1, p2}

This gives us three rather than four rows in the result.

4. QUANTITATIVE RESULTS

Reducing atomic relationships to molecular relationships seems to be a plausible idea, but does it really help? We set out to answer this question using several actual sets of authorization data in daily use within Morgan Stanley Dean Witter. The numbers we cite are:

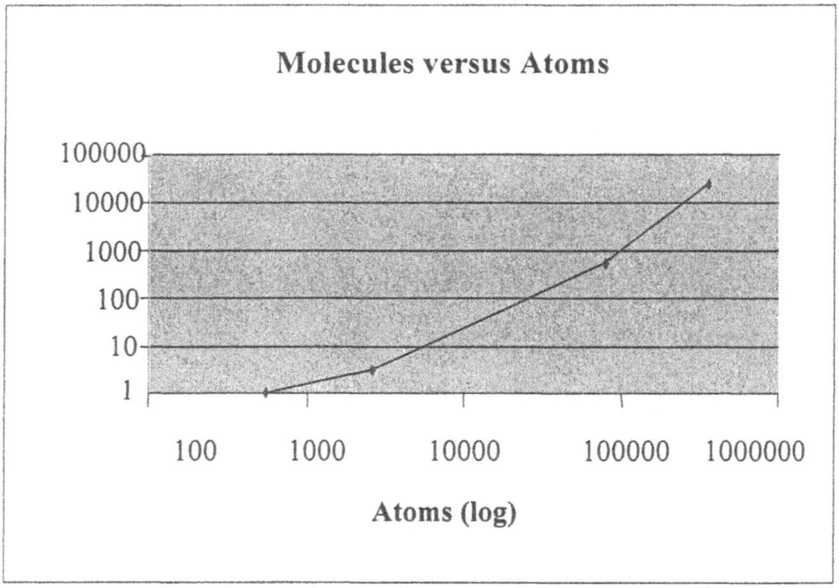

4.1.1 **the initial size of the atomic permissions table,**

4.1.2 **the size, following execution of the algorithm, of the molecular permissions table,**

4.1.3 **the sizes of each of the grouped entities: assets, userids, and privileges,**

4.1.4 **the number of groups: asset groups, user groups, and privilege groups**

4.2 Experiment 1:

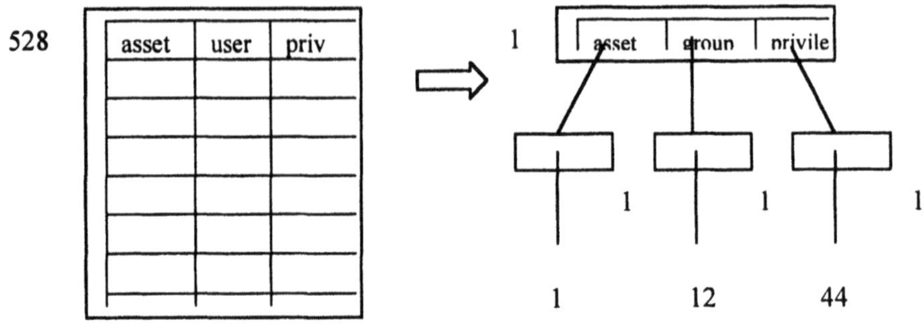

528 rows in PermissionsAtom became 1 row in Permissions Molecule.

- 1 asset grouped into 1 asset group
- 12 users grouped into 1 user group
- 44 privileges grouped into 1 privilege group

4.3 Experiment 2:

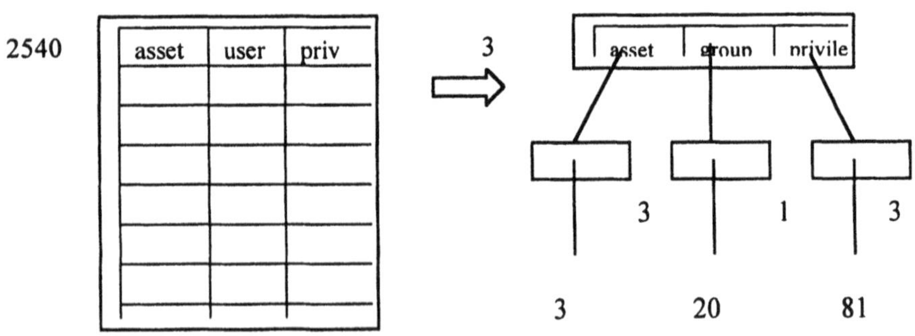

- 2540 rows in PermissionsAtom became
- 3 rows in PermissionsMolecule with
- 3 assets grouped into 3 asset groups
- 20 users grouped into 1 user group
- 81 privileges grouped into 3 privilege groups

4.4 Experiment 3:

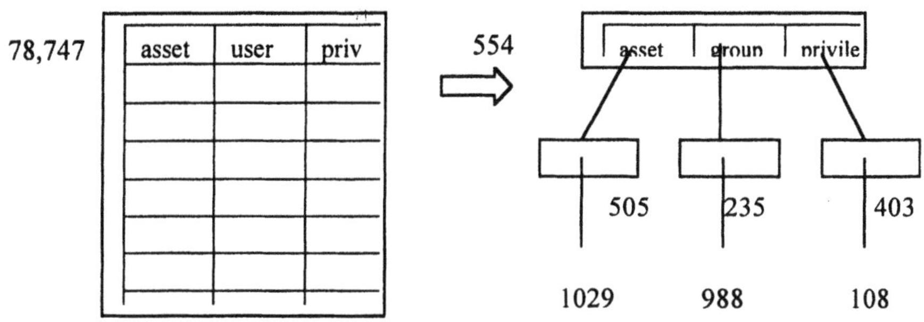

- 78,747 rows in Permissions Atom became
- 554 rows in PermissionsMolecule with
- 1029 assets grouped into 505 asset groups
- 998 users grouped into 235 user groups
- 108 privileges grouped into 403 privilege groups

4.5 Experiment 4: Top Secret Configuration

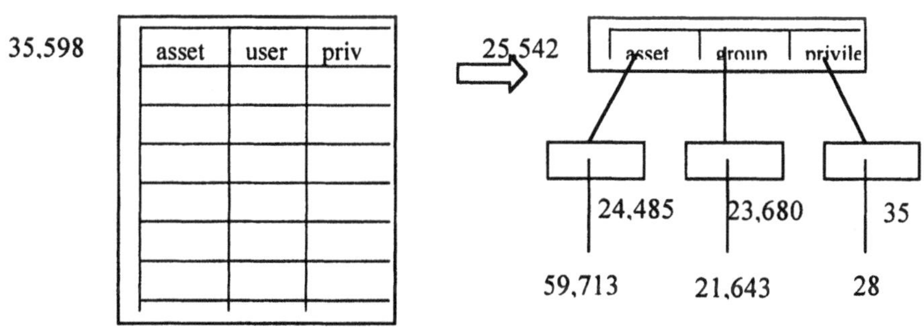

- 354,598 rows in Permissions Atom became
- 25,542 rows in PermissionsMolecule with
- 59,713 assets grouped into 24,485 asset groups
- 21,643 users grouped into 23,680 user groups
- 28 privileges grouped into 35 privilege groups

5. FUTURE WORK

We began this article by highlighting the plight of the auditors who must reconcile the representation of a security policy with regulations. We suggested that presenting a human being with hundreds of thousands of permission facts (354,598 in our case) was simply too unwieldy. Our algorithm reduced this number of facts to 25,542, definitely a step in the right direction but not yet a solution.

Achieving a solution requires "improving the hygiene" of the authorization data, i.e. data cleaning to eliminate typos, reduce inconsistencies and so on. An algorithm for data cleaning is an open problem, but we think the following ideas are worth exploring:

Suppose that our grouping to the molecular level produces several sets of users that are large and are mutually similar. The fact that they are not identical might be an indication of inconsistent treatment of these users. The same holds for assets and for privileges.

Sometimes we may be able to infer that permissions are missing.

Consider the following example of atomic permissions:

A	B	C
a1	b1	c1
a1	b1	c2
a1	b2	c1
a1	b2	c2
a1	b3	c1
a1	b3	c2
a2	b1	c1
a2	b1	c2
a2	b2	c1
a2	b2	c2
a2	b3	c1
a2	b3	c2

As it stands this can be reduced to one row:

AG	BG	CG
{a1,a2}	{b1,b2,b3}	{c1,c2}

Now, we notice that any break in that symmetry, for instance by removing one row, will cause the groups to break up quite a lot. For instance, if we remove the last row to give:

A	B	C
a1	b1	c1
a1	b1	c2
a1	b2	c1
a1	b2	c2
a1	b3	c1
a1	b3	c2
a2	b1	c1
a2	b1	c2
a2	b2	c1
a2	b2	c2
a2	b3	c1

Then grouping will lead to more rows in the result:

AG	BG	CG
{a1,a2}	{b1,b2,b3}	{c1}
{a1,a2}	{b1,b2}	{c2}
{a1}	{b3}	{c2}

In this case, we'd want to infer that we were missing:

a2	b3	c2

Additional information can also help the cleaning process. We have found the following heuristics to be useful for example when the organizational structure is supposed to imply homogeneous privileges: Find people whose permissions are inconsistent with most (say 80%) of their co-members in the supposedly homogeneous group. Alternatively, find permissions that most members of a group have and consider those to be a core. Question any permission outside the core.

Human judgement plays the critical role in managing security. Our hope is to provide tools that help people manage this sometimes-overwhelming task. This paper is one step in that direction.

6. REFERENCES

[1] "Role Based Access Control," D. Ferraiolo and R. Kuhn, NIST, http://hissa.ncsl.nist.gov/rbac/

[2] "Guide to the SQL Standard," H. Darwen and C. J. Date, 1997, Addison-Wesley, ISBN 0201964260.

[3] "A Unified Framework For Enforcing Multiple Access Control Policies," S. Jajoida, P. Samarati, V. S. Subrahmanian, and E. Bertino, Proceedings of ACM SIGMOD International Conference on Management of Data, 1997, pp 474-485

CHAPTER 27

Database Security 2000

John R. Campbell
National Security Agency, Fort Meade, MD 20755-6730

Abstract: Database systems are being more and more used, with larger sized databases, and as components of very complex systems, that include numerous protocols. Database security problems in the past have only partially been solved. Is there any hope to provide adequate security for the new database systems? This paper describes user and system requirements and provides a list of hints and techniques to better secure this type of system.

1. INTRODUCTION

Have we solved the DBMS Security Problem? No, the DBMS security problem was never completely solved. Parts of the problem were solved, but, in many cases, were not implemented by the popular vendors. Inference, aggregation and individual I&A in complex systems were never completely solved. In addition, DBMS's are constantly evolving to meet the current expectations of users. Therefore the means of securing the data must change with the changes in architectures, methodologies and applications. Existing solutions are now even more insufficient. However, the overall goals of database information security, that of information privacy, integrity, availability and nonrepudiation remains the same. The data must be protected.

2. Environment:

The environment continues to become more interesting and more difficult to work in. Databases are more widely used than ever. More formats and protocols are used to access and link to data sources. Web browser access is everywhere and interconnectivity is a keyword. But with such configurations, can we assure that only authorized persons are accessing the data? Do we have usable audit for such transactions? The configuration today could be cell phone request to data source. The cell phone or laptop could be located anywhere, possibly in an analog-only cell area, as could the data source. At a recent conference in Maryland, an attendee was accessing a California database during a break in the conference via a cell phone/laptop client. No one thought this act was unusual.

To make matters worse, there are now fewer trusted operating systems to mount database systems on. This trend is likely to continue. Trusted operating systems are not selling very well and few, if any potential users, have made their use mandatory. Components, in general, have low levels of assurance. What happens to security when you use low-assurance components, that are now more complex, in both hardware and software, and which are strung together in ever-larger strings?

Some of the old solutions may are not too useful anymore. Stand-alone systems are infrequently used and simple client-server systems are used less and less. New solutions and mechanisms may require new security solutions. For example, a new switching and transfer mode, such as the asynchronous transfer mode (ATM), may require new encryption equipment to match the ATM's format and speed. Fortunately some solutions exist for ATM. How good are these solutions? Does the security equipment exist for other new technical solutions? Is there an overall security policy? Is it written? Does the system comply with the security policy?

The widespread use of ActiveX, Java and other mobile codes causes more security concerns. Database management systems are using these codes for connectivity, flexibility and applications. The future promises even more use of these codes. While having many positive qualities, these codes also may have capabilities that the user, or database administrator may not be aware of, such as rebooting a target computer, or capturing passwords and files. Here the selection and proper use of an appropriate product may ease some of the security problems.

Database architectures have become more varied. In addition to 2-tier architectures, such as client/server architecture, there exist 3-tier architectures, that could include a transaction server, and n-tier architectures that may have multiple presentation, application and data tiers as well as a transaction manager. Is your security solution appropriate for the architecture that you are working with? Further considerations include whether the Distributed Component Object Model (DCOM) or Common Object Request Broker Architecture (CORBA) is being used.

Bigger databases, terabytes in length, exist. Data warehouses and marts are common. Data mining is in. Inference and aggregation, using a variety of techniques, is a prime goal. How do you prevent some and allow others to use these techniques?

What do users desire? They desire much more functionality, with widely distributed systems over varying communications, while preserving ease-of-use. These systems are complex, requiring the use and integration of many protocols. E-commerce has increased the perception of the user that data has real value, and with the additional perception that their systems may be vulnerable, users are requesting strong Identification and Authentication. Non-repudiation is now very important. In part, to satisfy these goals, smart cards, PCM cards, certificates or biometrics devices may be used. Users also want strong access controls to determine who accesses their database or file and what portion of a database an individual can see. Very important to the user is ease-of-use with many hoping for a single signon. The easiest way to have security bypassed is to make it too hard or complicated. Multiple, hard to remember, frequently changed passwords, which although in theory is good security, is a good example of a methodology that is frequently circumvented.

3. Tools/Solutions

Considering all these problems and complexities, what do we have to work with to build a secure system? First, we can look to mechanisms in existing commercial database management systems. The traditional roles, passwords, privilege settings, audit logs and backups still exist and are usable. New features have been added in some systems to make use of, for example, smart cards, Kerberos, CORBA compliance, encryption, certificates, including X.509 certificates, public key directories, and biometric authenticators.

Second, network and component operating systems still have security mechanisms and may also use some of the newer ones mentioned in the previous paragraph. In addition, OS and DBMS may be coupled in Trust relationships between the two.

Third, there has been a tremendous growth in firewalls of various types, intrusion detection systems, hashing integrity schemes to insure file integrity, public keys including infrastructure, virtual private networks, stronger encryption, and better use of encryption, including public key encryption. A potential problem is how well the Database System can use these improvements. Are the security features transparent to the user? Has the database vendor provided appropriate interfaces to "seamlessly" use these features? How easy are they to use? Do I have to write my own interfaces, or other code? How much assurance can I place in each feature and in the system security as a composable whole?

Fourth, one practical method to improve security is to limit the functionality of the system. A system that just needs to answer HTTP queries can be built more securely than a system that has to handle many protocols as protocol filtering is easier. A "read only" system is easier to protect than one where users can write into the database. If necessary, the users could enter data into another system, where it can be checked and verified before being copied over to the database. Or, I could use a one way mechanism, such as one way fiber, to fill a database, and then periodically refresh the database, a means of "throwing the data over the fence"?

Fifth, an Extranet or Intranet is easier to protect than the Internet, because I only have to worry, about "insiders", who can be screened and more easily disciplined. One level systems are easier to protect than multi-level systems. With one-level systems, I worry less about write-downs or spillage as I do with multilevel systems.

Sixth, If I need a multilevel system, because, say, ease of use, I could form a composite system based on risk. If the group that is putting information into the database is known and trusted to me, I may be willing to let them work at multiple levels, in effect, using a MLS system to input into a database. I may force each submitter to sign his data entry. If the groups that is obtaining data from the database only require it at one level, then I may restrict them to that level and to read only. If the groups that read the data read it in only one format, then I can protect even further.

Seventh, system configuration, as usual, is a weak point. Does system configuration for the system exist? Is the system baselined? Is there system configuration documentation? What documentation exists? What are the procedures for changing hardware or software? Have all the relevant patches been applied? How do you know? How does the next person, who replaces you, know? Are you using the latest version of virus detecting software? How do you know? And so on. It is very easy to get into problems at this point.

Eighth, defense in depth, using intrusion detection, operating systems with differing architectures, filters, firewalls, guards and encryption may increase security, if the system is designed properly.

Ninth, the entire system must be looked at. Remember we are protecting the data. In one system, I was asked to look at the security of a database server, and I did. But you can not stop with just looking at a component. An input to the system was downgraded data, and there was, in my opinion, much more risk associated with the downgrading equipment and procedures than there was with the single-level database server.

Tenth, as systems become more complex, standards, at all levels, become even more important. Levels of software, including security software have to interface, as do the various components. It's great if all hardware and software can be purchased from one vendor, both for compatibility and accountability reasons, and, also, hopefully, for security policy consistency. However, it has been my experience that we usually have to use multiple vendors, and, often, provide custom code to complete the system solution.

Eleventh, try to avoid projects where security is thought of as an after-thought. The ideal system is built from a pre-established list of functional and security requirements. I've had the good fortune of doing this once. However, the later in the system development security is regarded as needed, the poorer the security result is likely to be.

Finally, the physical, personnel, and procedural techniques that we have used in the past to secure systems are all the more important now, in this new era of complex, buggy yet critical systems.

CHAPTER 28
DECLARATIVE SEMANTICS OF BELIEF QUERIES IN MLS DEDUCTIVE DATABASES

Hasan M. Jamil
Department of Computer Science
Mississippi State University, USA
jamil@cs.msstate.edu

Abstract A logic based language, called *MultiLog*, for multi level secure relational databases has recently been proposed. It has been shown that MultiLog is capable of capturing the notion of user *belief*, of filtering unwanted and *"useless"* information in its proof theory. Additionally, it can guard against a previously unknown security breach – the so called *surprise stories*. In this paper, we outline a possible approach to a declarative characterization of belief queries in MultiLog in a very informal manner. We show that for *"simple programs"* with belief queries, the semantics is rather straight forward. Semantics for the general Horn programs may be developed based on the understanding of the model theoretic characterization of belief queries developed in this paper.

Keywords: Multi level security, belief queries, declarative semantics, completeness.

Introduction

In a recent research, Jukic and Vrbsky [8] demonstrate that users in the relational MLS model potentially have a cluttered view and ambiguous belief of "visible data", and that the extraction process of knowledge and belief about data from such databases is manual and thus, error prone. In an earlier research [4], we showed that ad hoc knowledge extraction is quite an undertaking in such models, and understanding what others believe is not easily possible. We also showed that a special form of security breach, called *surprise stories*, is still possible in the MLS models and thus, have devised ways to guard against such breaches in *MultiLog*, a query language for deductive MLS databases. We continue to argue that it is imperative for users to theorize about the beliefs of other users at different visible levels. Current models, unfortunately, do not provide any support to this end. We have addressed some of the issues we perceive as bottlenecks for contemporary proposals in [4]. We will not elaborate on those issues here for the sake of conciseness. We refer the readers to [3] for an introduction to MLS data model, and to [2, 8, 4] for a discussion of its shortcomings and possible enhancements. We also do not include a detailed discussion on the syntax and the proof theory of MultiLog in this paper due to space limitations. Interested readers may refer to [4] for a preparatory reading. But for the sake of completeness, we present the syntax of all types of atoms of MultiLog below. The formulas and clauses of MultiLog are constructed in a way similar to classical logic programs.

MultiLog syntax includes a variety of atoms constructed from the alphabet of MultiLog language $\mathcal{L}$. In this alphabet (i) p is a predicate symbol, and *order* and *level* are two distinguished predicates, (ii) $\boldsymbol{t}_i$s, $\boldsymbol{v}$ and $\boldsymbol{k}$ are terms, (iii) a is an attribute name, (iv) $\boldsymbol{l}, \boldsymbol{h}, \boldsymbol{s}$ and $\boldsymbol{c}$ are symbols representing security levels, (v) and finally, m is a belief mode representing *firm* (fir), *cautious* (cau) or *optimistic* (opt) belief of a user. The so called m-atoms are of the form $\boldsymbol{s}[p(\boldsymbol{k} : a \overset{\boldsymbol{c}}{\rightarrow} \boldsymbol{v})]$, and the b-atoms are constructed from m-atoms as $\boldsymbol{s}[p(\boldsymbol{k} : a \overset{\boldsymbol{c}}{\rightarrow} \boldsymbol{v})] \ll m$. The p-atoms (or general predicates) are of the form $p(\boldsymbol{t}_1, \ldots, \boldsymbol{t}_k)$, while two distinguished predicates called the l-atoms and h-atoms are respectively of the form $level(\boldsymbol{s})$, and $order(\boldsymbol{l}, \boldsymbol{h})$.

Our goals for this paper are two-fold: (i) to develop a direct Herbrand semantics for a subset of definite Horn clause fragment of MultiLog, called the *simple programs* by defining a model theory and a fixpoint theory, and (ii) to demonstrate on intuitive grounds that the equivalence of MultiLog's three characterizations – proof theory, model theory and fixpoint theory can be easily established for simple programs. Through this equivalence, we hope to convince readers that MultiLog's unique features and modeling capabilities, many of which are non-monotonic in nature, do not compromise the soundness and completeness of the language. This development is significant from a theoretical perspective, as it gives insight into the understanding of the logical behavior and mathematical foundations of the language. Complete details of the ideas discussed in this paper may be found in an extended version [6] elsewhere.

1. DECLARATIVE SEMANTICS OF MULTILOG

The Herbrand semantics of MultiLog databases can be defined in terms of a composite set-theoretic structure which provides a model for each of the security levels in the language $\mathcal{L}$ of MultiLog, including the level $s_\perp$ – the system level which is not part of any database universe. In other words, each model in the composite structure interprets formulas pertaining to the corresponding levels in the security hierarchy. The notion of *"belief"* in such a structure is then captured using a function level semantics over the sets in the Herbrand structure, not as a set membership. The notion of Herbrand universe $\mathcal{U}$ and base $\mathcal{H}$ is defined in a manner similar to the classical case. Formally, an *Herbrand structure* $\mathbf{H}$ of $\mathcal{L}$ is a tuple $\langle H(s) : s \in \mathcal{S} \rangle$ such that $H(s) \subseteq \mathcal{H}$ for every $s \in \mathcal{S}$. When $s \neq s_\perp$, $H(s)$ contains only m-atoms, otherwise $H(s_\perp)$ contains only p-, l- and h-atoms. Intuitively, every $H(s), s \neq s_\perp$ in $\mathbf{H}$ interprets the associated data items belonging to the level s as ground m-atoms that are true with respect to level s in $\mathbf{H}$. To make a distinction between an interpretation corresponding to a security level and the interpretation structures for our language $\mathcal{L}$, we henceforth call them interpretations and T-interpretations respectively, since the latter is actually a tuple of simple interpretations or sets.

Definition 1.1 (Satisfaction of Formulas) Let $\mathbf{H}$ be a T-interpretation, $\bar{u}$ be a user clearance level, $H(s)$ be any arbitrary interpretation in $\mathbf{H}$ where s is a security level in $\mathbf{H}$, and let n be the number of such security levels. Furthermore, let A and B denote ground atomic formulas, and F and G denote any arbitrary ground formulas. Then, the satisfaction of ground formulas with respect to $H(s)$ in $\mathbf{H}$, denoted $H(s)\models_{\mathbf{H},\bar{u}}A$, or $H(s)\models_{\mathbf{H},\bar{u}}F$, is defined as follows:

$$
\begin{array}{lll}
(1) & H(s)\models_{\mathbf{H},\bar{u}}A & \iff A \in H(s) \text{ where } depth(A) = s \text{ and } s \preceq \bar{u} \\
(2) & H(s)\models_{\mathbf{H},\bar{u}}A & \iff H(o)\models_{\mathbf{H},\bar{u}}A \text{ where } depth(A) = o \text{ and } s \neq o \\
(3) & H(i)\models_{\mathbf{H},\bar{u}}A \leftarrow B_1,\ldots,B_m & \iff H(i)\models_{\mathbf{H},\bar{u}}B_g,\ g=1,\ldots,m \Longrightarrow H(i)\models_{\mathbf{H},\bar{u}}A \\
(4) & H(i)\models_{\mathbf{H},\bar{u}}l[p(k:a \overset{c}{\rightarrow} v] \ll m & \iff H'\models_{\mathbf{H},\bar{u}}l[p(k:a \overset{c}{\rightarrow} v] \text{ where} \\
 & & \quad H' = \beta(\bigcup_{j=1}^{n} H(s_j), \bar{u}, m) \text{ such that} \\
 & & \quad \forall j, s_j \preceq l \text{ and } l \preceq \bar{u}
\end{array}
$$

Finally, we say that $\mathbf{H} \models_{\bar{u}} A$ if and only if $H(l)\models_{\mathbf{H},\bar{u}}A$, where $l = depth(A)$.

In the definition above, β is a belief function defined as follows. Let S be an arbitrary set of m-atoms, $\bar{u}$ be a clearance level, $A = l[p(k : a \overset{c}{\rightarrow} v)]$ be a ground m-atom, and m be a belief mode in $\mu = \{fir, cau, opt\}$. Then, the belief function $\beta : \mathcal{P}(\mathbf{S}) \times \mathcal{S} \times \mu \rightarrow \mathcal{P}(\mathbf{S})$, where $\mathbf{S}$ is a set of all possible m-atoms and $\mathcal{S}$ is the set of all security symbols, such that:

$$
\beta(S,\bar{u},m) = \left\{ \bar{u}[p(k:a \overset{c}{\rightarrow} v)] \quad \middle| \quad
\begin{array}{l}
\text{One of the following conditions hold:} \\
\text{- } m = fir \text{ and } \bar{u}[p(k:a \overset{c}{\rightarrow} v)] \in S \\
\text{- } m = cau \text{ and } \exists l'[p(k:a \overset{c}{\rightarrow} v)] \in S,\ l' \preceq \bar{u}, \text{ and} \\
\quad \neg\exists l''[p(k:a \overset{c'}{\rightarrow} v')] \in S,\ l'' \preceq \bar{u}, \text{ and } c \prec c'. \\
\text{- } m = opt \text{ and } l'[p(k:a \overset{c}{\rightarrow} v)] \in S \text{ and } l' \preceq \bar{u}
\end{array}
\right.
$$

Furthermore, the depth of a p-, l- or h-atom is defined to be $s_\perp$ and as $\boldsymbol{s}$ for m- or b-atoms of the forms $\boldsymbol{s}[p(\boldsymbol{k} : a \overset{\boldsymbol{c}}{\rightarrow} \boldsymbol{v})]$ and $\boldsymbol{s}[p(\boldsymbol{k} : a \overset{\boldsymbol{c}}{\rightarrow} \boldsymbol{v})] \ll m$ respectively. The notion of models (T-models to be precise) can be developed using the machinery above. We explain the idea through a couple of examples. In the examples that follow, a database D is said to be in level l, denoted $\langle D, l\rangle$, if a user with a clearance level l accesses the database that sets a context for the queries and the responses returned by the database.

Example 1.1 Consider the following database $\langle D_1, c\rangle$ below. In this example, and also throughout this paper, we consider only four security levels for simplicity. Namely, $s_\perp$, u, c, and s with a total order $s_\perp < u < c < s$. That is, we have in our database the atoms *order(u,c)*, and *order(c,s)*, and that *order*($s_\perp$,*u*) is implicit.

$$
\Lambda_{D_1} := \left|\begin{array}{ll}
r_1: & level(u). \\
r_2: & level(c). \\
r_3: & level(s). \\
r_4: & order(u,c). \\
r_5: & order(c,s).
\end{array}\right.
\qquad
\Sigma_{D_1} := \left|\begin{array}{ll}
r_6: & c[p(k:a \overset{u}{\rightarrow} v)]. \\
r_7: & c[p(k:a \overset{c}{\rightarrow} t)] \leftarrow p(j). \\
r_8: & s[p(K:A \overset{C}{\rightarrow} V)] \leftarrow \\
 & c[p(K:A \overset{C}{\rightarrow} V)] \ll cau.
\end{array}\right.
$$

$$
\Pi_{D_1} := \left|\ r_9:\ q(j).\right. \qquad \mathcal{Q}_{D_1} := \left|\ r_{10}:\ ?\ s[p(k:a \overset{u}{\rightarrow} v)]\right.
$$

For the database above, let the T-model be M_1, as shown below:

$$
\begin{array}{rcl}
M_1 & = & \langle \underbrace{\{level(u),\ level(c),\ level(s),\ order(u,c),\ order(c,s), p(j)\}}_{M_1(s_\perp)}, \underbrace{\emptyset}_{M_1(u)}, \\
 & & \underbrace{\{c[p(k:a \overset{u}{\rightarrow} v)], c[p(k:a \overset{c}{\rightarrow} t)]\}}_{M_1(c)}, \underbrace{\{s[p(k:a \overset{c}{\rightarrow} t)]\}}_{M_1(s)}\rangle
\end{array}
$$

In the T-model M_1 above, the first set in the interpretation belongs to level $s_\perp$, i.e., $M_1(s_\perp)$. The second set belongs to u, the third to level c, and the last to s. Now, several observations can be made here. Note that the database is at level c. Also note that $s[p(k : a \stackrel{c}{\rightarrow} t)] \in M_1$, $M_1(s)$ to be precise. Still $M_1 \not\models_c s[p(k : a \stackrel{c}{\rightarrow} t)]$. This is because $M_1(s) \not\models_{M_1,c} s[p(k : a \stackrel{c}{\rightarrow} t)]$ as it does not satisfy condition 1 of definition 1.1 of formula satisfaction, i.e., $s \not\preceq c$. But $M_1 \models_c c[p(k : a \stackrel{u}{\rightarrow} v)]$, and also $M_1 \models_c c[p(k : a \stackrel{c}{\rightarrow} t)]$. Yet, it is interesting to verify that $M_1 \models_c c[p(k : a \stackrel{c}{\rightarrow} t)] \ll cau$ but $M_1 \not\models_c c[p(k : a \stackrel{u}{\rightarrow} v)] \ll cau$. This observation follows from the definition of cautious belief in β for Herbrand sets.

But not every T-model is *"intended"* and the construction of an intended T-model is not so straightforward. Recall that the satisfaction of b-atoms depends on the belief function β which makes use of the Herbrand sets in **H**. Also recall that the set computed by β depends on the elements in the Herbrand sets corresponding to security levels dominated by user clearance $\bar{u}$ (alternatively, by the level of the database). While the satisfaction of b-atoms is not affected by elements not required for a structure to be a T-model for a database $\langle \Delta, \bar{u} \rangle$, it potentially affects the beliefs of users as unwanted models may result. The following example helps clarify this point.

Example 1.2 Consider a level s database $\langle D_2, s \rangle$. Assume that database D_2 is derived from database D_1 of example 1.1 by replacing rule r_6 with $u[p(k : a \stackrel{u}{\rightarrow} v)]$, rule r_8 by $s[p(k : a \stackrel{u}{\rightarrow} v)] \leftarrow c[p(k : a \stackrel{u}{\rightarrow} v)] \ll cau$, and finally by deleting rule r_9 and adding two rules $r_{11} : p(X) \leftarrow r(X)$ and $r_{12} : r(X) \leftarrow q(X)$. Now for database $\langle D_2, s \rangle$ as defined, the intended T-model M_2 may be identified as follows:

$$M_2 = \langle \underbrace{\{level(u),\ level(c),\ level(s),\ order(u,c),\ order(c,s)\}}_{M_2(s_\perp)}, \underbrace{\{u[p(k : a \stackrel{u}{\rightarrow} v)]\}}_{M_2(u)}, \underbrace{\emptyset}_{M_2(c)}, \underbrace{\{s[p(k : a \stackrel{u}{\rightarrow} v)]\}}_{M_2(s)} \rangle$$

However, it is easy to verify that M_2' or M_2'' below are not intended although they are T-models for D_2.

$$M_2' = \langle \underbrace{\{level(u),\ level(c),\ level(s),\ order(u,c),\ order(c,s)\}}_{M_2'(s_\perp)}, \underbrace{\{u[p(k : a \stackrel{u}{\rightarrow} v)]\}}_{M_2'(u)}, \underbrace{\{c[p(k : a \stackrel{c}{\rightarrow} t)]\}}_{M_2'(c)}, \underbrace{\emptyset}_{M_2'(s)} \rangle$$

$$M_2'' = \langle \underbrace{\{level(u),\ level(c),\ level(s),\ order(u,c),\ order(c,s), p(j)\}}_{M_2''(s_\perp)}, \underbrace{\{u[p(k : a \stackrel{u}{\rightarrow} v)]\}}_{M_2''(u)}, \underbrace{\{c[p(k : a \stackrel{c}{\rightarrow} t)]\}}_{M_2''(c)}, \underbrace{\emptyset}_{M_2''(s)} \rangle$$

M_2' and M_2'' are not intended because they make $s[p(k : a \stackrel{u}{\rightarrow} v)]$ false, i.e., $M_2' \not\models_s s[p(k : a \stackrel{u}{\rightarrow} v)]$ and $M_2'' \not\models_s s[p(k : a \stackrel{u}{\rightarrow} v)]$, for similar but different reasons (for $c[p(k : a \stackrel{c}{\rightarrow} t)]$ being in $M_2'(c)$ and as well as in $M_2''(c)$ that made satisfaction of $c[p(k : a \stackrel{u}{\rightarrow} v)] \ll cau$ not possible, instead forced $c[p(k : a \stackrel{c}{\rightarrow} t)]$ to be believed, but cautiously, at level c). If either one of these T-models were minimal, it would have modeled $s[p(k : a \stackrel{u}{\rightarrow} v)]$, as dictated by logical entailment and implication. A careful observation will reveal that if the component models are the smallest (no extra atoms present than needed to be a model), then the composite T-interpretation stands a chance to be an *intended T-model.*

1.1. FIXPOINT THEORY

The issue now is – can the intended model of a database be constructed algorithmically? In this section, we present a constructive way of defining the least T-model for a MultiLog database $\langle \Delta, \bar{u} \rangle$. The key idea is to construct the least T-model $\mathbf{M}_\Delta$ of a database $\langle \Delta, \bar{u} \rangle$ by means of a bottom-up least fixpoint computation based on an immediate consequence operator $\mathbf{T}^{\bar{u}}_\Delta$. Since our T-interpretations are tuples of interpretations, we define $\mathbf{T}^{\bar{u}}_\Delta$ in terms of the immediate consequence transformation of each of the levels in $\langle \Delta, \bar{u} \rangle$.

Definition 1.2 (Fixpoint Operator) Let Δ be a "closed" database and let $\widehat{\Delta} = \langle \widehat{\Lambda}, \widehat{\Sigma}, \widehat{\Pi}, \widehat{Q} \rangle$ be its Herbrand instantiation defined as usual. Let I be an Herbrand interpretation for Δ. We define $\mathbf{T}^{\bar{u}}_\Delta$ to be the immediate consequence operator such that $\mathbf{T}^{\bar{u}}_\Delta = \langle T^{\bar{u}}_\Delta(I(s)) : s \in \mathcal{S} \rangle$. The operator $T^{\bar{u}}_\Delta$ for each component $I(s) \in I$ is defined similar to the classical case as $T^{\bar{u}}_\Delta : \mathcal{P}(\mathcal{H}) \mapsto \mathcal{P}(\mathcal{H})$, such that

$$T^{\bar{u}}_\Delta(I(s)) = \{A \mid A \leftarrow G \in \widehat{\Delta}, depth(A) = s \text{ and } I(s) \models_{I,\bar{u}} G\}$$

Unfortunately, the fixpoint of $\mathbf{T}^{\bar{u}}_\Delta$ does not yield the the intended model of $\langle \Delta, \bar{u} \rangle$ in general. This is because the belief function β is non-monotonic in nature (recall the case of overriding of less strict data item in a cautious mode), and thus the behavior of β depends on the stage of computation. While it does not affect the monotonicity of the $\mathbf{T}^{\bar{u}}_\Delta$ operator, it does spoil the intended model computation process. The following example exposes the unscrupulous nature of $\mathbf{T}^{\bar{u}}_\Delta$.

Example 1.3 Consider the database $\langle D_3, s \rangle$ derived from database D_2 in example 1.2 by adding the rule $r_{13} : q(j)$ in Π_{D_3}. For the database $\langle D_3, s \rangle$, the intended T-model M_3 may be identified as follows:

$$M_3 = \langle \underbrace{\{level(u),\ level(c),\ level(s),\ order(u,c),\ order(c,s),\ q(j),\ r(j),\ p(j)\}}_{M_3(s_\perp)}, \underbrace{\{u[p(k : a \stackrel{u}{\rightarrow} v)]\}}_{M_3(u)}, \underbrace{\{c[p(k : a \stackrel{c}{\rightarrow} t)]\}}_{M_3(c)}, \underbrace{\emptyset}_{M_3(s)} \rangle$$

However, if we consider the sets computed at every stage of $T^{\bar{u}}_\Delta$, we have the following sequence,

$$\begin{aligned}
\delta_1 &= \{level(u),\ level(c),\ order(u,c),\ q(j),\ u[p(k : a \stackrel{u}{\rightarrow} v)]\} \\
\delta_2 &= \{r(j),\ s[p(k : a \stackrel{u}{\rightarrow} v)]\} \\
\delta_3 &= \{p(j)\} \\
\delta_4 &= \{c[p(k : a \stackrel{c}{\rightarrow} t)]\}
\end{aligned}$$

giving us the T-model

$$M_3' = \langle \underbrace{\{level(u),\ level(c),\ level(s),\ order(u,c),\ order(c,s),\ q(j),\ r(j),\ p(j)\}}_{M_3'(s_\perp)}, \underbrace{\{u[p(k : a \stackrel{u}{\rightarrow} v)]\}}_{M_3'(u)}, \underbrace{\{c[p(k : a \stackrel{c}{\rightarrow} t)]\}}_{M_3'(c)}, \underbrace{\{s[p(k : a \stackrel{u}{\rightarrow} v)]\}}_{M_3'(s)} \rangle$$

which is not intended as the component model $M_3'(s)$ is not minimal, i.e., $M_3'(s) \neq \emptyset$. As such the query returns the answer true.

It turns out that if b-atoms are allowed only in the queries, and not in the clauses, then the intended models can be constructed fairly easily. Such restricted databases (or programs) are called *simple* databases (or programs). For simple databases it is easy to prove the following results.

Proposition 1.1 (Existence and Uniqueness of Intended Models) For any consistent database $\langle \Delta, \bar{u} \rangle$ [4, 6] and a least consistent T-model I of $\langle \Delta, \bar{u} \rangle$ [6], I is the unique intended model of $\langle \Delta, \bar{u} \rangle$ if $\langle \Delta, \bar{u} \rangle$ is simple.

Theorem 1.1 (Least T-models) Let $\langle \Delta, \bar{u} \rangle$ be a database and $\mathbf{M}_\Delta$ be its least T-model. Then, $\mathbf{M}_\Delta = lfp(\mathbf{T}_\Delta^{\bar{u}}) = \mathbf{T}_\Delta^{\bar{u}} \uparrow^\omega$.

The equivalence between the model theoretic semantics and the proof theory can now be established as follows.

Theorem 1.2 (Equivalence) Let $\langle \Delta, \bar{u} \rangle$ be a database, $\mathbf{M}_\Delta$ be its least T-model, and G be a ground goal. Then, we have

$$\langle \Delta, \bar{u} \rangle \vdash_\epsilon G \iff \mathbf{M}_\Delta \models_{\bar{u}} G$$

2. CONCLUSION

For simplicity of presentation, we have assumed that our databases are simple, and have essentially made them free from b-atoms while we still allowed b-atoms in the queries. This restriction can be removed by considering a more elaborate model theoretic treatment similar to stratification [1], or by taking an approach similar to the overriding concept developed in [7]. Our recent work on parametric inheritance [5] also provides additional formal basis for the belief function we have introduced in [4], and used in this paper. Intuitively, the rules containing b-atoms should be placed at the highest possible stratum so that the belief computation kicks off when the m-atoms are completely computed. But if the computation of m-atoms depends upon b-atoms, the scenario will become complicated and we will possibly have to settle for multiple minimal models. These are some of the issues we seek to investigate in our future research. The details may be found in an extended version of this paper in [6].

References

[1] M. Bugliesi and H. M. Jamil. A stable model semantics for behavioral inheritance in deductive object oriented languages. In *Proc ICDT*, pages 222–237, 1995.

[2] F. Cuppens. Querying a multilevel database: A logical analysis. In *VLDB Proc.*, pages 484–494, 1996.

[3] S. Jajodia and R. Sandhu. Toward a multilevel secure relational data model. In *ACM SIGMOD*, pages 50–59, 1991.

[4] Hasan M. Jamil. Belief reasoning in MLS deductive databases. In *ACM SIGMOD*, pages 109–120, 1999.

[5] H. M. Jamil. A logic based language for parametric inheritance. In *Proc KR'2000.*

[6] Hasan M. Jamil and Gillian Dobbie. Logical characterization of multi-level secure databases. Technical report, Department of Computer Science, Mississippi State University, USA, October 2000.

[7] Hasan M. Jamil and L. V. S. Lakshmanan. A declarative semantics for behavioral inheritance and conflict resolution. In *Proc ILPS*, pages 130–144, December 1995.

[8] N. A. Jukic and S. V. Vrbsky. Asserting beliefs in MLS relational models. In *SIGMOD Record*, pages 30–35, Ithaca, NY, 1997.

CHAPTER 29

Trust Management in Distributed Databases

James B. Michael and Leonard T. Gaines
Naval Postgraduate School, Computer Science Department, Monterey, CA

Key words: Trust, Trust Management, Internet Security, Distributed Databases

Abstract: Businesses and the military must be able to incorporate information from a number of sources in different formats to remain competitive. As the need for information increases, more applications are utilizing distributed databases. Data is collected from multiple sources in multiple formats and is combined into data warehouses or datamarts. For example, military applications are incorporating distributed databases to combine sensor information for use in command and control. Intelligent agents can already search the web for information sources. However, issues of interconnectivity among the agents and information sources, data overflow, data validity, and security remain to be addressed. This article addresses the security and data validity issues. Specifically, the article addresses trust management and its application to obtaining information utilizing an inherently untrustworthy medium.

1. INTRODUCTION

The Internet has created an opportunity for organizations to gather more quantitative and qualitative information for decision makers. The ability to analyze information faster and more efficiently than the competition permits organizations to better position themselves in the marketplace so as to react quickly to changes in the business environment.

As applications such as online analytical processing (OLAP) tools become more sophisticated, the need to gather and filter information will become crucial. Soon these tools will begin to incorporate intelligent agents to gather information. These agents can search a distributed system for information, or they can monitor sites, reporting on significant or changing information. Once the agents obtain data, they can pass it to a data warehouse that can be accessed by the application tools.

The use of intelligent agents and distributed databases raises a number of concerns about trust. The Internet and other distributed systems that encompass two or more administrative domains for security (i.e., enclaves) are inherently untrustworthy. Authentication of users and nodes (e.g., web sites) can be difficult, and the paths that data packets traverse are not always owned or controlled by entities that use them. The presence of viruses, Trojan horses, and hackers also adds to the public's mistrust of distributed systems. How does user know that the information retrieved by a system is from a reputable source? How can a system verify the legitimacy of a node? Can a user trust the owners or users of a particular node in a distributed system?

Concerns associated with trust in distributed databases can be addressed, to some extent, by utilizing a trust-management system. Members of an organization tend not to want to use data and information from sources that they do not trust. The motivation for the work reported here is to explore the extent to which trust-management systems can assist the members of an organization, to decide, based on consideration of policy about trust, whether to access data or information from a particular source in a distributed database system.

2. TRUST AND DISTRIBUTED SYSTEMS

Many believe that cryptography is the key to security on the Internet, but it does not address all of the pertinent security issues. When connecting with a server and exchanging information utilizing secure socket layer (SSL), how do you know that you have connected to the correct server? Site spoofing involves using URLs that are similar to popular web pages in the hopes that people will incorrectly type a URL and land on the rogue site. A good example is Whitehouse.com, which is a pornography site instead of the government site located at Whitehouse.gov. The site may look exactly like the site you want, but unless you open the certificate and compare the name on the certificate to the site, SSL will allow you to transact business with the rogue site.

Intelligent agents can check certificates to validate sites, but how can they determine the accuracy of the information located at the sites? Additionally, how does the agent verify whether a reputable organization issued the certificate? The Internet Information Server can create its own certificate. When downloading information from a web site, how does the agent know whether the information contains malicious code? Additionally, if a client downloads Java applets or Active X code, how does the client know whether the mobile code is malicious until it is too late to prevent the malicious code from executing?

In summary, the user must form an opinion concerning the extent to which he or she trusts the developers of the downloadable program and the web site that is distributing the program. However, a user must be able to analyze the risks and be knowledgeable enough to make an informed decision on matters of trust, which can be difficult when dealing with complex technical issues. Trust-management systems are designed to assist the user by evaluating the action to be taken, gathering the information required to form a decision, and determining whether the action to be taken is consistent with a policy about trust.

3. TRUST MANAGEMENT

In order for intelligent agents to interact with the Internet, in a secure manner, a methodology must be developed for identifying and validating web sites and their information. One of the methods to accomplish this is to add labels to the web sites that contain their certificates and outline the information contained in each site. Additional labels can attest to a form of validation similar to the Trusted Computer Security Evaluation Criteria (TCSEC) model. These validations can consist of a level of security, organization of data, an evaluation of the sources of information, and possibly insurance information covering the site. Utilizing these labels, organizations would be better able to evaluate the information they are receiving from the Internet. However, a trust-management system would still need to be implemented to ensure that the information gathered from a distributed database system met with certain organization-wide and user-defined trust criteria.

Trust models have been used to mimic human trust, dissect trust into element parts, categorize trust, and assign metrics to trust. The designers of the trust models try to communicate a notion of trust from one entity to another. Since trust is a subjective belief, one must assign a metric to beliefs that will have value when evaluating trust.

According to Gaines, trust management has a number of definitions. (Gaines, L., 2000) Some believe it is the process of translating a trust model into a practical application by combining trust variables associated with authentication with those of integrity and confidentiality. Others believe it is a system for protecting open, decentralized systems by analyzing, codifying, and managing trust decisions.

The authors of the REFEREE trust-management system argue that trust management provides a systematic means for deciding whether a requested action, supported by credentials, conforms to a specific policy. (Chu, Y., Feigenbaum, J., LaMacchia, B., Resnick, P., and Strauss, M., 1997) Another view of trust management is that it is a new philosophy for codifying, analyzing, and managing decisions about trust, with regarding to the overarching question "Is someone trusted to take action on some object?" (Khare, R. and Rifkin, A., June, 1998, p. 2)

In order to implement a trust-management system with OLAP tools, we must first develop a way to identify all of the principals (i.e., the entities involved). The use of digital certificates within a public-key infrastructure (PKI) is an example of one way to accomplish this. The second step is to list the various elements of the system, and for instance, use external metadata labels. These labels can be bound by a URL to a specific web-based resource. These labels can be in a Platform for Internet Content Selection (PICS) format. The final step is to specify the authorization decisions according to some policy. The REFEREE trust-management system (discussed later) addresses these steps. In addition, REFEREE makes trust decisions based upon a target, a principal, a proposed action, and policy. (Khare, R. and Rifkin, A., June, 1998)

Trust management systems such as REFEREE take as input a subject, action, and statements about the subject, matching these to a module containing the corresponding policy. For each action, there are specific policies that govern which statements are valid.

Khare and Rifkin discuss three types of approaches to framing policies. The first approach based on principal-centric policies, which forward a notion that only certain people can be trusted. The policy-enforcement mechanism checks the clearance of each principal to determine whether that principal can perform an action on an object. Another approach is based on object-centric policy. Handles, tokens, combinations, and cryptographic keys are the essence of object-centric policy. A principal must have a trusted object that represents permission to execute actions on another object. The third approach relies on action-centric policy, that is, policy that specifies that only certain actions can be trusted: the policy-enforcement mechanism must ensure that any action taken by a principal on an object is approved. (Khare, R. and Rifkin, A., 30 November, 1997.)

REFEREE has four major components: the metadata format, the trust protocol, the trust-policy languages, and the execution environment. The REFEREE system was designed to incorporate these four components. (Chu, Y., June 1997) PICS labels contain metadata about the site. The metadata can be queried. The information contained in the metadata is applied to heuristics and trust protocols to determine whether an action is permitted by policy.

The trust-policy languages must be capable of interpreting the various forms of metadata and applying the information to internal trust protocols. The trust protocols consist of gathering all of the necessary information or assertions to determine if a given request complies with a trust policy. The trust protocols process the query on the metadata.

> The execution environment is the place where a request is evaluated against a trust policy and the pertinent metadata information. It accepts requests and interprets the truth policies that pertain to the requests. It also triggers the trust protocols to gather the necessary information to make a decision. Then it provides an answer to the request along with an explanation.

For a given user request, REFEREE invokes the appropriate user policy and interpreter module and returns to the host application an answer of whether or not the request complies with the policy. The basic computing unit is a module. It is an executable block of code that processes the input arguments, compares the input to policies, and outputs an answer. The module consists of a policy and zero or more interpreters. Modules can delegate tasks to other modules if necessary. Modules can also be easily added or deleted; they are contained in a module database that cross-references the requested action with the appropriate module and interpreter.

REFEREE is a good trust management system in that it is one of the first to combine all of the categories of trust management into one system. The other system, Microsoft's Authenticode, also combines all of the categories into one system, but its application is limited. Authenticode does not have the flexibility that is inherent in REFEREE. (Chu, Y., 13 June 1997)

4. JØSANG'S TRUST MODEL

An important part of REFEREE is authentication through the use of certificates. However, cryptography does not address issues of trust associated with the public-key infrastructure (PKI).

Jøsang's trust model was developed for use in the authentication of public keys. In an open environment such as the Internet, certificates alone cannot validate authenticity. The trust in the binding of a certificate key and its owner is essential in providing a level of legal culpability (i.e., digital certificates and non-repudiation). The certification authority that created the certificate must also be assessed for trustworthiness. Do they properly check identification before issuing a certificate? The authenticity of a key can be validated with its corresponding public or private key. However, the certificate that holds the key is what needs to be validated.

Jøsang defined trust as a subjective measure: the belief that a system will resist malicious attacks. Trust in humans was defined as the belief that he or she will cooperate and not defect. (Jøsang, A., 1999) In his model, he assumes that the outcome of a transaction depends on whether an agent defects or cooperates. Thus, probabilities are not assigned to possible outcomes. Instead, trust measures are used as input to a decision mechanism.

In Jøsang's trust model the truth-value of a statement must be crisp (i.e., they are either true or false). Whenever the truth of a statement is assessed, it is always done by an individual, and therefore represents a subjective determination of trust. The belief in a statement cannot be purely binary. Humans do not have perfect knowledge, so it is impossible to know with certainty whether a statement is true or false. We can only have "opinions" about the veracity of a statement. These opinions represent degrees of belief, disbelief, and uncertainty. Jøsang expresses "opinions" mathematically as $b + d + u = 1$ and $b,d,u \in [0,1]$, where b, d, and u represent belief, disbelief, and uncertainty, respectively.

Jøsang's trust model is founded on subjective logic. Subjective logic defines the various logical operators for combining opinions. These operators are conjunction, disjunction, negation, recommendation, and consensus: they are the same operators as those found in classical and subjective logics, but they are applied to trust.

A conjunction of two opinions combines an individual's opinions on two distinct binary statements into one opinion that reflects the belief in the truth of both statements. If x and y are two distinct statements, the conjunction of the belief in x, represented by $W_x = (b_x, d_x, u_x)$ and y represented by $W_y = (b_y, d_y, u_y)$ represents an individual's opinion about both x and y being true.

If we represent the conjunction of an individual's opinions on statements x and y as $W_{x \wedge y}$, then $W_{x \wedge y} = (b_{x \wedge y}, d_{x \wedge y}, u_{x \wedge y})$. In order to compute the conjunction, the individual values of belief, disbelief, and uncertainty must be combined for the opinions on both statements. In contrast, the disjunction operation represents an individual's opinion about statements x or y or both being true, that is, $W_{x \vee y} = (b_{x \vee y}, d_{x \vee y}, u_{x \vee y})$.

A negation of an opinion represents the belief that a statement is false. If W_x represents an opinion, $W_{\neg x}$ represents the negation of W_x such that $W_{\neg x} = (b_{\neg x}, d_{\neg x}, u_{\neg x})$.

Subjective logic can also be used to convey values for recommendation. Recall that trust in humans is the belief that the human will cooperate and not defect. Agent A has an opinion about B's willingness to cooperate and not defect. Agent B has an opinion about a statement or proposition x. A recommendation consists of combining B's opinion about x with A's opinion about B's cooperation, so A can form an opinion about statement x.

An assumption underlying the recommendation operator is that the agents do not defect or change their recommendations depending on whom they interact with. In addition, there is an assumption that the opinions that are recommended are independent. If a chain of recommenders is needed to gain information about a proposition x, it is assumed that only first-hand knowledge is transmitted. If second-hand knowledge is passed as a recommendation, opinion independence is violated. Additionally, the order in which the opinions are combined is significant.

Subjective logic has consensus operators. A consensus operator allows two independent agents to form a consensus opinion based on each agent's individual opinions concerning a proposition x.

Jøsang provides an example of how subjective logic can be used to measure the trust in a certificate. In some PKI architectures, a certificate authority issues certificates containing an individual's public key. If agent *A* knows certification authority *B*'s public key k_b and *B* knows agent *C*'s public key k_c, then *B* can send *C*'s public key to *A* signed by *B*'s private key k_{-1b}. Agent *A* will verify the certificate with *B*'s public key, and if correct, will know that it has received a correct copy of *C*'s public key.

Unfortunately, this exchange does not convey *A*'s trust that it has received a correct copy of *C*'s public key. In order to trust in a certificate, *A* must have an opinion about the validity of *B*'s public key. *A* must also form an opinion on agent cooperation, which measures *A*'s trust in *B* to properly certify other keys. *A* must also evaluate the recommendation of *B* as to the validity of *C*'s public key.

In order to validate the authenticity of the certificate, *A* must first evaluate the recommendation from certification authority *B*. *A* will combine its opinion of *B*'s key authentication with its opinion about *B*'s agent cooperation. This will determine *A*'s opinion about *B*'s capability as a recommender. Then *A* must combine its opinion about *B*'s recommendation ability with *B*'s recommendation about *C*'s public key. (Jøsang, A., 1998)

Jøsang has demonstrated the versatility of his model by showing that it is capable of chaining trust and certificate relationships using multiple recommendation operators. The model also supports measuring trust along multiple trust-paths and combining them into a single representation, and assigning utility values (i.e., weights) to levels of trust.

5. PRACTICAL APPLICATION

In order to provide trust-based decision-making support for applications that rely on distributed databases a combination of Jøsang's public-key-authentication trust model and REFEREE can be used. Such a combination can permit an application to validate a web site and utilize metadata to determine whether the data can be trusted. This section contains a practical application utilizing an OLAP tool. The discussion here is based on a portion of the thesis research conducted by Gaines. (Gaines, L., 2000)

In response to a request generated by the front-end, the OLAP server queries the data source. If additional information is needed, intelligent agents are deployed to collect the pertinent data. When an agent arrives at a web site, it examines the site's metadata; contained in this metadata is the site's certificate. In order to authenticate this site, the certificate is passed to the OLAP server.

The OLAP server, when receiving a certificate, can utilize Jøsang's model to compute a level of trust in the certificate. If a chain of trust is needed to validate the certificate, then the system can generate the queries necessary to collect recommender information. The OLAP server can compute a probability-expectation value and compare this value to a value in user-defined policy. If the certificate is trusted, then additional metadata will need to be collected. Otherwise, the agent will not access that site.

In this scenario, metadata includes a rating level from an outside entity that evaluates the way data is organized, evaluates data sources, and judges an organization's reputation. The agent passes the metadata to the referee system along with a statement such as "can this agent access this web site?" The trust protocol can collect the necessary metadata and pass it to the execution environment. The trust-policy language can then be used to select the syntax to apply so that a policy can be compared to the metadata. The execution environment analyzes the statement, the metadata information, and compares both to a corresponding preset policy about trust. The execution environment returns an answer: access permitted or denied.

Suppose that two different agents pose the same query to different web sites. The query results turn out to be different, even partially inconsistent with one another. The agents each have their own opinions as to the trustworthiness of the sources. However, by combining their opinions using the consensus operator in Jøsang's model, it may be possible for the agents to reduce their combined level of uncertainty about the trustworthiness of the sources.

REFEREE is designed to determine whether an agent should perform a potentially dangerous task, such as downloading unknown Java applets. The agent asks the system for permission to execute a particular task. The system evaluates the task and the metadata information and compares it to a policy about trust. If the REFEREE system trusts the site or the software being downloaded, then it will allow the agent to perform some action on that site or use the software that was downloaded.

The foregoing example is somewhat oversimplified. For example, we ignored the complexities associated with composing heterogeneous trust-management systems. In addition to the need for semantic interoperability between heterogeneous database systems, Hansen, for instance, points out the necessity for both technical and functional interoperability between the public-key infrastructures that are used by the U.S. Department of Defense and other branches of government to manage trust. (Hansen, A., 1999)

6. CONCLUSION

Users of distributed database systems can rely to some extent on trust-management systems, in conjunction with their portfolio of other types of security services, to partially automate both reasoning about and enforcing policy about trust. Instead of placing universal trust in an object or node within a distributed database system, the decision-maker can take steps to gauge the trustworthiness of the object or node, in addition to passing his or her trust in the object or node to another party.

Trust-management systems provide applications with the ability to make informed decisions about actions performed by their distributed databases, including the actions of intelligent agents. Trust-management systems are not a silver bullet for addressing all of the challenges associated with trust-based decision-making in distributed database systems, but they do provide an avenue for managing trust, and hence, managing risk associated with trusting a source of data and information.

Disclaimer

The views and conclusions contained herein are those of the authors and should not be interpreted as necessarily representing the official policies or endorsements, either expressed or implied, of the U.S. Government. The U.S. Government is authorized to reproduce and distributed reprints for Government purposes not withstanding any copyright annotations thereon.

List of References

Chu, Y., "Trust Management for the World Wide Web," Master's thesis, Massachusetts Institute of Technology, 1997.

Chu, Y., Feigenbaum, J., LaMacchia, B., Resnick, P., and Strauss, M., "REFEREE: Trust Management for Web Applications," [http://www.research.att.com/~bal/papers/www6-referee/www6-referee.html], 1997.

Dousette, P., Danesh, A., and Jones, M., "Command and Control using World Wide Web Technology," [http://turing.acm.org:8005/pubs/citations/proceedings/ada/289524/p212-dousette], 1998.

Gaines, L. T., "Trust and its Ramifications for the DOD Public Key Infrastructure," Master's Thesis, Naval Postgraduate School, 2000.

Hansen, A. P., "Public Key Infrastructure Interoperability: A Security Services Approach to Support Transfer of Trust," Master's thesis, Naval Postgraduate School, 1999.

Jøsang, A., "An Algebra for Assessing Trust in Certification Chains," in *Proceedings of the Network and Distributed Systems Security (NDSS'99) Symposium*, Internet Society, 1999.

Jøsang, A., "A Subjective Metric of Authentication," in *Proceedings of the Fifth European Symposium on Research in Computer Securit)*, Springer-Verlag, 1998.

Jøsang, A., "Trust-Based Decision Making for Electronic Transactions," in *Proceedings of the Fourth Nordic Workshop on Secure Computer Systems*, 1999.

Khare, R., and Rifkin, A., "Trust Management on the World Wide Web," [http://www.firstmonday.dk/issue3_6/khare/], June 1998.

Khare, R. and Rifkin, A., "Weaving a Web of Trust," [http://www.cs.caltech.edu/~adam/local/trust.html], 30 November 1997.

CHAPTER 30

Active Authorization as High-level Control

Daniel Cvrček
PhD. student on DCSE, Brno University of Technology
Božetěchova 2, 61266 Brno
Czech Republic
cvrcek@dcse.fee.vutbr.cz

Key words: authorization system, workflow, active authorization

Abstract: The paper introduces several issues that have one common target - secure cooperation of autonomous information systems. We show that Active authorization model may be an abstract layer that allows simple, efficient and secure management of heterogeneous system's security properties.

1. INTRODUCTION

Nowadays commercial sector demands possilibity to specify well-defined tasks that represent usual business processes. It means that users may work with intuitive tasks like *process customer order* or *prepare contract of insurance* and so on.

The tasks' definitions may be divided into two abstract levels. The lower level contains tasks representing atomic (relatively simple) actions. The higher level comprises workflows, tasks that may be invoked by external subjects (e.g. users) or other applications.

Commercial environment implies existence of users that can not be fully trusted and will never be experts in security. Communication among physically distant information systems is usually performed via insecure channels and quality of access controls and used models differs. Those facts demand existence of very tight security permissions that allow application of *need-to-know* and *need-to-do* principles. Ideal seems to be authorization model that preservers and joins one security state with each particular task. General properties of such a model have been given in [6].

2. OVERVIEW OF SECURITY IN DISTRIBUTED SYSTEMS

The first thing we have to do for solving security issues is to split the distributed system into *homogenous* (from the security point of view) parts that are centrally administered. We shall call them *autonomous information system* or *s-node.*At this moment, we may solve secure cooperation among s-nodes. The identified problems are:

a) Access control in s-node - this problem comprises access control to resources local in s-node and is solved by access control model implemented in the local platform. Each autonomous system may have implemented other access control model.
b) Global administration of system - distributed system has to solve problems with heterogeneity of its s-nodes and enforce uniform administration of security properties.
c) Flow control - we are talking about systems that allow space distributivity of computational tasks. Those tasks use data with different sensitivity, stored on many s-nodes. Flow control enforces uniformity throughout the system - *reference monitor* [1].

We may control several different types of resource accesses (with increasing abstraction).

1. Access to resources on s-node
2. Access to resources in workflow
3. Access to workflows
4. Data flow in workflows

It is clear that *discretionaryon control* is sufficient for the lowest level of access control. The mandatory or some other type of axiomatic access control (e.g. RBAC [2,3,4]) has to be on the other side used for access control to workflows and their resources (e.g. RBAC) when a common security policy is to be enforced.

3. COOPERATION WITH ACCESS CONTROL

Cooperation between global authorization model (AAM) [5] see items 2-4 above and local authorization models (item 1) is the crucial aspect of successful enforcement of access control rules throughout the distributed system. We do not know about any work that solves problems rising from this cooperation. Existing papers explicitly use only RBAC model for determination of subjects able to activate tasks.

We try to generalize cooperation between AAM and s-nodes' access control systems. The basic condition is made by introducing general function $\Phi(\mathfrak{S}, P_I^t) \rightarrow \mathfrak{S}_0^t$ that allows determination of subjects - initiators, able to run a task, from the set of all subjects according to the set of privileges necessary for initialization of the task.

We do not say which way is the set obtained. We do not say what model is used for that purpose. It may be a function that finds all users that are specified in a given UNIX group or a function cooperating with RBAC model that uses much more sophisticated ways for the purpose.

3.1 Examples of Local Access Control Models

There are vital differences among different access models. Because of the lack of space we only name the most important. DAC models such as HRU, Take-Grant, Acten. MAC models Bell-LaPadula, Biba or Dion and also object oriented models ORION, Iris.

Generally, one may say that basic DAC (discretionary access control) models do not offer any properties that can be used for generalization of access control and there are problems with centralized administration. To solve those problems we have to create layer isolating system with DAC model from external subjects (users).

MAC (mandatory access control) models contain general axioms that may be used for common security. Those axioms express certain general rules that may be used for centralized administration.

The first problem that has to be solved is general architecture of authorization system as a whole. We are interested in heterogeneous distributed systems composed from s-nodes that are able to communicate among themselves. Each s-node contains resources it is able to work with (files, peripheral devices, ...). It also has a system that manages access to resources (operational system, database management system) and there is an access (or authorization) control model that is used for managing access to resources. The control model has to be a part of authorization system.

3.2 Basic Layering of Authorization System

It is useful to create a basic layering of authorization system based on the architecture of the distributed system.

We have already said that s-nodes contain (or use) access control model. This is the first layer and we call it *Local Access Control*. This layer should be able to create new users or user groups and provide instruments that allow authentication of more abstract systems (or its users).

Definition 1: Local Access Control L_i is n-tuple $L_i=\{S_i, O_i, A_i, f_i\}$ that consists of set of users S_i, set of resources (or objects) O_i set of access modes A_i and authorization function f_i that is defined as follows:

$$f_i: S_i \times O_i \times A_i \rightarrow \{True, False\}$$

The function f_i is able to decide access requests. ■

The second layer of our architecture should be able to convert global definition of privileges into a form applicable in Local Access Controls and vice versa. This layer shall be called *Conversion Layer*. This is the first element that creates some general (global) framework.

Definition 2: Conversion Layer represents two functions σ_i' and σ_i'' that take set of users and set of resources from the underlying Local Access Control $L_i=(S_i, O_i, A_i, f_i)$, set of resource categories C^k and returns subset of users that are authorized to access specified resources.

$$\sigma_i'' : C^k \times S_i \rightarrow S_i$$

uses σ_i' to translate resource categories C^k into the set of resources O_i^k

$$\sigma_i' : C^k \rightarrow O_i^k$$

and of course the function f_i to determine the final subset of users with privileges to access all elements from the set of resources O_i^k. ■

Next layer should allow specification of tasks executable in the distributed system. We distinguish two types of tasks.

- Tasks that are executed on one s-node and by one user. We call those tasks *atomic tasks*. The description of those tasks is dependent on the particular s-node.
- Tasks that may be executed on several s-nodes and/or by several users. We call them *workflows* and their specification is *platform independent*.

Atomic tasks are described by means of given s-node. Particular layer is *Atomic Task Manager*. The last one, *Workflow Manager* is completely s-node independent. It allows its implementation by means satisfying execution on various systems. Workflow Manager may be split into two parts, one concerning *static authorizations* of workflows (authorizations that are specified during workflow creation) and one concerning *dynamic authorizations*.

3.3 Communication of Security Layers

Authorization system of any distributed system has to be *active*. We do not know all users of the distributed system in one central place and s-nodes have to be able to determine whether and where are users able to run particular task or workflow step.

How to perform a workflow? Imagine that someone on s-node S_i has started a workflow and executed the first step of it. We need to find all s-nodes that are potentially able to execute next step of the workflow.

(1) We have to address all s-nodes in the distributed system. (2) Each s-node identifies users that are able to continue the workflow and wait until one of the identified users initiates execution of the task. (3) When the *active* user is on the s-node S_j, then S_j responds to S_i. (4) S-node S_i recalls its request on all s-nodes except S_j. And (5) execution of the workflow moves to the new s-node S_j and the *active* user may execute next step.

The most important is step (2). Communication among layers of the authorization system on particular s-nodes is performed here. The Workflow Manager receives the first impulse. It has to ask the Atomic Task Manager, if the particular task is defined there. In the case of success, the Atomic Task Manager has to determine set of users authorized (static rights) to run the task (either directly with Local Access Control or in cooperation with Conversion Layer). The same task but with the dynamic authorization is done by Workflow Manager, Conversion Layer and Local Access Control. There are received two sets of users. Their intersection is a set of users authorized to execute the workflow's task.

3.4 The Conversion Layer

Conversion Layer is the place, where two considerably different models are in touch. Very important is to find criterion for general specification of authorization requirements. The following possibilities were identified.

- Hierarchy in the organization.
- Name of subject (user).
- Privilege for data access (analogy with MAC).
- Reference to a common hierarchy (absolute or relative (from-to)).
- Reference to another predefined role (group) structure.
- Types of resources that have to be accessed.

The classification we shall use has to be very stable and must be applicable for all s-nodes. We have assumed that the most general and stable classification should be based on resource categories (defined according to data content) that form a non-hierarchical set of elements C^k that depends on the environment.

When using just category of resource, subject is able to perform all possible operations over accesible resources. We have got no information to restrict set of operations. The restriction in this direction is enforced through the tasks' definitions.

Resource categorization is the fixed point that allows global definition of workflows. All task definitions use categorization (or classification) to specify security requirements for data access (resources and workflows). During execution of particular task step are categories converted into form that the s-node's Local Access System is able to use to determine authorized users and to determine needed resources (functions Φ and Θ). Atomic Task Manager performs this conversion especially in Conversion Layer and partially.

4. CONCLUSION

We have proposed base ideas of the problem of unification of security administration and secure cooperation among autonomous information systems. The offered approach consists of two cornerstones. The first one is existence of uniform security classification (or categorization) of resources. This fact constitutes fixed point that consolidates security administration of s-nodes. The second one is design of authorization system in such a way that allows separation of particular platforms from active subjects (especially users). This structure allows uniform definition of workflows on any s-node in the distributed system.

The result is the architecture of authorization system that allows secure execution of workflows, centralized administration of the whole distributed system and decentralized definition of workflows.

5. BIBLIOGRAPHY

[1] D.E. Bell and L.J. LaPadula, Secure computer systems: Unified exposition and multics interpretation Technical Report MTR-2997, Bedford (MA), The Mitre Corporation, March 1976.

[2] E. Bertino, E. Ferrari, and V. Atluri, A Flexible Model Supporting the Specification and Enforcement of Role-based Authorizations in Workflow Management Systems, Proceedings of the Second ACM Workshop on Role-Based Access Control (Fairfax, VA), November 1997.

[3] R. S. Sandhu et al., Role-based Access Control Models, IEEE Computer, February 1996, p. 38-47.

[4] R.S. Sandhu, Role Hierarchies and Constraints for Lattice-Based Access Controls, Proc. Fourth European Symposium on Research in Computer Security, September 1996.

[5] D. Cvrcek, Mandatory access control in workflow systems, Knowledge-based Software Engineering - Proc. of the JCKBSE - Conference, 2000, pp. 247-254.

[6] R.K. Thomas and R.S. Sandhu, Towards a Task-based Paradigm for Flexible and Adaptable Access Control in Distributed Applications, Proceedings of the Second New Security Paradigms Workshop (Little Compton, Rhode Island), IEEE Press, 1993.

CHAPTER 31

Conference Key Agreement Protocol using Oblivious Transfer

Ari Moesriami Barmawi, Shingo Takada, Norihisa Doi
Department of Computer Science, The Graduate School of Science and Technology, Keio University, JAPAN

Key words: conference key, individual key, oblivious transfer

Abstract: The basic idea of our protocol is establishing a conference key based on oblivious transfer which can be used in either asymmetric or symmetric cryptography, such that we can reduce the number of decryptions for the key confirmation without sacrificing the level of security. In our proposed method, we break the conference key into several individual secret keys in accordance with the amount of members within the group. This individual key will be used by each member to sign (encrypt (asymmetrically)) the established conference key in the key confirmation procedure. Then, each member multiplies all signed conference keys and decrypting (asymmetrically) the multiplied signed conference key using the multiplicative inverse of his locally calculated conference key.

Thus, each member only needs to perform one decryption for the key confirmation. Furthermore, by using the individual secret key, each member can directly communicate with each other by a support of the leader, while the leader does not gain any knowledge of messages which is exchanged between the communicating members. The last features can not be found in the previous method except in Li-Pieprzyk's. However, for the key generation we need only a less modular exponentiations than the former.

1 INTRODUCTION

There are many key agreement protocols which have been proposed for establishing session key between more than two users, such as those proposed by Burmester-Desmedt [1], Mike Just et. al. [2], Colin Boyd [3,4], Li-Pieprzyk [5], etc. Suppose for the key confirmation, each member signed the conference key which is calculated by himself. To verify whether all members are holding the same conference key, each member of the group needs to verify all members signed keys. In this case, the previous protocols need several decryptions which increase computational burden to the group. Besides, the previous proposed protocols except Li-Pieprzyk's, did not provide any facilities for the two members in the group to communicate securely with each other (i.e. other members of the group outside the communicating members learn nothing about messages that have been exchanged between the two communicating members). Our protocol provides this facility, but it is more efficient than the Li-Pieprzyk's, since for the key generation, our protocol needs less modular exponentiations than Li-Pieprzyk's..

We propose a protocol for generating the conference and the individual secret keys at once, using oblivious transfer. Using our method, we can establish a conference key which can be used in either symmetric or asymmetric cryptography.

At the end of our proposed protocol each member of the group can calculate the conference and his individual keys (i.e., a key which has to be kept secret between the leader and a certain member of the group). The conference key is used to encrypt (symmetrically and asymmetrically) messages which can be decrypted by all members of the group. The individual key of member U_i is used to encrypt (symmetrically) messages which can be decrypted (symmetrically) only by member U_i itself and the leader of the group. In the key confirmation, this individual key is used for signing the established conference key. Then, each member can verify that all members have the same conference key by multiplying all signed keys and decrypt (asymmetrically) the result using the multiplicative inverse of his locally calculated conference key. Hence, for the key confirmation, each member has to perform only one decryption. Thus, instead of being used for encrypting/decrypting message symetrically, the conference key can be used for encrypting message asymmetrically as well.

This individual key can be used for signing a contract. Suppose there is a contract which has to be signed by all members. The leader broadcasts a message, then each member signs this message using his individual key and sends it back to the leader. Furthermore, the leader can verify whether the message he sent has been signed by all members only by multiplying all signed messages and decrypting (asymmetrically) it with the multiplicative inverse of the conference key, instead of decrypting each message (one by one). Thus, in this case the computational burden of the leader will be decreased.

This paper first describes the features of the supporting protocols. Section 2 describes the detailed proposed protocol. Section 3 describes the security analysis. And the comparison with the previous protocols. Section 4 makes concluding remarks.

2 The Proposed Protocol

In order to realize our proposed protocol, we invoke oblivious transfer [6] and multiplicative-additive share converter proposed by Gilboa [7]. However, due to space we will not describe the detail of these protocols. In our proposed protocol we assumed that the group is predetermined and one of the users is the leader whose commands must be authenticated and has public and secret keys. Thus, the leader's public key should be publicly known.

2.1 Detailed Proposed Protocol

Suppose a group has r members (including the group leader) who are honest. Furthermore, the conference key is actually the product of r individual keys. The individual key of each member is determined by each member's randomly chosen number and the leader's one. For obtaining the conference and individual keys the group has to execute the following protocol:

1. All members and the leader have to agree on the size of their randomly chosen numbers n_i that will determine the conference and their individual keys (suppose the size of each n_i is l bit) and a large strong prime θ. Let $\beta=\Phi(\theta)$ (where $\Phi(\theta)$ is the Euler Totient Function of θ). Furthermore, they choose a number α which is the generator of $\mathbf{Z}_{\beta}$*.
2. Let U_1 be the group leader, and U_i (for $i=2,\ldots,r$) are members. Suppose each member as well as the leader has their own public and secret keys, where the public key of each member is known only by the leader.
3. Each member U_i chooses any integer dum_i, encrypts it with the leader's public key, and sends it to the leader.
4. Each member privately chooses a number n_i.
5. Suppose U_1 chooses n_1 as his multiplicative share whose size is l (we set n_γ as the γth bit of n_i, for $(\gamma=1,\ldots,l)$ and $s_{1,1},\ldots,s_{1,l}$. He then sets l pairs of $(t_{1,\gamma}^{0}, t_{1,\gamma}^{1})$ where $(t_{1,\gamma}^{0}=2^{\gamma}\, n_1+s_{1,\gamma})$ and $(t_{1,\gamma}^{1}=s_{1,\gamma})$. Each member U_i has his own multiplicative share n_i which consists of l bits $(n_{1,1},\ldots,n_{1,l})$. U_1 and all members invokes one out of two oblivious transfer, such that $(n_1 n_i=x_1+x_i)$ (where x_i and x_1 are the secret additive shares of user U_i (for $i=2,\ldots,r$) and U_1 respectively) using Gilboa's method. In this case, $x_1=-\sum_{\gamma=1,\ldots l} s_{1,\gamma}$ and $x_i=\sum_{\gamma=1,l} t_{i,\gamma}\, n_{i,\gamma}$.
6. Each member U_i broadcasts ($y_i\equiv \alpha^{x_i+dum_i} \bmod \beta$) encrypted with his secret key and y_i itself.

7. The leader verifies whether y_i comes from U_i by decrypting the encrypted message using the member's public key and comparing the value of y_i which is obtained from the signed message and the plaintext one. If they are equal (i.e. the leader verifies that this message was signed by the legitimate sender) then he executes the following procedure:
   - Calculating $(\alpha^{x}{}_i \bmod \beta \equiv (y_i\alpha^{-dum}{}_i) \bmod \beta)$
   - Calculating $(P\equiv\alpha^{[(r-1)x_1+\Sigma_{i=2,r} x_i]} \bmod \beta)$. The leader chooses a number dum_1 such that P' (where $(P'=[P(\alpha^{dum}{}_1)]^{t} \bmod \beta)$) is not congruent to □□$1 \bmod \beta$. The individual key of the leader is defined as follows:□□□□ $K_1\equiv B^t \bmod \beta$, where $B \equiv \alpha^{dum}{}_1 \bmod \beta$. Then the conference key K is
     $K=P \bmod \beta$ (1)
     where t should be agreed upon in advance by all members of the group and t is not congruent to $0 \bmod \lambda(\beta)$ (where λ is the Carmichael Function [8]).
   - Broadcasting the size of $(\alpha^{((r-1)x_1+dum_1-\Sigma_{i=2,r} dum_i)} \bmod \beta)$ denotes as u
     along with $(\alpha^{n}{}_1 \bmod \beta)$ and the signed $H(\alpha$^ $^{((r-1)x_1+dum_1-\Sigma_{i=1,r} dum_i)} \bmod \beta)$ (where H has to be agreed upon in advance by all members and the leader). Otherwise, he will interrupt the protocol execution, and then repeat the protocol from the beginning.
8. U_1 sends $[\alpha^{(r-1)x_1+dum_1-\Sigma_{i=2,r} dum_i} \bmod \beta]$ by executing u one out of two obli-vious transfer.
9. Each member U_i verifies whether the leader is a legitimate one by comparing the values of the conference key K by using the following equation:
   $K=[\alpha^{(r-1)x_1+dum_1-\Sigma_{i=2,r} dum_i} \prod_{i=2,r} y_i]^t \bmod \beta$ (2)
10. Each member U_i can calculate its individual key as follows:
    $K_i = \alpha^{n_1 n_i t} \bmod \beta$ (3)
    and the leader can calculate U_i's individual key by using the following equa-tion:
    $K_i = \alpha^{(x_i+x_1)t} \bmod \beta$ (5)
11. To verify whether all members (including the leader) hold the same conference key, each party broadcasts $\{K\}_{Ki}$ whose value is equal to $SK_i = K^{K_i \bmod \beta} \bmod \theta$. Then each member calculates
    $K\equiv (\prod_{i=1,r} SK_i)^{(K_{\square}^{-1}) \bmod \beta} \bmod \theta$ (6)
    If the value of equation (6) and the value of K which is locally calculated by a member are equal then the member can verify that all members hold an equal value of K.

2.2 Communication Among the Members

Our proposed protocol provides the facility for each member to be able to commu-nicate with other member securely via the leader using the individual key. In this case, the leader helps the members to communicate with each other, but he does not any knowledge concerning the messages. The procedure is as follows:

1. First of all we assume that the leader is honest. During the communication, the two communicating members and the leader use asymmetric crypto-system.
2. Suppose member U_i will send a message M (where $M \square Z_\theta$) to member U_j. Then, U_i sends U_j and the leader $(M^{K_i R_i \bmod \beta} \bmod \theta)$ where R_i and R_j are any integer chosen by U_i and U_j respectively, and $gcd(R_i,\beta)=1$; $gcd(R_j,\beta)=1$. Besides, $K_i R_i$ and $K_j R_j$ should not be congruent to $(0 \bmod \lambda(\beta))$.
3. The leader sends U_j message $(M^{R_i K_j \bmod \beta} \bmod \theta)$
4. Member U_j calculates $(M^{R_i K_j K_j \square' \bmod \beta} \bmod \theta)$ for obtaining $(M^{R_i \bmod \beta} \bmod \theta)$ and calculate $G=M^{(K_i R_i K_j R_j) \bmod \beta} \bmod \theta$. Furthermore, member U_j sends G to U_i.
5. U_i then calculates: $E=G^{(R_i K_i) \square' \bmod \beta} \bmod \theta$, and sends it to U_j along with $(M^{R_i \bmod \beta} \bmod \theta)$.
6. U_j obtains M by calculating: $D \equiv E^{(K_j R_j) \square' \bmod \beta} \bmod \theta \equiv M \bmod \theta$.
7. To verify whether U_i is the legitimate member, U_j compares the values of $(M^{(R_i) \bmod \beta} \bmod \theta)$ sent by the leader and U_i. If they are equal then U_i is the legitimate member, otherwise he is an adversary.

Since the leader does not know the values of R_i and R_j, it is not possible for him to obtain M.

3 Security Analysis

This section discusses the security of our proposed scheme against passive and active intruder.

3.1 Passive Attacks

First, we assume that all members of the group (including the leader) are honest. Passive attacks whose aim is key recovery for a given session involves eavesdropping on message passed between participants for that session.

Then, the conference key recovery will be successful if the adversary can guess t and $a^{(r-1)x_1 + dum_1 \cdot \Sigma_{i=2,r} dum_i} \bmod \beta$ after eavesdropping y_i and u.

If we assume that all members are honest and the size of t is $|t|$ bits, then there are $2^{|t|}$ possible values of t. Thus, the probability for obtaining the value of K is equal to $(1/[(\lambda(\beta)-1)\ (2^{|t|}\ )])$ (where $(\lambda(\beta))$ is the Carmichael Function of β[8]).But since the largest possible order of an integer modulo β is $(\lambda(\beta)-1)$ while $((2^{|t|})(\lambda(\beta)-1)) > \lambda(\beta)-1)$, the probability for obtaining K is equal to $1/(\lambda(\beta)-1)$. Thus, the protocol will be secure if we choose a large strong prime of β such that $\lambda(\beta)$ is large as well.

3.2 Active Attack

Active attack is usually defined as an impersonation attack. Recall that a key agreement protocol is successful if each of the members accept the identity of the other and terminate with the same key. In our proposed protocol, the adversary who will impersonate a member of the group (for example member U_i) may choose his/her random number n_i', performing Gilboa's method with the leader for obtaining his/her additive share x_i' and calculating y_i'. Thus, the probability for impersonating the legitimate member depends on the probability of finding t and the secret key of U_i. Suppose the size of t is $|t|$ and the probability for finding U_i 's secret key is δ, then the probability for breaking the protocol is $[(\delta)/(2^{|t|})]$.

4 Comparison with Previous Proposed Protocols

Suppose that for the key confirmation each member of the group and the leader has to broadcast the conference key signed (asymmetrically) with each mem-ber's secret key. Thus, for verifying that all members of the group and the leader hold the same conference key, each member has to decrypt all encrypted messages which are sent by the other members. Using the previous protocols, this will contribute a higher computational burden for all members of the group in the key confirmation if they use signature such as RSA signature to sign the conference key, because each member has to decrypt several signed messages. In our proposed protocol each member signs/encrypts (asymmetrically) the established conference key using his individual key and broadcasts it. A member can verify whether all members have an equal value of conference key by comparing the conference key which is signed by all members and the one he has calculated. This will reduce the computational burden of each member for the key confirmation, since using our proposed protocol each member needs to perform only one (asymmetric) decryption.

Suppose a member of a group U_i is going to propose a project, and he asks other members for approval of the proposal. Using the previous schemes, U_i has to do ***(r-1)*** verifications to check whether all members of the group agree or not. It means that U_i has to do ***(r-1)*** (asymmetric) decryptions. This will increase the com-putational burden for U_i. In our proposed scheme, each member of the group has his/her own individual secret key which can be used to sign his/her agreement. So, all members will sign the agreement and U_i will verify all members agreement by doing ***one*** verification which means that he/she needs to perform only one (asymmetric) decryption for verifying all members' agreements.

Compared with Li-Pieprzyk's protocol our proposed protocol is more efficient, since using Li-Pieprzyk protocol, for establishing the conference key, each member has to perform about $(2r^2 + 3r + 1)$ exponentiations, but using our proposed method each member needs to perform not more than *10* exponentiations (roughly) and $l+u$ oblivious transfers.

5 Conclusion

We proposed a new key agreement protocol which is based on oblivious transfer. Our proposed scheme introduced individual keys which can be used by each user to sign a common message, which is not included in the previously proposed protocols. By using individual keys, we can reduce the number of verifications and also redu-ce the computational burden for the verifier. Besides, using this individual key a member can communicate securely with the other members via the leader, while the leader can not gain any knowledge about the message sent among his members.

Our proposed scheme will be secure as long as the value of t and the secret num-ber chosen by each member are kept secret.

References

[1] Burmester, M. and Desmedt, Y. G., *Efficient and Secure Conference Key Distribution*, Proceeding of Security Protocols International Workshop Cambridge, United Kingdom, Springer-Verlag, LNCS 1189, April 1996, pp. 119-129.

[2] Just, M. and Vaudenay, S., *Authenticated Multy-Party Key Agreement*, Advances in Cryptology ASIACRYPT '96, Springer-Verlag, LNCS 1163, 1996.

[3] Boyd, C., *On key agreement and Conference Key Agreement*, Proceeding of Information Security and Privacy Australasian Conference (ACISP), Springer-Verlag, LNCS 1270, 1997, pp 294-302,

[4] Boyd, C., *Towards a Classification of Key Agreement Protocols*, Proceeding of Computer Security Foundation Workshop,1995, pp. 38-43.

[5] Li, C. and Pieprzyk, J., *Conference Key Agreement from Secret Sharing*, Proceeding of ACISP 1999, Springer-Verlag, pp 64-76.

[6] Goldreich, O., *Secure Multy-Party Computation*, Working Draft, Download from the Internet, June 1998.

[7] Gilboa, N., *Two RSA Key Generation*, Crypto 99, LNCS1666, Springer Verlag, 1999, pp. 116-129.

[8] Adler, A. and Coury, John E., *The Theory of Numbers*, Jones and Barlett, 1995.

CHAPTER 32

An Integration Model of Role-Based Access Control and Activity-Based Access Control Using Task

Sejong Oh, Soeg Park
Sogang University

Key words: Access control, RBAC, Task, Role, Enterprise environment

Abstract: Role-based access control (RBAC) and activity-based access control (ABAC) models are well known and recognized as a good security model for enterprise environment. (ABAC model is represented as 'workflow'). But these models have some limitations to apply to enterprise environment. Furthermore, enterprise environment needs application both RBAC and ABAC models.

In this paper we propose integration model of RABC and ABAC. For this we describe basic concept and limitations of RBAC and ABAC models. And we introduce concept of classifications for tasks. We use task by means of connection RBAC and ABAC models. Also we discuss the effect of new integration model.

1. INTRODUCTION

In general, today's companies manage business information with computer systems. Access control is an important security issue in the enterprise environment. Access means the ability to perform work such as reading, writing, and the execution of the system resources. Access control is the way to control the ability for performing the work.

From an access control point of view, enterprise environment can be expressed in Figure 1. In general, users in the company belong to the organization structure and they are performing their assigned job functions according to their job positions. Organization structure reflects authorization structure. Users read or write information resources for executing their job functions. There are two ways that users access information resources. First, users can access information resources directly for their some job functions. Second, some job functions are connected with others in the business process, and direct access of information resources is restricted by the status of business process. Passive access control applies to the first case, and active access control applies to the second case.

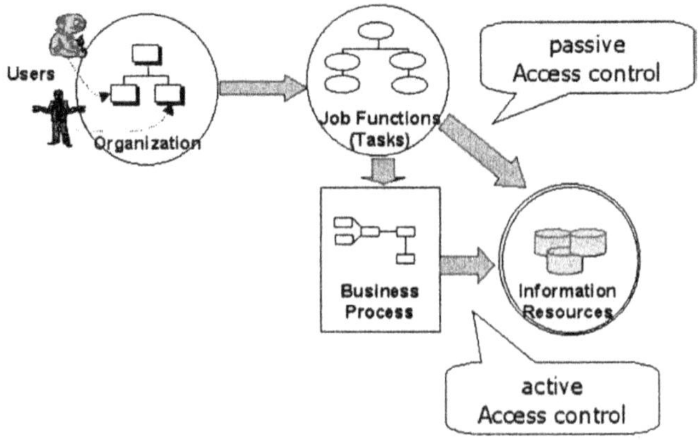

Figure 1. *Enterprise Environment*

Note. *We will use the term '**task**' instead of '**job function**'. In this paper, task has a meaning of unit of job that accesses information resources.*

Researchers have developed some access control models such as discretionary access control (DAC)[1], mandatory access control (MAC)[2], and role-based access control (RBAC). Activity-based access control (ABAC) model, which was motivated by workflow environment, was introduced recently. RBAC and ABAC are more suitable for enterprise environment than MAC and DAC. RBAC and ABAC have a good point of security, but also have constraints about applications for enterprise environment. So it is necessary to investigate more proper model for enterprise environment.

The purpose of this paper is to propose an improved access control model for enterprise environment through the integration of the RBAC and ABAC models. At first we reviews the limitations of RBAC and ABAC models, and then introduces our improved access control model.

2. RBAC AND ABAC MODELS

Role-based access control (RBAC)[5][6] has the central notion of preventing users from accessing company information discretionarily. Instead, access rights are associated with roles, and users are assigned to appropriate roles.

RBAC model has limitations as follows.

- RBAC supports passive access control. For example, if an access right is assigned to a user, then he/she can use the access right at any time. But enterprise environment include workflow, and it needs a dynamic activation of access right. RBAC cannot support dynamic activation of access right.
- Basic RBAC model has a role hierarchy concept that higher role inherits all access rights of lower role in the role hierarchy, and it is not suitable for real world. For example, *manager* is a higher job position than that of *clerk*, however, manager doesn't automatically inherit the *'register purchase'* job function of *clerk*. Full inheritance of role hierarchy has undesirable side effects by violating 'need-to-do' principle.

Activity-based access control (ABAC) model [3] [8][9] is investigated for a collaborative work environment represented as 'workflow'. Workflow is defined as a set of activities (tasks) that are connected to achieve a common goal. ABAC separates access right assignment for users and access right activation. Even if a user was allocated access rights on the workflow template, he/she can exercise his rights during the activation of the task in the specific workflow instance. ABAC model has limitations in the enterprise environment as follows.

- There exist many tasks that don't belong to workflow in the company, and ABAC model doesn't deal with them. So extra access control methods should be added to ABAC model.
- In the real world, a superior officer supervises and reviews execution of tasks of his/her inferior clerks. It's important for security and integrity; however, ABAC model doesn't take review and supervision into consideration.

3. INTEGRATION MODEL OF RBAC & ABAC

3.1 Problems in the Integration of RBAC & ABAC Models

As we can see, enterprise environment needs both passive and active access controls. (See Figure 1). We choose RBAC for passive access control model. Some researchers proposed injection of RBAC to workflow security [4][7]. But their approach doesn't deal with RBAC and ABAC models on an equal footing. Their approach is based on ABAC model, and adopts concept of 'role' as a meaning of group. There are some problems in the integration of RBAC and ABAC models as follows.

First, task is a unit of permission in the ABAC model. But RBAC, as a passive access control model, assigns information objects such as file or record to role. Task is higher level than information object. Integration model needs consistent unit of permission between RBAC and ABAC models.

Second, as we pointed out in section 3, there exist many tasks that don't belong to workflow in the company. In this case passive access control is more proper than active access control.

Third, as we pointed out in section 2, full inheritance of role hierarchy in RBAC has undesirable side effects. These side effects bring about serious security problems in active access control such as domination of 'need to do' principle.

3.2 Task Classification Concept

Before we propose integration model RBAC and ABAC that solves above problems, we introduce task classification concept. We will use a task concept as a connecter of RBAC and ABAC model.

By observation of the enterprise environment, we found that there are three classes of tasks such as in Table 1. If a user U_1 has tasks that belong to class S, their related access rights are inherited to user Un who has a higher job position than U_1 in the organization structure. But class W and class P do not have such inheritance characteristics. Tasks belong to class W, which has a relation with workflow and show the characteristics of an ABAC model. Passive security model is applied to class S and class P. Access control of the enterprise environment needs a proper method to deal with three classes of tasks through different ways. Our suggested model is based on the classification of tasks.

Table 1. *Classification of tasks.*

Classification of tasks		Class id	Example tasks	Characteristics	Inherited to higher job positions	Applied security model
Supervision Tasks		Class S	✔ supervise ✔ review ✔ delegation	✔ has a access right inheritance ✔ access right hierarchy is similar to organization hierarchy	O	Passive
Essential tasks	Workflow oriented tasks	Class W	✔ *drafting & approval* ✔ chained job	✔ similar to transaction ✔ needs active access control ✔ always includes write operation	X	Active
	Non workflow oriented tasks	Class P	✔ *analysis* ✔ planning ✔ decision making	✔ private tasks (has no relationship with other tasks or other job positions)	X	Passive

3.3 Integration of RBAC and ABAC

Now we propose the integration model of RBAC and ABAC models based on task classification. *(Note. We will call new integration model as T-RBAC. It means that Task-Role-Based Access Control).* Figure 2 shows a brief of T-RBAC. The most difference between T-RBAC and RBAC is that the access rights are assigned to task in T-RBAC, rather than access rights are assigned to role in RBAC. In the real world access rights are needed for the user to perform tasks. So assignment of access rights to task is reasonable. Another difference is role hierarchy. We use supervision role hierarchy (S-RH) instead of general role hierarchy. In the S-RH, higher role doesn't inherit all access rights of lower role in the role hierarchy. Only access rights of class S are inherited from lower role to higher role.

Tasks in the class W are used to compose workflow. Workflow creates the workflow instances that are set of task instances. Access rights are assigned to tasks in the class W statically. But the access rights are bound and activated during execution of task instance. Task instance has three attributes such as activation condition, time constraint, and cardinality. Time constraint is an available time after the task is activated. Cardinality is the number of specific task instance at the same time. How to specify and manage security constraint is remained research issue.

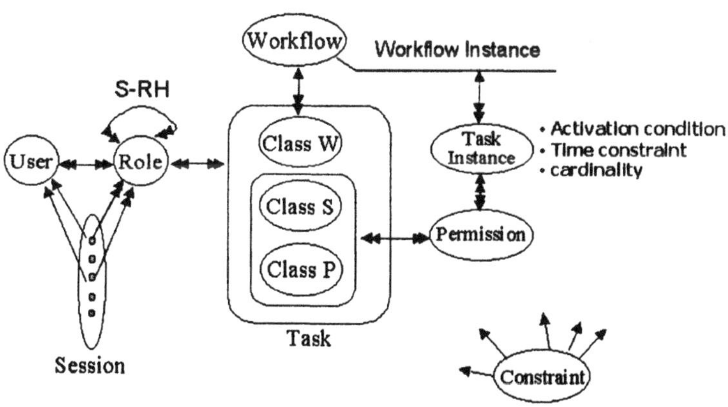

***Figure 2. T-RBAC**: Integration model of RABC and ABAC models*

The step of authority check in T-RBAC is as follows. When a user request accessing to some information objects, RBAC system checks the validity of the user's role, task. If the user's role and task are correct, then RBAC system checks the validity of permission. If the task belongs to class S or class P, RBAC system checks that permission is assigned to the task or not. If the task belongs to class W, RBAC system specifies task instance and checks activation condition, time constraint, and cardinality of the task instance. After checking permission, RBAC system checks security and integrity constraints. And RBAC system decides to accept or reject user's request.

In T-RBAC model, the concept of session and user-role assignment (URA) follows RBAC.

4. CONCLUSION

There are two central ideas in the T-RBAC. One is the classification of enterprise tasks (job functions) according to their characteristics. The other is to use intermediate tasks between access rights and roles instead of assigning access rights to roles. It makes possible that roles can be linked to access rights through intermediate tasks. Moreover, it makes the point of contact that RBAC could be integrated to ABAC model. The T-RBAC model has following effect from their characteristics.

- T-RBAC can support more elaborate access control. In the RBAC model, the unit of separation of duty and delegation is a role unlike in the T-RBAC where the unit is task. Task unit has more small scope of access rights than role unit
- It offers the criterion that which task/access rights can be inherited to higher roles from lower roles on the supervision role hierarchy (S-RH). Only the tasks belong to class S has an inheritance characteristic. It solves problems of general role hierarchy in RBAC.
- T-RBAC deals each class by different way according to its class. It is also possible to apply *active security model* to tasks that belong to class W and apply the general *passive security model* to tasks that belong to class S or P. Thus, task is a base concept for the integration of RBAC and ABAC.

REFERENCES

[1] C.P.Pfleeger, Security in Computing, second edition, Prentice-Hall International Inc.,1997.

[2] E.G.Amoroso, Fundamentals of Computer Security Technology, PTR Prentice Hall, 1994, 253-257.

[3] Dagstull, G.Coulouris, and J.Dollimore, "A Security Model for Cooperative work : a model and its system implications", Position paper for ACM European SIGOPS Workshop, September 1994.

[4] G.J.Ahn, R.S.Sandhu, M.Kang, and J.Park, "Injecting RBAC to Secure a Web-based Workflow System", Proc. of 5th ACM Workshop on Role-Based Access Control, 2000.

[5] R.S.Sandhu, E.J.Coyne, H.L.Feinstein, and C.E.Youman, "Role-Based Access Control Method", IEEE Computer, vol.29, Feb. 1996.

[6] D.Ferraio, J.Cugini, and R.Kuhn, "Role-based Access Control (RBAC): Features and motivations", Proc. of 11th Annual Computer Security Application Conference, 1995.12.

[7] W.K.Huang and V.Atluri, "SecureFlow: A Secure Web-enabled Workflow Management System", Proc. of 4th ACM Workshop on Role-Based Access Control, 1999.

[8] G.Herrmann and G.Pernul, "Towards Security Semantics in Workflow Management", Proc. of the 31st Hawaii International Conference on System Sciences, 1998.

[9] R.K.Thomas and R.S.Sandhu, "Task-based Authorization Controls (TBAC): A Family of Models for Active and Enterprise-oriented Authorization Management", Proc. of the IFIP WG11.3 Workshop on Database Security, 1997.

CHAPTER 33

Authorization Model in Object-Oriented Systems

Keiji Izaki, Katsuya Tanaka, and Makoto Takizawa
Dept. of Computers and Systems Engineering Tokyo Denki University
{izaki, katsu, taki}@takilab.k.dendai.ac.jp

Abstract In object-oriented systems, data and methods of a class are inherited by lower-level classes according to the is-a hierarchy. It is difficult to specify access rules for every class and object, because the system is composed of various types of classes, and objects which are dynamically created and dropped. If access rules on some class could be reused for other classes, the access rules are easily specified. This paper discusses how to inherit access rules in hierarchical structure of classes and objects.

Keywords: Access Control, Inheritance, Object-oriented systems

Introduction

Various kinds of distributed applications (Dittrich *et al.* 1989) are required to be realized in secure information systems. Various kinds of access control models are discussed so far, e.g. basic model (Lampson *et al.* 1971) and lattice-based model (Bell *et al.* 1975, Denning *et al.* 1982). An access rule $\langle s, o, op \rangle$ means that a subject s is allowed to manipulate an object o by an operation op. An access rule which a subject granted can be granted the to another subject in the discretionary model like relational database systems (Oracle *et al.* 1999). In the role-based model (Sandhu *et al.* 1996), a *role* is modeled to be a collection of access rights. A subject is granted a role.

Distributed systems are now being developed according to object-oriented frameworks like CORBA (Object *et al.* 1997). The papers (Dittrich *et al.* 1989, Samarati *et al.* 1997) discuss a *message filter* in an object-oriented system to prevent illegal information flow. The paper (Spooner *et al.* 1989) points out some problems to occur in the inheritance hierarchy, but does not discuss to make the system secure.

The paper (Yasuda *et al.* 1989) discusses the *purpose-oriented* access control model in an object-based system.

The object-oriented system is composed of various kinds of classes and objects which are dynamically created and destroyed. It is cumbersome to specify access rules for all classes and objects. If access rules for a class are inherited by subclasses, access rules are easily specified for classes. We discuss how to inherit access rules on classes and objects structured the *is-a* relation in a discretionary way.

In section 2, we briefly review the object-oriented model. In section 3, we discuss how to inherit access rules in the object-oriented model.

1. OBJECT-ORIENTED MODEL

The object-oriented system is composed of multiple classes and objects. A class c is composed of a set π_c of *attributes* A_{c1}, ..., A_{cm_c} ($m_c \geq 1$) and a set μ_c of *methods* op_{c1}, ..., op_{cl_c} ($l_c \geq 1$). An object o is created from the class c by allocating memory area for storing values of the attributes. Let μ_o be a set of methods of o. The methods are inherited from c, i.e. $\mu_o = \mu_c$. The object o is allowed to be manipulated only through methods in μ_o. o is referred to as *instance of* the class c.

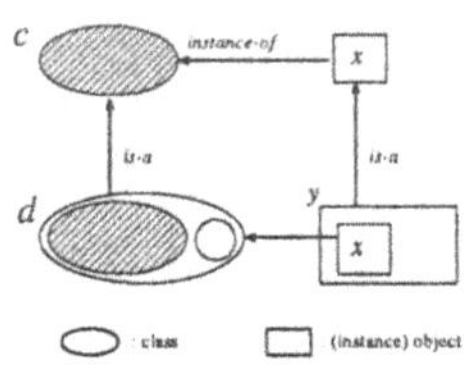

Figure 1 Classes and objects.

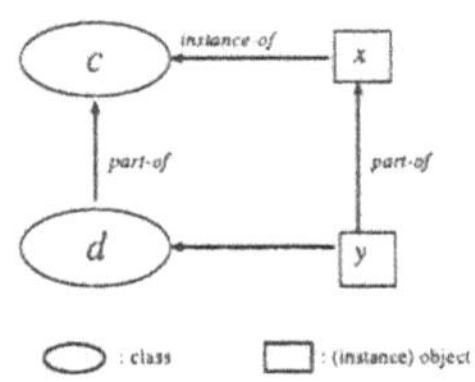

Figure 2 Part-of relation.

Classes and objects are hierarchically structured with *is-a* and *part-of* relations. A new class d is derived from an existing class c, where d inherits attributes and methods from c. Here, d is in an *is-a* relation with c, i.e. d is a *subclass* of c. Additional methods and attributes can be defined for the subclasses. Furthermore, attributes and methods inherited from c can be overridden for d. Figure 1 shows an *is-a* relation between a pair of classes c and d, i.e. d is a subclass of c. d inherits attributes and methods from c. In addition, the object y is in an *is-a* relation with x, i.e. the values of x are inherited by y. $\sigma_x \subseteq \sigma_y$ and $\mu_x \subseteq \mu_y$. Let $y.c$ denote values of y inherited from x. The object y in fact does not have the value of x, in order to reduce the storage space. A class c can be composed of other classes c_1, ..., c_n. Here, each class c_i is a *part* or *component* class of c. Let d be a component class of a class c [Figure 2]. Let x and y be objects of the classes c and d, respectively.

y is also a component object of x. However, there is neither *is-a* nor *part-of* relation between objects in the traditional systems.

A *manipulation* method manipulates values of attributes in the object. Another one is a *schema* method, by which classes and objects are created and destroyed, e.g. *create object*.

2. INHERITANCE OF ACCESS RULES

2.1. INSTANCE-OF RELATION

First, suppose an object x is created from a class c. An owner of the class c grants a subject an access right to create an object from c. Then, the subject creates an object x from c and is an owner of x. Suppose a set α_c of access rules are specified for c. The object x inherits the access rules α_c from c in addition to the attributes and methods. Here, a set α_x of access rules for the object x is $\{\langle s, x, op\rangle \mid \langle s, c, op\rangle \in \alpha_c$ and op is manipulation method$\}$.

Every subject s granted an access right $\langle c, op\rangle$ is granted $\langle x, op\rangle$ for every objet x of the class c. Only access rules on manipulation methods are inherited by the object x. The owner of x can define additional access rules and can revoke the access rules inherited from c.

There are *class* and *object* access rules. A *class* access rule $\langle s, c, op\rangle$ is specified for a class c. Here, every object x of c inherits the rule $\langle s, x, op\rangle$. If $\langle c, op\rangle$ is revoked from s, $\langle x, op\rangle$ is automatically revoked from s. If a new class rule $\langle s, c, op\rangle$ is specified, $\langle s, x, op\rangle$ is also inherited by every object x of c. The class access rules are allowed to be changed only by the owner of the class c. On the other hand, the object access rules of a class c are inherited by the objects created from c, but can be changed by the owner of the object. In fact, the object access rules of c are copied to the object x while the class rules are maintained in the class c [Figure 4(1)].

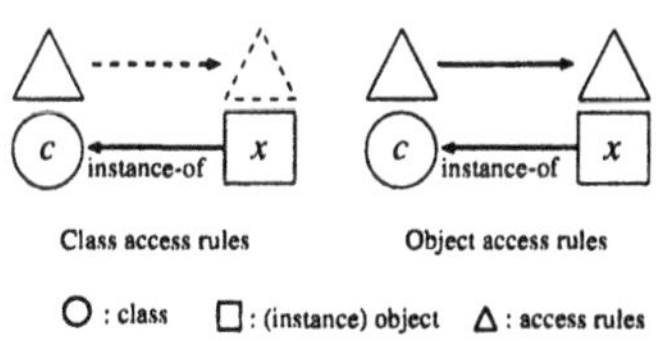

Figure 3 Access rules.

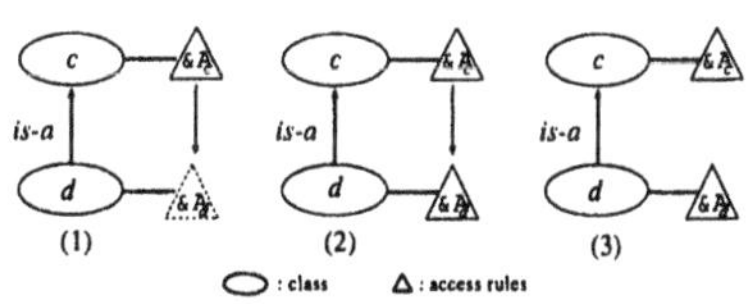

Figure 4 Inheritance of access rules.

2.2. IS-A RELATION OF CLASSES

Suppose a class d is a subclass of a class c as shown in Figure 1. The access rules of c are inherited by d. Let α_c and α_d be sets of access rules of c and d, respectively. There are following ways on how to inherit access rules α_c from c to d [Figure 4]; (1) the access rules α_c are inherited by d, (2) the access rules α_c are copied to d, and (3) no access rule α_c is inherited by d. In the first case, the access rules inherited by the subclass d depend on c. Values of attributes of c are manipulated through a manipulation method *op*. Here, *op* is also performed on the attribute $d.c$ in the class d. If the access rules in α_c are changed in c, the access rules in d are also changed. If a new rule $\langle s, c, op\rangle$ is specified for c, $\langle s, d, op\rangle$ is automatically *authorized*. The access rules are in fact maintained only in the class c and are not in the subclass d. c is referred to as *home* class of the access rule. Next, let us consider how to inherit access rights on a schema method *op* of the class c. For example, suppose an access rule $\langle s, c, op\rangle$ is specified for the class c. Here, $\langle s, c, op\rangle$ is inherited by d. If d is derived from c, the subject s can create an object from d.

In the second case, the access rules α_c of the class c are copied in the subclass d [Figure 4 (2)]. The access rules of d are independent of c. For example, even if a new access rule is authorized for c, the access rule is not authorized for d. In the last case, the access rules of c are not inherited by d. The access rules of d are defined independently of c.

Suppose an access rule $\langle s, c, op\rangle$ is specified for a class c. There are *mandatory* and *optional* access rules. Suppose a class d is derived from c. If an access rule $\langle s, c, op\rangle$ is *mandatory*, d is required to inherit an access rule $\langle s, d, op\rangle$ from c. The rule $\langle s, d, op\rangle$ cannot be changed for d. Each time the class d and its objects are manipulated, the access rules of the class c are checked. Next, let us consider an optional rule $\langle s, c, op\rangle$. Here, every subclass d of the class c can decide whether or not d inherits $\langle s, c, op\rangle$. The rule $\langle s, d, op\rangle$ can be one of the types *inherit* and *copy* in the subclass d. If $\langle s, d, op\rangle$ is *inherit* type, $\langle s, d, op\rangle$ cannot be changed. $\langle s, d, op\rangle$ is not maintained in d as discussed for *mandatory* inheritance for c. If $\langle s, d, op\rangle$ is a *copy* type, $\langle s, d, op\rangle$ is independent of $\langle s, c, op\rangle$. Every mandatory rule $\langle s, c, op\rangle$ cannot be specified as *copy* in d. The mandatory access rule is automatically an *inherit* type in d.

In Figure 5, an access rule α is mandatory while β and γ are normal for the class c. The classes d and e inherit α from c. c is the home class of α. β is a *copy* type and γ is an *inherit* type for d. If α and γ are changed for c, α for d and e and γ for d are also changed. However, even if β is changed for c, β of d is not changed. If β of d is changed, β of e is changed. The home class of β of e is d.

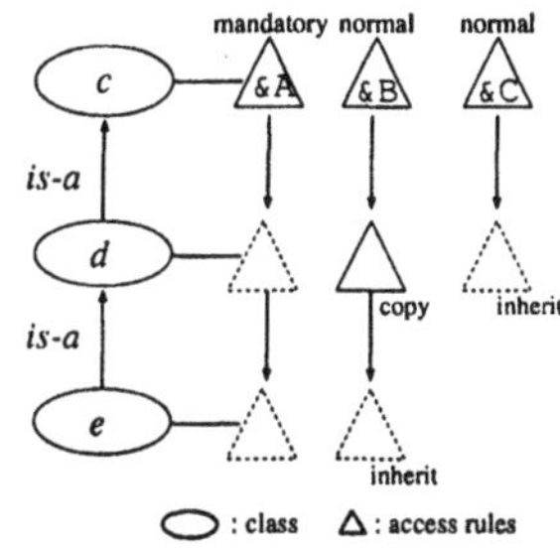

Figure 5 Types of Inheritance.

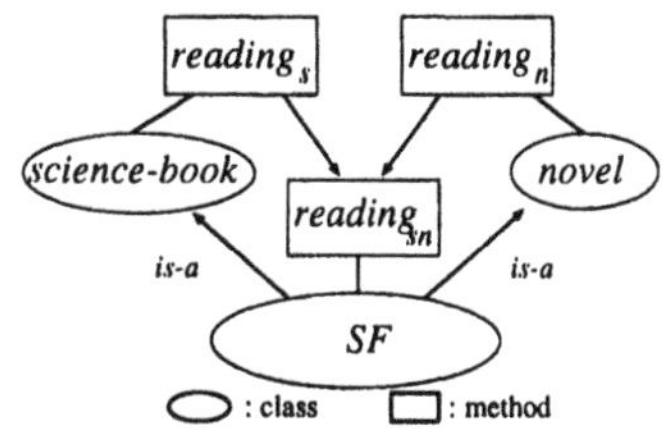

Figure 6 Multiple inheritance.

2.3. MULTI-INHERITANCE

Let us consider *novel* and *science-book* classes each of which supports a manipulation method *reading*. An $SF(science\ fiction)$ class is derived from *novel* and *science-book*. SF inherits *reading* from *novel* and *science-book*. Suppose a subject s is granted an access right $\langle novel, reading\rangle$ but not $\langle science\text{-}book, reading\rangle$. Question is whether or not s can *read* SF. The subject s cannot read *science-book* while it can read *novel*. Thus, the access rights from *science-book* and *novel* conflict. Here, let $\sim\langle s, c, op\rangle$ show that an access rule $\langle s, c, op\rangle$ is not authorized for a class c. $\sim\langle s, c, op\rangle$ is *negative* rule of a *positive* one $\langle s, c, op\rangle$. If a subclass c inherits a pair of access rules $\langle s, c, op\rangle$ and $\sim\langle s, c, op\rangle$ from classes, the inheritance is referred to as $conflict$.

If $\langle s, c, op\rangle$ is not specified for a class c, a negative rule $\sim\langle s, c, op\rangle$ is assumed to be authorized. There are two types of inheritance of negative rules as discussed for positive rules. We have to specify which negative rules are mandatory. In addition, negative rules can be explicitly specified for each class. If $\sim\langle s, c, op\rangle$ is mandatory in a class c, every subclass d is required to inherit $\sim\langle s, c, op\rangle$ from c. Here, if d inherits both $\langle s, d, op\rangle$ and $\sim\langle s, d, op\rangle$ through the mandatory type of classes, the inheritances conflict in d. Suppose a subclass d is derived for classes c_1 and c_2. d inherits an access rule α_1 for c_1 and α_2 for c_2. Suppose c_1 and c_2 conflict. If α_1 is mandatory in c_1 and α_2 is optional in c_2, d inherits α_1. If α_1 and α_2 are optional in c_1 and c_2, the subclass d can inherit either α_1 or α_2, but not both. If α_1 and α_2 are mandatory in c and c_2, d cannot be defined from c_1 and c_2.

3. CONCLUDING REMARKS

This paper discussed a discretionary access control model in the object-oriented system. The object-oriented system supports inheritance of properties. We made clear how to inherit the access rules in the *instance-of* and *is-a* relations. By using the inheritance of the access rules, it is easy to grant and revoke access rules in systems which are composed of various kinds of classes and objects.

References

Bell, D. E. and LaPadula, L. J., "Secure Computer Systems: Mathematical Fousdations and Model," *Mitre Corp. Report*, No.M74-244, 1975.

Dittrich K R, Haertig M, Pfefferle H., "Discretionary Access Control in Structurally Object-Oriented Database Systems," *Database Security* 2, pp105-121, 1989.

Grosling, J. and McGilton, H., "The Java Language Environment," *Sun Microsystems*, Inc., 1996.

Lampson, B. W., "Protection," *Proc. of the 5th Princeton Symp. on Information Sciences and Systems*, 1971, pp.437-443.

Thuraisingham, M. B., "Mandatory Security in Object-Oriented Database Systems," *ACM Sigplan Note,* Vol. 24, No. 10, 1989 pp.203-210.

Object Management Group Inc., "The Common Object Request Broker : Architecture and Specification," Rev. 2.1, 1997.

Oracle Corporation,"Oracle8*i* Concepts", Vol. 1, Release 8.1.5, 1999.

Samarati, P., Bertino, E., Ciampichetti, A., and Jajodia, S., "Information Flow Control in Object-Oriented Systems," *IEEE Trans. on Knowledge and Data Engineering,* Vol. 9, No. 4, 1997, pp. 254–238.

Sandhu, R. S., Coyne, E. J., Feinstein, H. L., and Youman, C. E., "Role-Based Access Control Models," *IEEE Computer,* Vol. 29, No. 2, 1996, pp. 38–47.

Spooner, D., "The Impact of Inheritance on Security in Object-Oriented Database System," *Database Security* 2, 1989, pp. 141–150

Stroustrup, B., "The C++ Programming Language (2nd ed.)," *Addison-Wesley*, 1991.

Yasuda, M., Higaki, H., and Takizawa, M., "A Purpose-Oriented Access Control Model for Information Flow Management," *Proc of 14th IFIP Int'l Information Security Conf. (IFIP'98)*, 1998, pp. 230–239.

CHAPTER 34

Panel 2

Reind van de Riet, Raban Serban, Sylvia Osborn, Arnie Rosenthal, Vijay Atluri, Joachim Biskup, Gio Weiderhold

Moderator: Reind van de Riet, Vrije Universiteit, Amsterdam

Members of the panel:

Arnie Rosenthal, Mitre, USA

Radu Serban, Vrije Universiteit, Amsterdam

Sylvia Osborn The University of Western Ontario, Canada

Vijay Atluri, Rutgers University, USA

Joachim Biskup, University of Dortmund, Germany

Gio Wiederhold, Stanford University, California

Contribution by: **Reind van de Riet**, vdriet@cs.vu.nl

The Panel discussed two themes: 1. Are there better ways to protect data from misuse? and 2. Should security be built in at the Applications level? For item 1, in our group we worked on: a) fire walls, objects which are agents, which explode when misused (See Serban's contribution). b) other ways to define access rules: protection in Mokum is provided indirectly by structuring the objects: persons, doctors, nurses, insurance company employees. In this way 90\% of all security is defined. This in contrast to the way security in an ERP system is defined with hundreds of class definitions for thousands of certificates. Another advantage is that security can be proved correct. Item 2 leads in the direction of ERP and WorkFlow systems. In current ERP systems security rules are enforced using a variety of certificates, the possession of which depends on roles persons have in the organization. Using WorkFlows, one can use them for security and privacy protection (See Atluri's contribution).

Contribution by: **Radu Serban**, serbanr@cs.vu.nl
Privacy protection depends on informedness (awareness of threats and vulnerabilities, trust in the technical infrastructure and in the other participants and strict regulations. Apart from legal and technical measures to increase privacy, the designers of future Cyberspace protocols have to consider self-regulatory measures, such as an awareness mechanism based on reputation, a language for specifying scenarios and policies and the adoption of preventive measures. Several principles have been suggested to be enforced by the privacy assistant of an individual: purpose-binding, informed consent, need-to-know (control by source) and appropriate value exchange. In order to increase the informedness of the individual, a model for privacy analysis would require more formal definitions for key notions such as ownership, visibility, responsibility, vulnerability, and provability. In future Cyberspace it is likely that agents representing an individual in an electronic transaction will encapsulate a great deal of personal information and will have more autonomy. Such a privacy assistant has the role of monitoring online transactions, ensuring personal management and keeping the individual informed with respect to his privacy status. It also assesses privacy violation risks, investigates privacy violations and takes corrective measures. We have proposed an architecture of such a privacy assistant, that assists an individual to fine tune the control of his own personal data and keeps him informed with respect to his privacy status. To protect personal information, the privacy assistant has to create and coordinate several user agents, termed fireballs, which encapsulate personal information together with their policies for specific applications. The fireballs cannot enforce protection by themselves, but only function in special trusted environments in which commitments for privacy compliance hold. In this respect, the barriers to effective privacy protection seem to be social, more than technical: the collectors of personal data have to make binding commitments to protect privacy, otherwise software solutions for privacy protection are fundamentally limited.

Contribution by: **Sylvia Osborn**, sylvia@csd.uwo.ca
As a reaction to both themes, I would like to pose the following question: how do different existing software architectures interact with security mechanisms? I think that many newly proposed techniques will not be adopted unless they can be used with existing platforms, existing software architectures and existing software practices. A related question is: can the same security models or mechanisms be used at different stages of the software lifecycle? Is any attention being paid to mechanisms that are appropriate during software development? What tools should be available

and incorporated into software once it is deployed? Are current models/mechanisms adequate for all of these stages?

Contribution by: **Arnie Rosenthal**, arnie@mitre.org
The Grand Challenge is: How can we make enterprise-level administration of security so simple that *ordinary* organizations will do it well? A subsidiary challenge is: How do we modularize the technology, so that vendors will build it? And, what would it take to administer a distributed, heterogeneous, redundant, semi-autonomous system (e.g., databases, business objects, ERP objects) as much as possible as an ordinary system? Discussion: Large enterprises are trying to build systems that make data widely available, in terms of objects that the recipient can interpret (which are rarely the same as those naturally produced by sources). In such architectures, security policies will be specified in detail), examined, and enforced in many positions in a system-databases, object managers, applications (e.g., ERP). Policies will be needed for many derived objects. We need a technical approach that places responsibility where there are both the needed skills (or tools) and the motivation. The best way forward on administration is to provide automated aids for policy propagation and integration and a modular service for each kind of information to be administered (e.g., access permissions, grant permissions, roles, groups, both "info" and "physical" access permissions.

Contribution by: **Vijay Atluri**, atluri@cimic3.rutgers.edu
Workflow management systems (WFMSs) are today used in numerous application domains. The various tasks in a workflow are carried out by several users according to the organizational rules relevant to the process represented by the workflow. Security policies of a given organization are usually expressed in terms of the roles within the organization rather than individuals. With traditional role-based access control (RBAC), roles are assigned to users based on their qualifications, and tasks in turn are assigned to roles, thereby assigning permissions to users. Such a simple model of RBAC is not adequate in WFMS as a full-fledged authorization system should consider the following additional requirements: (1) Permissions should be granted only during the execution of a task, that is, authorization flow must be synchronized with the workflow. (2) Need to assign different roles to tasks based on the outcome of the prior task. (3) Need to grant different permissions to roles based on the outcome of the prior task. (4) Need to deal with authorization constraints such as separation of duties at runtime. (5) Capable to specify different authorizations for different instances of the same workflow. (6) Authorization specification need to be based on the context and based on the responsibilities to be performed by

individuals, and therefore need to be driven by the application. (7) Need for temporal and dynamic role-permission assignment and user-role assignment.

Contribution by: **Joachim Biskup**, biskup@ls6.cs.uni-dortmund.de
We all see the need to build computing systems that are "more secure" than the present ones. We should be careful with our expectations: there is no linear order for "degrees of security", rather we have to deal with several coordinates, governed by specific questions. The most important questions are: 1. Whose security is meant? 2. Which security interests (availability, integrity, authenticity, confidentiality) are affected? and 3. In which application contexts do these interests arise? Further questions deal with costs (in terms of time, space) and willingness of participants to accept the burden of using the security mechanisms? The corresponding coordinates (participants, interests, contexts, costs, acceptance) have to be studied in a common framework. This view on the security problem has some immediate consequences: * Each participant (or each group of participants) needs a toolbox consisting of technical mechanisms each of them is suitable to enforce specific interests in specific application contexts. Unfortunately, such a toolbox is not available yet. * The technical enforcement mechanisms should be composable, interoperable and combinable with application systems. * The effectiveness of the above mechanisms should be founded on a selection of trusted agencies, in order to provide the necessary informational infrastructure. The toolbox must contain "multi-party"-primitives. There are already a few examples, for instance "fair exchange" or "cooperative access rights".

Contribution by: **Gio Wiederhold**, gio@cs.stanford.edu
A novel issue in the security arena deals with protecting children from receiving inappropriate, typically pornographic, content. A law, passed in 1998 by the US Congress, the Children On-line Protection act (COPA), not yet implemented, which makes Internet Service Providers liable for failing to control such transmissions. Hearings on the social, legal, and technical issues have taken place under aegis of a specially constituted commission, which invited a wide range of comments, including organizations outside of the US. Its web page is http://www.copacommission.org/. In October 2000 a final report was released. My testimony can be found at my website. Part of the recommendation included the establishment of green and red top-level Internet domains (TLDs): .kids and .xxx. This November, ICANN (the Internet Corporation for Assigned Names and Numbers) rejected those proposals, mainly because of the problem of assigning authority for those TLDs. For the green TLD, a candidate was the Internet Content Rating Association (http://www.icra.org/), who collects input from volunteer raters.

I know of no such organization for the proposed red TLD. By providing tools for parents and other organizations the actually filtering decisions (who, what, when, how and to whom) can be devolved on people taking a specific and beneficial interest in the issue. At Stanford we have developed a very effective filtering program that recognizes classes of images: WIPE. This technology can support identification of candidates sites for the red TLD. WIPE uses wavelet analysis to extract features from images, and has been trained on pornographic and benign images that are available on the web. WIPE has a recognition rate of 95\% for individual images, and over 99% when identifying porno websites where there are multiple such images.

CHAPTER 35

Conference Summary

Bhavani Thuraisingham
The MITRE Corporation, Bedford, MA, USA

Abstract: This report summarizes the IFIP 11.3 Working Conference on Database Security held in Schoorl, The Netherlands from August 21 to August 23, 2000.

1. INTRODUCTION

This conference was the 14th IFIP Working Conference on Database Security. It had presentations and panels on a variety of topics including traditional ones such as Multilevel Security as well as emerging technologies such as XML security. Section 2 summarizes the papers and Section 3 provides directions.

2. SUMMARY OF PAPERS AND PANELS

One of the major focus areas of this conference was XML security and web security. The keynote presentation the first day was on related policy issues followed by papers on XML as well as web security. In addition, the first day consisted of papers on distributed object security and secure architectures as well as on encryption. The day ended with a lively panel on web security. This was followed by an interesting cultural event with a presentation on paintings related to Schoorl as well as musical concerts by conference participants.

The second day started with a keynote on privacy issues related to medical applications and was followed by papers on federated systems security and policies. In addition, we also had a session on multilevel security. To keep up with the traditions, we had the afternoon of the second day off and we enjoyed an organ recital by the conference chair at the local church followed by a bicycle ride and then dinner by North Sea. We also had a business meeting after lunch on the second day.

The third day started with a keynote on applying data mining for intrusion detection. This was followed by papers on workflow security and language security. The afternoon of the third day considered of several short paper presentations followed by a closing panel that discussed directions.

3. DIRECTIONS

Everyone was very enthusiastic about the conference and felt that we must continue with this conference for many more years. We discussed the 2001 conference to be held near Niagara Falls, and then for 2002 there was strong support to have this conference in South Africa. Participants felt that while web and e-commerce security will be dominant over the next several years, we cannot forget about the traditional areas and need to continue research in these areas. There was record attendance at this conference with over 50 participants. The participants thoroughly enjoyed the atmosphere in Schoorl, The Netherlands.

Index